3x3

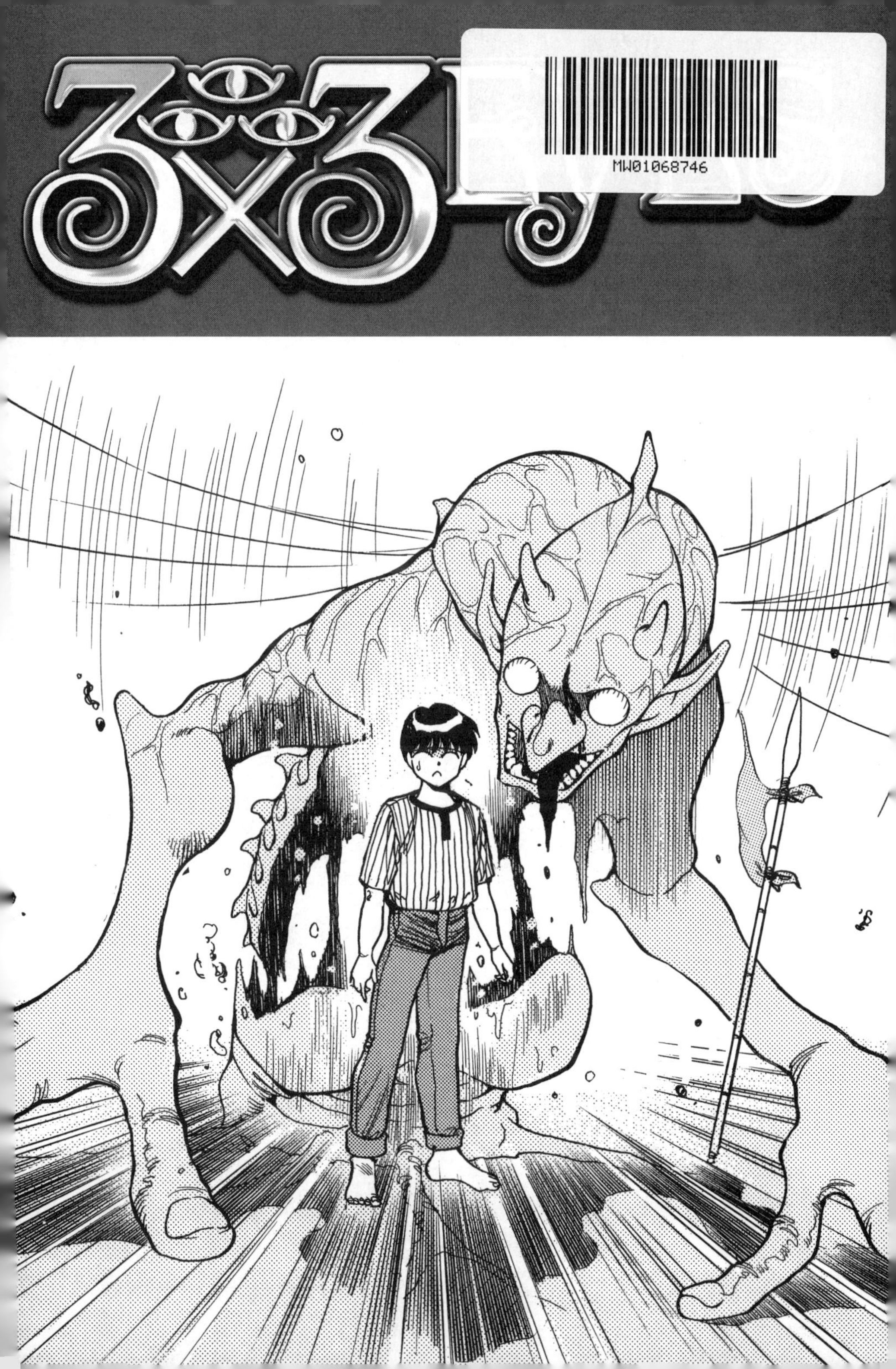

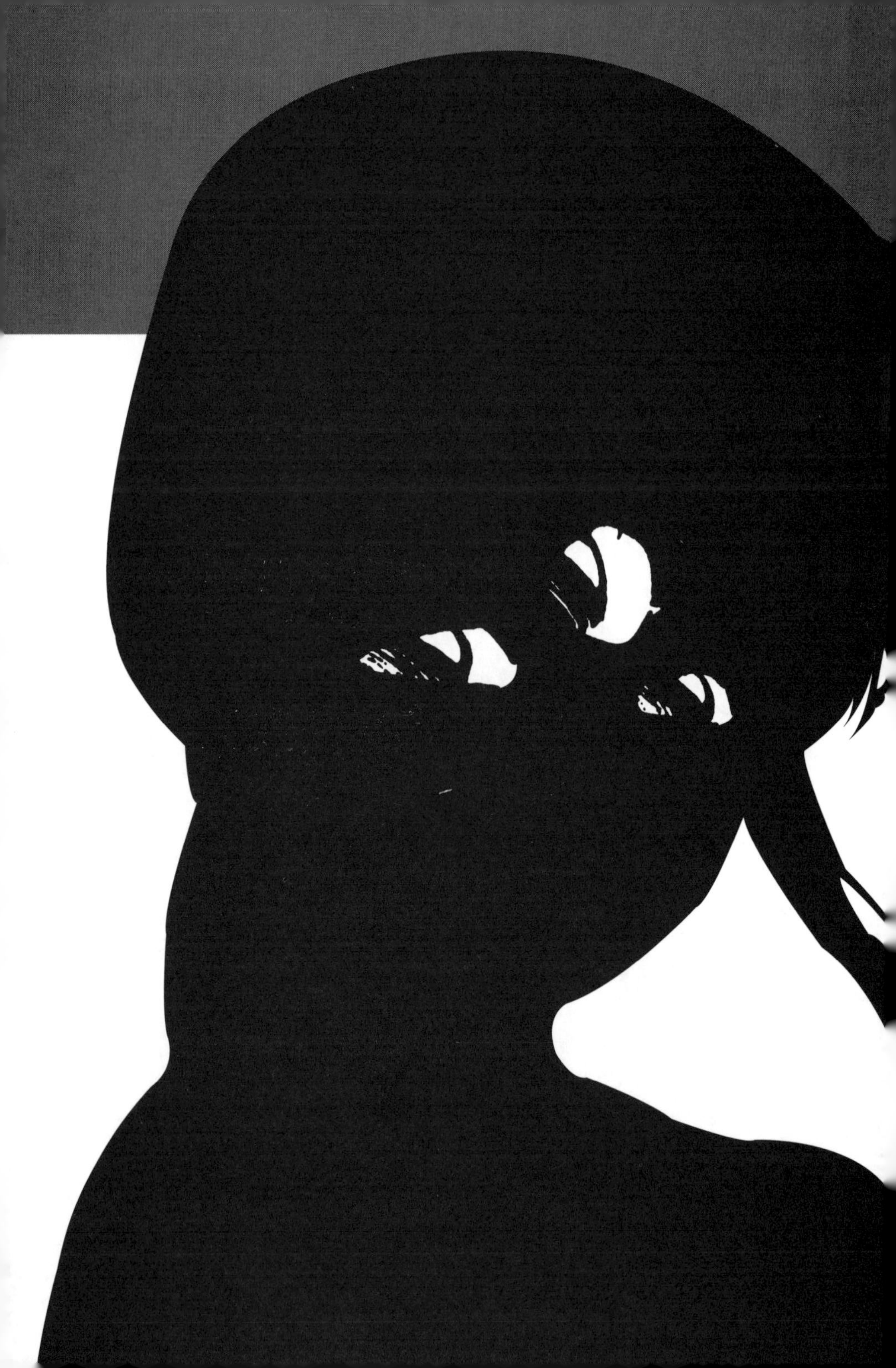

3x3 EYES

Flight of the Demon

story and art

Yuzo Takada

translation

**Hisashi Kotobuki, Elin Winkler,
Lea Hernandez, Christopher Lewis,
& Toren Smith**

lettering and touch-up

**Pat Duke & Radio Comix,
Chris Chalenor, Digital Chameleon**

Dark Horse Comics®

publisher *Mike Richardson*

series editor *Mike Hansen*

series executive editor *Toren Smith*
for *Studio Proteus*

collection editor *Chris Warner*

collection designer *Darin Fabrick*

art director *Mark Cox*

**English-language version produced by Studio Proteus,
Radio Comix, and Dark Horse Comics, Inc.**

3x3 Eyes: Flight of the Demon

This volume collects **3x3 Eyes** stories from issues one through seven of the
Dark Horse comic-book series **Super Manga Blast!**

Published by
Dark Horse Comics, Inc.
10956 SE Main Street
Milwaukie, OR 97222

www.darkhorse.com

To find a comics shop in your area, call the Comic Shop Locator Service toll-
free at 1-888-266-4226

First edition: November 2001
ISBN: 1-56971-553-X

10 9 8 7 6 5 4 3 2 1

Printed in Canada

Flight of the Demon

part 1

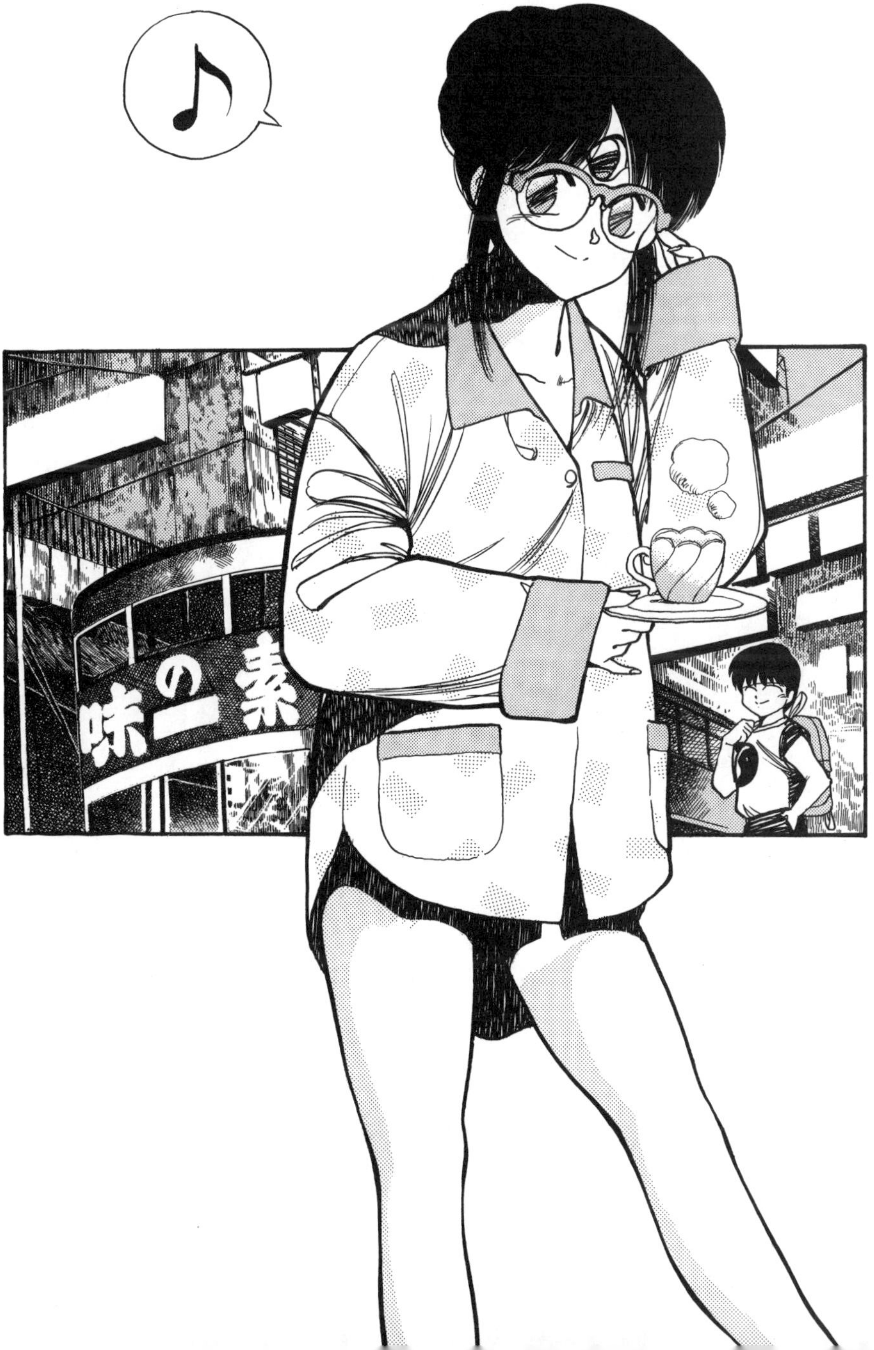
♪
味の素

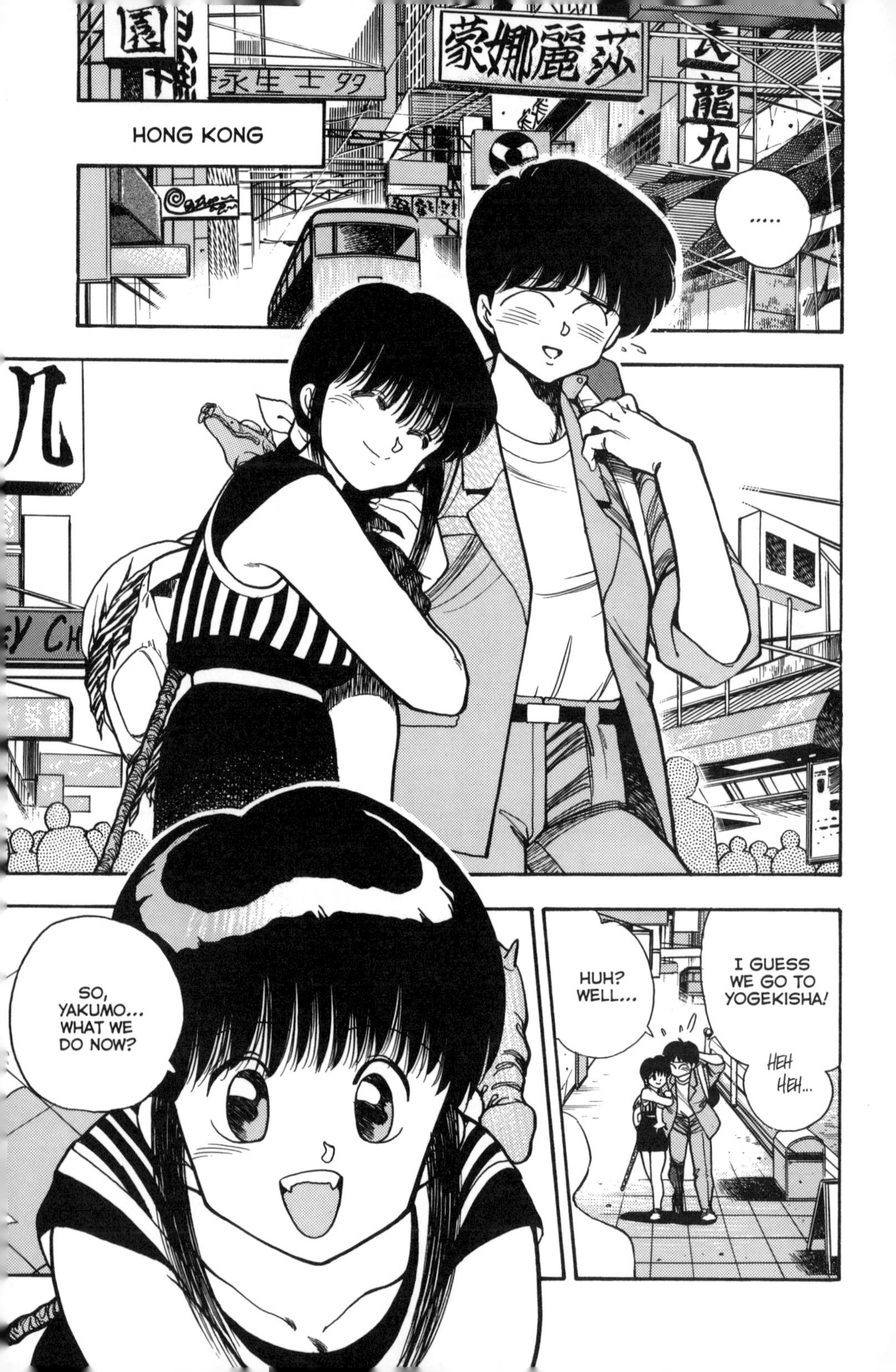
HONG KONG
蒙娜麗莎
.....
SO, YAKUMO... WHAT WE DO NOW?
HUH? WELL...
I GUESS WE GO TO YOGEKISHA!
HEH HEH...

TAA-DAA! ♪♪♪
POST CARD
AIR MAIL
藤井八雲様
JAPAN
像のありか
つきとめた
詳細は
香港にて
鈴鈴
JUST BEFORE WE LEFT JAPAN, THIS CAME IN THE MAIL!
"I FOUND THE LOCATION OF THE STATUE. MORE DETAILS WHEN YOU GET TO HONG KONG."
LING-LING
"STATUE"...?
AH!! SHE MEAN "FIGURE OF MAN"...?!

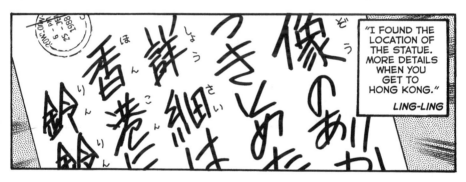

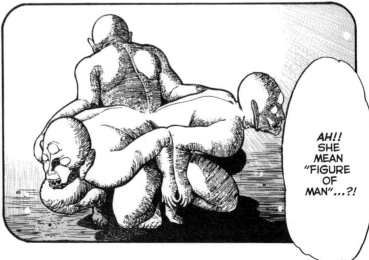

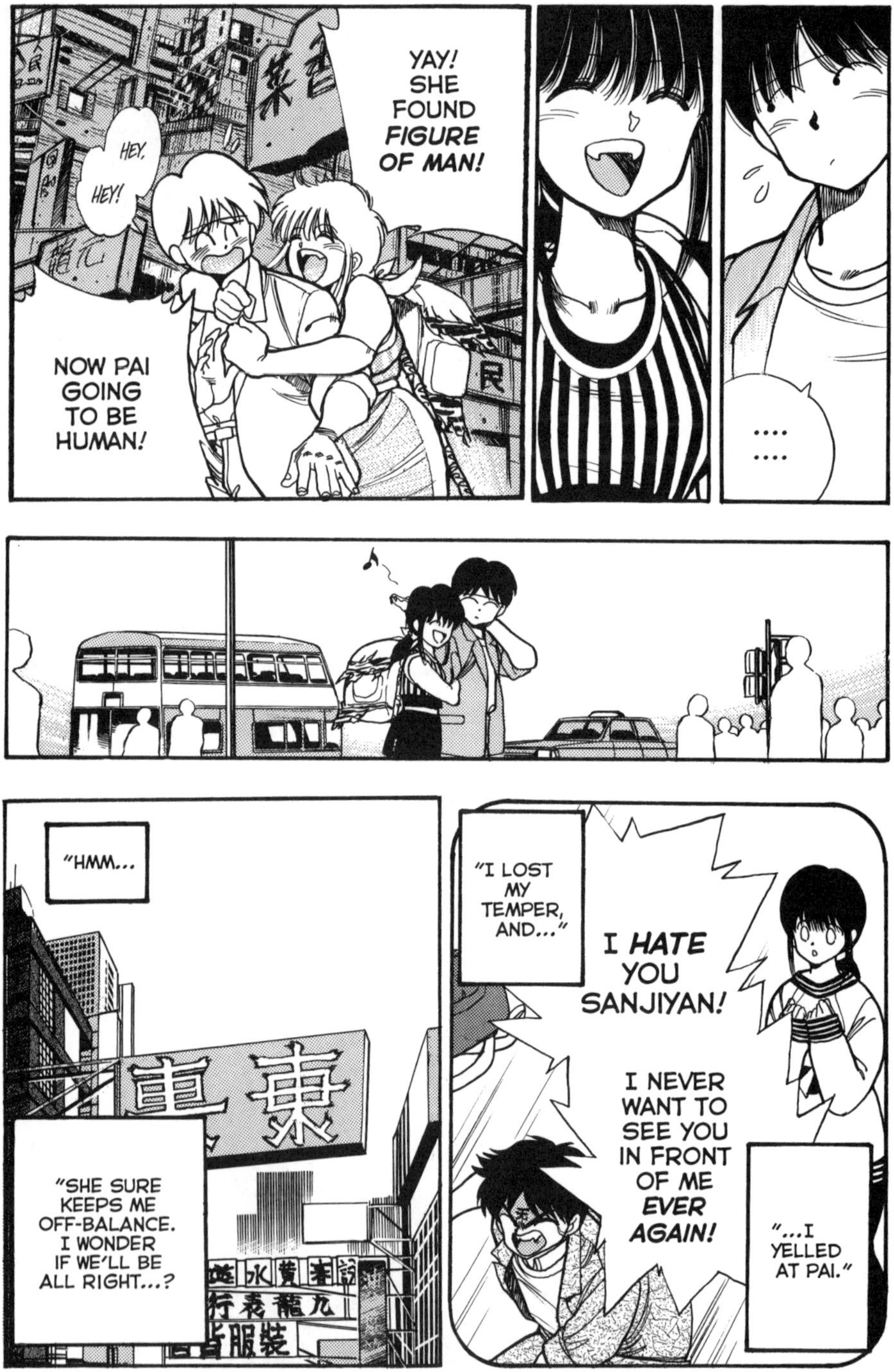
YAY! SHE FOUND FIGURE OF MAN!
HEY, HEY!
NOW PAI GOING TO BE HUMAN!
....
"HMM...
"SHE SURE KEEPS ME OFF-BALANCE. I WONDER IF WE'LL BE ALL RIGHT...?
"I LOST MY TEMPER, AND..."
I HATE YOU SANJIYAN!
I NEVER WANT TO SEE YOU IN FRONT OF ME EVER AGAIN!
"...I YELLED AT PAI."

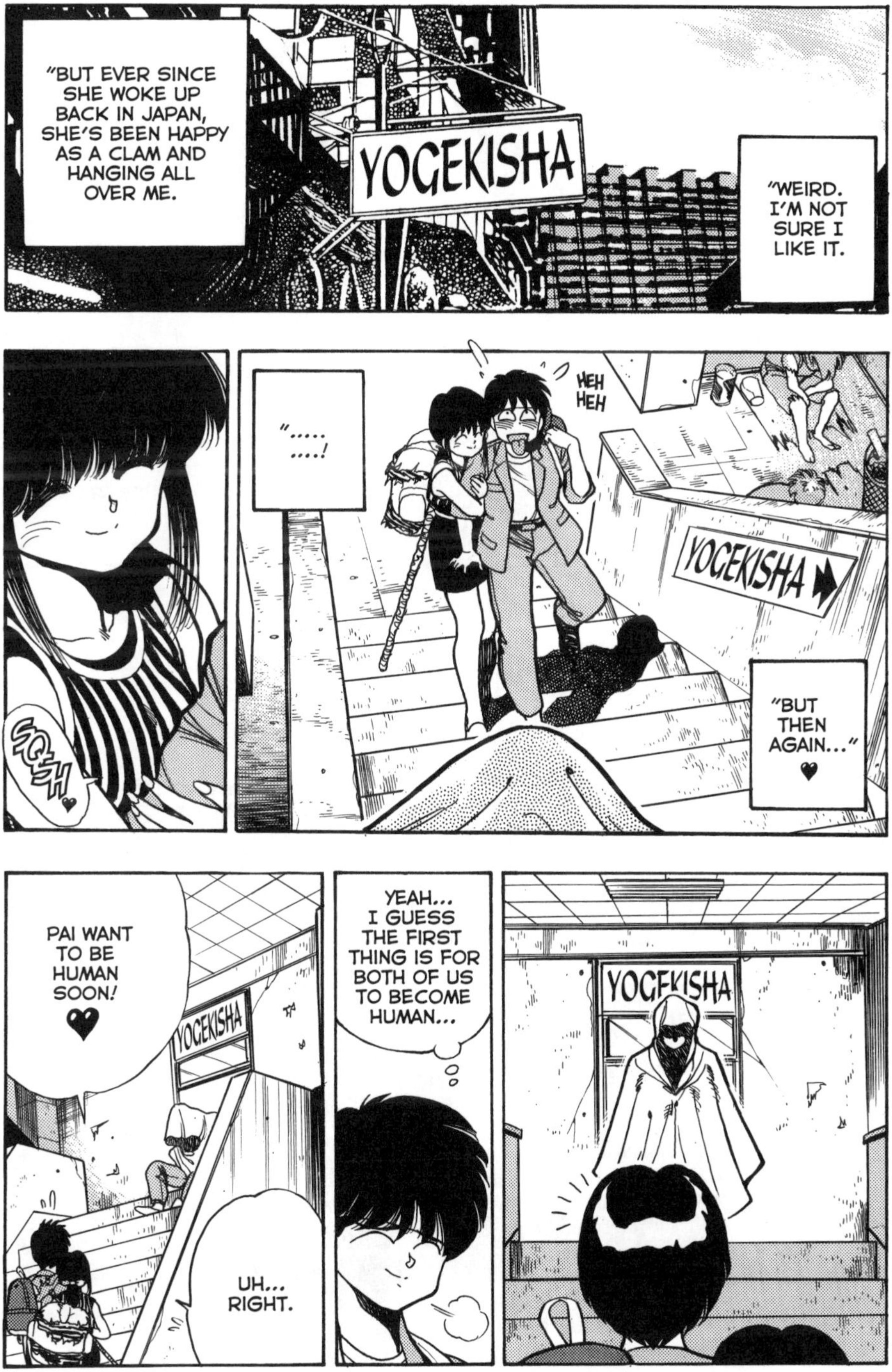
"BUT EVER SINCE SHE WOKE UP BACK IN JAPAN, SHE'S BEEN HAPPY AS A CLAM AND HANGING ALL OVER ME.
YOGEKISHA
"WEIRD. I'M NOT SURE I LIKE IT.
SQSH ♥
"...... .....!
HEH HEH
YOGEKISHA
"BUT THEN AGAIN..." ♥
PAI WANT TO BE HUMAN SOON! ♥
YOGEKISHA
UH... RIGHT.
YEAH... I GUESS THE FIRST THING IS FOR BOTH OF US TO BECOME HUMAN...
YOGEKISHA

▼ CANTONESE

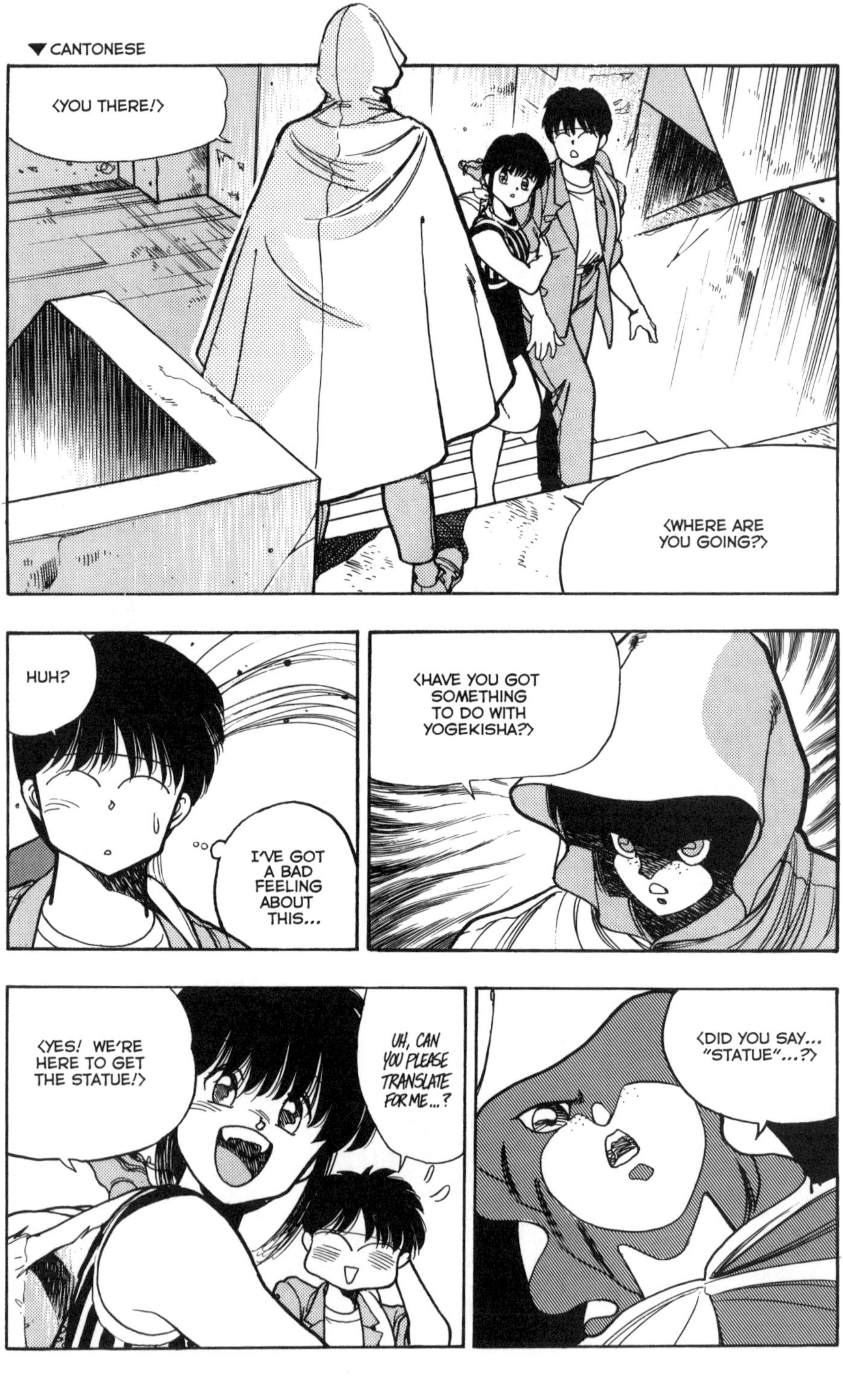
〈YOU THERE!〉
〈WHERE ARE YOU GOING?〉
HUH?
I'VE GOT A BAD FEELING ABOUT THIS...
〈HAVE YOU GOT SOMETHING TO DO WITH YOGEKISHA?〉
〈YES! WE'RE HERE TO GET THE STATUE!〉
UH, CAN YOU PLEASE TRANSLATE FOR ME...?
〈DID YOU SAY... "STATUE"...?〉

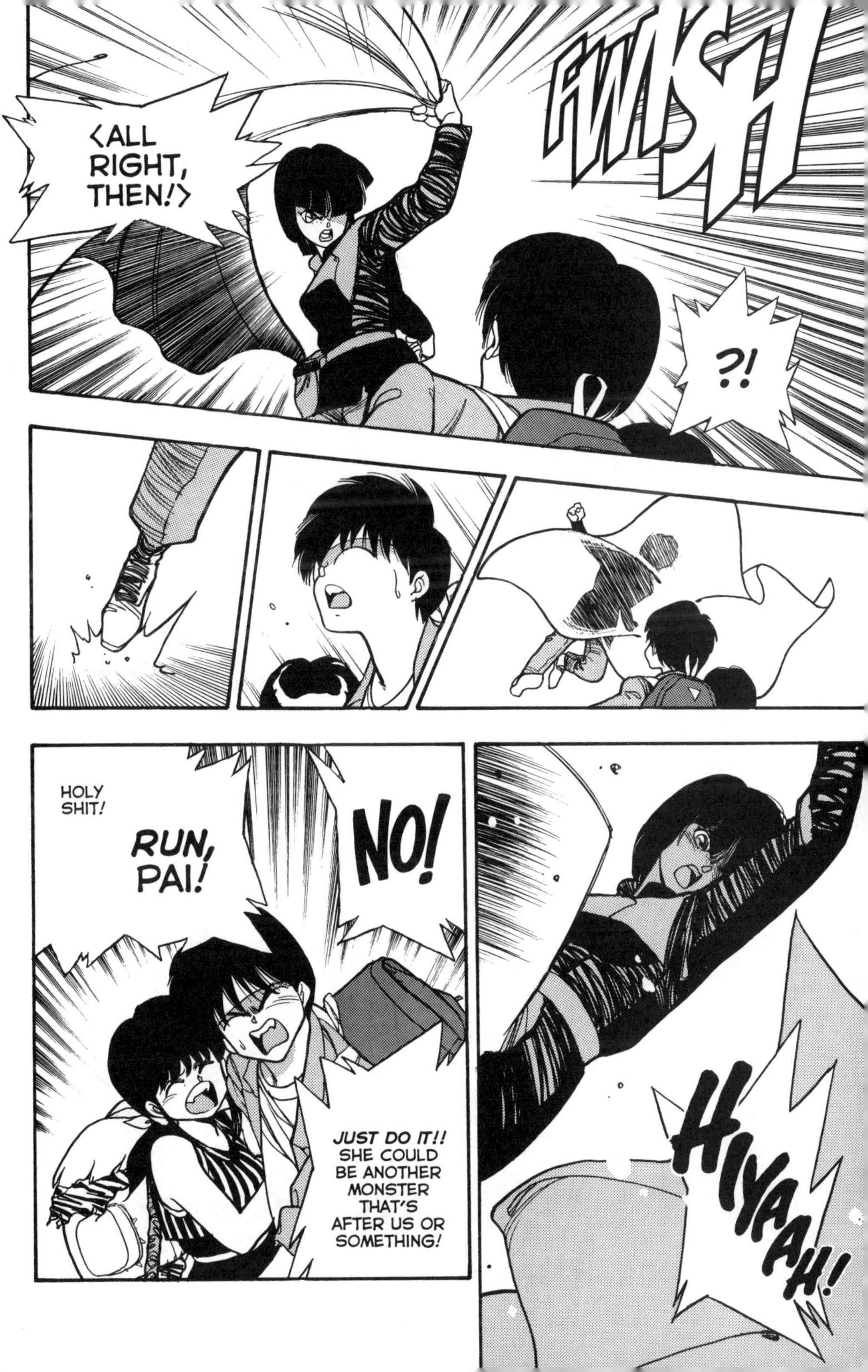
<ALL RIGHT, THEN!>
FWASH
?!
HOLY SHIT!
RUN, PAI!
NO!
JUST DO IT!! SHE COULD BE ANOTHER MONSTER THAT'S AFTER US OR SOMETHING!
HIYAAH!

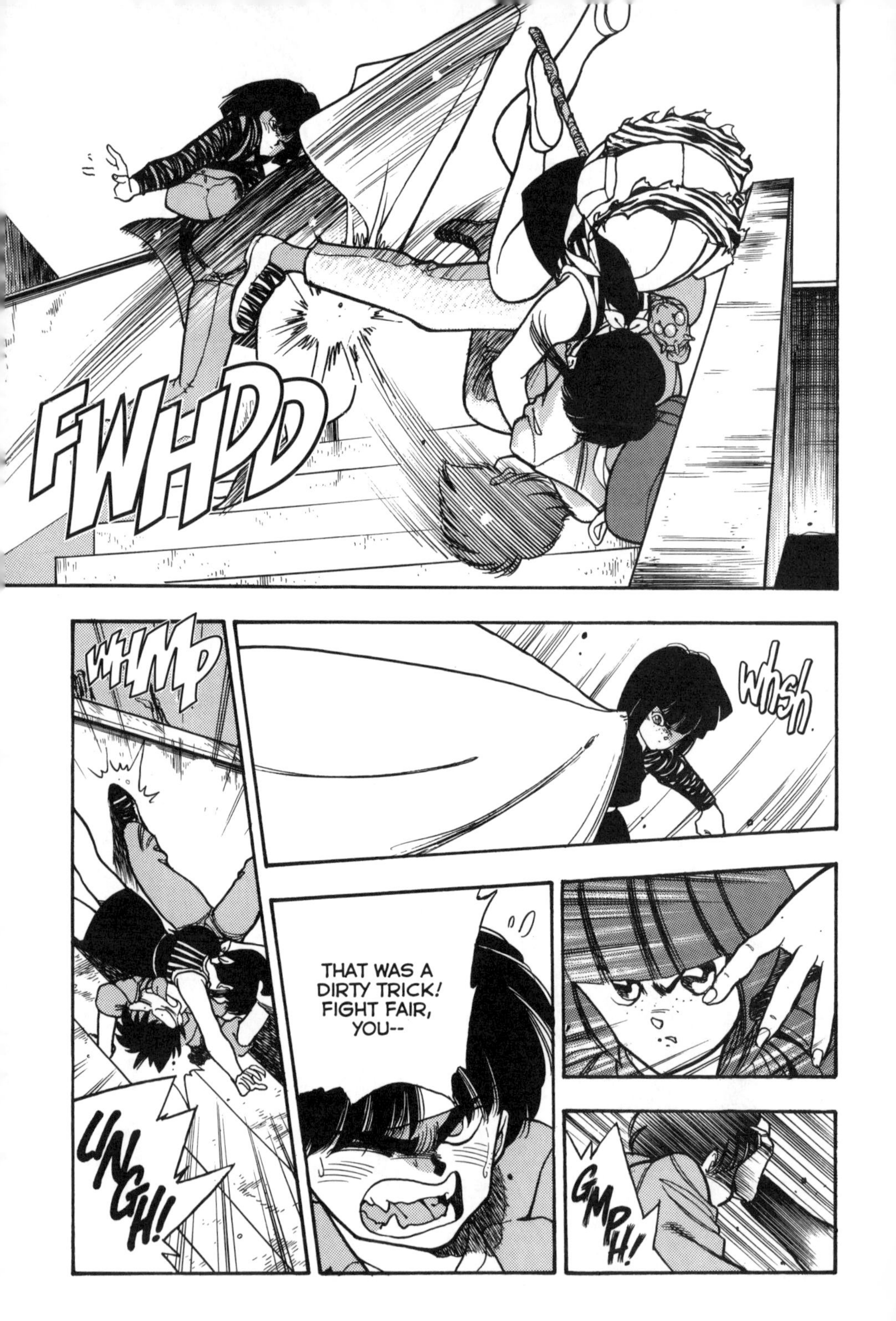
FWHDD
WHMP
whsh
THAT WAS A DIRTY TRICK! FIGHT FAIR, YOU--
UNGH!
GMPH!

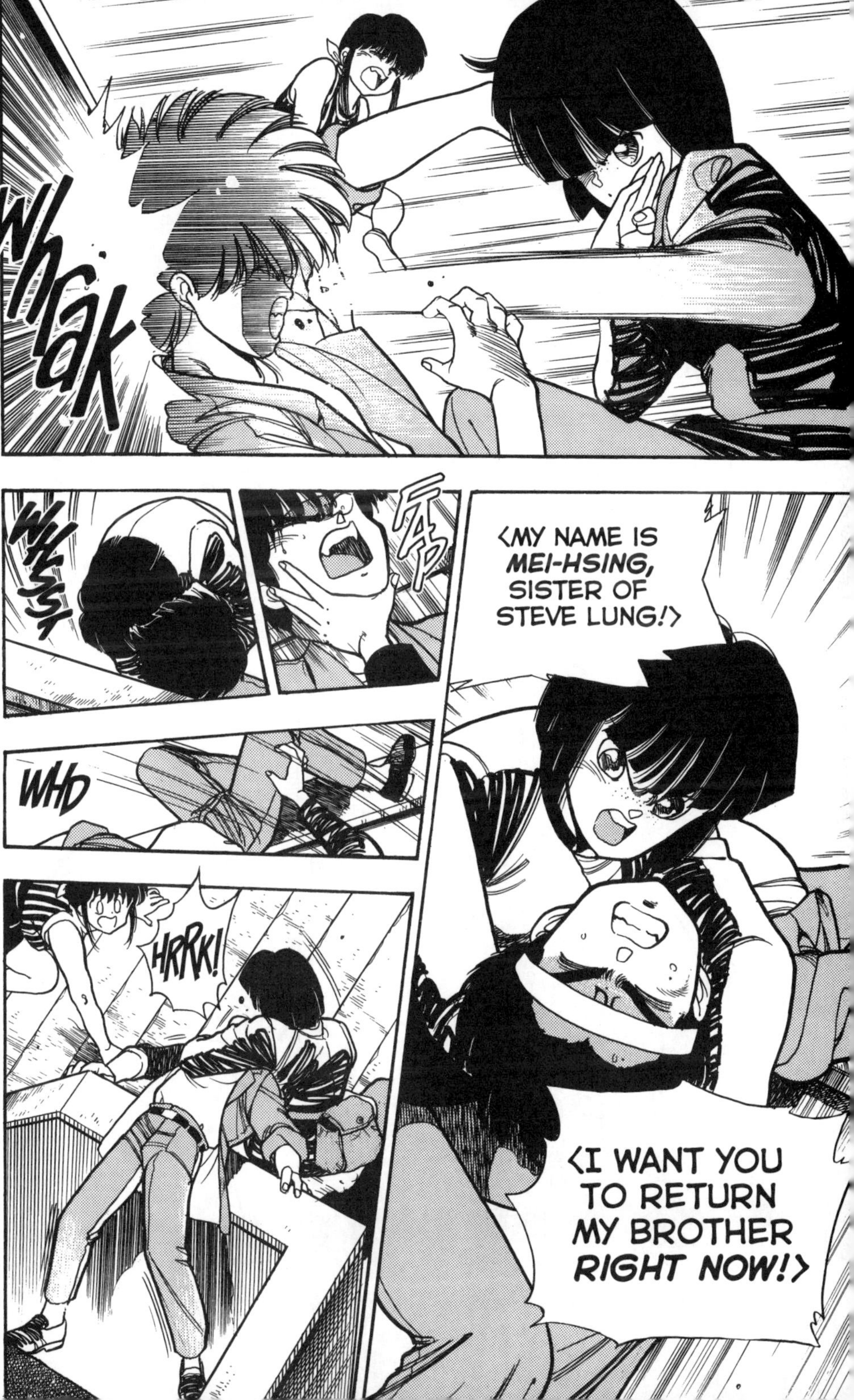

WHRAK
WHSSSK
FAP
WHD
HRRK!
<MY NAME IS *MEI-HSING*, SISTER OF STEVE LUNG!>
<I WANT YOU TO RETURN MY BROTHER *RIGHT NOW!*>

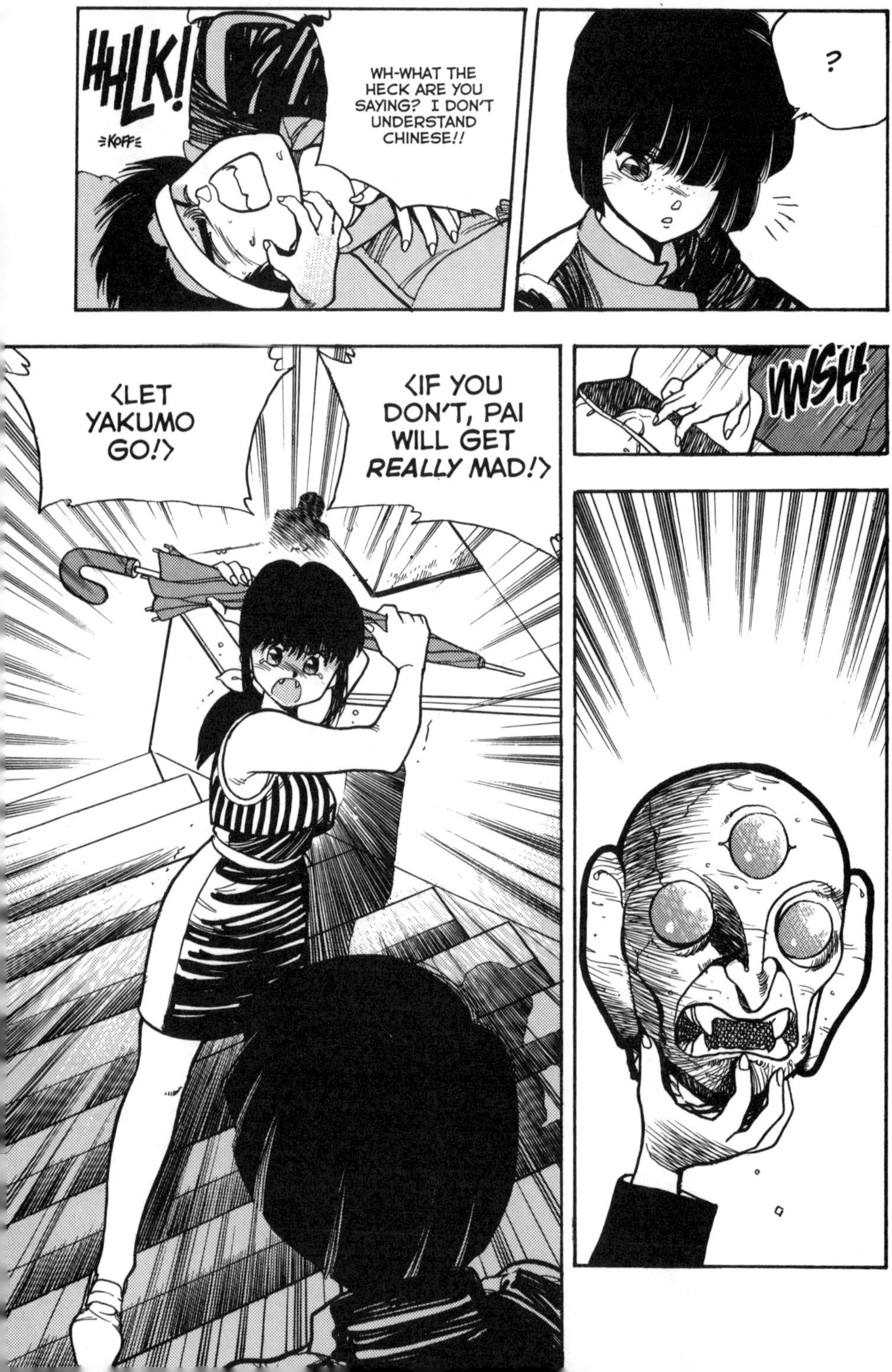
HHLK!
KOFF
WH-WHAT THE HECK ARE YOU SAYING? I DON'T UNDERSTAND CHINESE!!
?
<LET YAKUMO GO!>
<IF YOU DON'T, PAI WILL GET *REALLY* MAD!>
VWSH

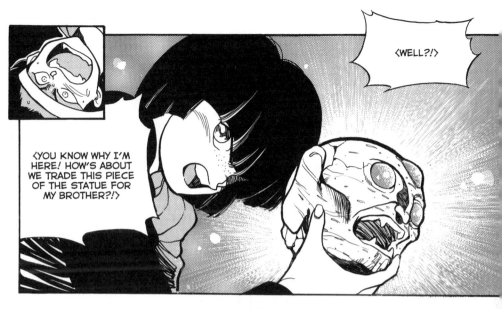

‹WELL?!›

‹YOU KNOW WHY I'M HERE! HOW'S ABOUT WE TRADE THIS PIECE OF THE STATUE FOR MY BROTHER?!›

‹WE DON'T KNOW *ANYTHING* ABOUT YOUR BROTHER!›

‹*PLEASE* LET YAKUMO GO...›
≥ SNIFF ≤

· · · ·

FWMP

· · · ·

‹YOU *REALLY* DON'T KNOW ANYTHING...?›

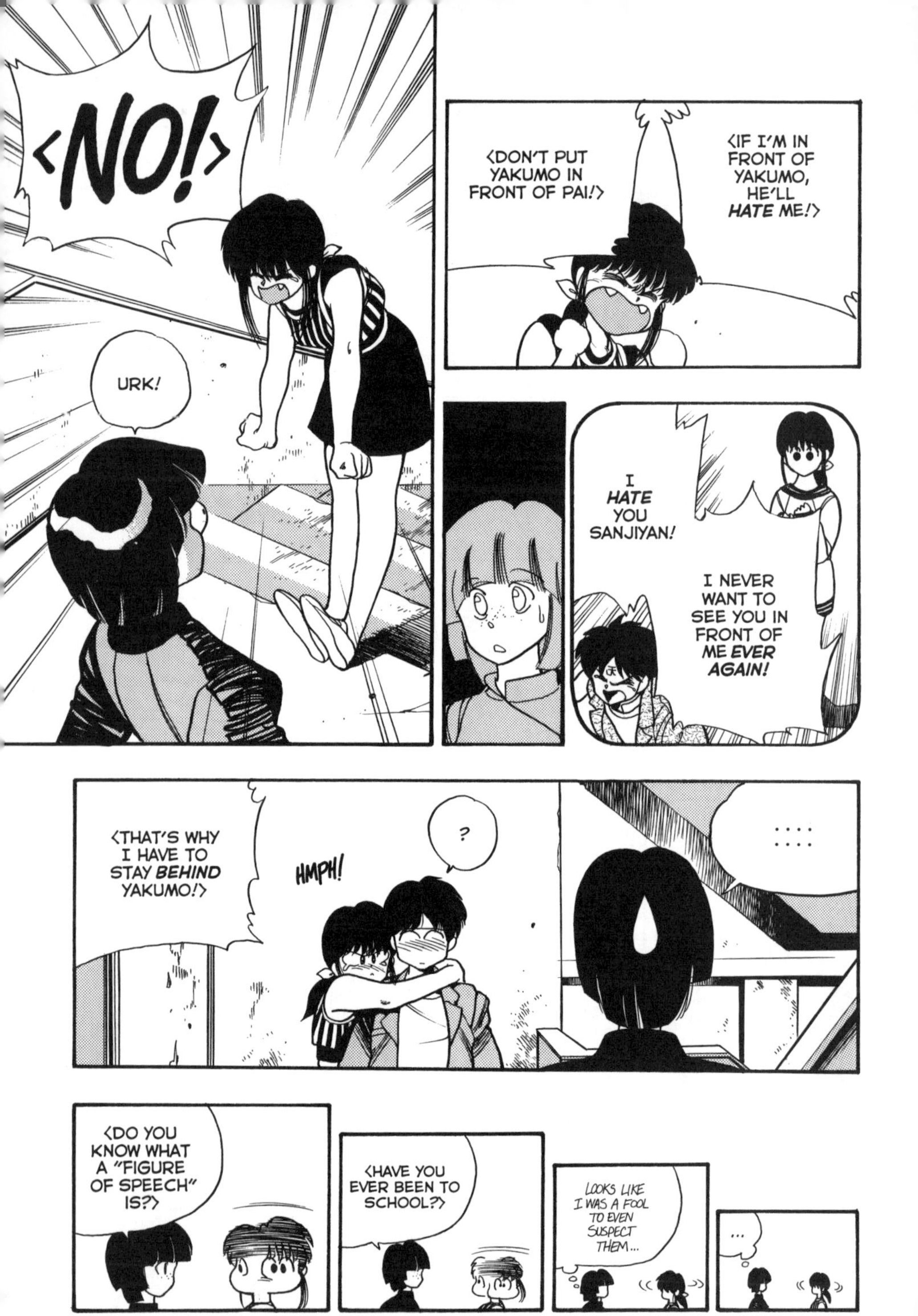

<NO!>
URK!
<DON'T PUT YAKUMO IN FRONT OF PAI!>
<IF I'M IN FRONT OF YAKUMO, HE'LL HATE ME!>
I HATE YOU SANJIYAN!
I NEVER WANT TO SEE YOU IN FRONT OF ME EVER AGAIN!
<THAT'S WHY I HAVE TO STAY BEHIND YAKUMO!>
HMPH!
?
....
<DO YOU KNOW WHAT A "FIGURE OF SPEECH" IS?>
<HAVE YOU EVER BEEN TO SCHOOL?>
LOOKS LIKE I WAS A FOOL TO EVEN SUSPECT THEM...
...

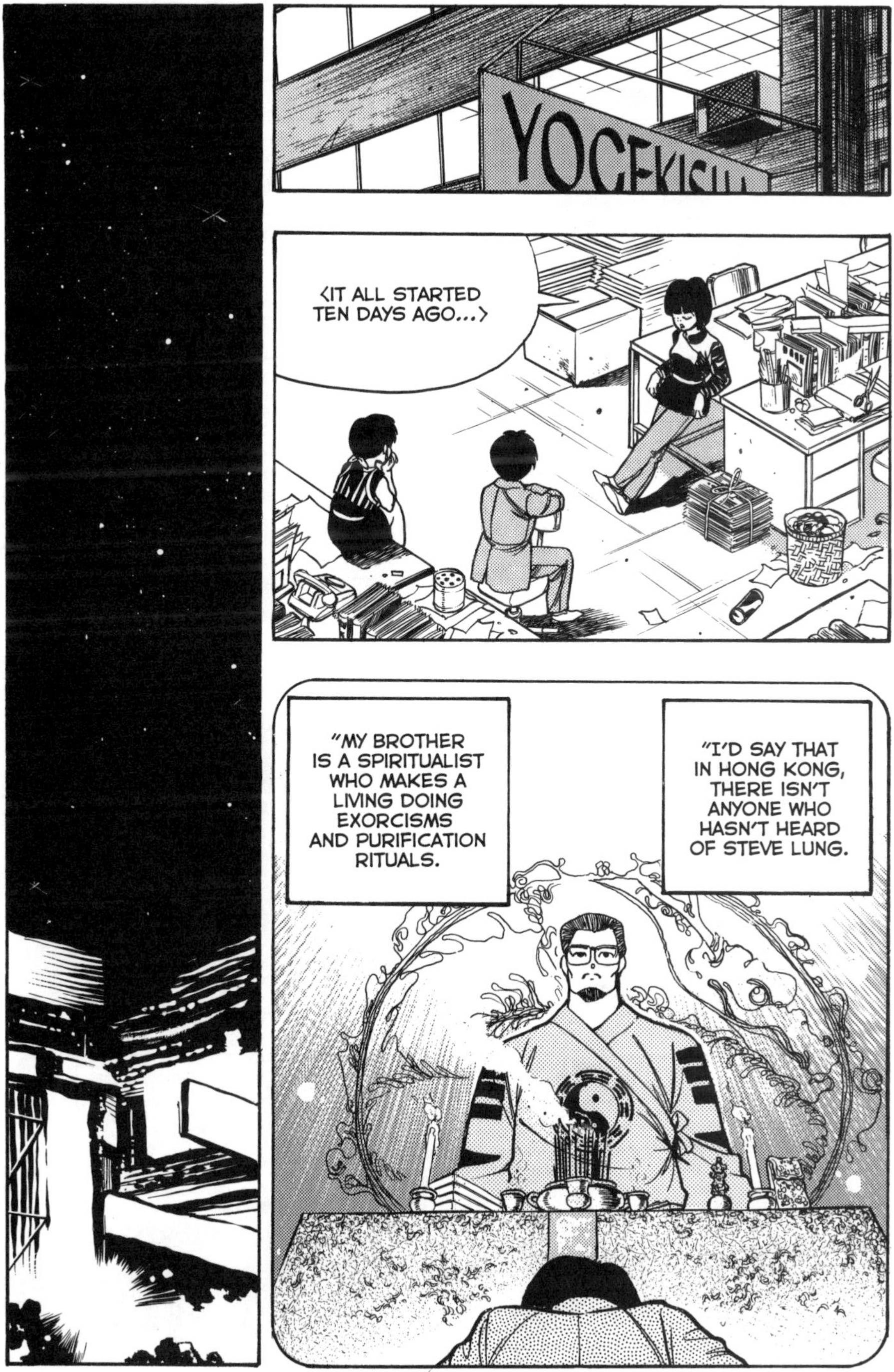
<IT ALL STARTED TEN DAYS AGO...>
"MY BROTHER IS A SPIRITUALIST WHO MAKES A LIVING DOING EXORCISMS AND PURIFICATION RITUALS.
"I'D SAY THAT IN HONG KONG, THERE ISN'T ANYONE WHO HASN'T HEARD OF STEVE LUNG.

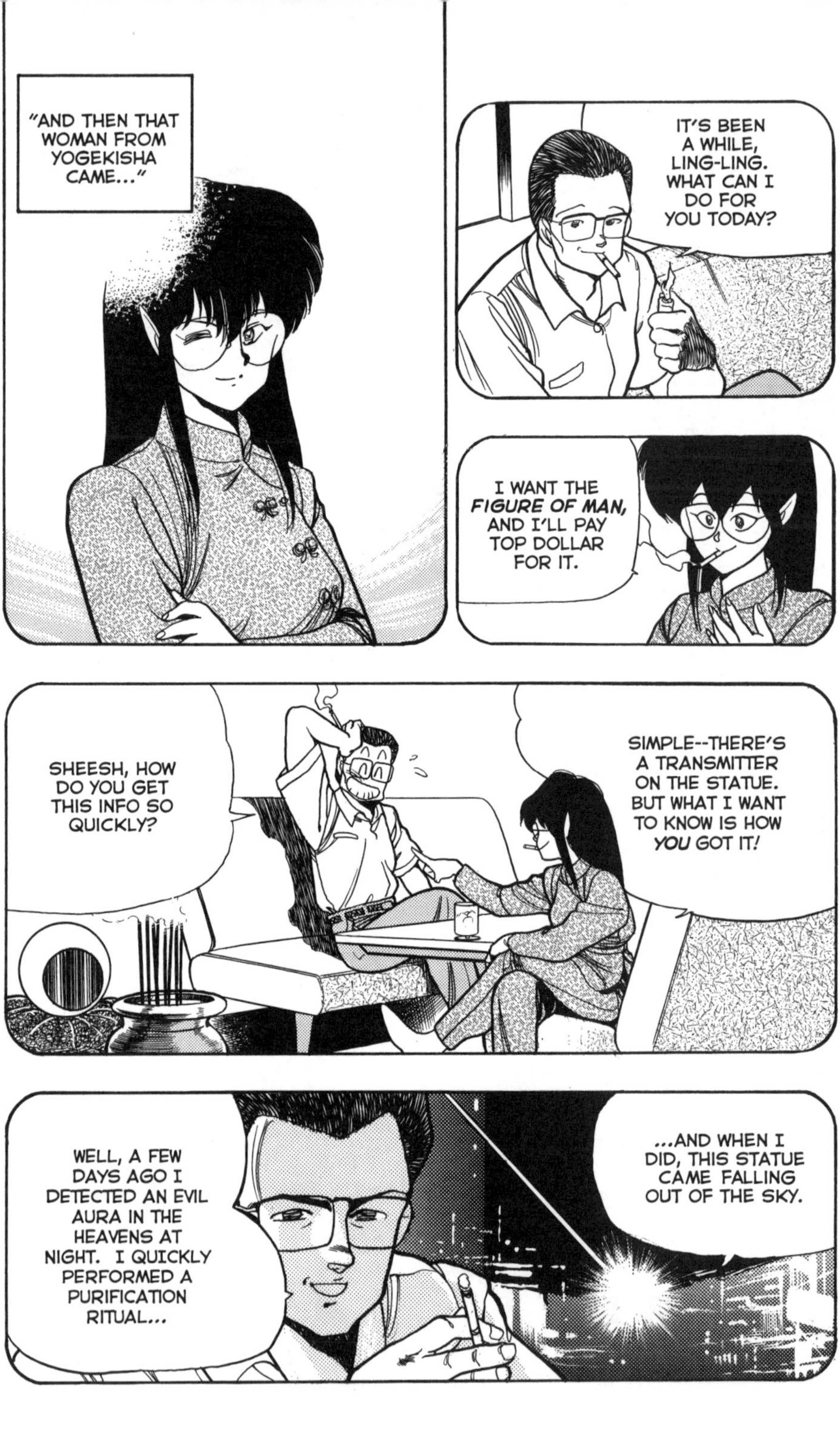

"AND THEN THAT WOMAN FROM YOGEKISHA CAME..."
IT'S BEEN A WHILE, LING-LING. WHAT CAN I DO FOR YOU TODAY?
I WANT THE *FIGURE OF MAN,* AND I'LL PAY TOP DOLLAR FOR IT.
SHEESH, HOW DO YOU GET THIS INFO SO QUICKLY?
SIMPLE--THERE'S A TRANSMITTER ON THE STATUE. BUT WHAT I WANT TO KNOW IS HOW *YOU* GOT IT!
WELL, A FEW DAYS AGO I DETECTED AN EVIL AURA IN THE HEAVENS AT NIGHT. I QUICKLY PERFORMED A PURIFICATION RITUAL...
...AND WHEN I DID, THIS STATUE CAME FALLING OUT OF THE SKY.

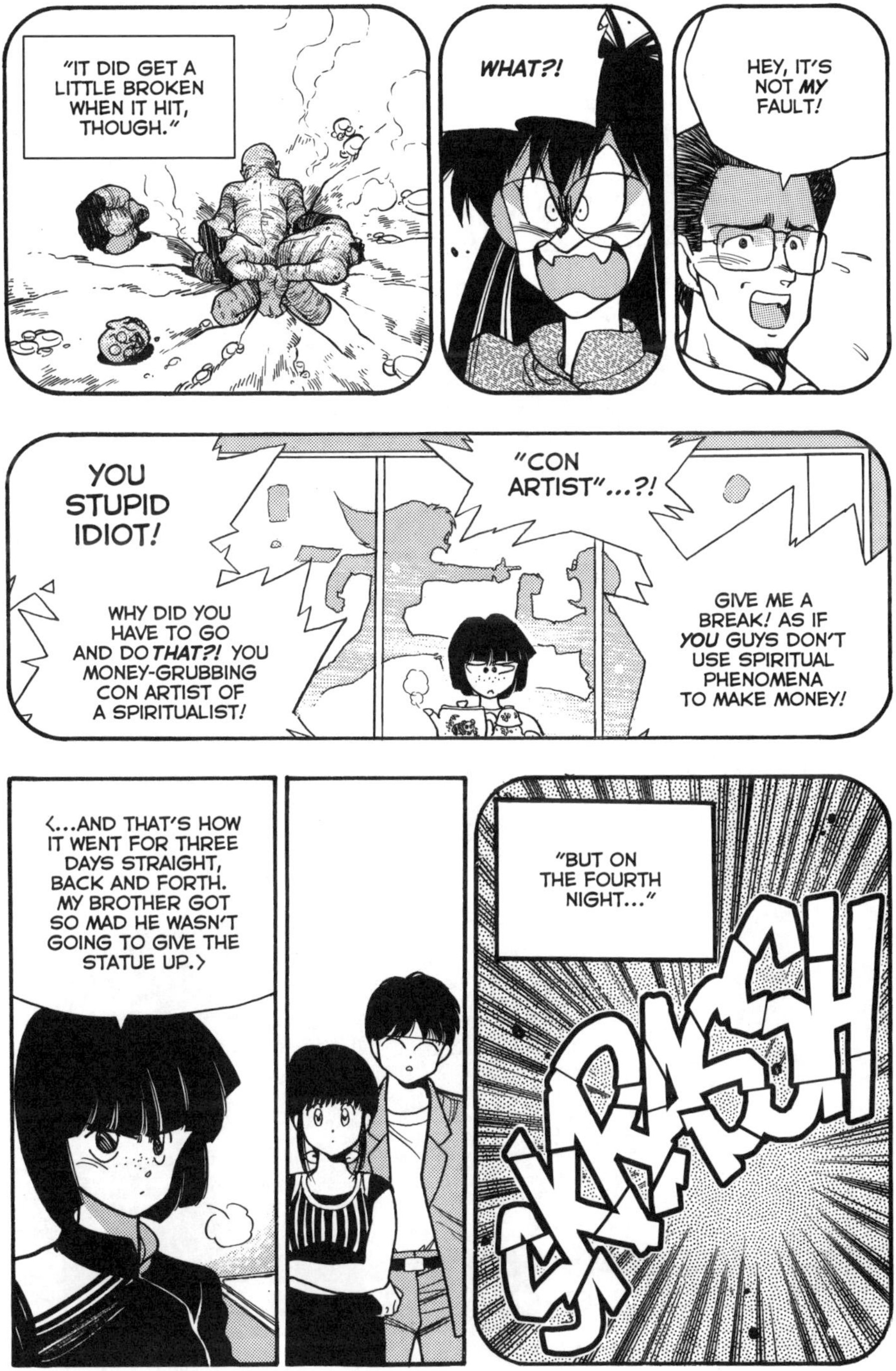
"IT DID GET A LITTLE BROKEN WHEN IT HIT, THOUGH."
WHAT?!
HEY, IT'S NOT *MY* FAULT!
YOU STUPID IDIOT!
WHY DID YOU HAVE TO GO AND DO *THAT?!* YOU MONEY-GRUBBING CON ARTIST OF A SPIRITUALIST!
"CON ARTIST"...?!
GIVE ME A BREAK! AS IF *YOU* GUYS DON'T USE SPIRITUAL PHENOMENA TO MAKE MONEY!
<...AND THAT'S HOW IT WENT FOR THREE DAYS STRAIGHT, BACK AND FORTH. MY BROTHER GOT SO MAD HE WASN'T GOING TO GIVE THE STATUE UP.>
"BUT ON THE FOURTH NIGHT..."
SKRASCH

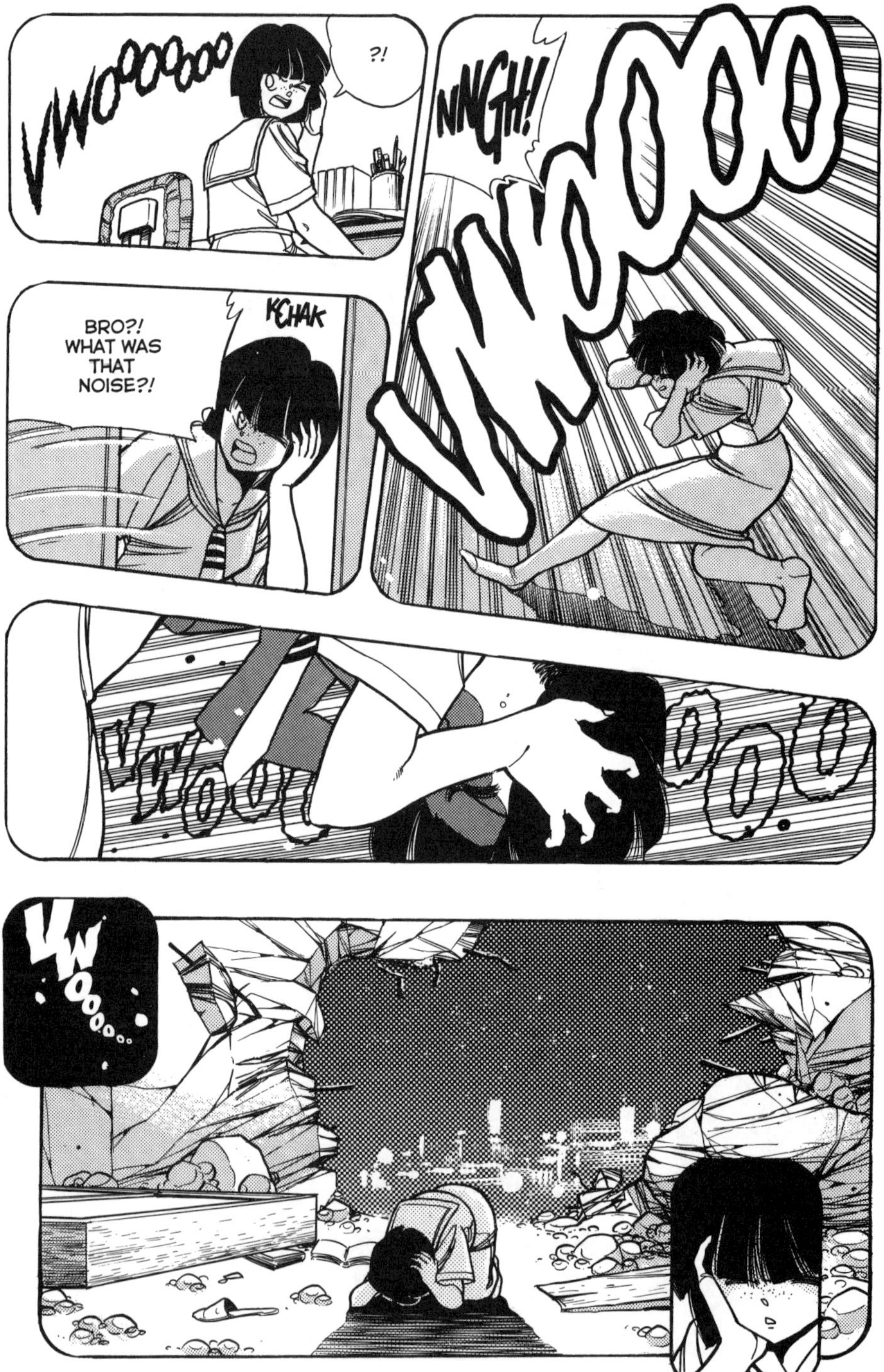
VWOOOOOOO
?!
BRO?! WHAT WAS THAT NOISE?!
KCHAK
NNGH!
VWOOOOO
VWOOOOOOOOO
VWOOOOOO

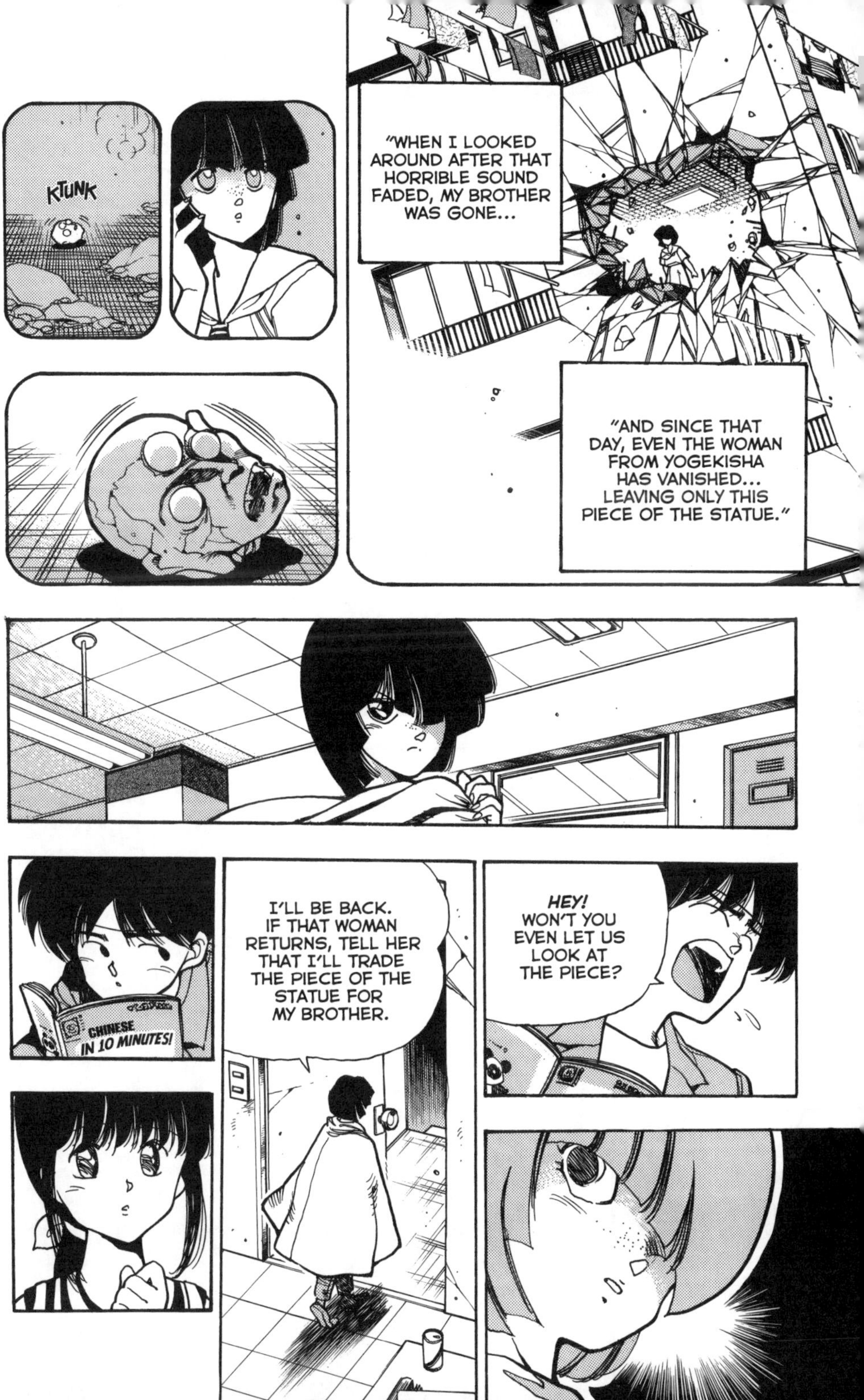
KTUNK
"WHEN I LOOKED AROUND AFTER THAT HORRIBLE SOUND FADED, MY BROTHER WAS GONE...
"AND SINCE THAT DAY, EVEN THE WOMAN FROM YOGEKISHA HAS VANISHED... LEAVING ONLY THIS PIECE OF THE STATUE."
CHINESE IN 10 MINUTES!
I'LL BE BACK. IF THAT WOMAN RETURNS, TELL HER THAT I'LL TRADE THE PIECE OF THE STATUE FOR MY BROTHER.
HEY! WON'T YOU EVEN LET US LOOK AT THE PIECE?

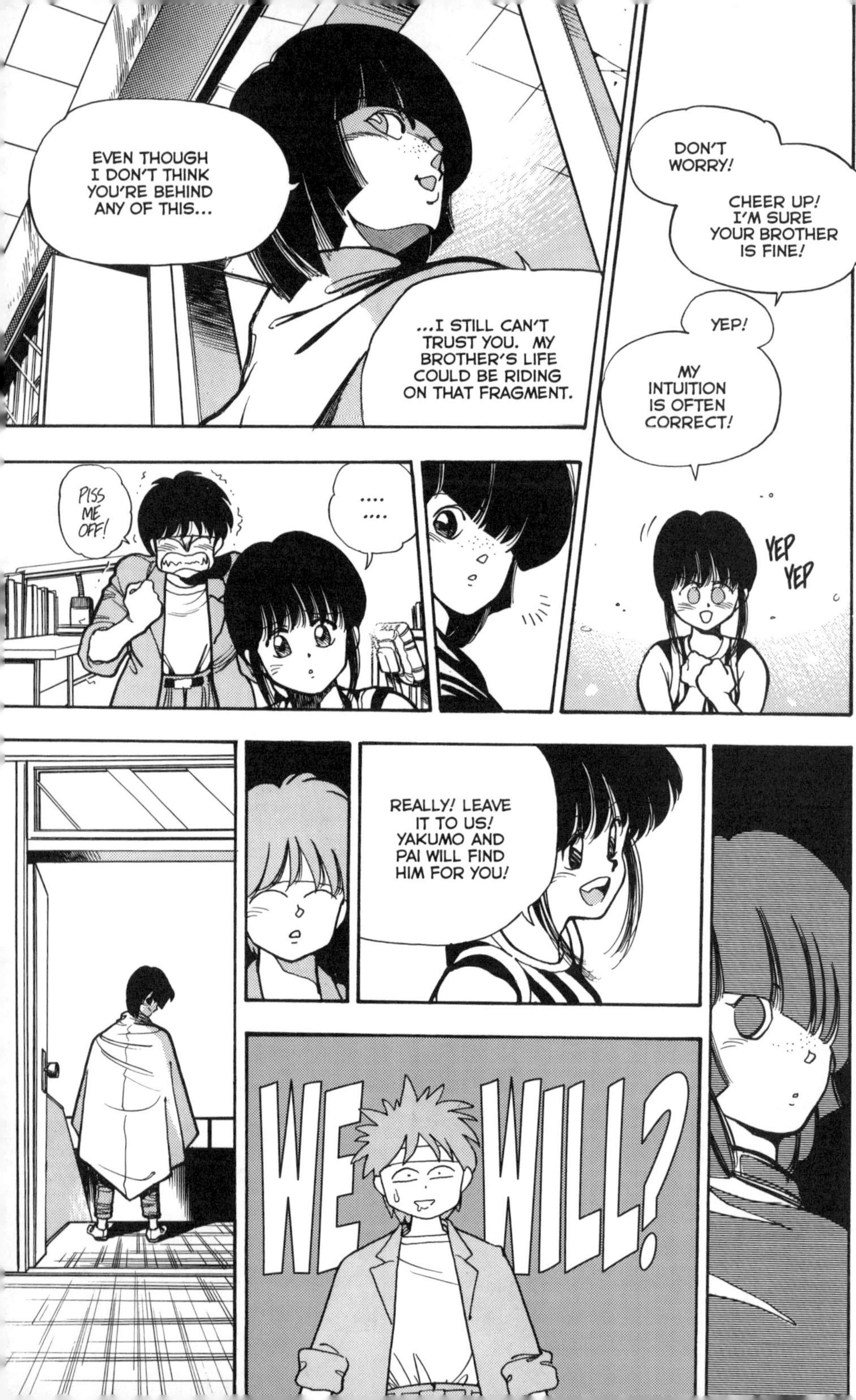
EVEN THOUGH I DON'T THINK YOU'RE BEHIND ANY OF THIS...
...I STILL CAN'T TRUST YOU. MY BROTHER'S LIFE COULD BE RIDING ON THAT FRAGMENT.
PISS ME OFF!
....
DON'T WORRY!
CHEER UP! I'M SURE YOUR BROTHER IS FINE!
YEP!
MY INTUITION IS OFTEN CORRECT!
YEP YEP
REALLY! LEAVE IT TO US! YAKUMO AND PAI WILL FIND HIM FOR YOU!
WE WILL?

I WON'T BE HOLDING MY BREATH!

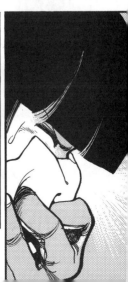

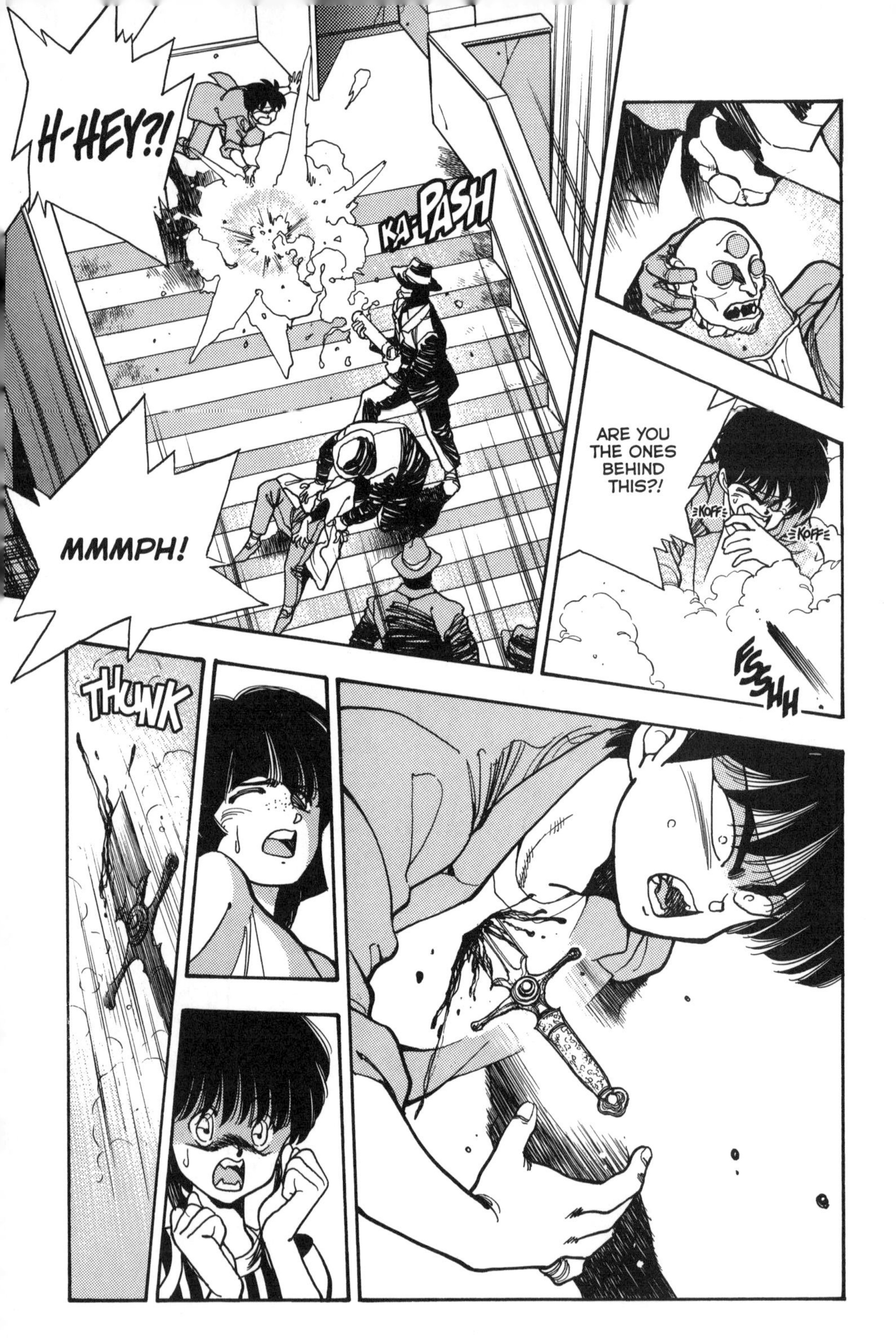
H-HEY?!
KA-PASH
MMMPH!
ARE YOU THE ONES BEHIND THIS?!
KOFF
KOFF
FSSHH
THUNK

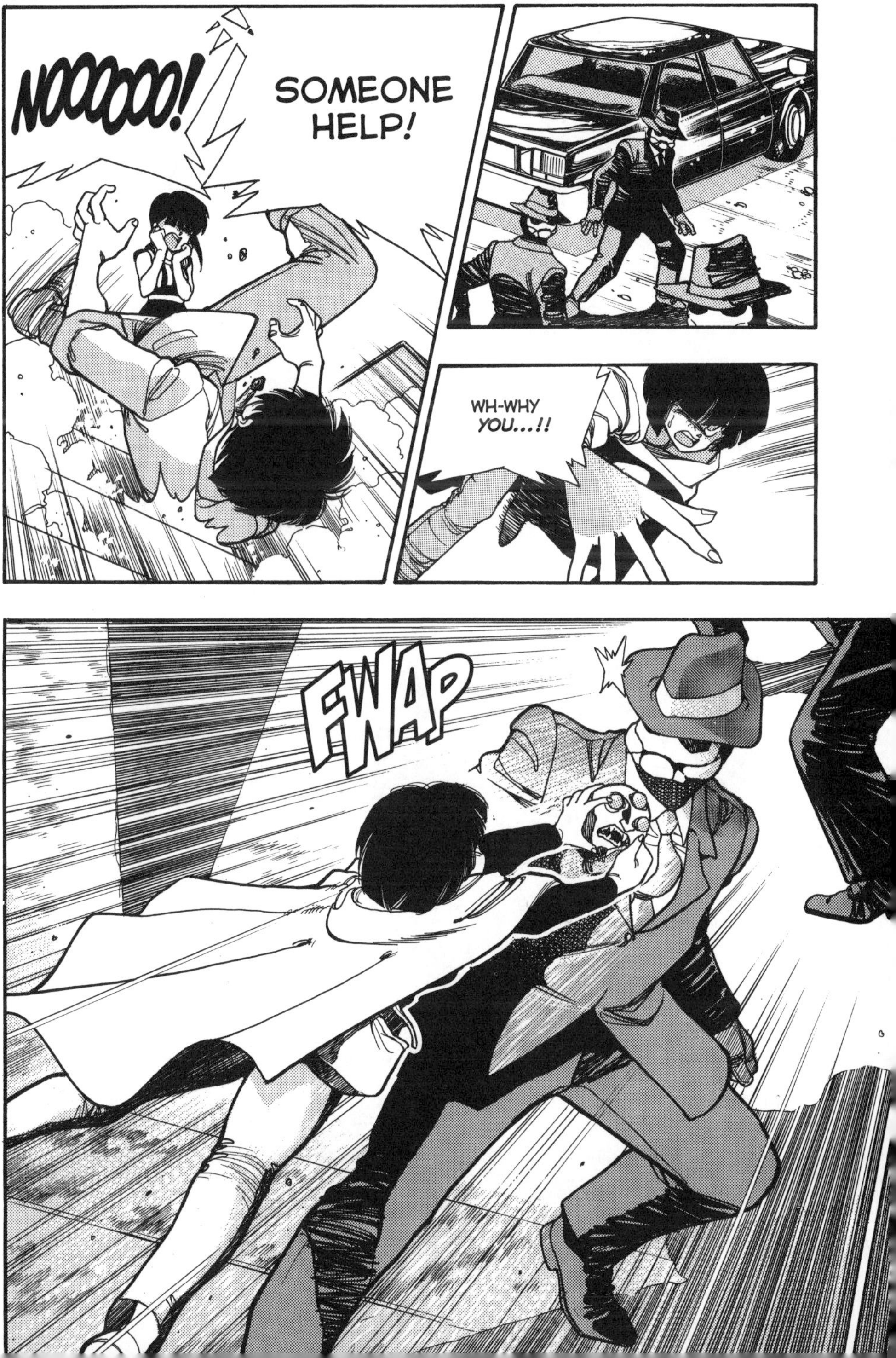
NOOOOOO!
SOMEONE HELP!
WH-WHY YOU...!!
FWAP

SOMEONE HELP US! *PLEASE!!*

YOU'LL GET THIS OVER MY DEAD BODY!

SNIK

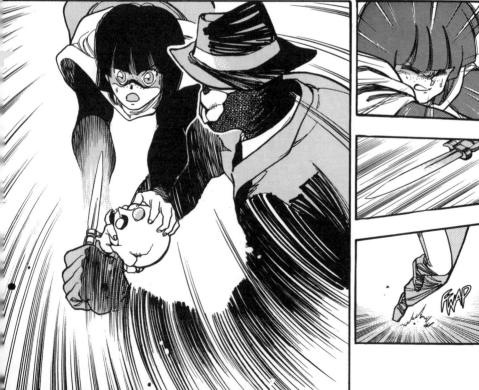

FWAP

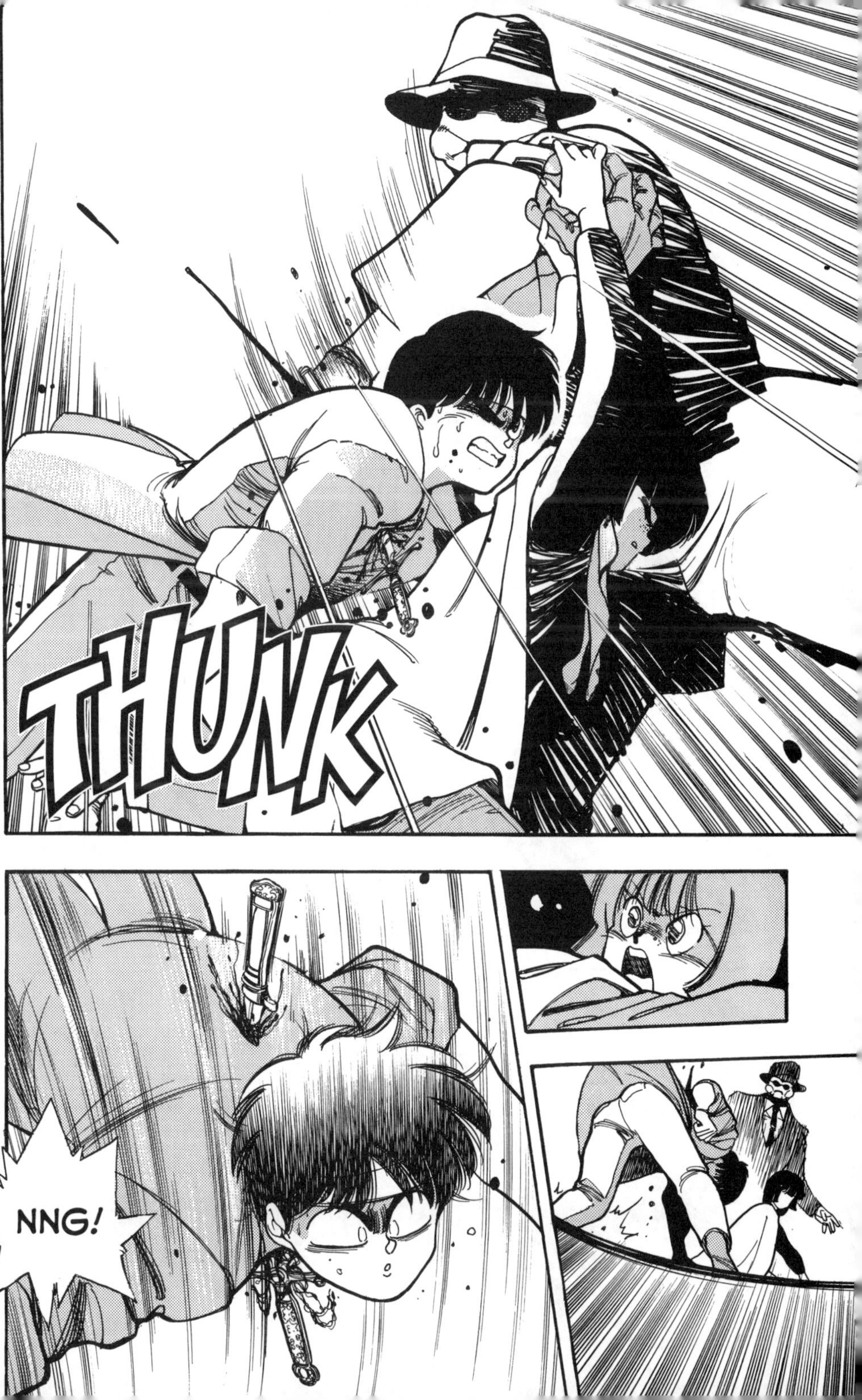
THUNK
NNG!

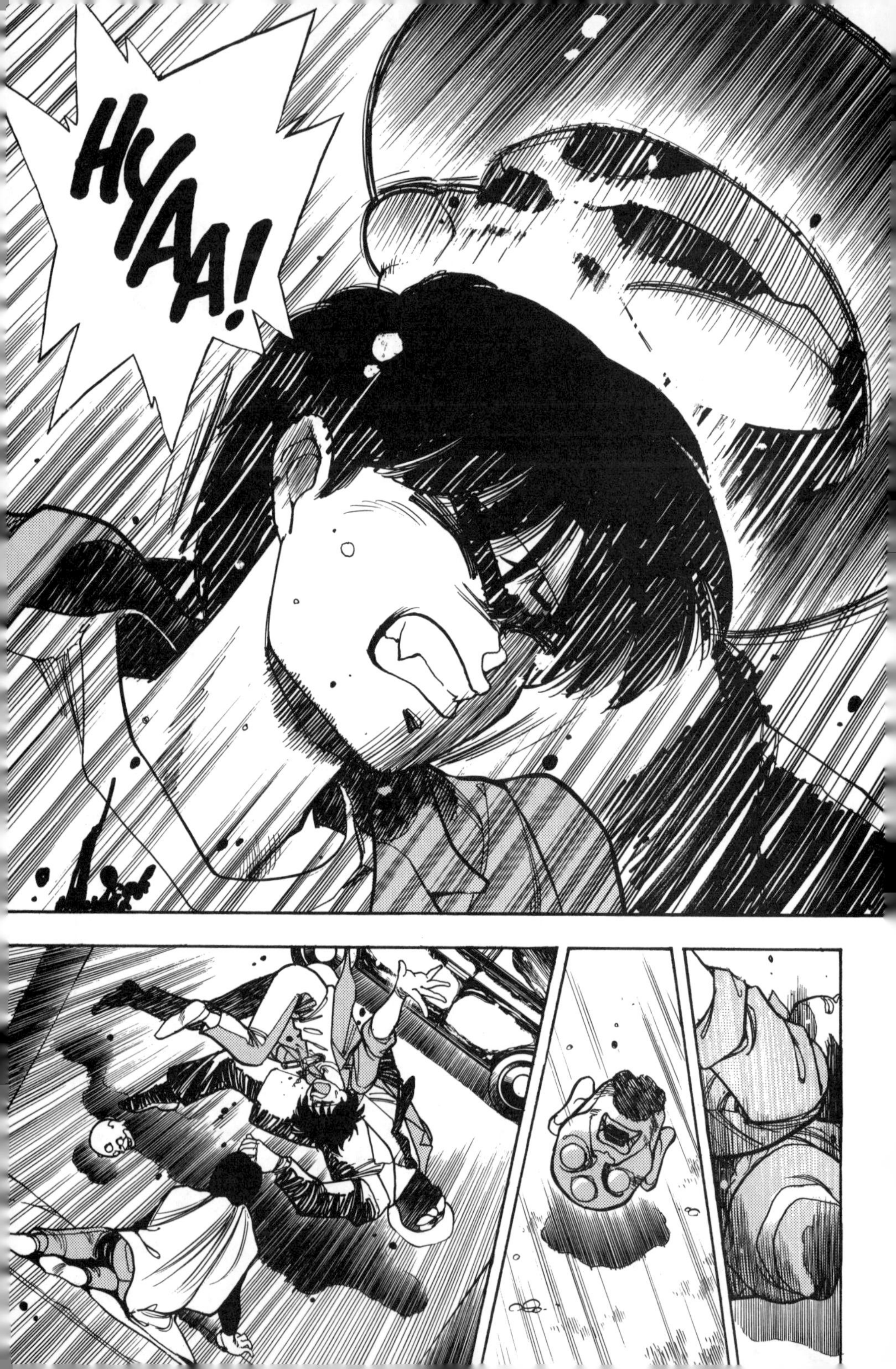
HYAAA!

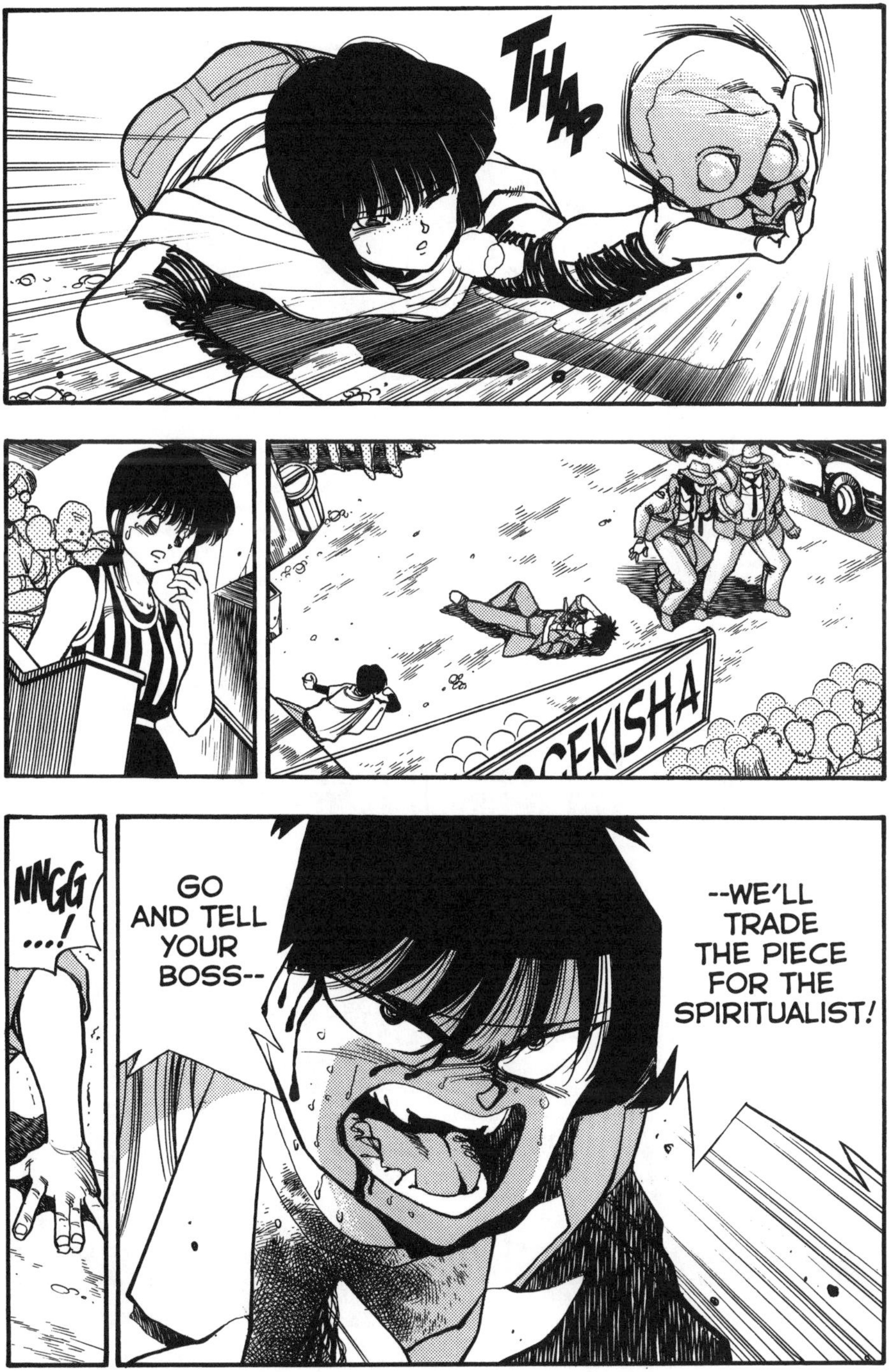
THAP
GEKISHA
NNGG ...!
GO AND TELL YOUR BOSS--
--WE'LL TRADE THE PIECE FOR THE SPIRITUALIST!

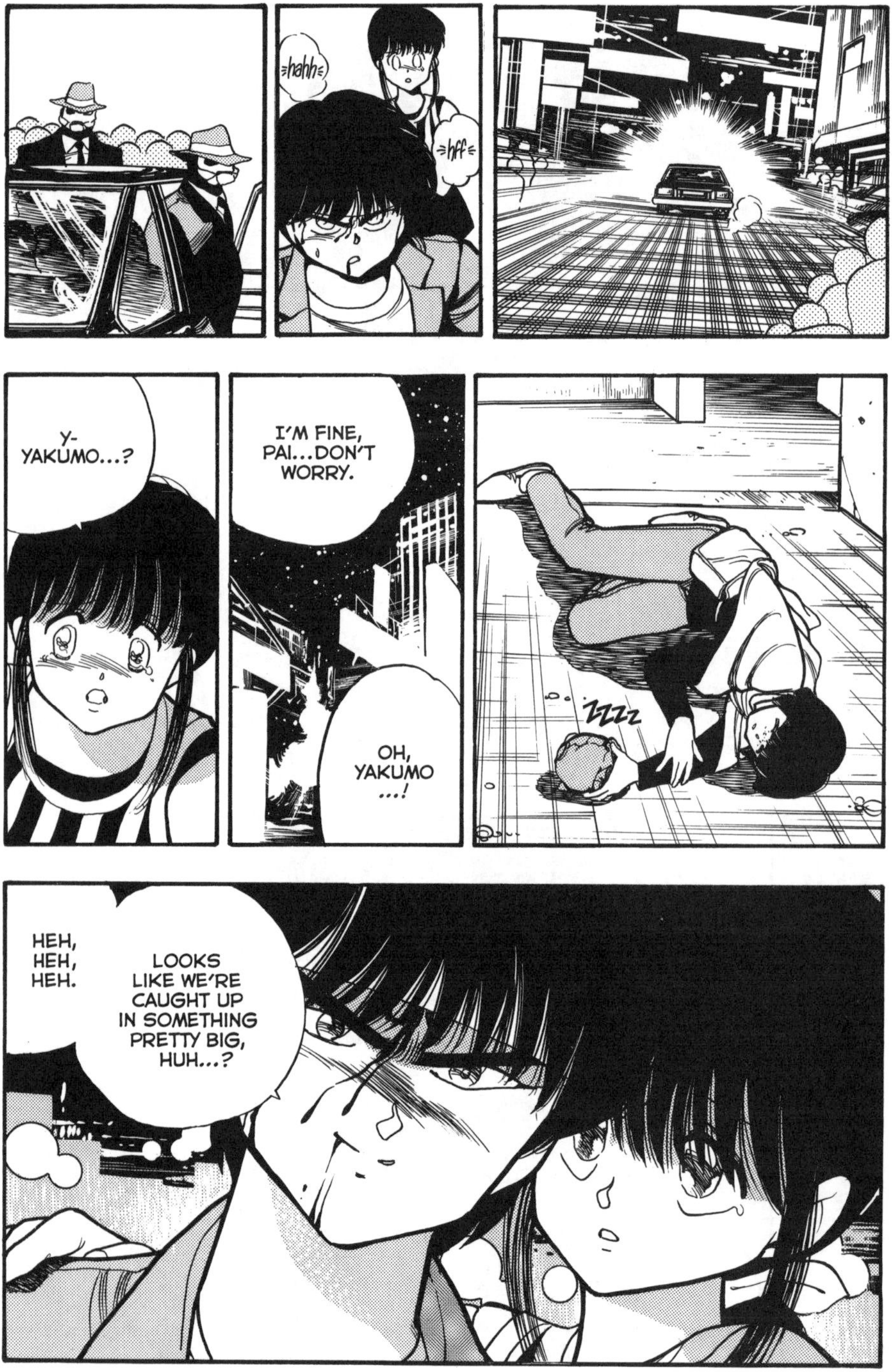
hahh
hff
Y-
YAKUMO...?
I'M FINE, PAI...DON'T WORRY.
OH, YAKUMO ...!
ZZZZ
HEH, HEH, HEH.
LOOKS LIKE WE'RE CAUGHT UP IN SOMETHING PRETTY BIG, HUH...?

Flight of the Demon
part 2

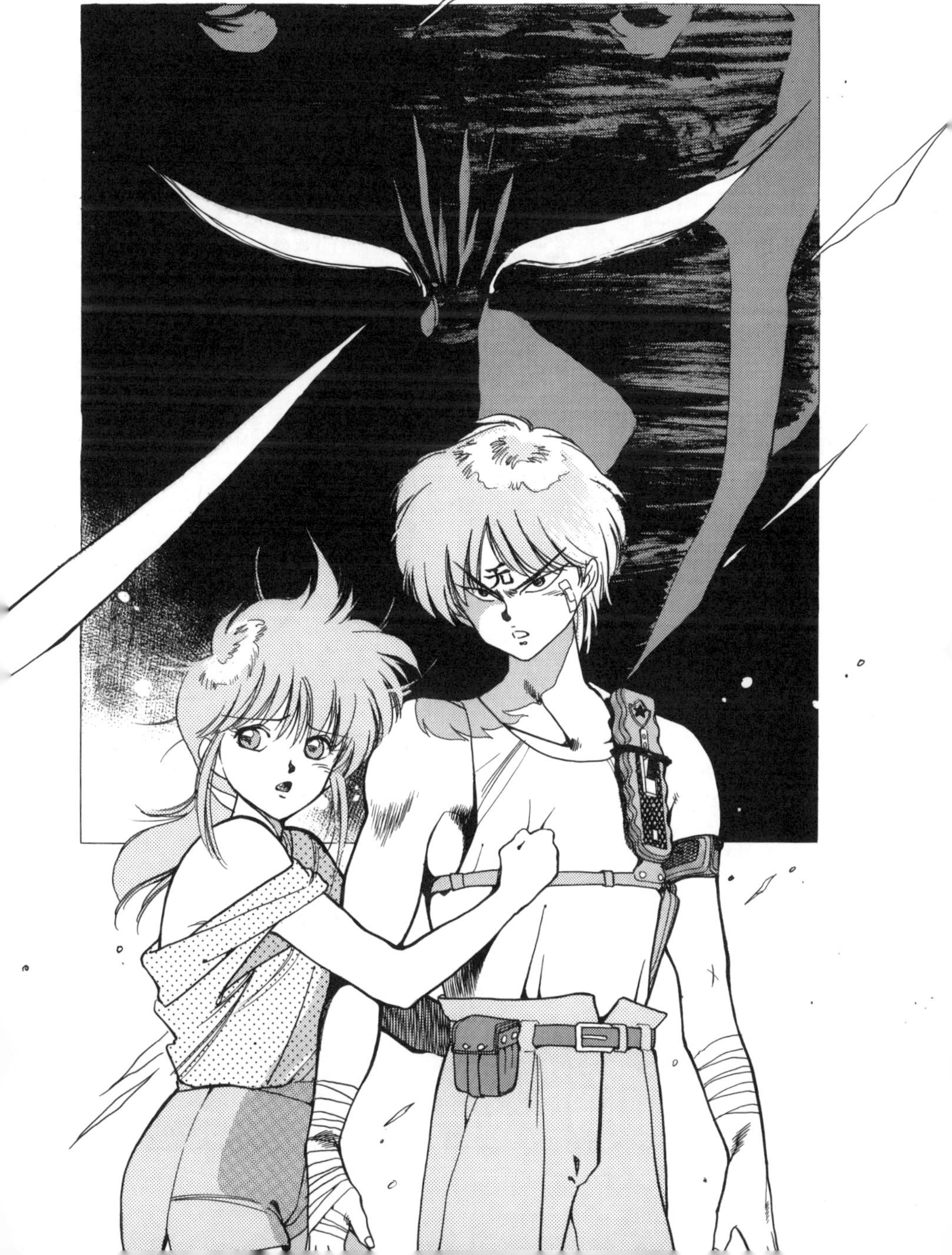

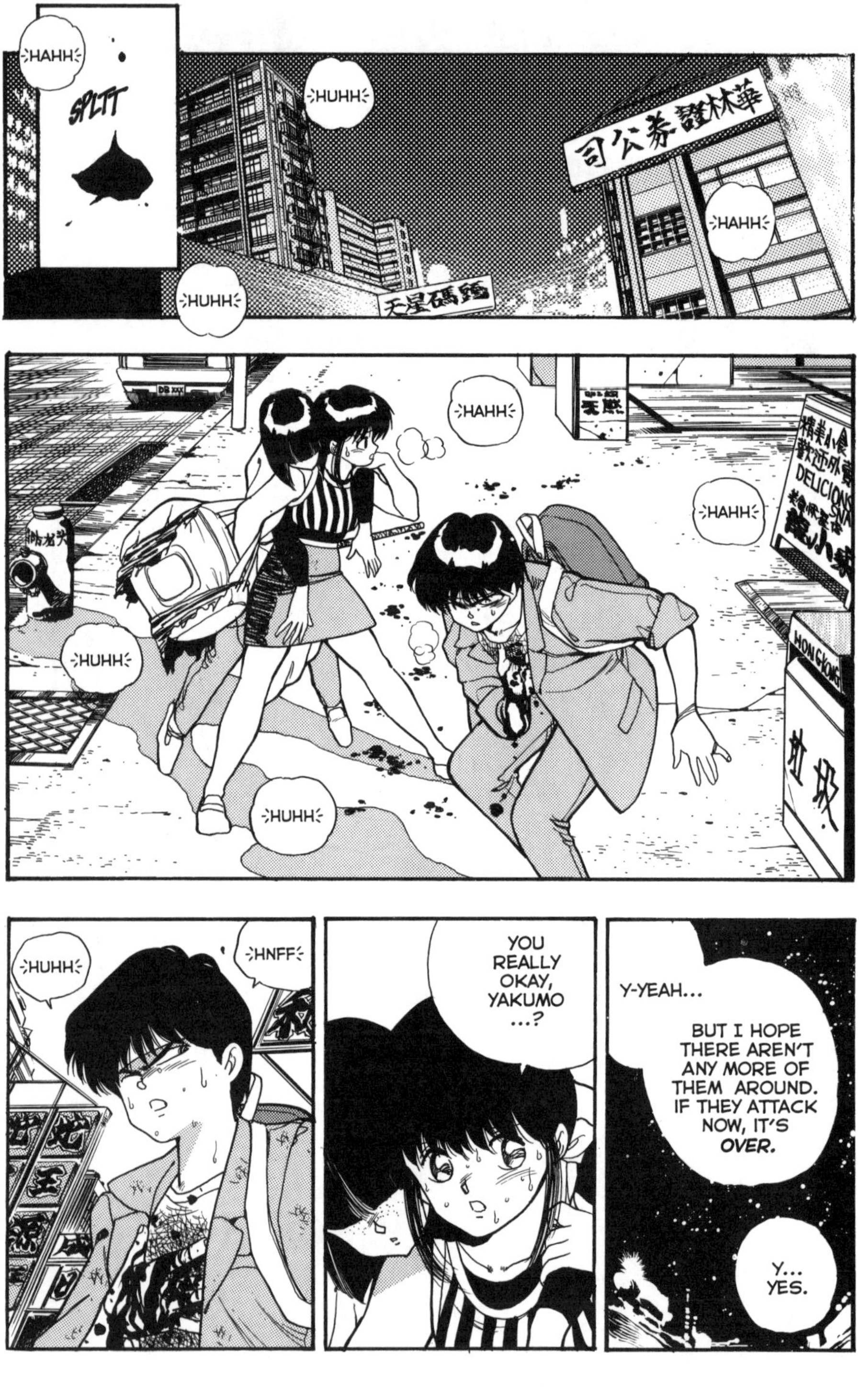HAHH
SPLTT
HUHH
HAHH
HUHH
HAHH
HAHH
HUHH
HUHH
HUHH
HNFF
YOU REALLY OKAY, YAKUMO ...?
Y-YEAH...
BUT I HOPE THERE AREN'T ANY MORE OF THEM AROUND. IF THEY ATTACK NOW, IT'S *OVER.*
Y... YES.

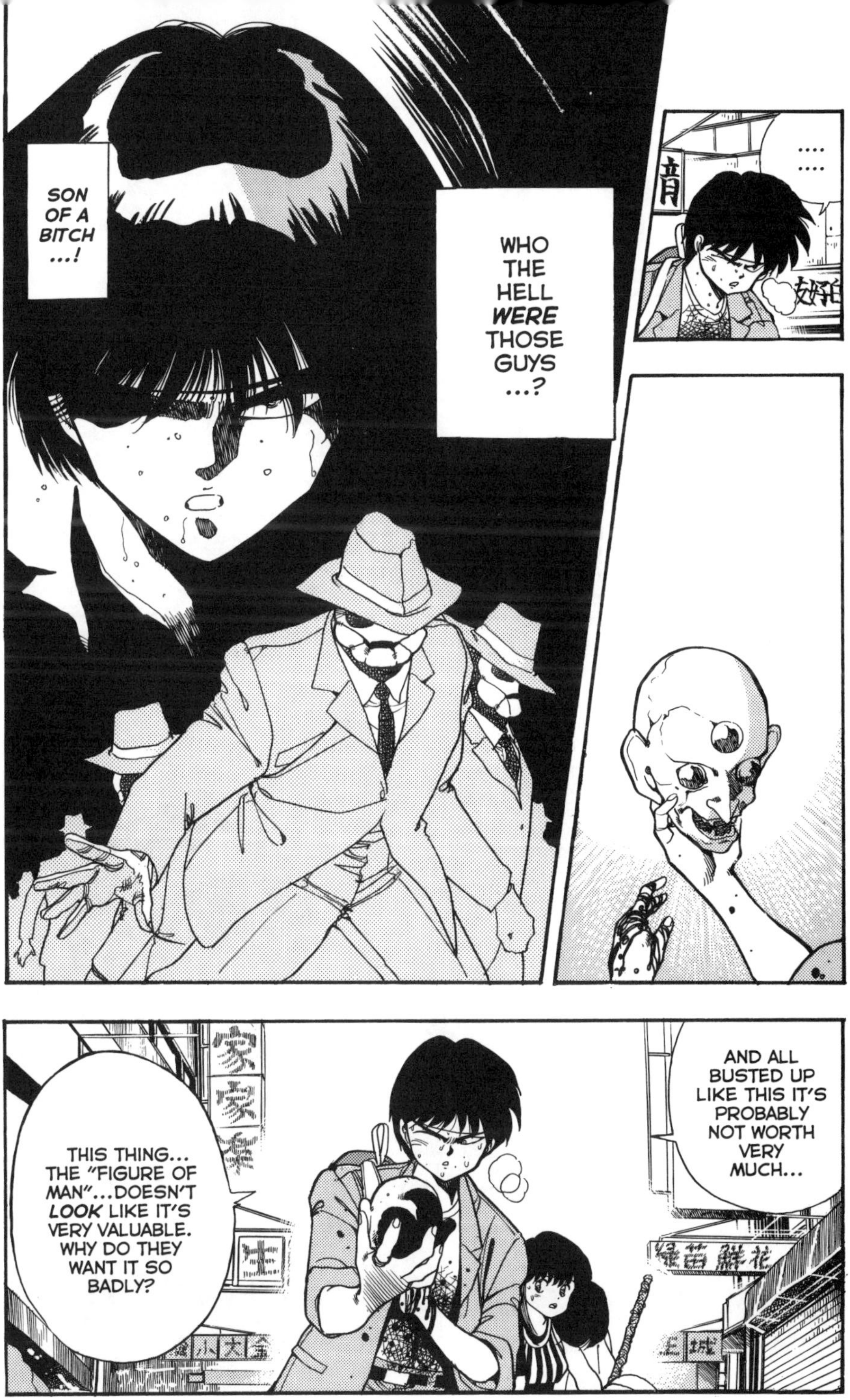
SON OF A BITCH ...!
WHO THE HELL *WERE* THOSE GUYS ...?
....
....
THIS THING... THE "FIGURE OF MAN"...DOESN'T *LOOK* LIKE IT'S VERY VALUABLE. WHY DO THEY WANT IT SO BADLY?
AND ALL BUSTED UP LIKE THIS IT'S PROBABLY NOT WORTH VERY MUCH...

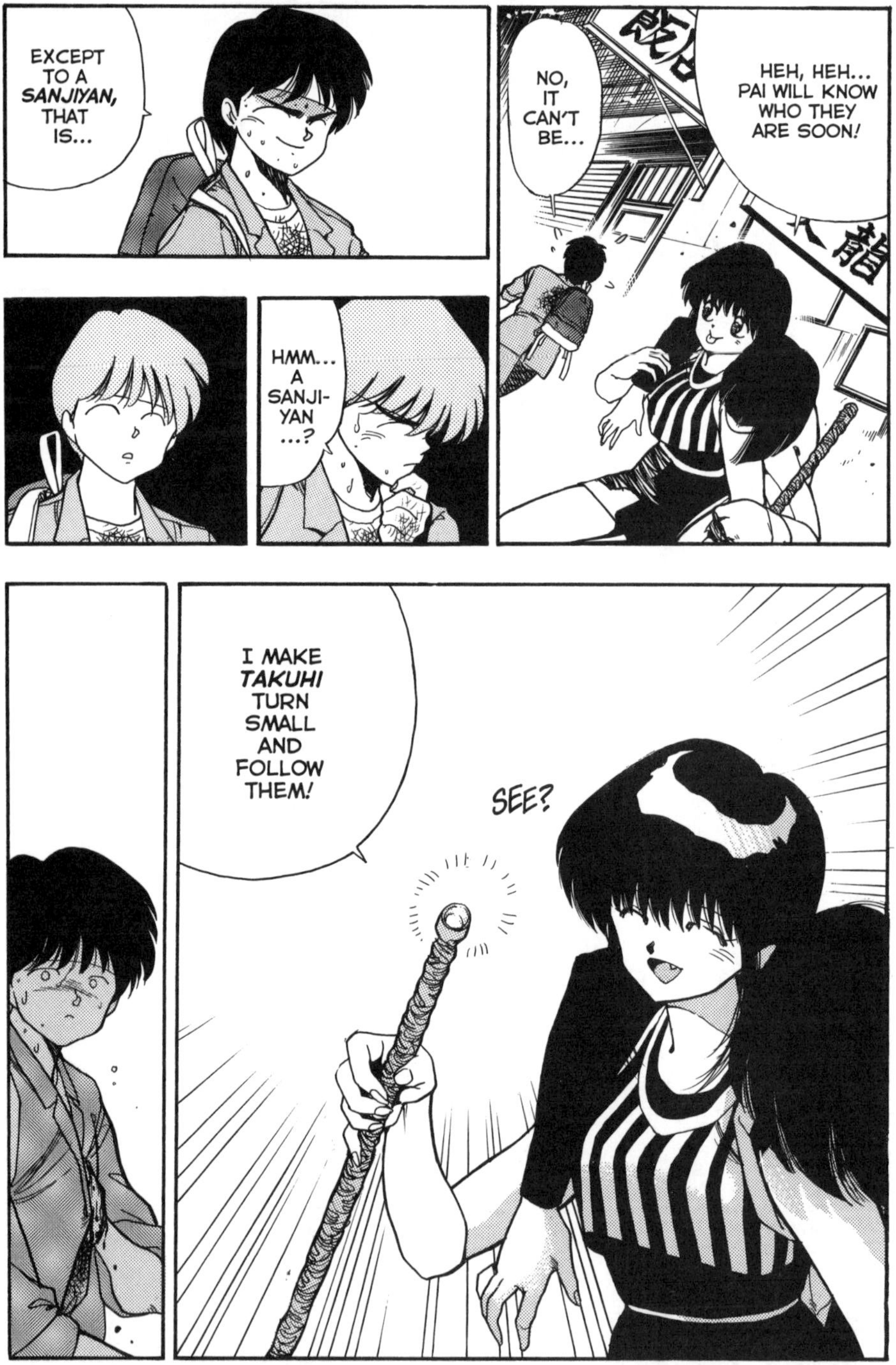
EXCEPT TO A *SANJIYAN,* THAT IS...
HMM... A SANJI-YAN ...?
NO, IT CAN'T BE...
HEH, HEH... PAI WILL KNOW WHO THEY ARE SOON!
I MAKE *TAKUHI* TURN SMALL AND FOLLOW THEM!
SEE?

PAI AND TAKUHI JOINED NOW, MIND TO MIND!

WHAT TAKUHI SEE, PAI SEE ALSO! ♥

ALL RIGHT!

THAT'S GREAT, PAI! YOU'RE THE BEST!

OOH, SAY MORE! ♥

TELL PAI SHE DID GOOD! ♥

PAI LOVES THAT!

THIS IS GREAT! IF ALL GOES WELL, NOT ONLY WILL WE BE ABLE TO FIND LING-LING AND THAT SPIRITUALIST GUY...

...BUT WE MAY FIND THE REST OF THE "FIGURE OF MAN," TOO!

THEN-- WE CAN FINALLY BECOME HUMAN!

OKAY, LET'S GO FIND SOMEPLACE TO HIDE OUT.

'KAY!

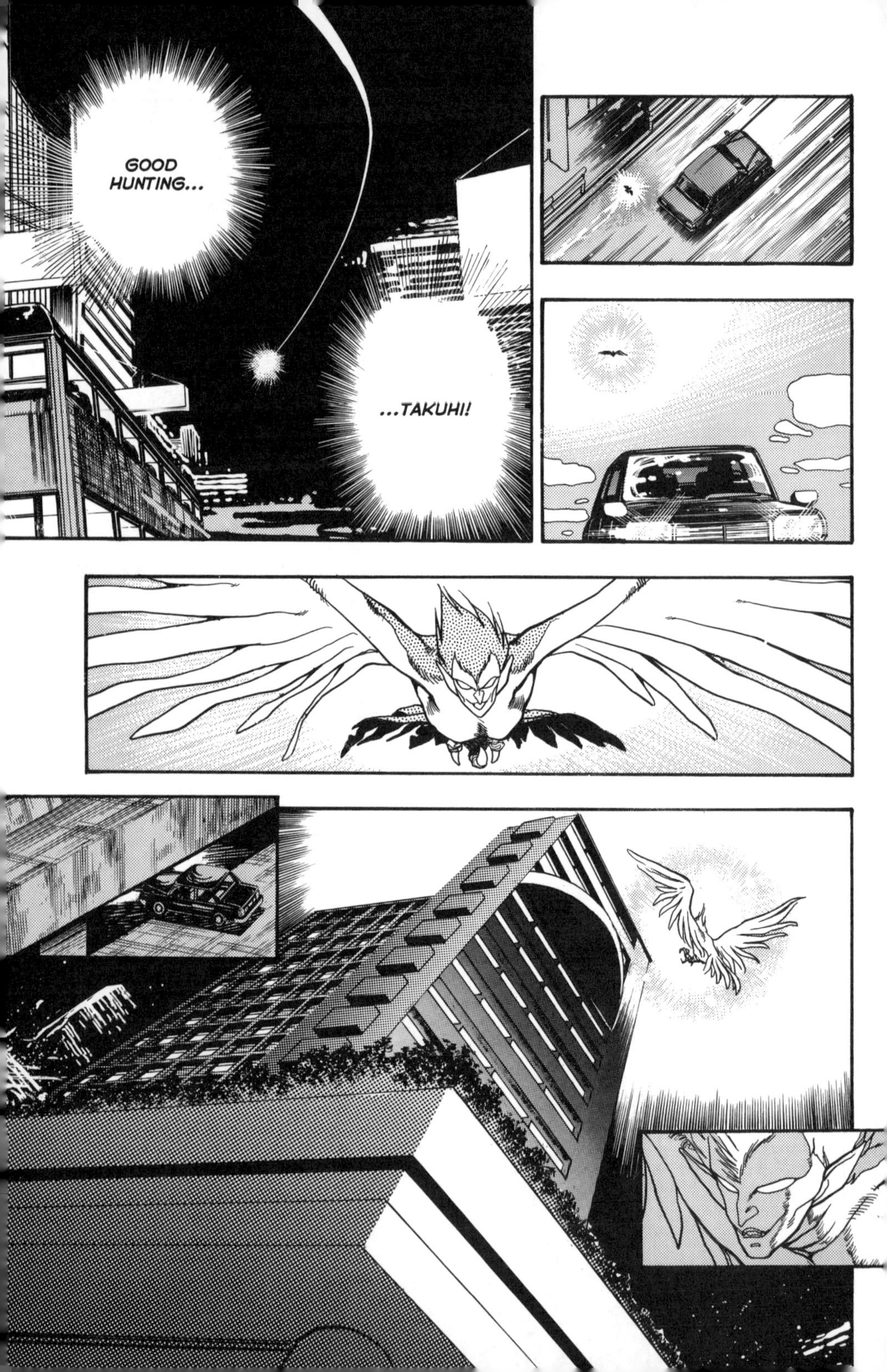
GOOD HUNTING...
...TAKUHI!

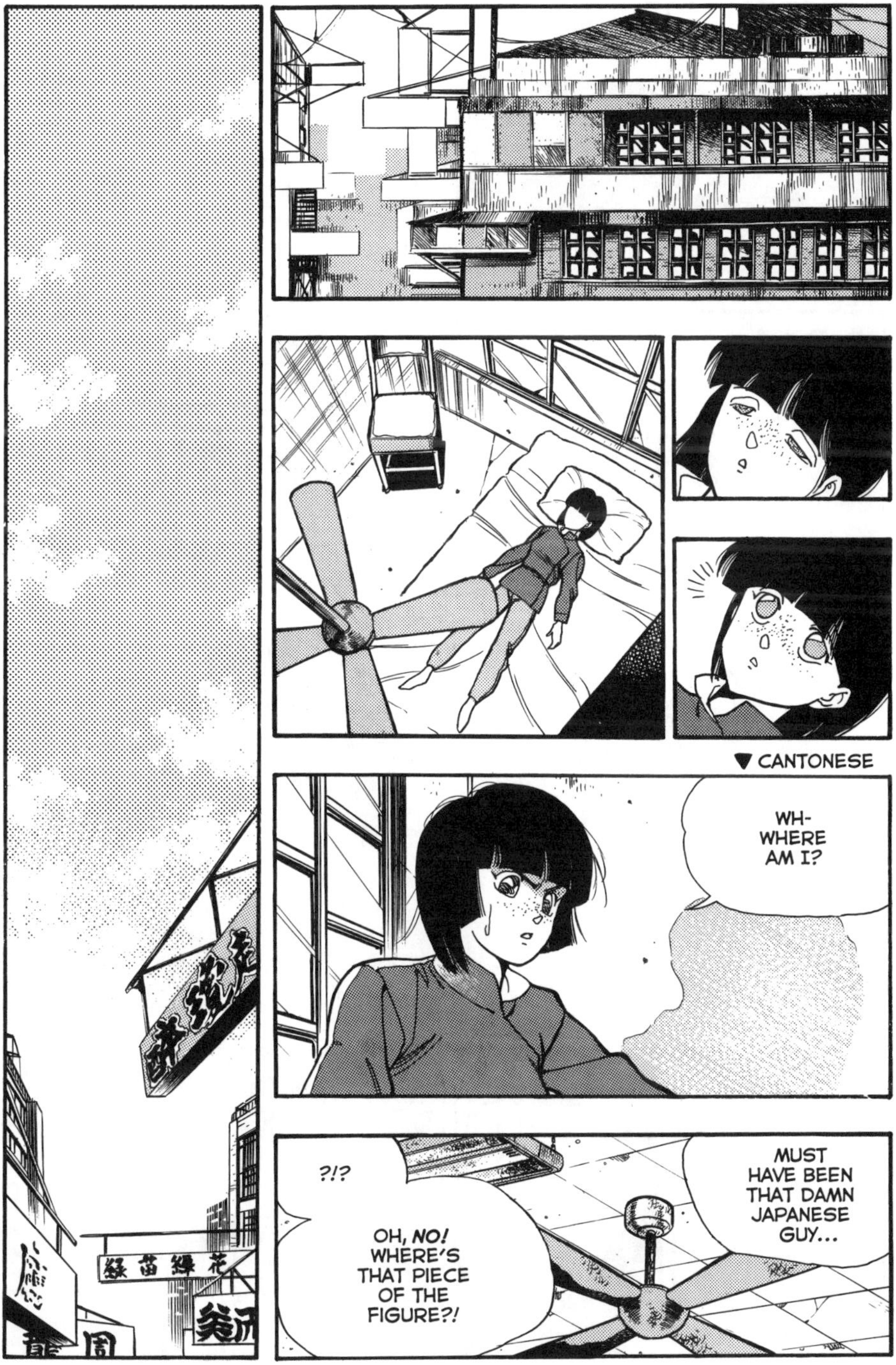
▼ CANTONESE
WH- WHERE AM I?
?!?
MUST HAVE BEEN THAT DAMN JAPANESE GUY...
OH, *NO!* WHERE'S THAT PIECE OF THE FIGURE?!

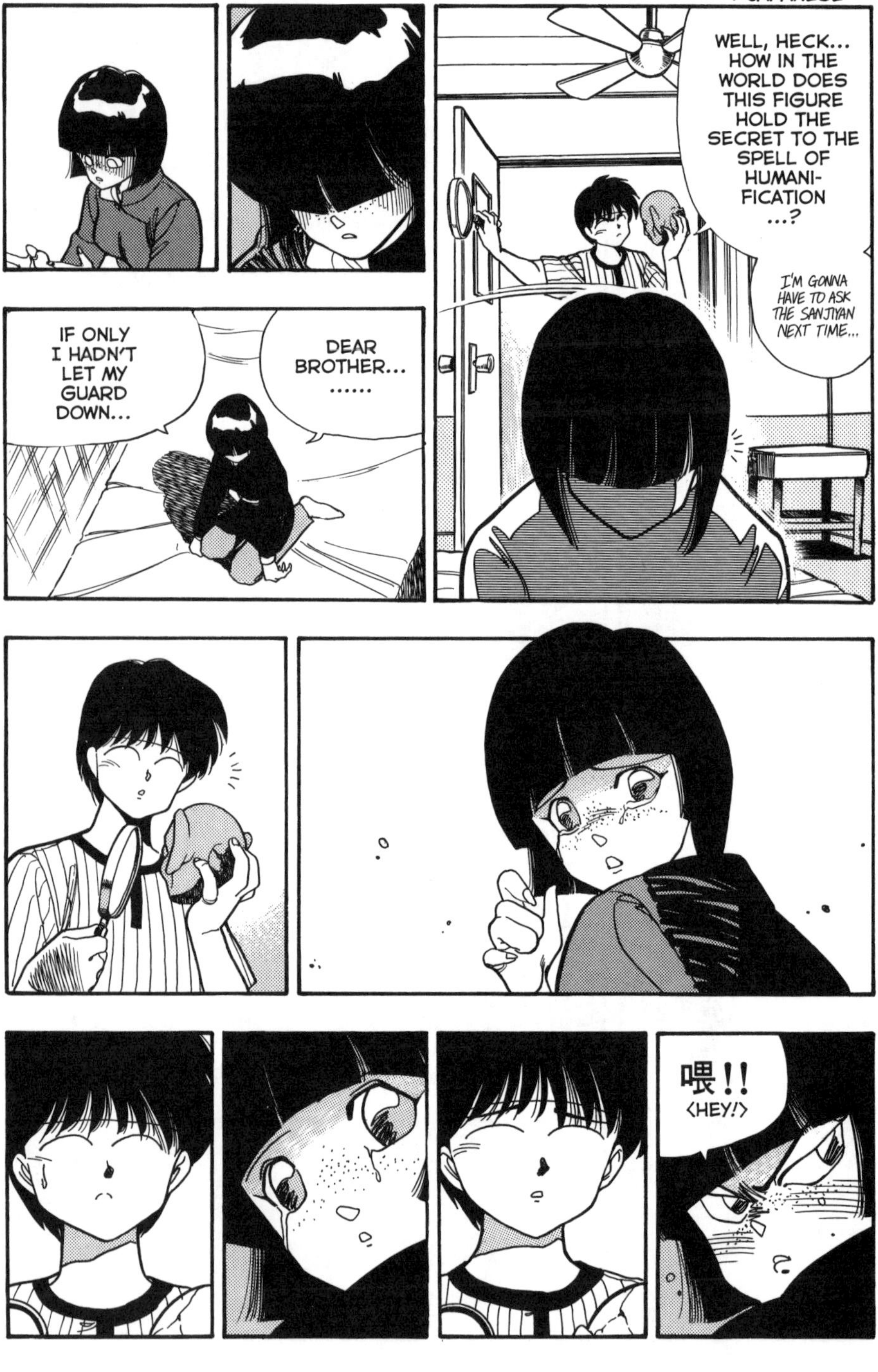
WELL, HECK... HOW IN THE WORLD DOES THIS FIGURE HOLD THE SECRET TO THE SPELL OF HUMANI-FICATION ...?
I'M GONNA HAVE TO ASK THE SANJIYAN NEXT TIME...
IF ONLY I HADN'T LET MY GUARD DOWN...
DEAR BROTHER... ......
喂!!
〈HEY!〉

〈GIVE ME BACK THAT PIECE OR I'LL RIP YOUR LUNGS OUT!〉

YEEOW!

C-CALM DOWN, GIRL!

I SAVED YOUR LIFE, REMEMBER...?!

〈KILL!〉

YEEEK!

SLLLP

??

〈WHOOPS!〉

WAAAAH!

HEY, LOOK OU--

?!

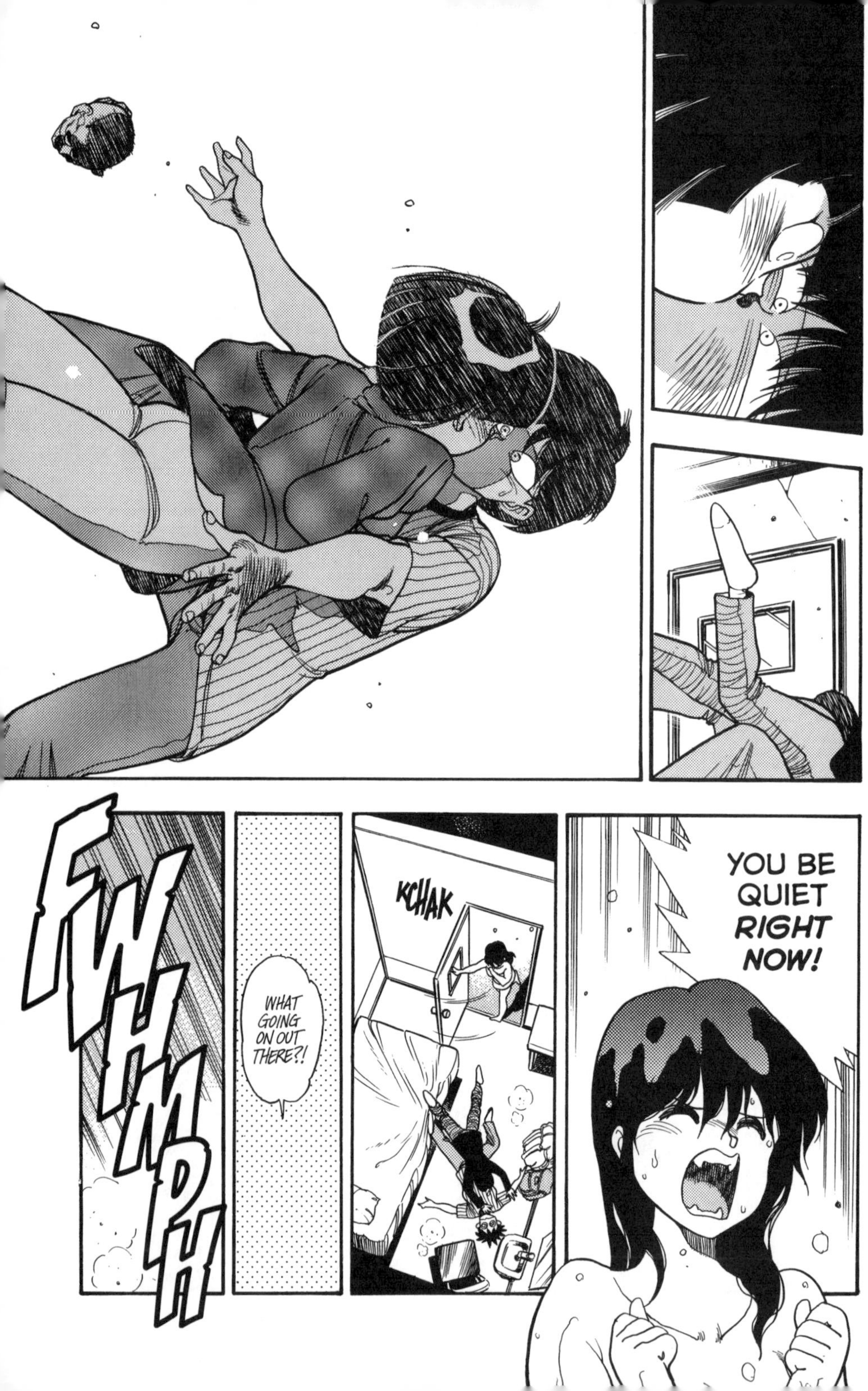
FWHMMPH
WHAT GOING ON OUT THERE?!
KCHAK
YOU BE QUIET RIGHT NOW!

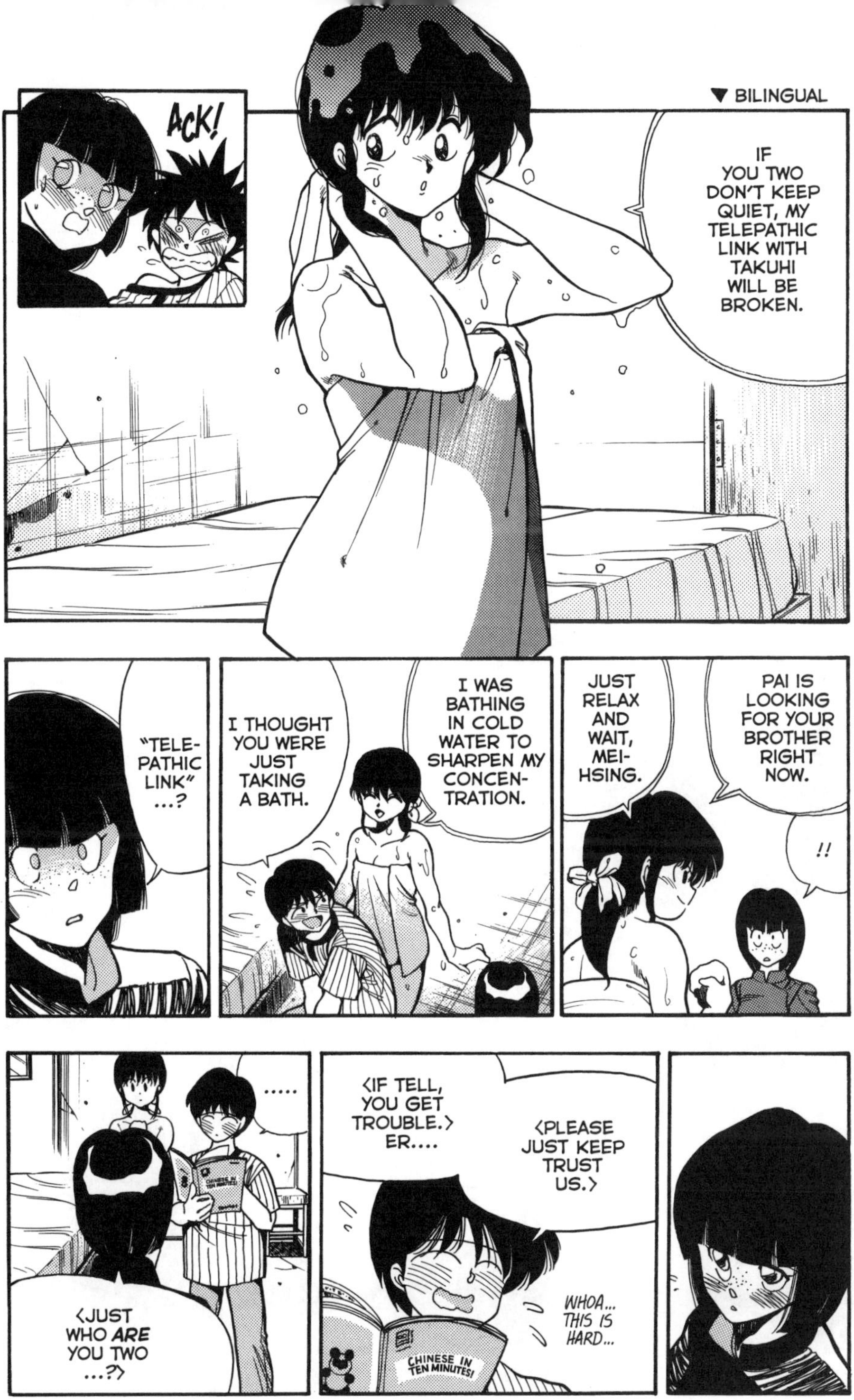
▼ BILINGUAL
ACK!
IF YOU TWO DON'T KEEP QUIET, MY TELEPATHIC LINK WITH TAKUHI WILL BE BROKEN.
"TELE-PATHIC LINK" ...?
I THOUGHT YOU WERE JUST TAKING A BATH.
I WAS BATHING IN COLD WATER TO SHARPEN MY CONCEN-TRATION.
JUST RELAX AND WAIT, MEI-HSING.
PAI IS LOOKING FOR YOUR BROTHER RIGHT NOW.
!!
.....
<JUST WHO *ARE* YOU TWO ...?>
CHINESE IN TEN MINUTES!
<IF TELL, YOU GET TROUBLE.> ER....
<PLEASE JUST KEEP TRUST US.>
WHOA... THIS IS HARD...
CHINESE IN TEN MINUTES!

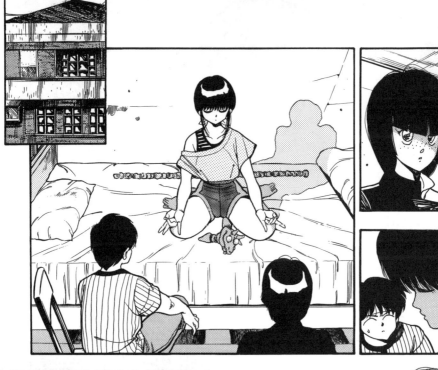

A HOTEL...

HOTEL...

ROYAL
SOARER...
HONG
KONG...

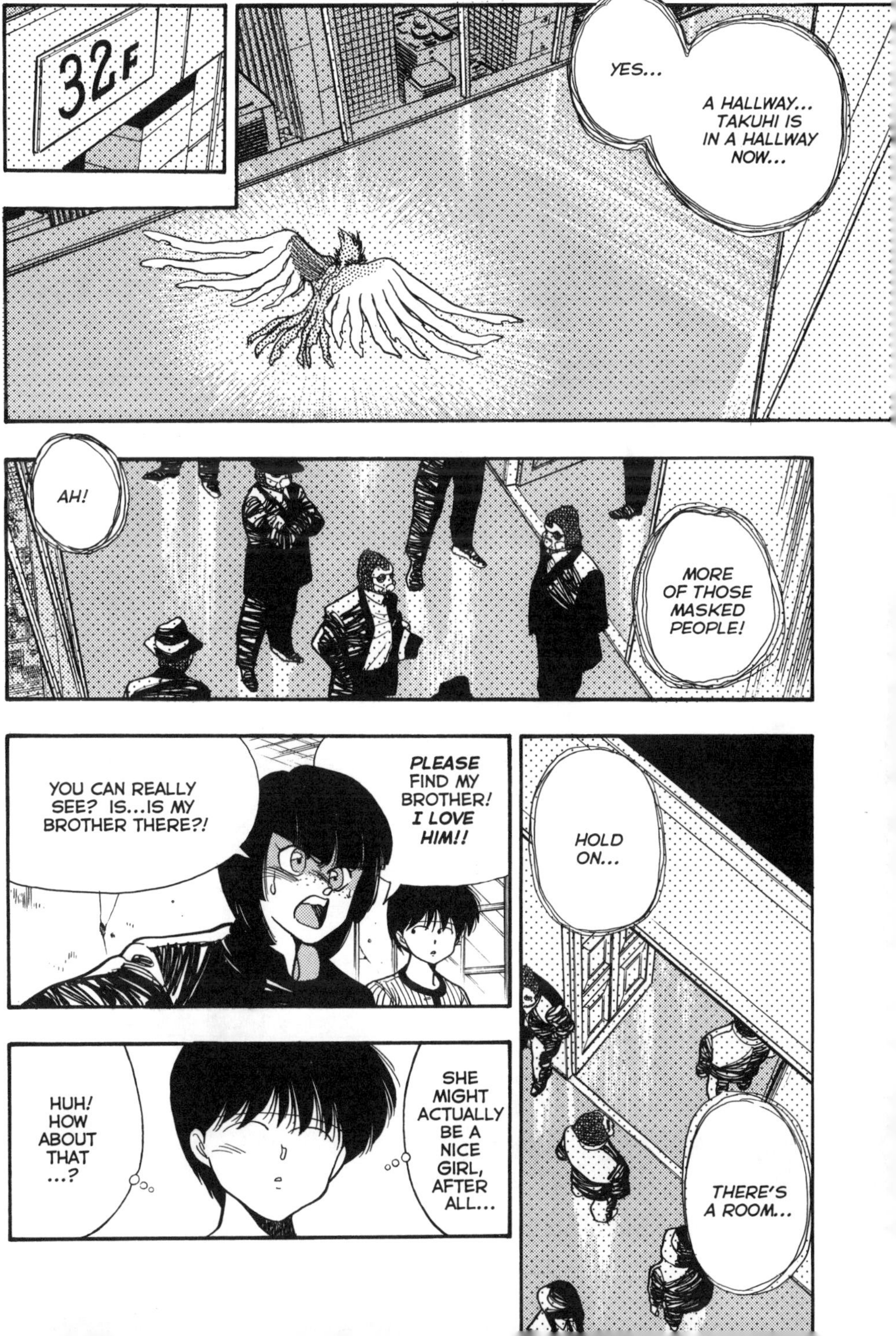
32F
YES...
A HALLWAY... TAKUHI IS IN A HALLWAY NOW...
AH!
MORE OF THOSE MASKED PEOPLE!
YOU CAN REALLY SEE? IS...IS MY BROTHER THERE?!
PLEASE FIND MY BROTHER! I LOVE HIM!!
HUH! HOW ABOUT THAT ...?
SHE MIGHT ACTUALLY BE A NICE GIRL, AFTER ALL...
HOLD ON...
THERE'S A ROOM...

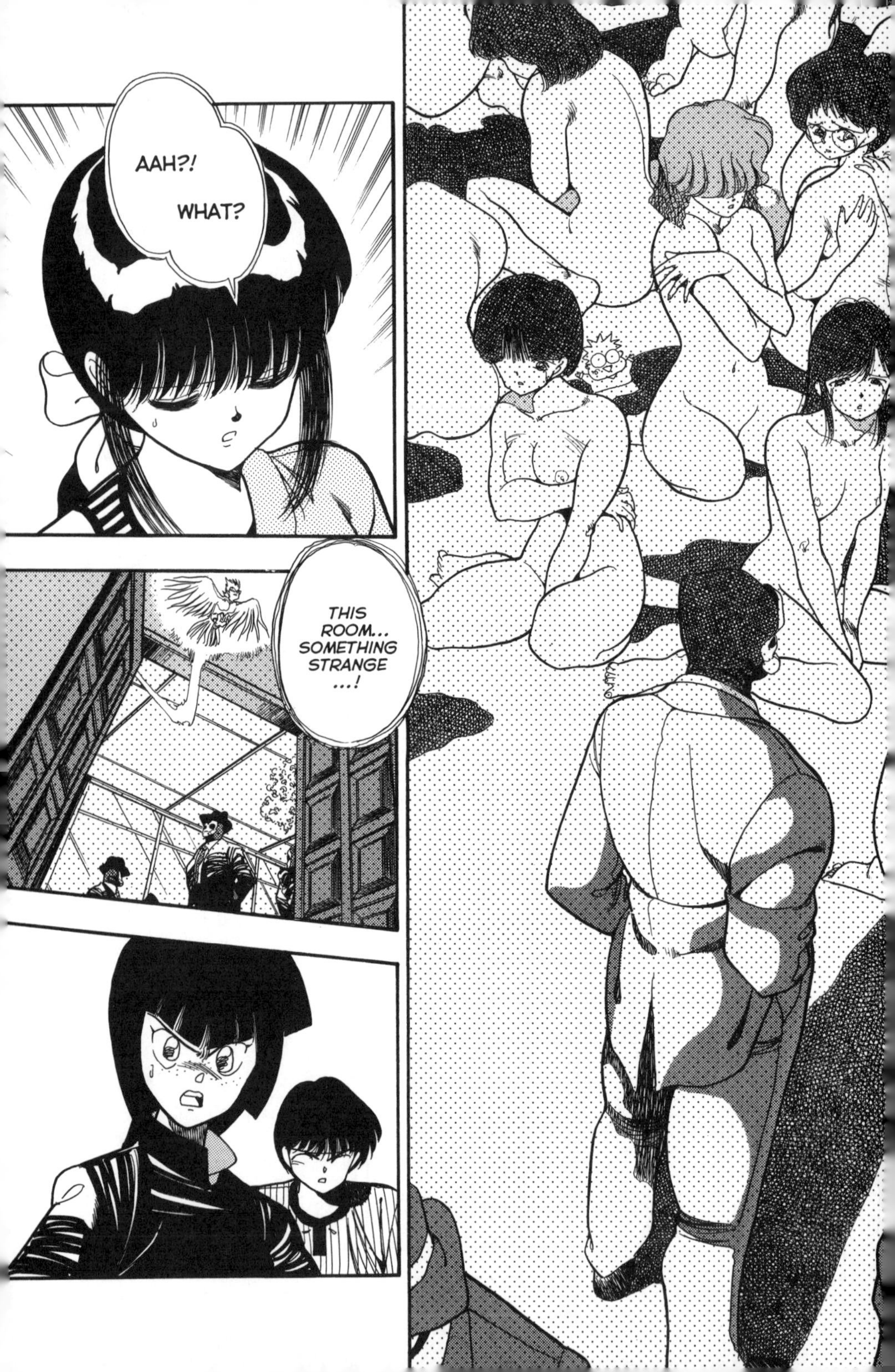
AAH?!
WHAT?
THIS ROOM... SOMETHING STRANGE ...!

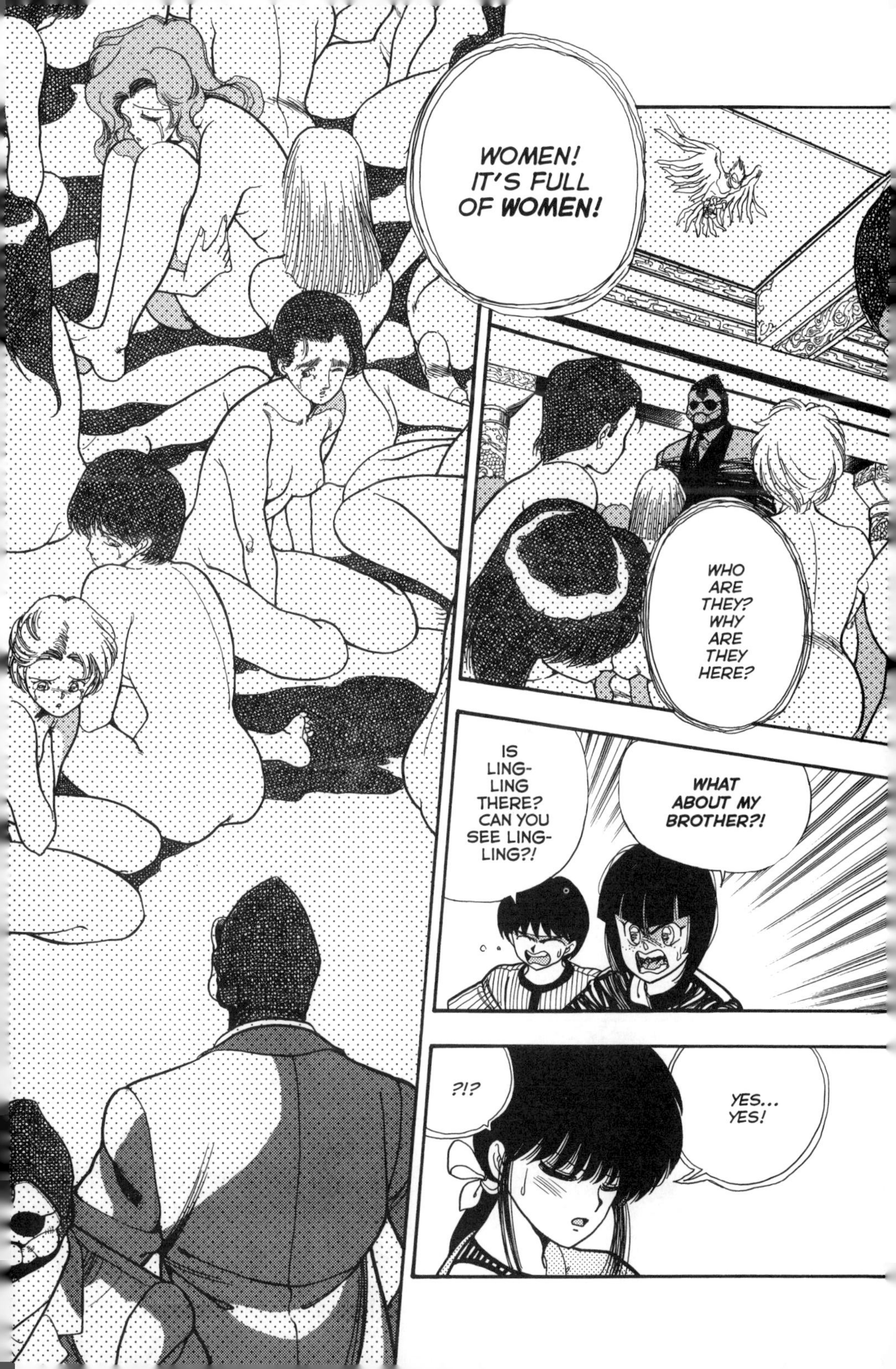
WOMEN! IT'S FULL OF WOMEN!
WHO ARE THEY? WHY ARE THEY HERE?
IS LING-LING THERE? CAN YOU SEE LING-LING?!
WHAT ABOUT MY BROTHER?!
?!?
YES... YES!

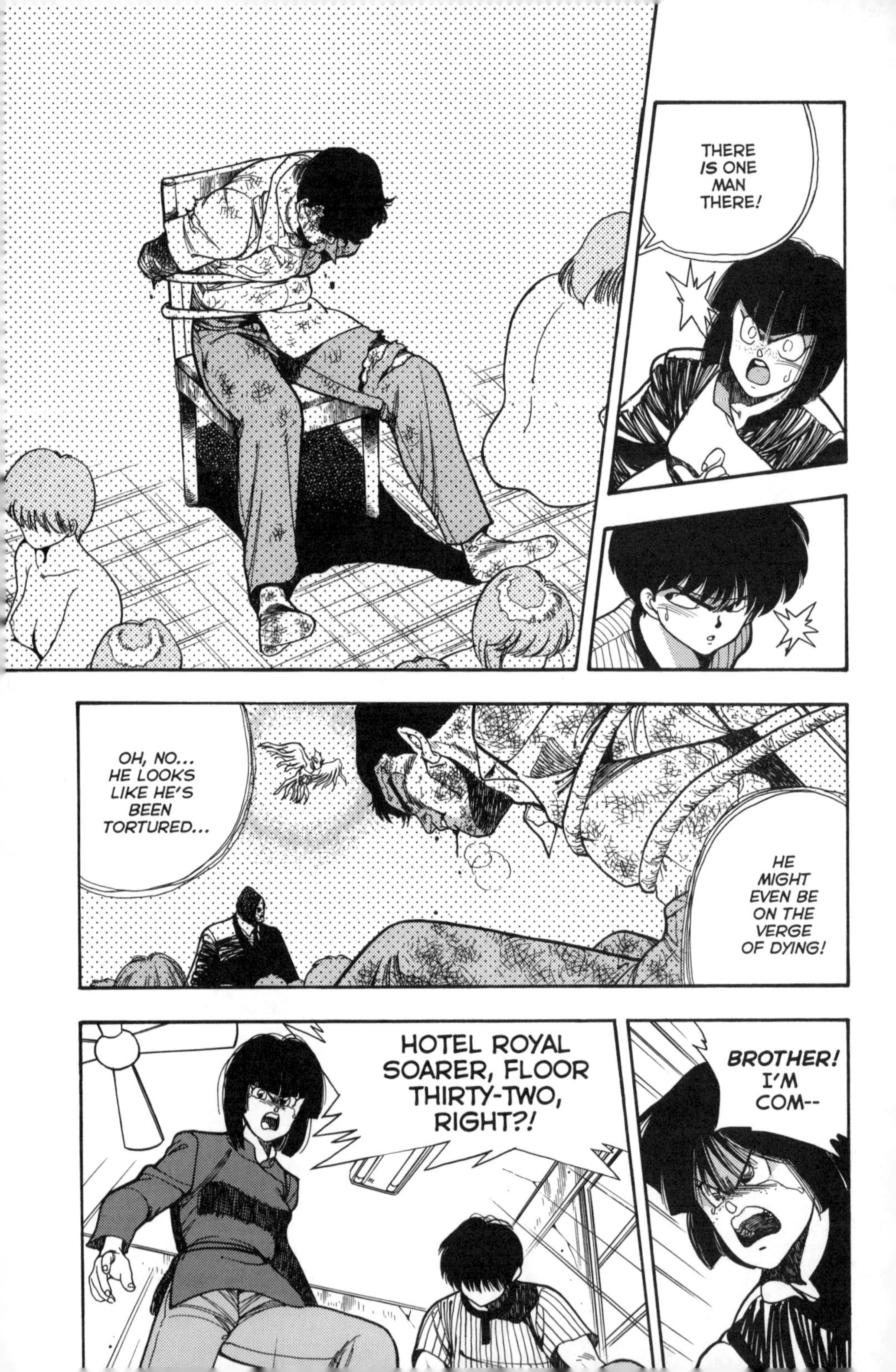
THERE *IS* ONE MAN THERE!
OH, NO... HE LOOKS LIKE HE'S BEEN TORTURED...
HE MIGHT EVEN BE ON THE VERGE OF DYING!
HOTEL ROYAL SOARER, FLOOR THIRTY-TWO, RIGHT?!
BROTHER! I'M COM--

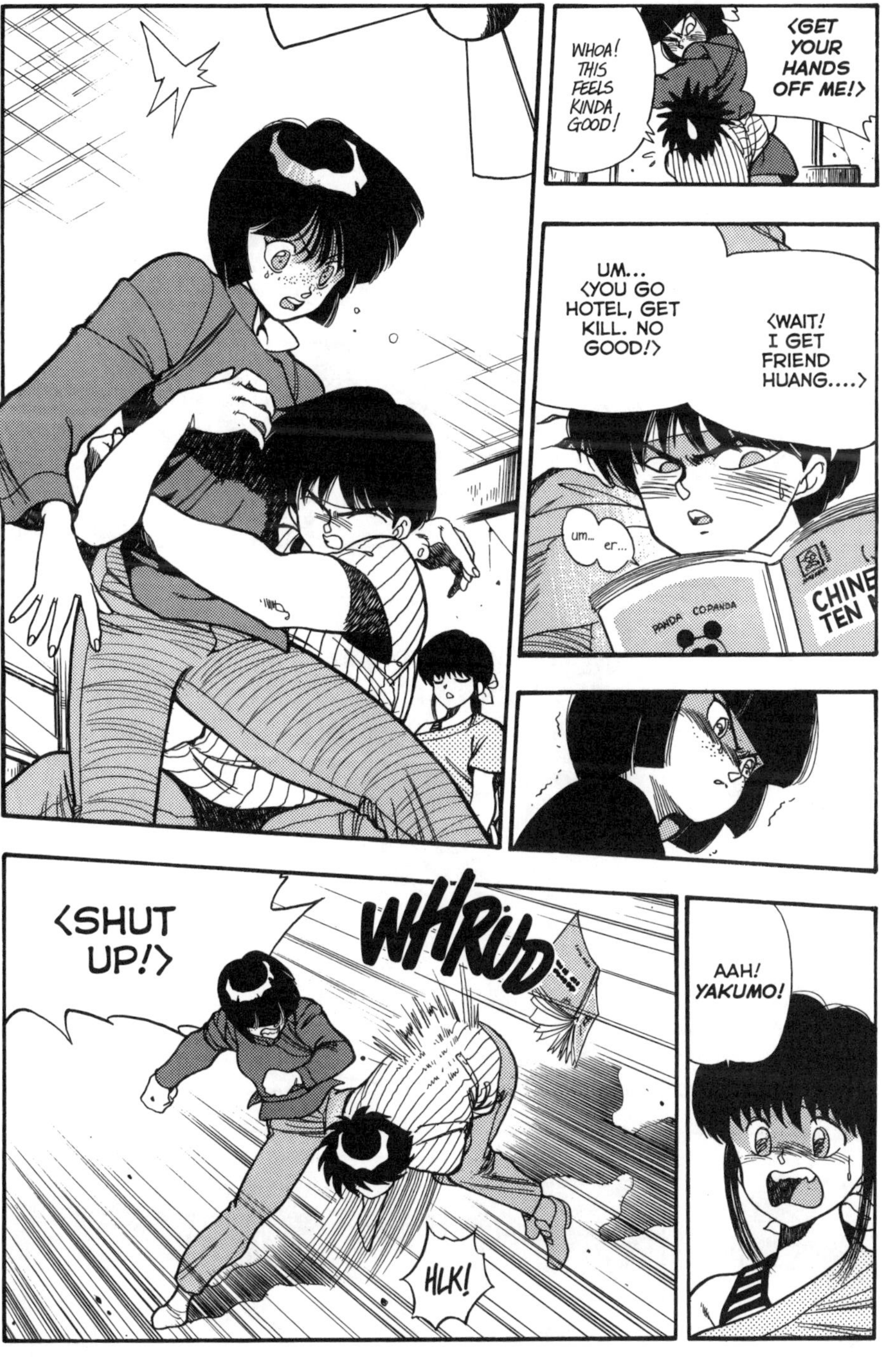

WHOA! THIS FEELS KINDA GOOD!
<GET YOUR HANDS OFF ME!>
UM... <YOU GO HOTEL, GET KILL. NO GOOD!>
<WAIT! I GET FRIEND HUANG....>
um... er...
PANDA COPANDA
CHINE TEN
<SHUT UP!>
WHRUD
HLK!
AAH! YAKUMO!

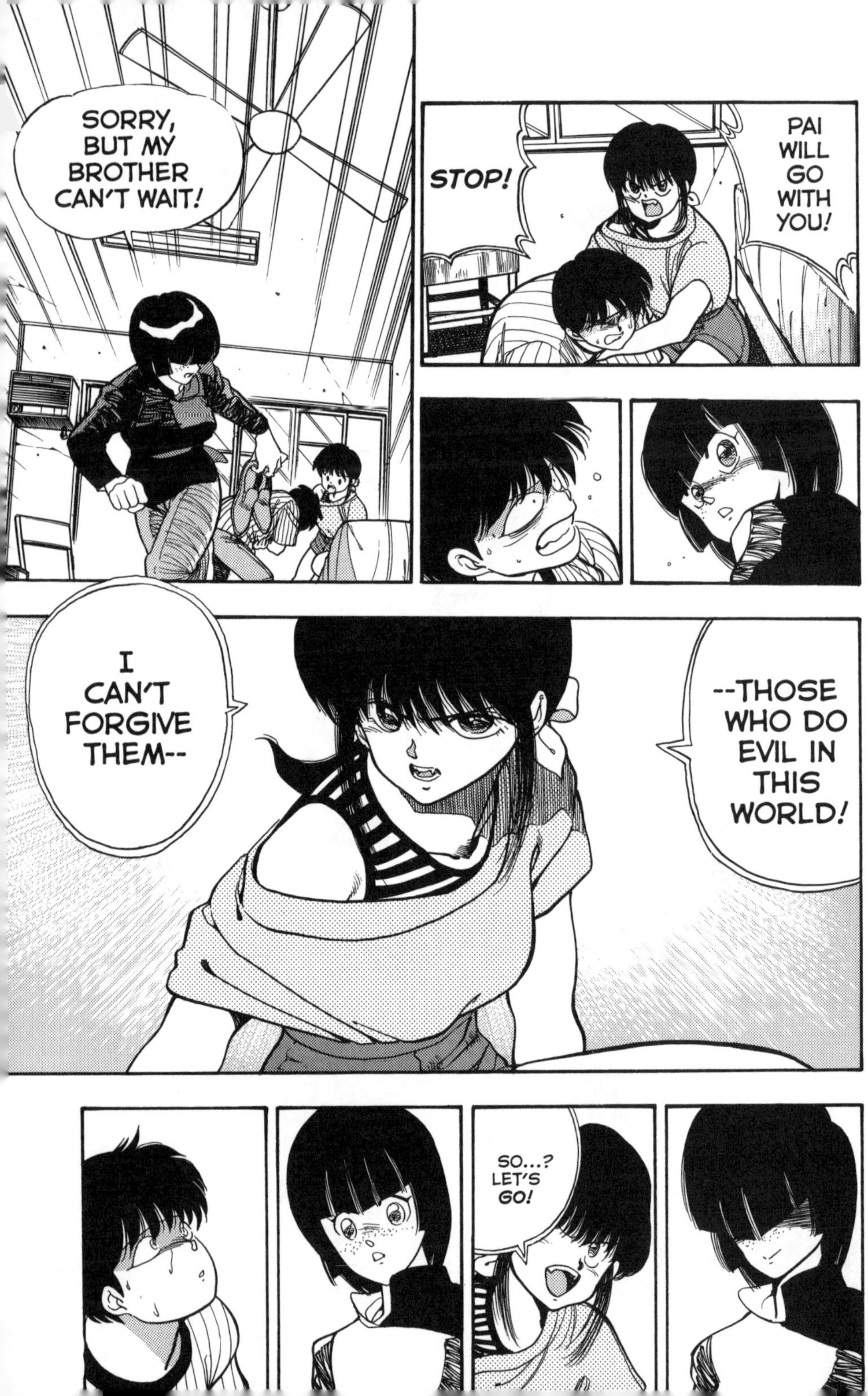
SORRY, BUT MY BROTHER CAN'T WAIT!
STOP!
PAI WILL GO WITH YOU!
I CAN'T FORGIVE THEM--
--THOSE WHO DO EVIL IN THIS WORLD!
SO...? LET'S GO!

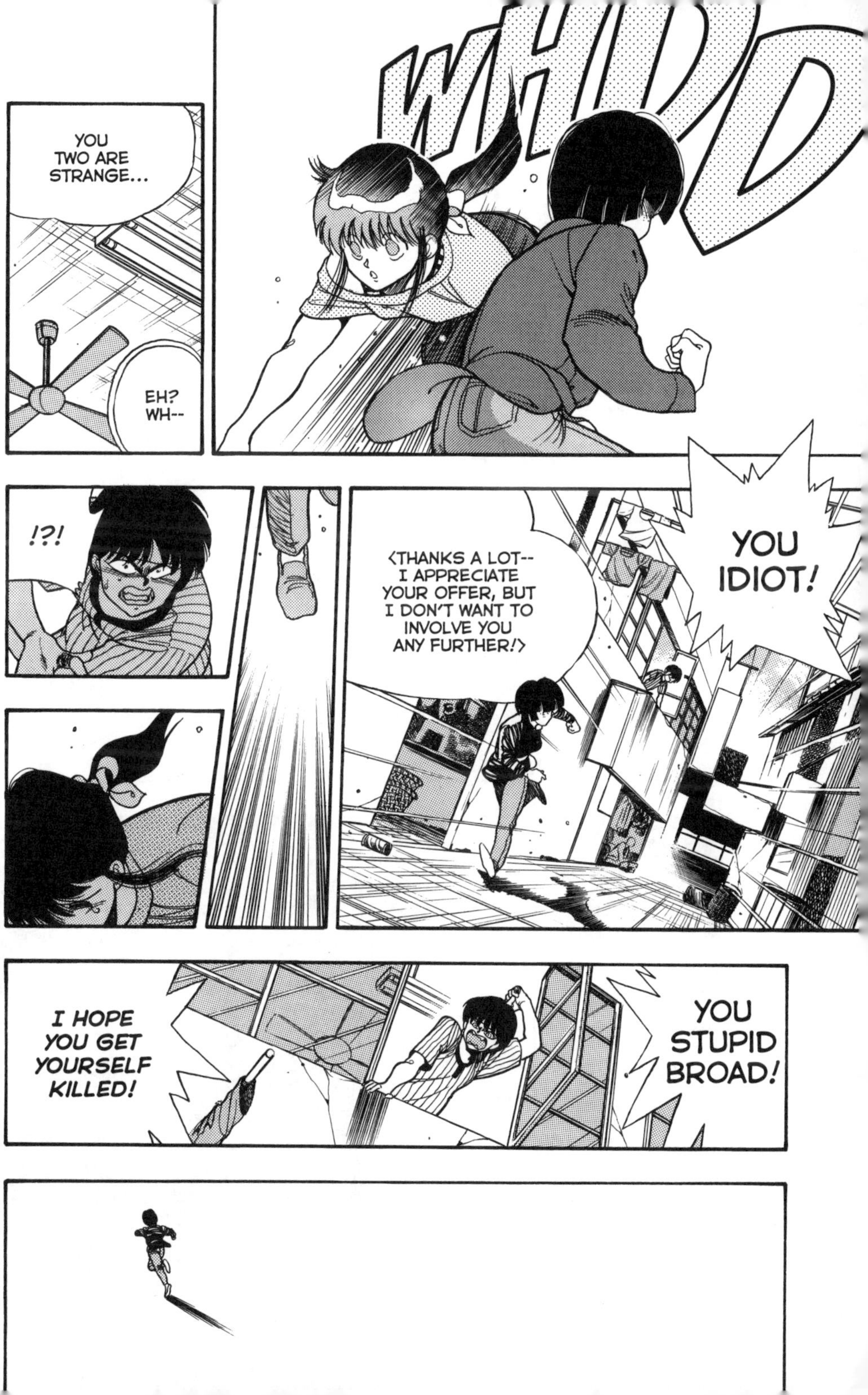
YOU TWO ARE STRANGE...
EH? WH--
WHIPP
!?!
<THANKS A LOT-- I APPRECIATE YOUR OFFER, BUT I DON'T WANT TO INVOLVE YOU ANY FURTHER!>
YOU IDIOT!
I HOPE YOU GET YOURSELF KILLED!
YOU STUPID BROAD!

ARE YOU ALL RIGHT, PAI?

Y... YES. ....

WE HAVE TO GO! HELP MEI-HSING!

GIMME A BREAK! WE'RE BETTER OFF WITH HER GONE, ANYWAY.

NO!

PAI *LIKE* MEI-HSING.

DOESN'T YAKUMO...?

N-NO WAY! I COULDN'T CARE LESS ABOUT...

ABOUT... HER...

UM...

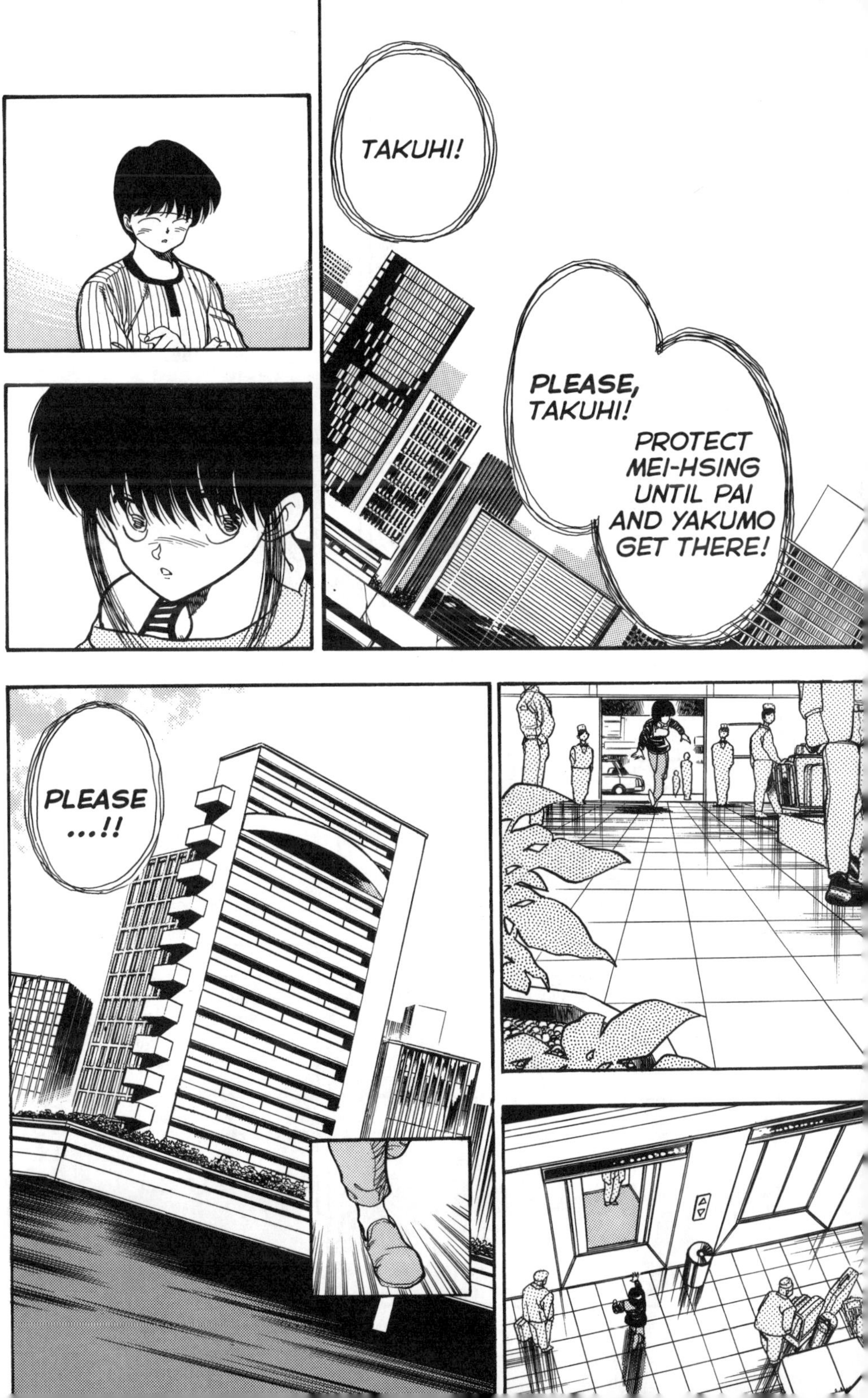
TAKUHI!
PLEASE, TAKUHI!
PROTECT MEI-HSING UNTIL PAI AND YAKUMO GET THERE!
PLEASE ...!!

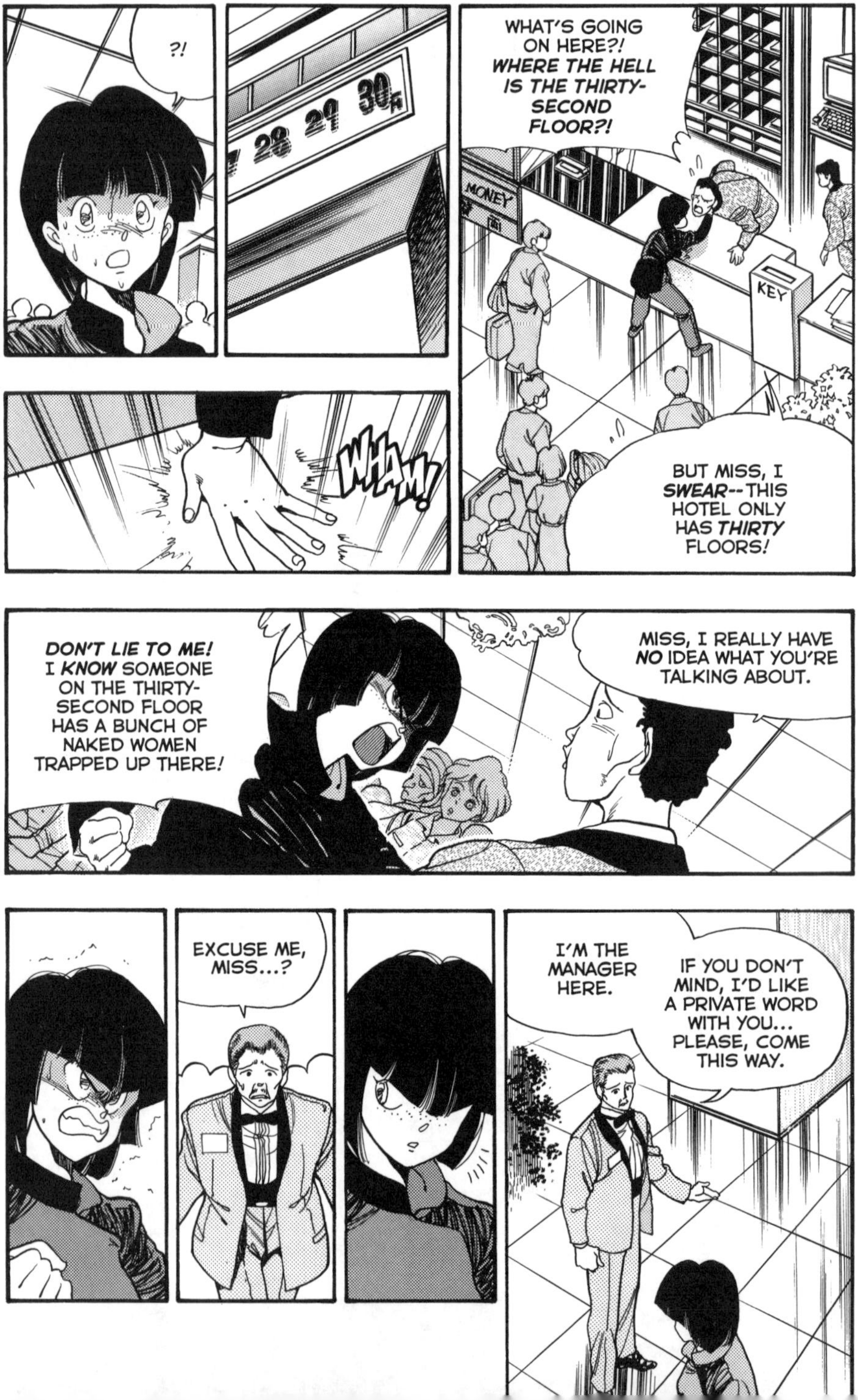
?!
28 29 30F
WHAT'S GOING ON HERE?! *WHERE THE HELL IS THE THIRTY-SECOND FLOOR?!*
MONEY
KEY
BUT MISS, I *SWEAR*--THIS HOTEL ONLY HAS *THIRTY* FLOORS!
WHAM!
DON'T LIE TO ME! I *KNOW* SOMEONE ON THE THIRTY-SECOND FLOOR HAS A BUNCH OF NAKED WOMEN TRAPPED UP THERE!
MISS, I REALLY HAVE *NO* IDEA WHAT YOU'RE TALKING ABOUT.
EXCUSE ME, MISS...?
I'M THE MANAGER HERE.
IF YOU DON'T MIND, I'D LIKE A PRIVATE WORD WITH YOU... PLEASE, COME THIS WAY.

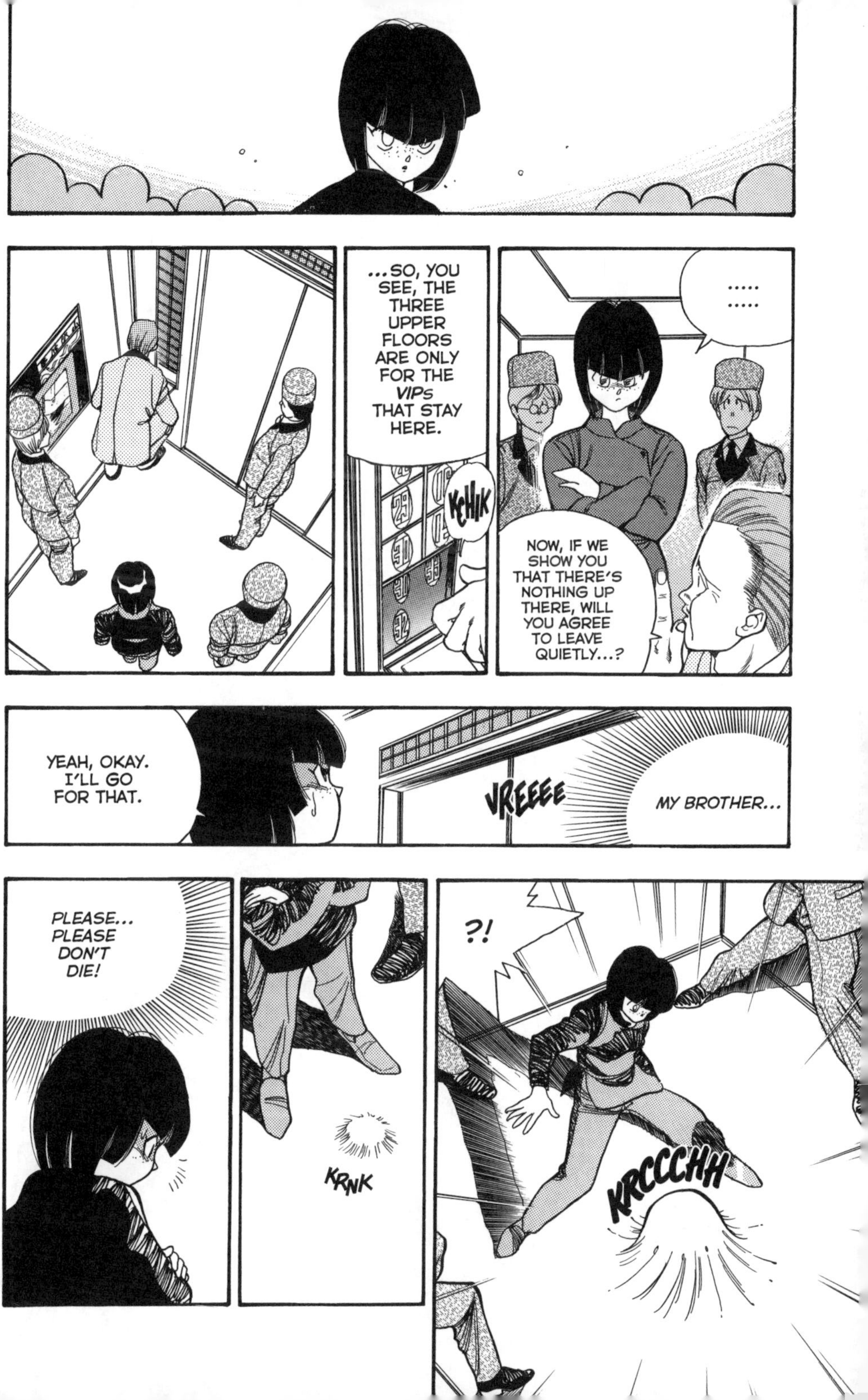
...SO, YOU SEE, THE THREE UPPER FLOORS ARE ONLY FOR THE VIPs THAT STAY HERE.
KCHIK
.....
.....
NOW, IF WE SHOW YOU THAT THERE'S NOTHING UP THERE, WILL YOU AGREE TO LEAVE QUIETLY...?
YEAH, OKAY. I'LL GO FOR THAT.
VREEEE
MY BROTHER...
PLEASE... PLEASE DON'T DIE!
KRNK
?!
KRCCCHH

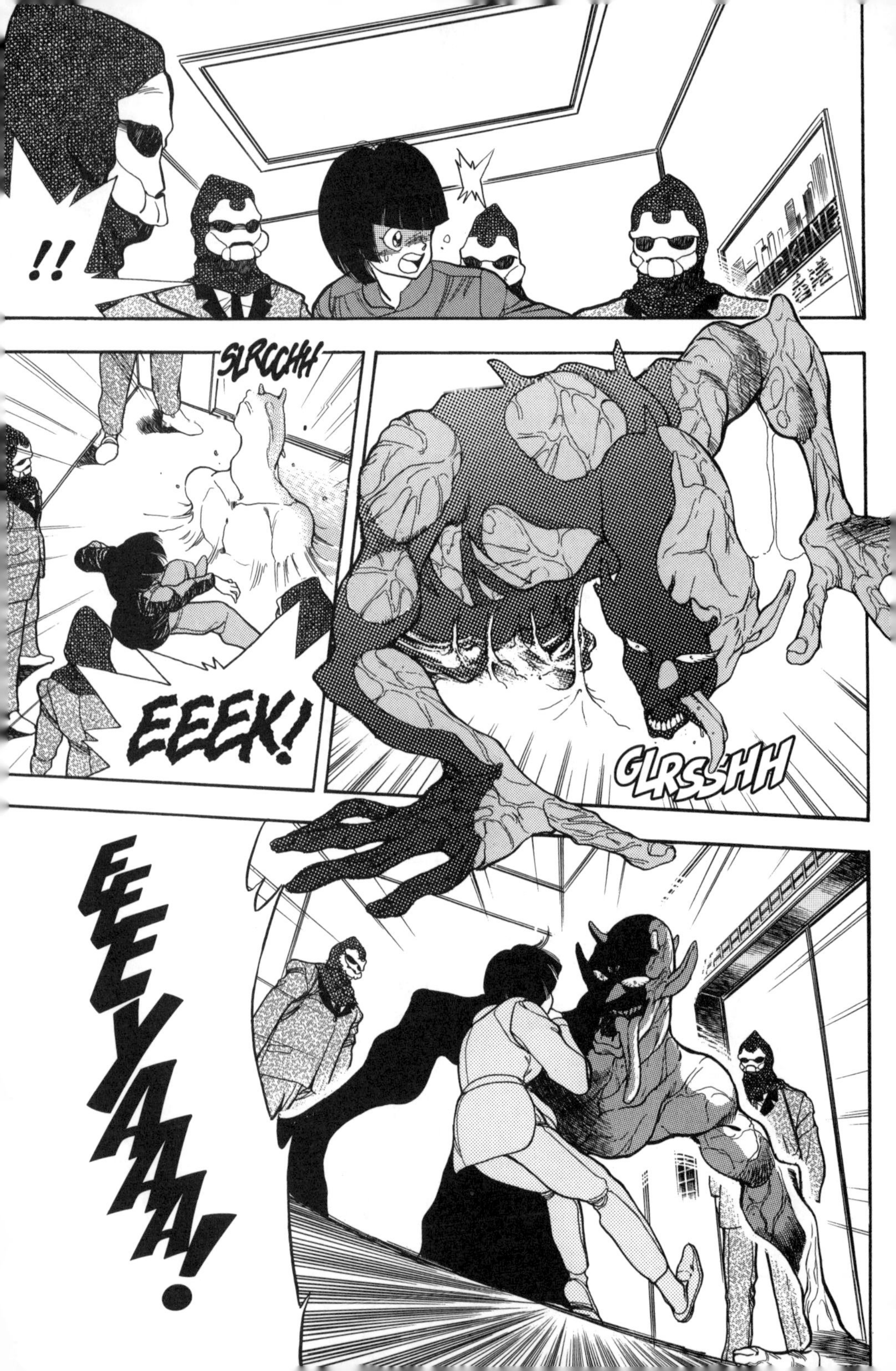
!!
SLRCCHH
EEEK!
GLRSSHH
EEEYAAA!

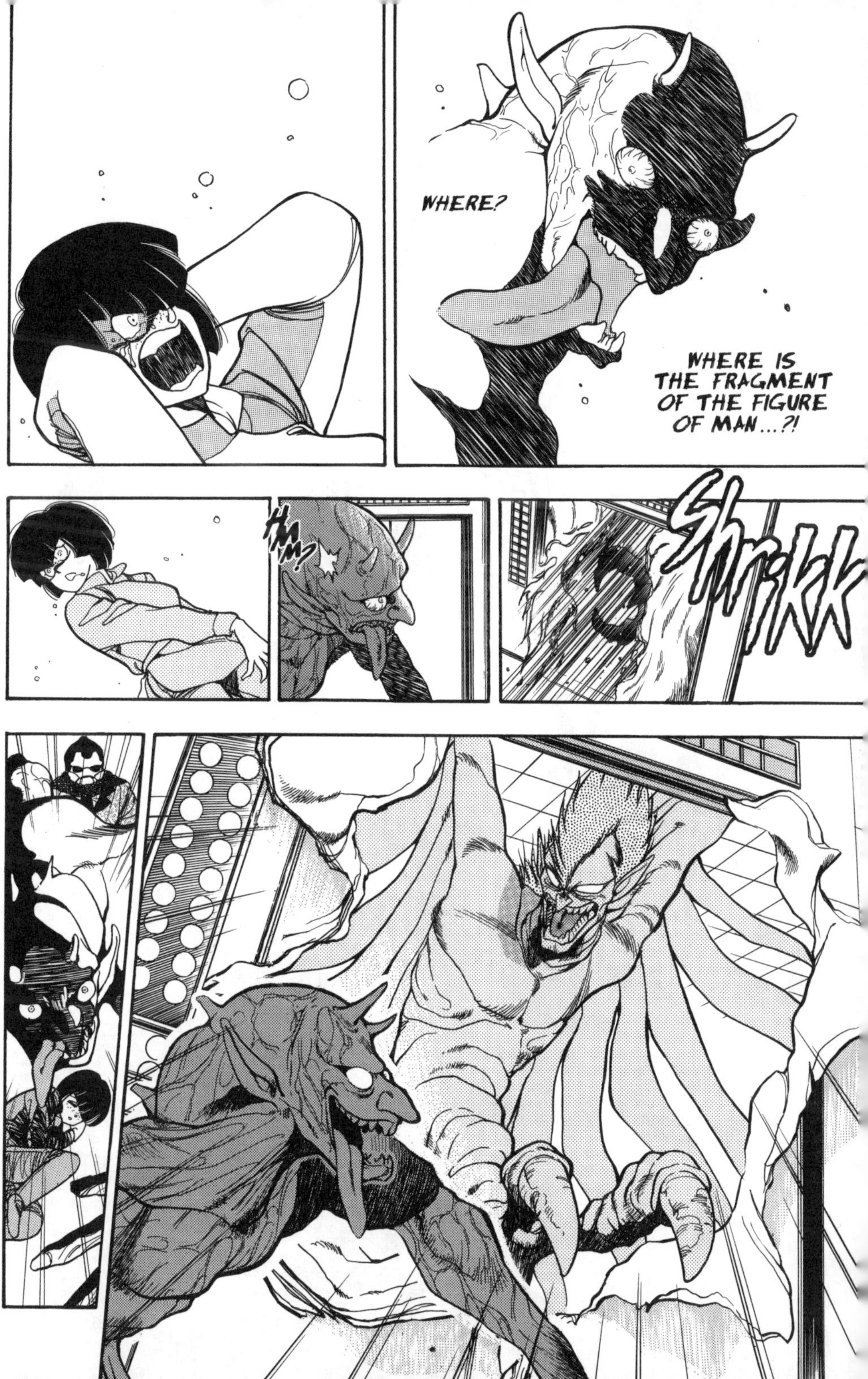
WHERE?
WHERE IS THE FRAGMENT OF THE FIGURE OF MAN...?!
HM?
Shrikk

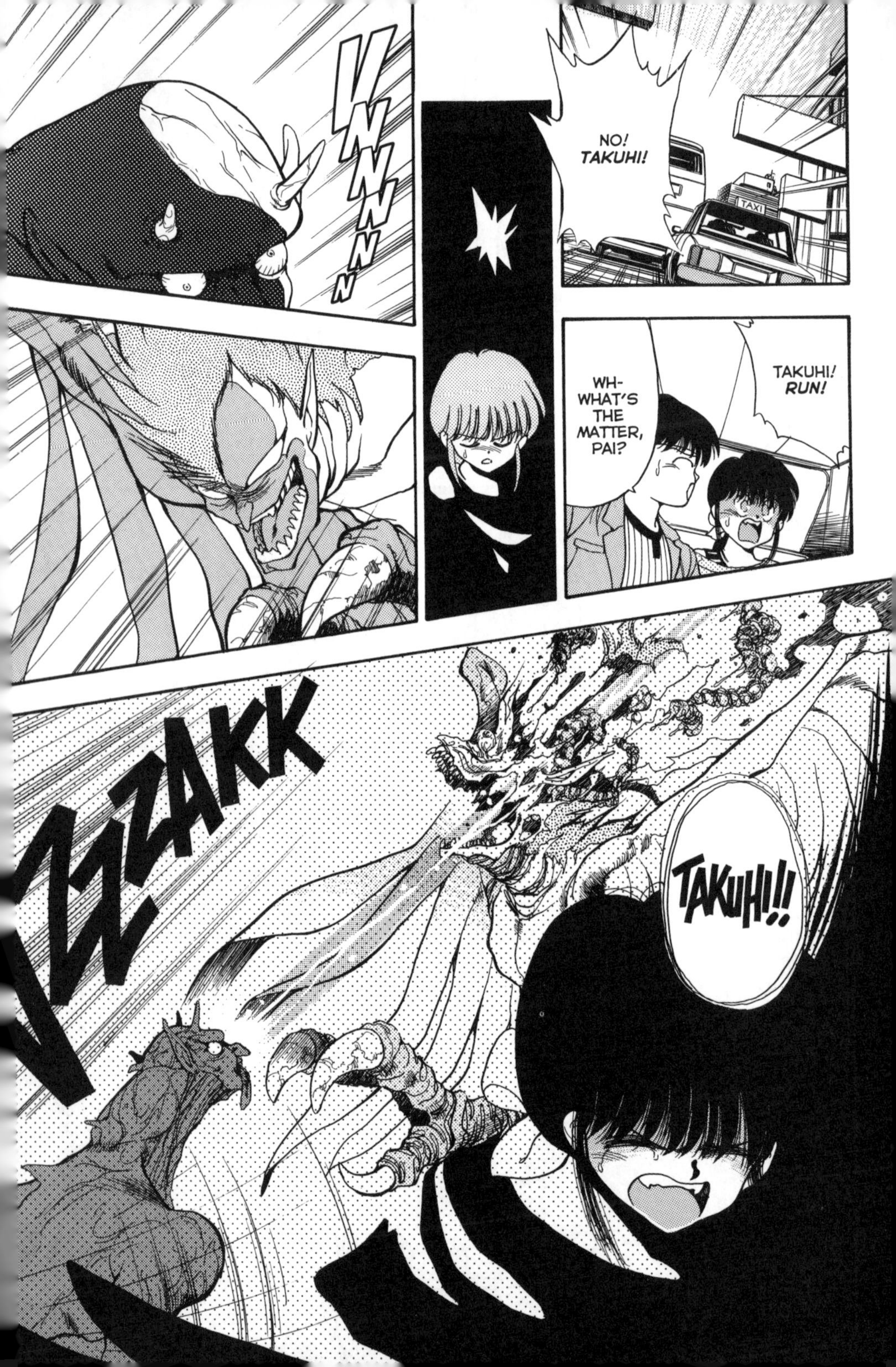

VNNNNNN
NO! TAKUHI!
WH- WHAT'S THE MATTER, PAI?
TAKUHI! RUN!
ZZZAKK
TAKUHI!!

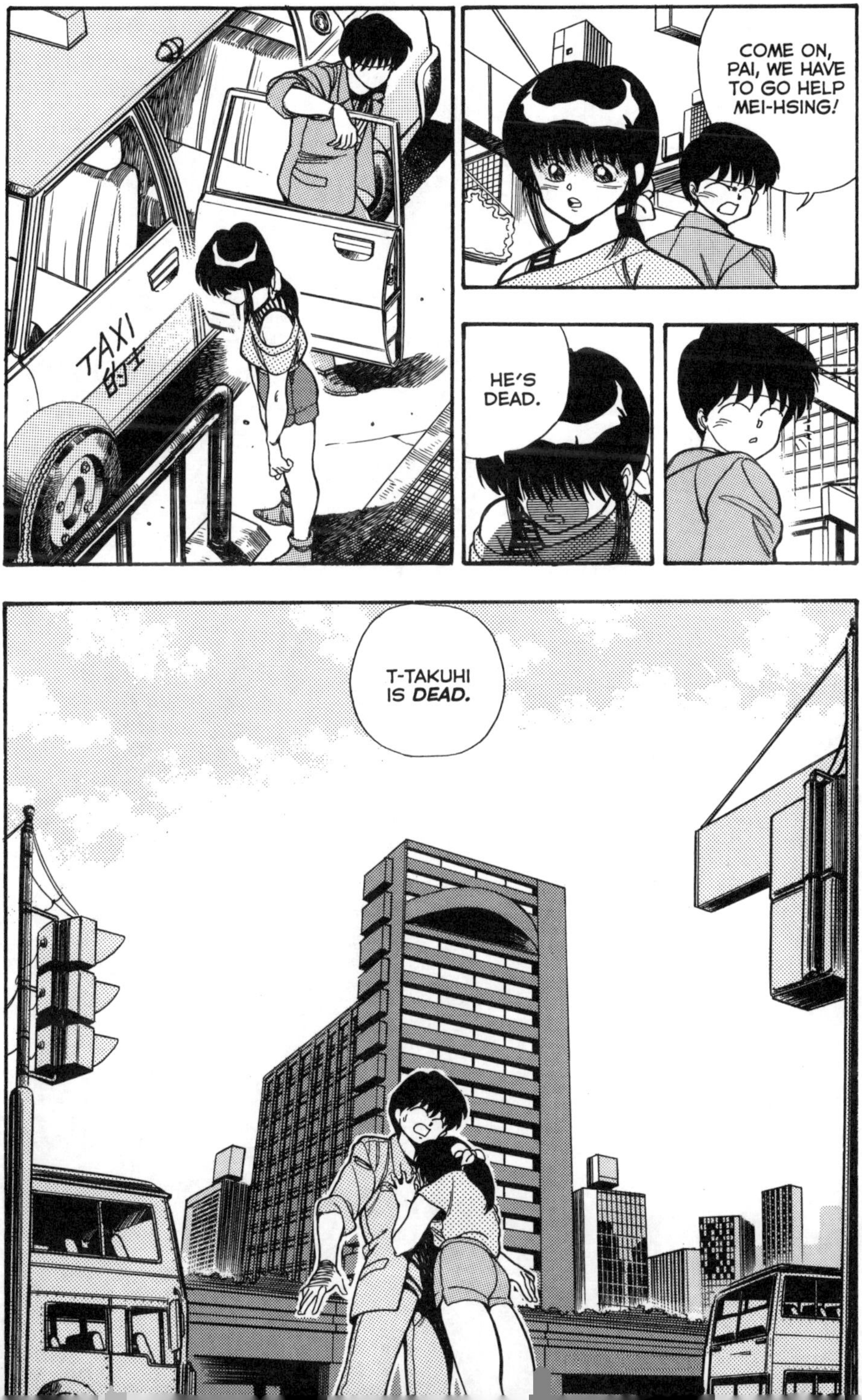
TAXI
的士
COME ON, PAI, WE HAVE TO GO HELP MEI-HSING!
HE'S DEAD.
T-TAKUHI IS *DEAD.*

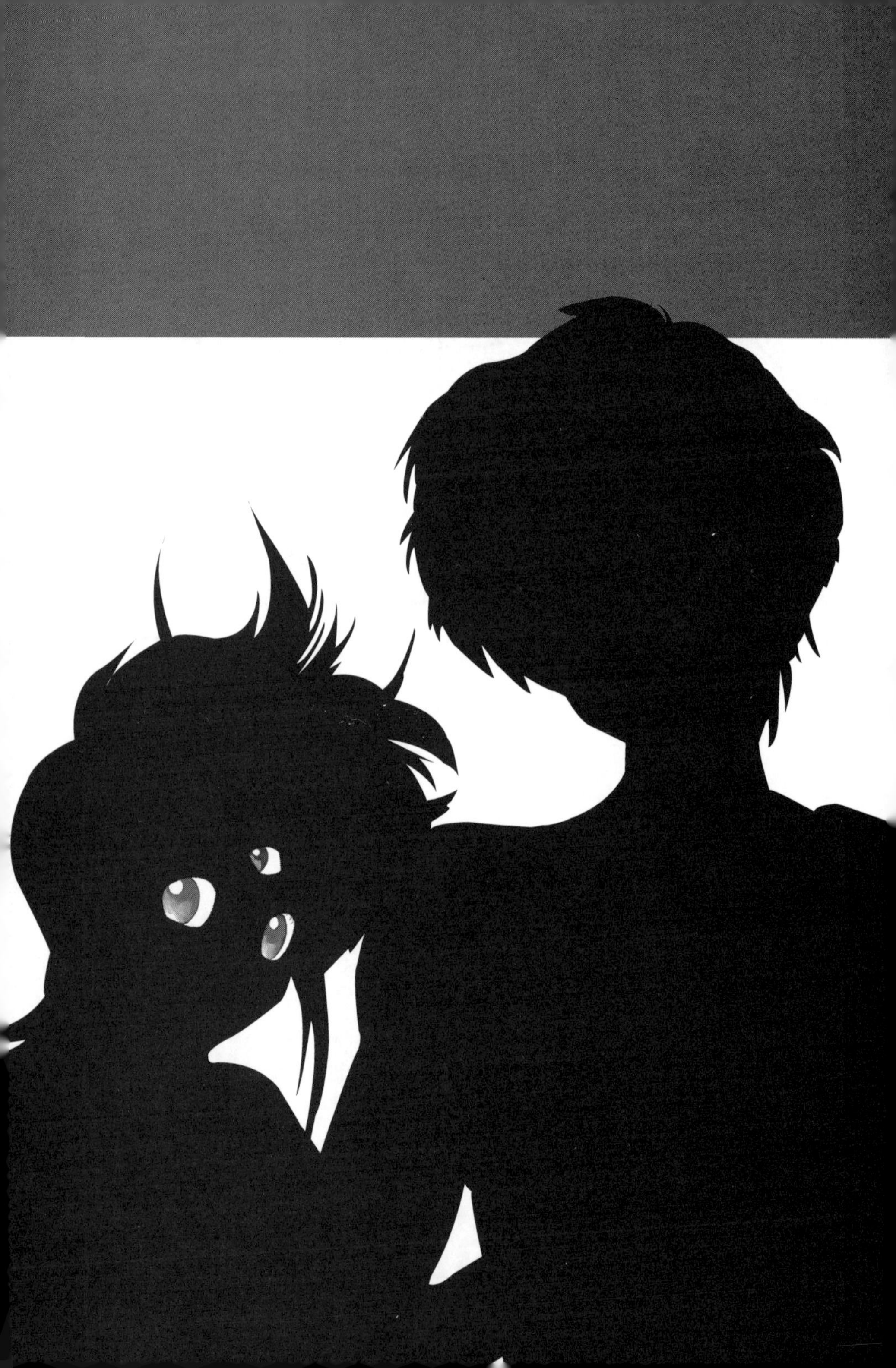

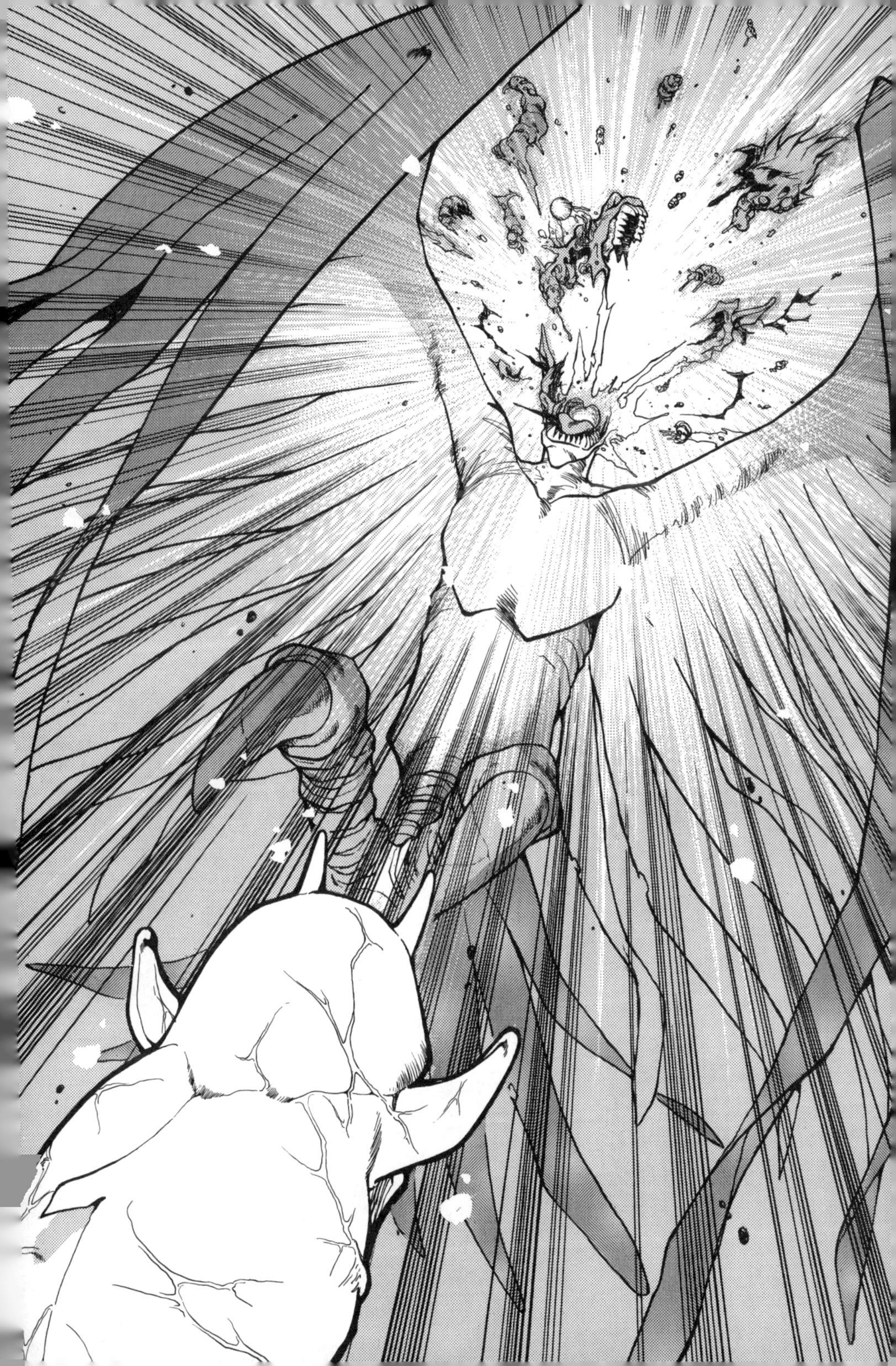

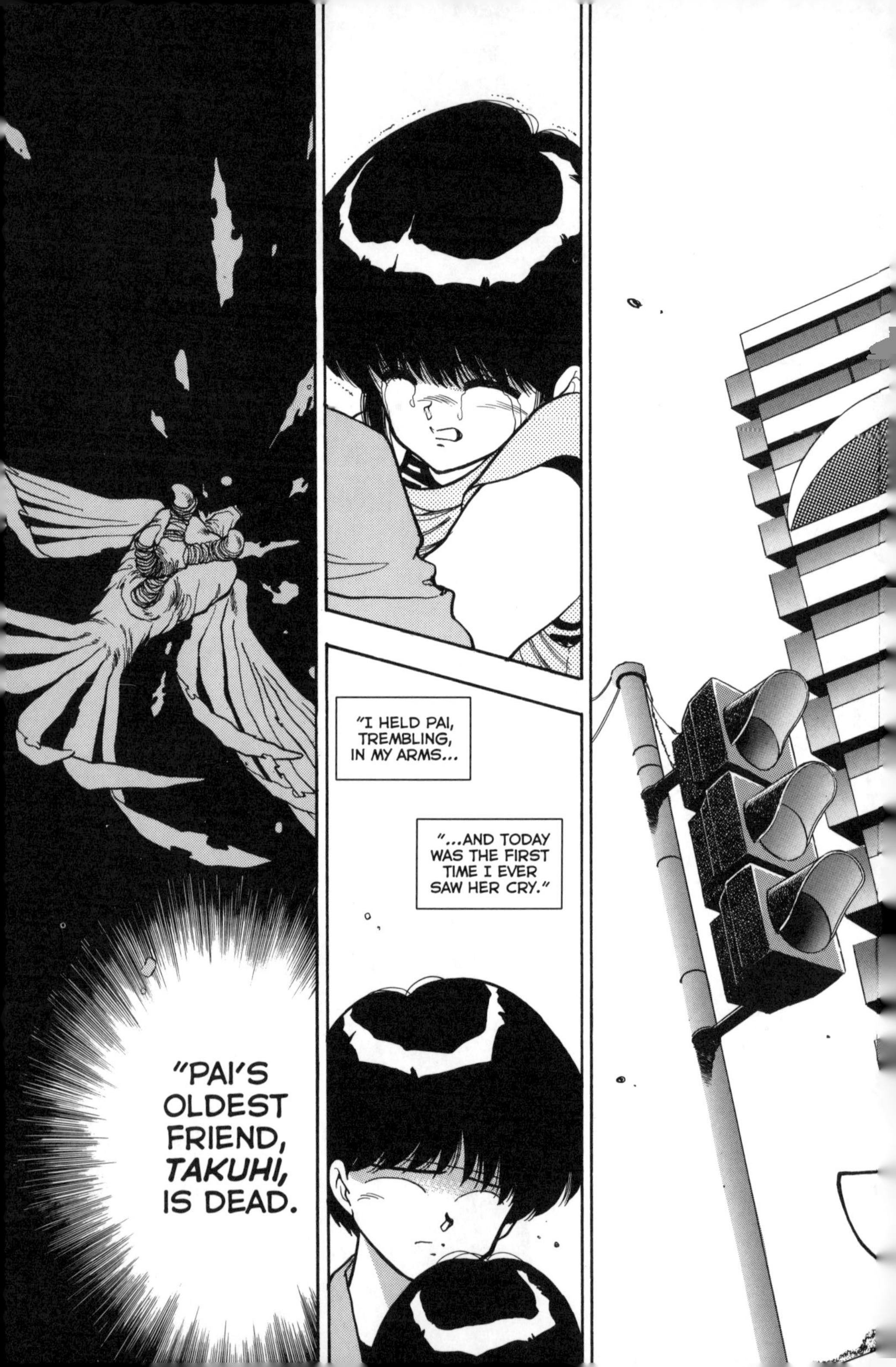
"PAI'S OLDEST FRIEND, *TAKUHI*, IS DEAD.
"I HELD PAI, TREMBLING, IN MY ARMS...
"...AND TODAY WAS THE FIRST TIME I EVER SAW HER CRY."

Flight of the Demon
part 3

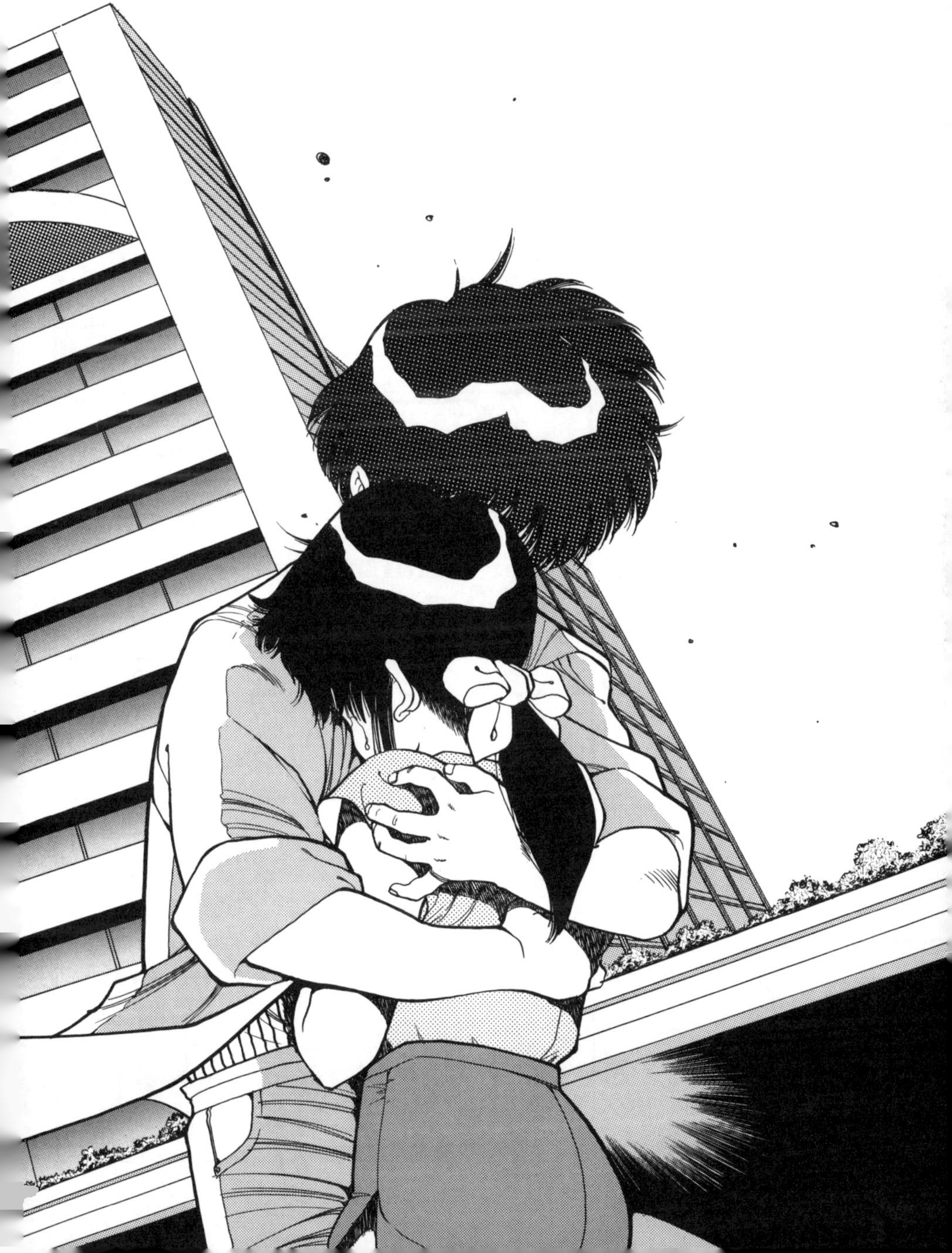

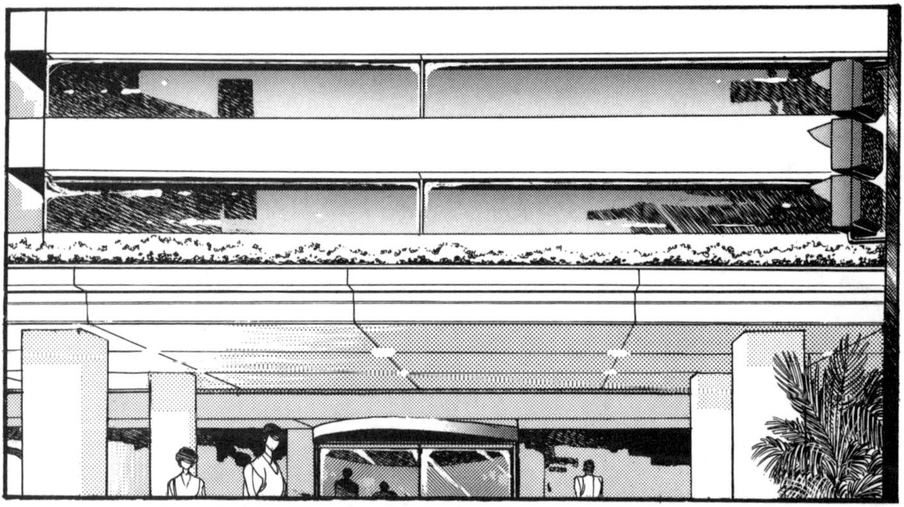
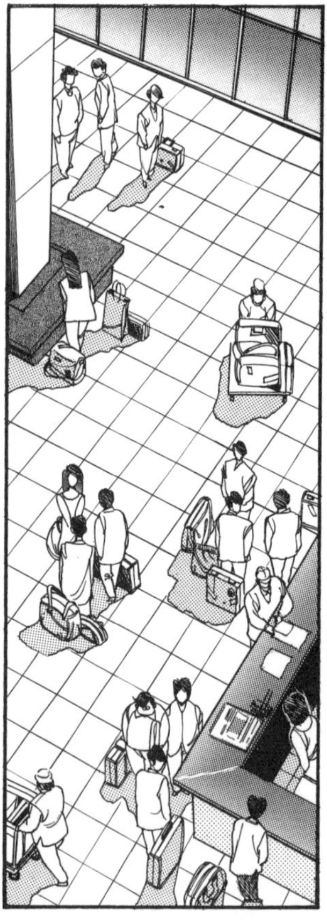
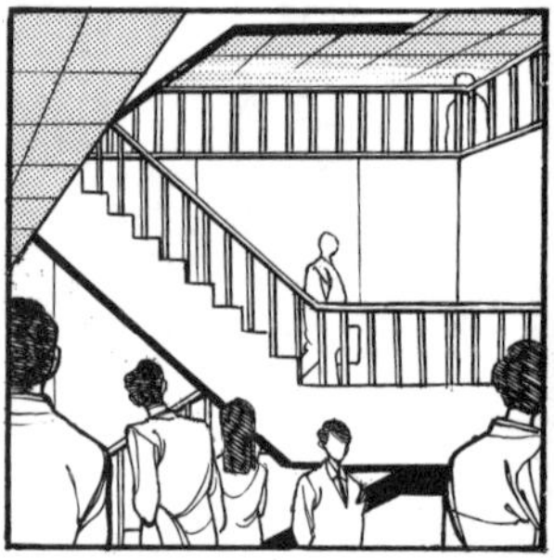
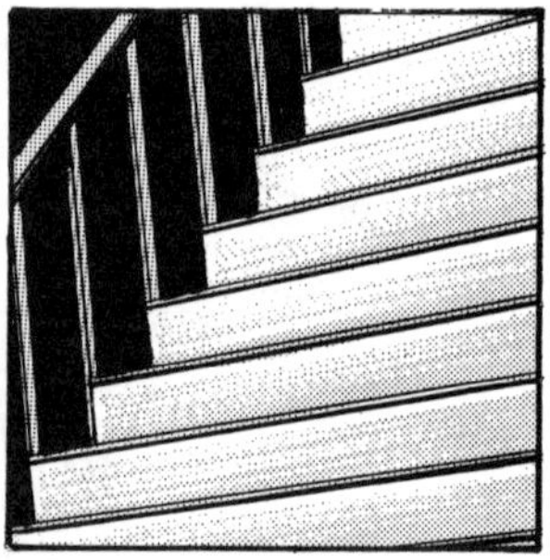
30th FLOOR
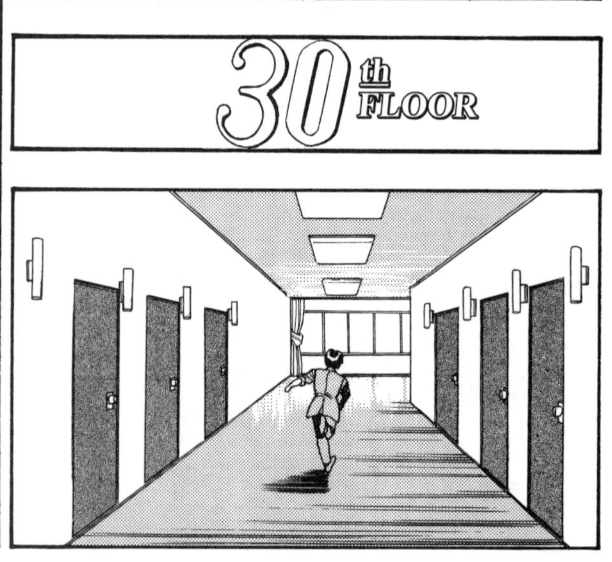

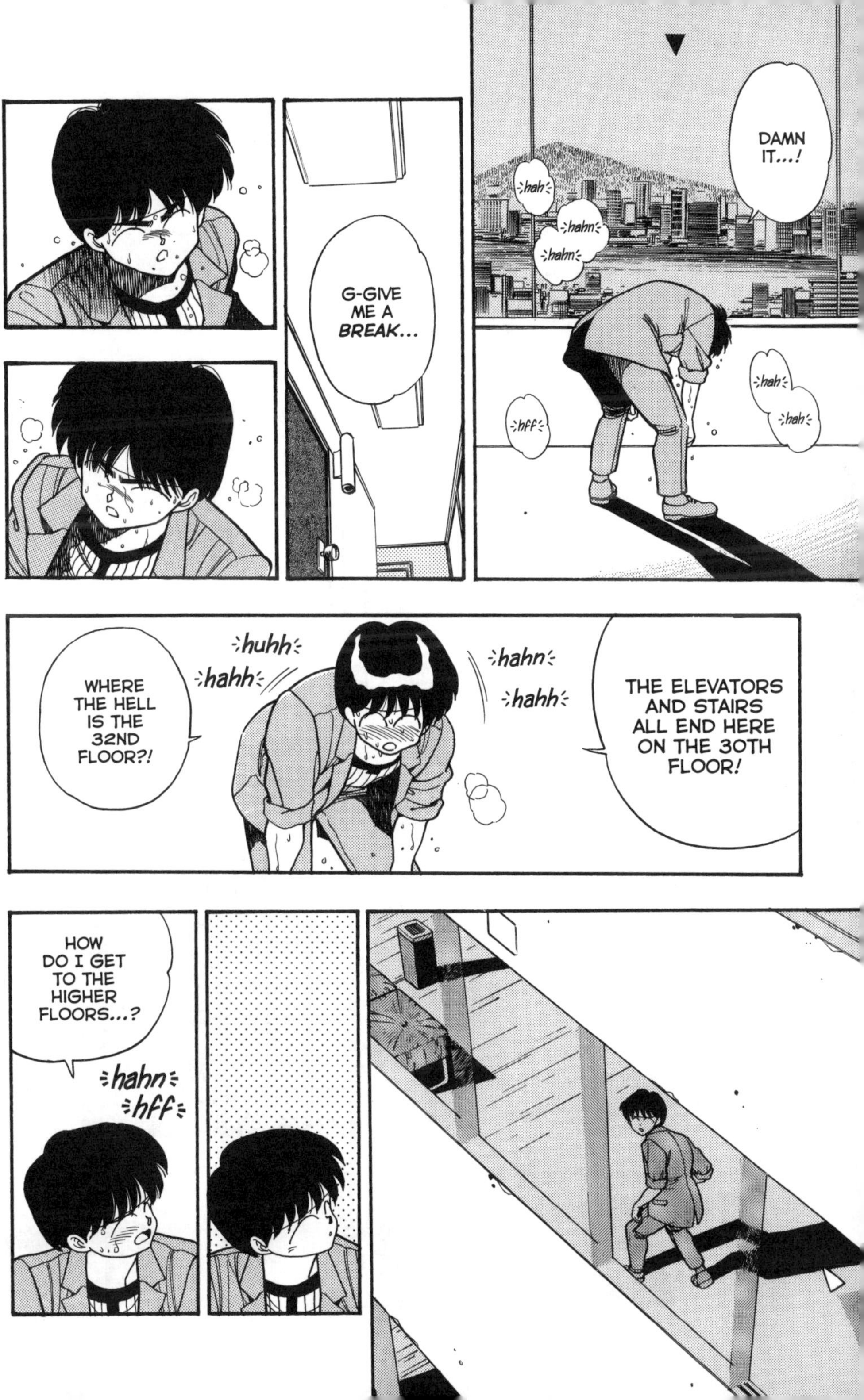
G-GIVE ME A BREAK...
hah
hahn
hahn
DAMN IT...!
hff
hah
hah
WHERE THE HELL IS THE 32ND FLOOR?!
huhh
hahh
hahn
hahh
THE ELEVATORS AND STAIRS ALL END HERE ON THE 30TH FLOOR!
HOW DO I GET TO THE HIGHER FLOORS...?
hahn
hff

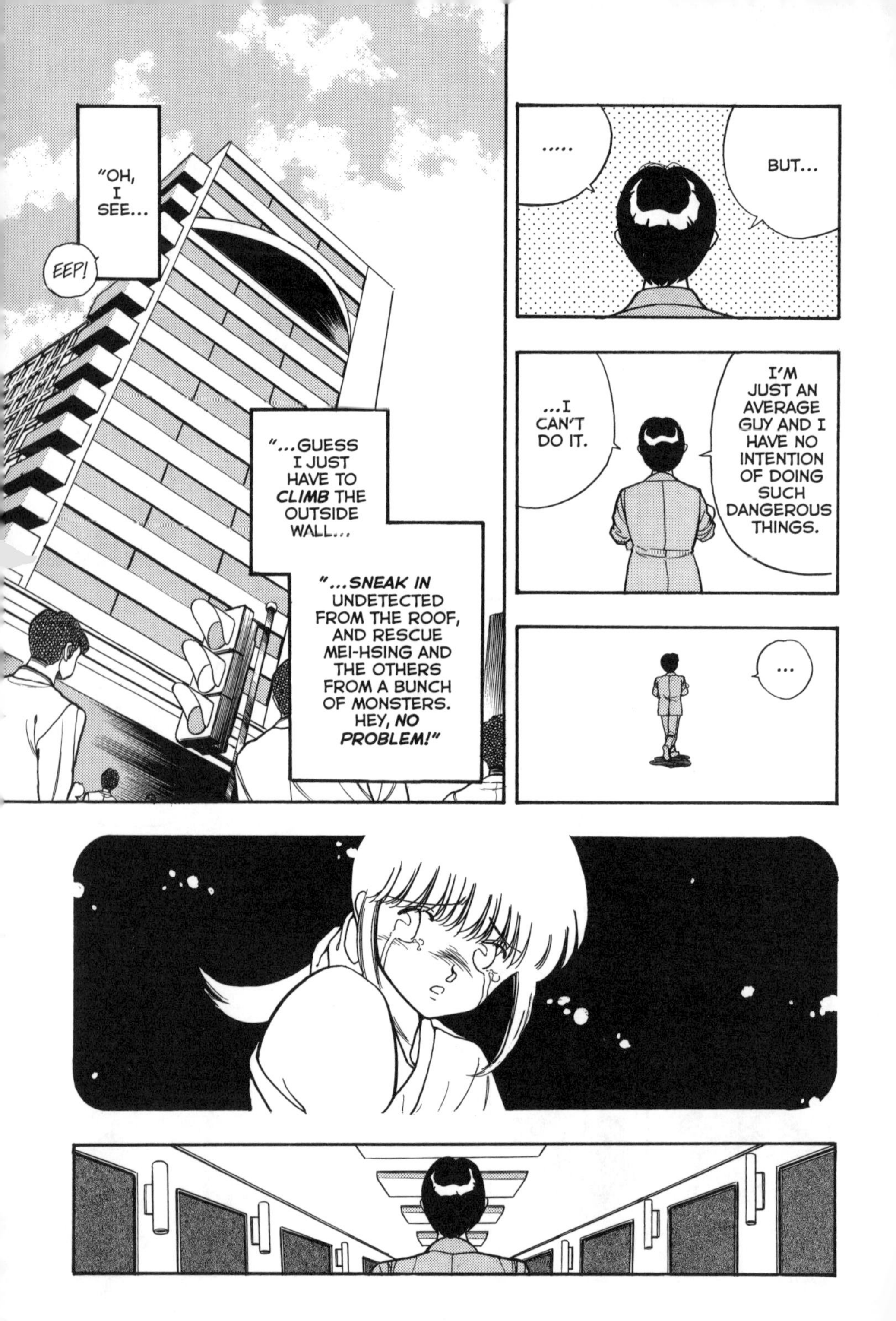
"OH, I SEE...
EEP!
"...GUESS I JUST HAVE TO CLIMB THE OUTSIDE WALL...
"...SNEAK IN UNDETECTED FROM THE ROOF, AND RESCUE MEI-HSING AND THE OTHERS FROM A BUNCH OF MONSTERS. HEY, NO PROBLEM!"
.....
BUT...
...I CAN'T DO IT.
I'M JUST AN AVERAGE GUY AND I HAVE NO INTENTION OF DOING SUCH DANGEROUS THINGS.
...

"MAYBE IT'S TOO SOON TO CRY, PAI..."

I MEAN-- YOU NEVER KNOW. TAKUHI'S A *MONSTER*, RIGHT?

MAYBE HE WON'T DIE JUST BECAUSE HIS HEAD GOT BLOWN OFF... RIGHT?

TAKUHI'S HEAD NOT JUST *DECORATION*, YOU KNOW!

HEY, *MY* HEAD GOT KNOCKED OFF, TOO, REMEMBER? AND I'M ALL RIGHT!

EEH? YAKUMO'S HEAD ONLY DECOR-ATION?!

KABOOMF

SO TAKUHI *COULD* STILL BE ALIVE... RIGHT?

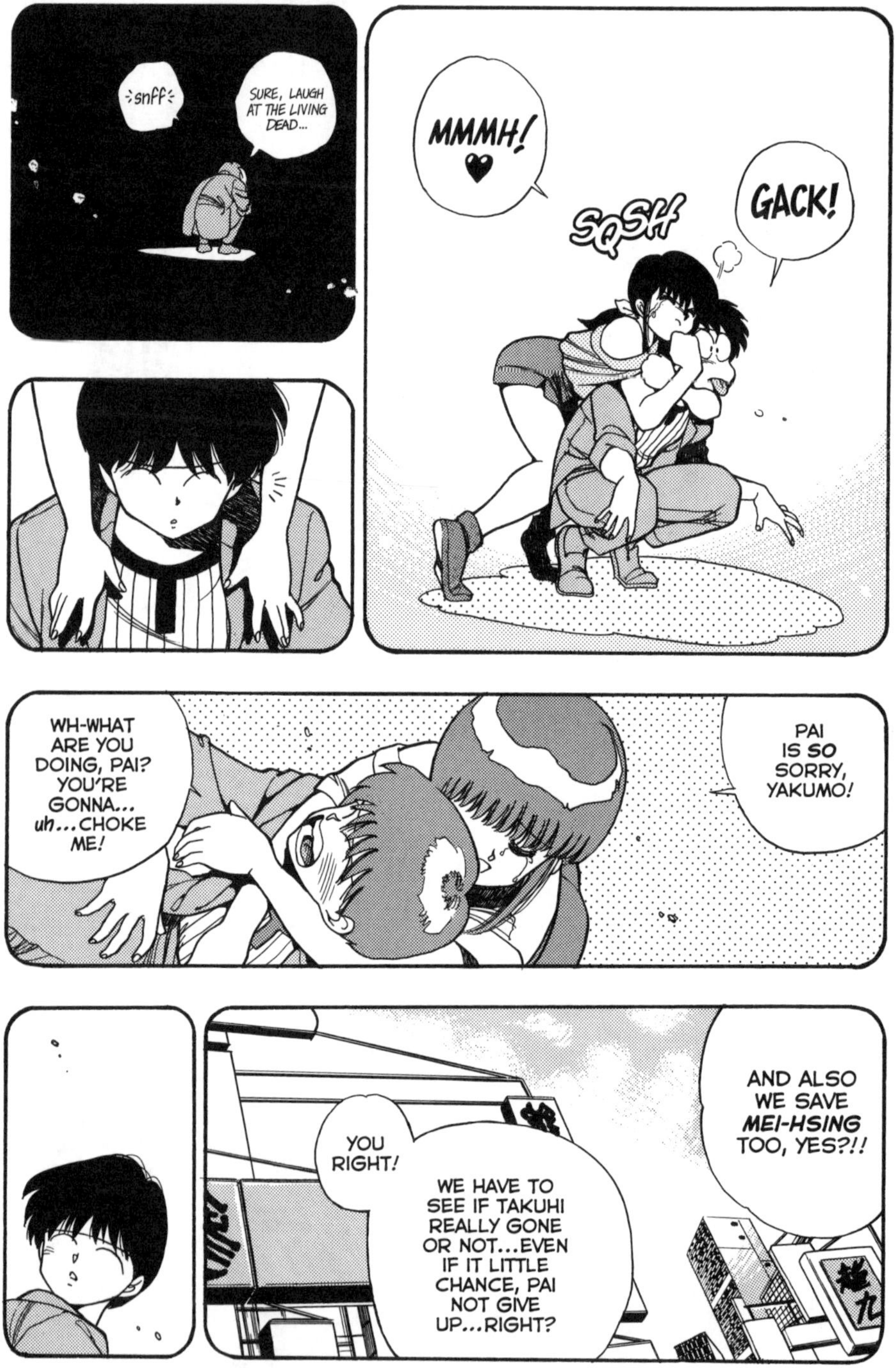
snff
SURE, LAUGH AT THE LIVING DEAD...
MMMH! ♥
SQSH
GACK!
WH-WHAT ARE YOU DOING, PAI? YOU'RE GONNA... uh...CHOKE ME!
PAI IS SO SORRY, YAKUMO!
YOU RIGHT!
WE HAVE TO SEE IF TAKUHI REALLY GONE OR NOT...EVEN IF IT LITTLE CHANCE, PAI NOT GIVE UP...RIGHT?
AND ALSO WE SAVE MEI-HSING TOO, YES?!!

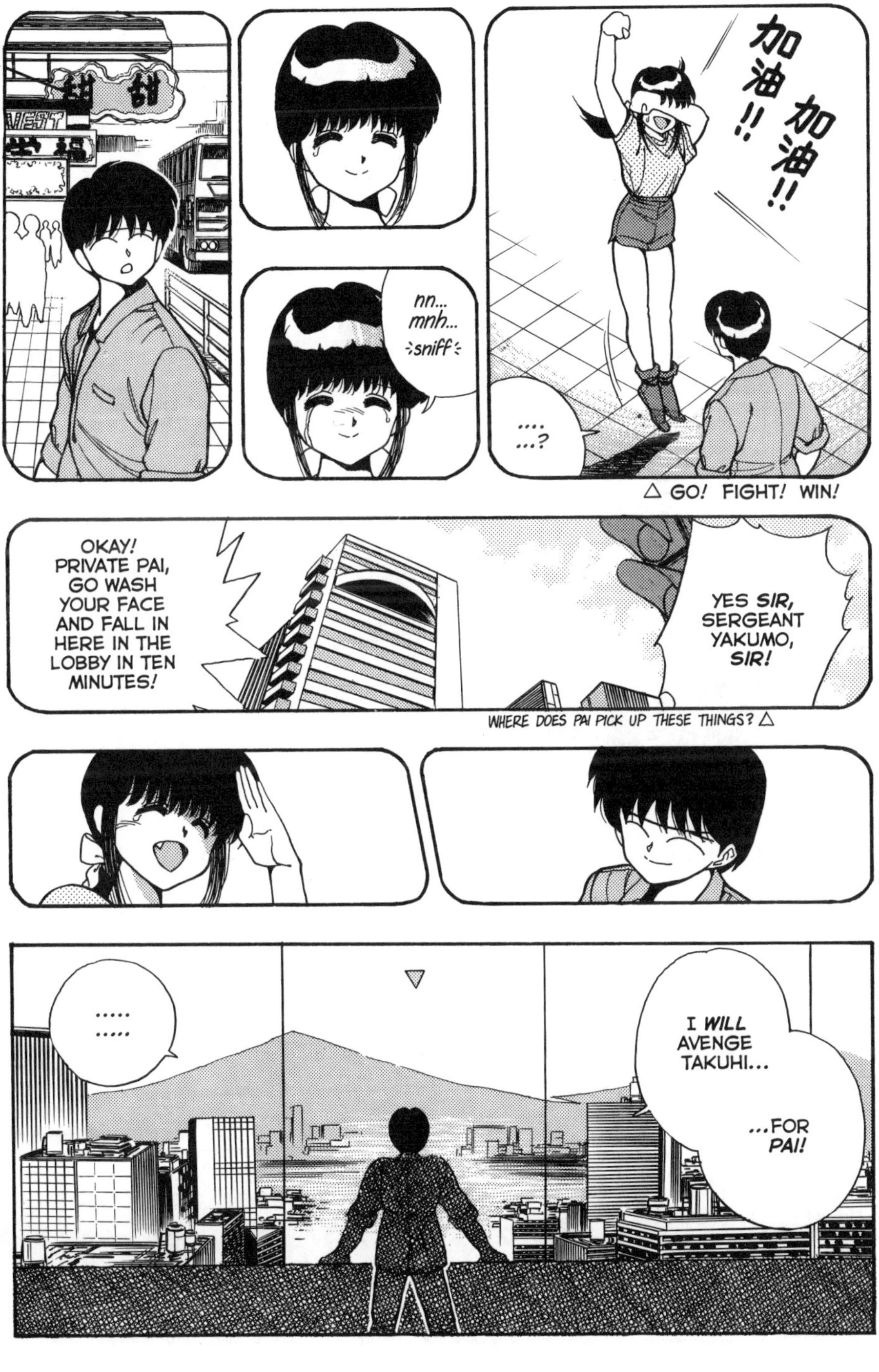
nn... mnh... sniff
加油!!
加油!!
....
...?
GO! FIGHT! WIN!
OKAY! PRIVATE PAI, GO WASH YOUR FACE AND FALL IN HERE IN THE LOBBY IN TEN MINUTES!
YES SIR, SERGEANT YAKUMO, SIR!
WHERE DOES PAI PICK UP THESE THINGS?
.....
.....
I WILL AVENGE TAKUHI...
...FOR PAI!

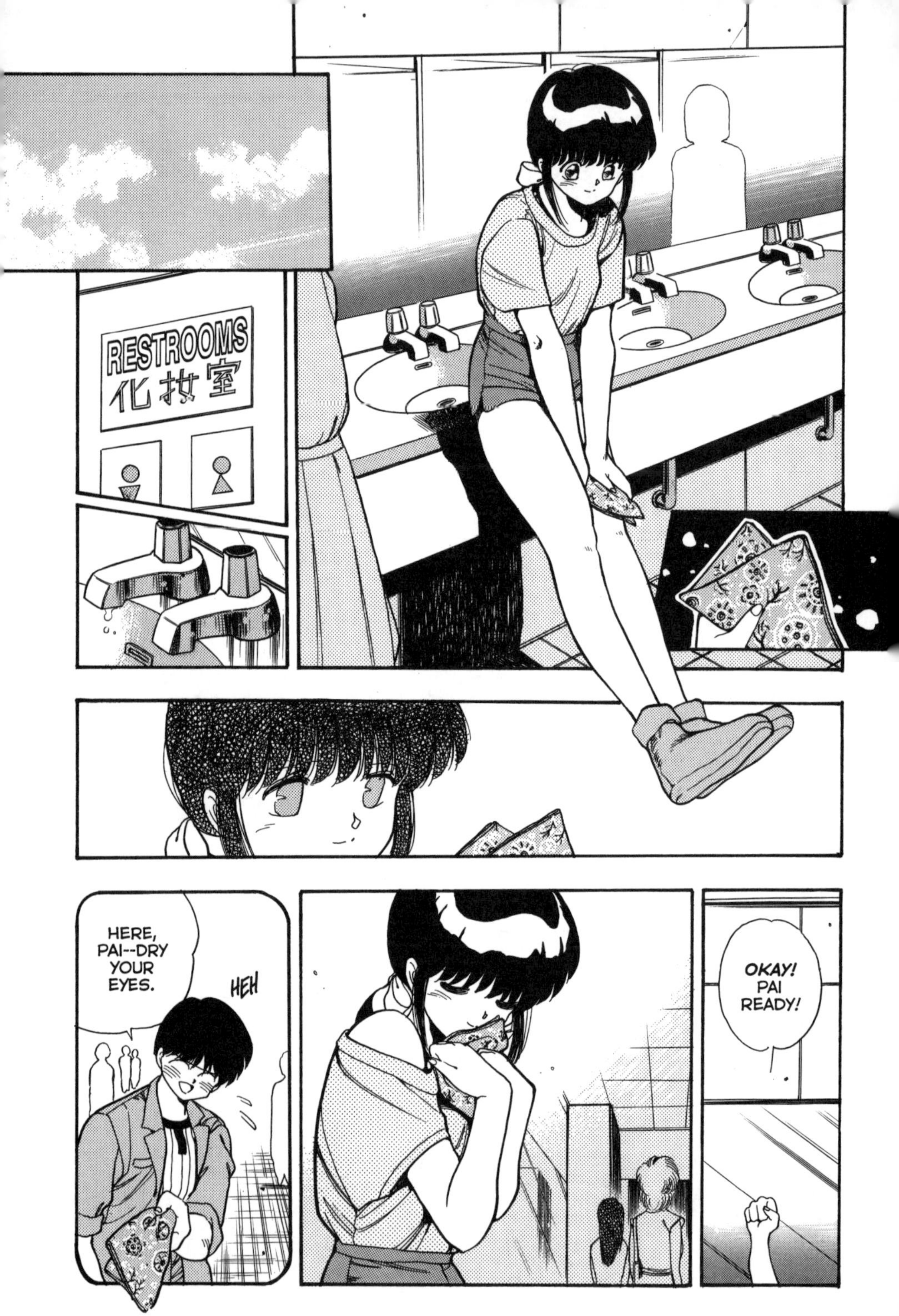

RESTROOMS
化妆室
HERE, PAI--DRY YOUR EYES.
HEH
OKAY! PAI READY!

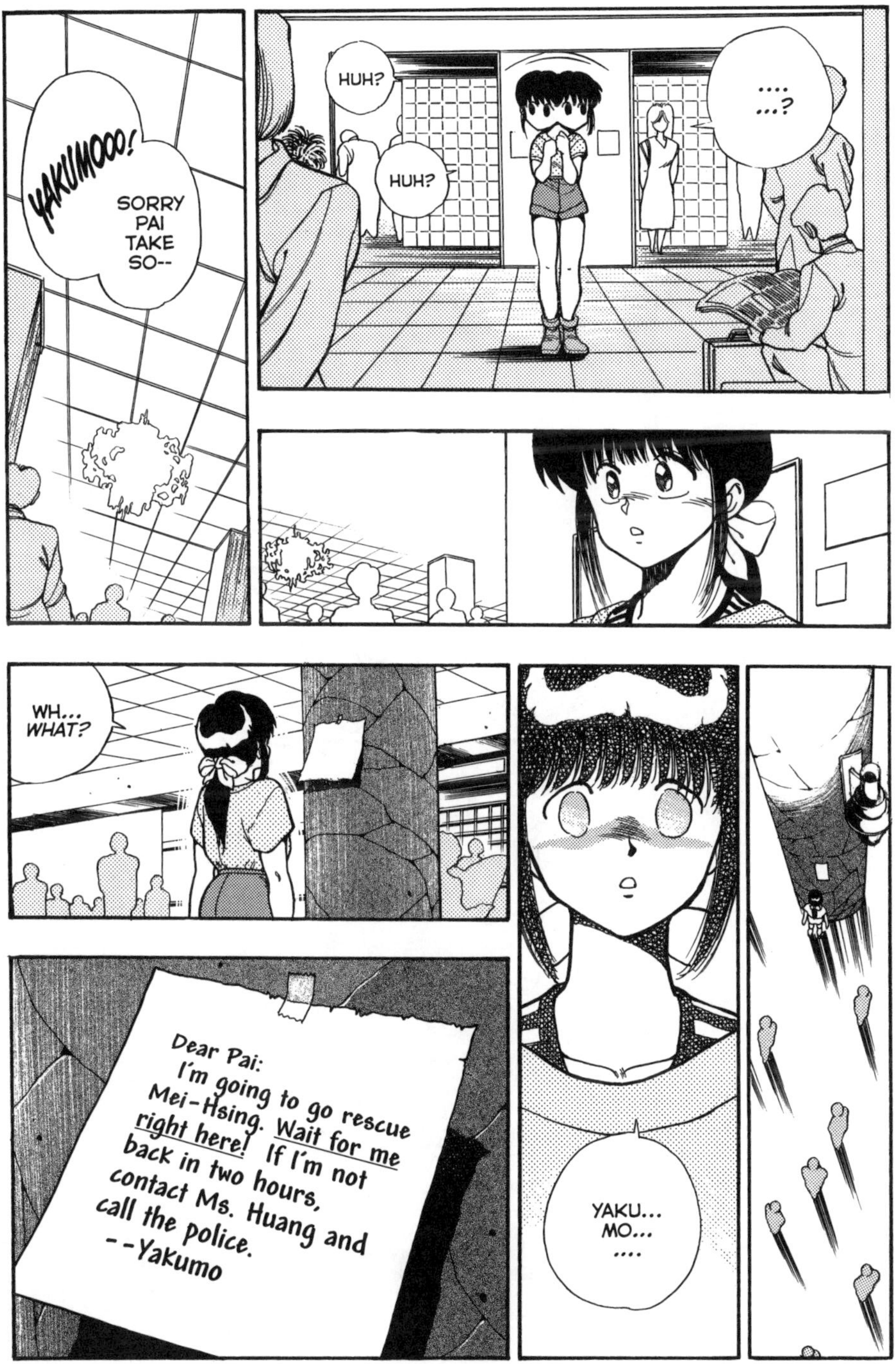
YAKUMOOO!
SORRY PAI TAKE SO--
HUH?
HUH?
....?
WH... WHAT?
Dear Pai: I'm going to go rescue Mei-Hsing. Wait for me right here! If I'm not back in two hours, contact Ms. Huang and call the police. --Yakumo
YAKU... MO... ....

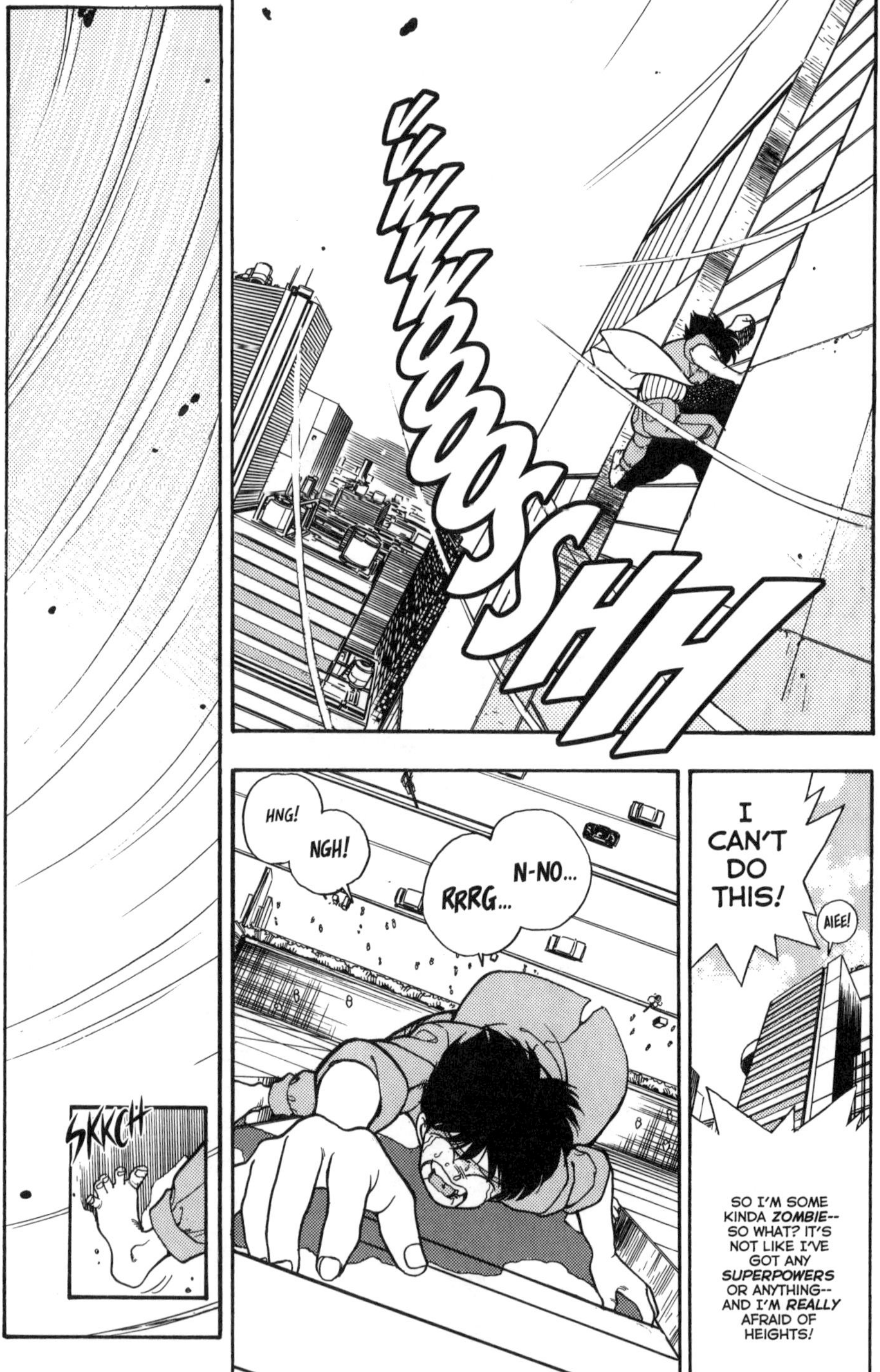
SKKCH
WWWHOOOOOSHH
HNG!
NGH!
N-NO... RRRG...
I CAN'T DO THIS!
AIEE!
SO I'M SOME KINDA *ZOMBIE*-- SO WHAT? IT'S NOT LIKE I'VE GOT ANY *SUPERPOWERS* OR ANYTHING-- AND I'M *REALLY* AFRAID OF HEIGHTS!

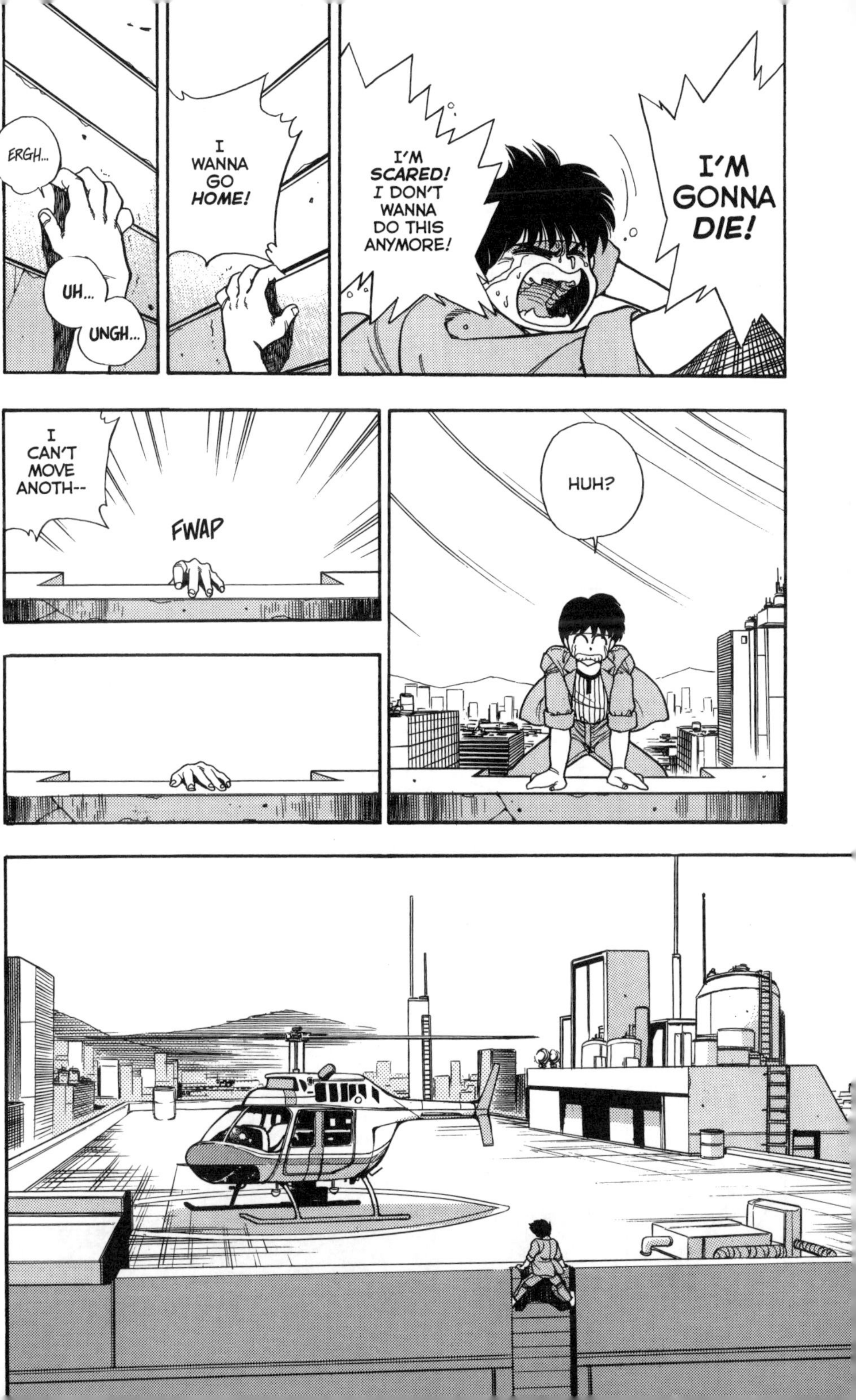
ERGH...
UH...
UNGH...
I WANNA GO HOME!
I'M SCARED! I DON'T WANNA DO THIS ANYMORE!
I'M GONNA DIE!
I CAN'T MOVE ANOTH--
FWAP
HUH?

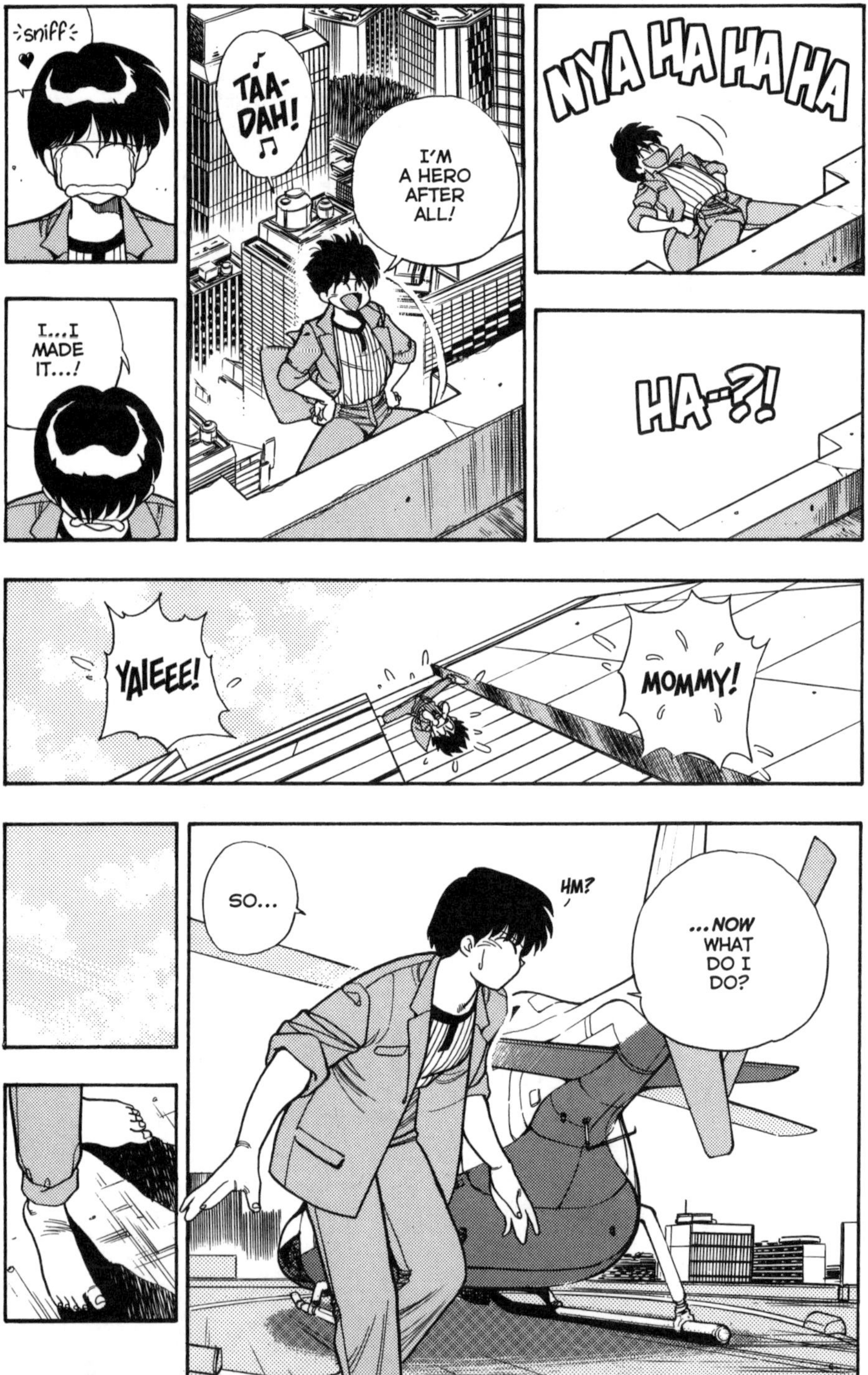
sniff
I...I MADE IT...!
TAA-DAH!
I'M A HERO AFTER ALL!
NYA HA HA HA HA
HA--?!
YAIEEE!
MOMMY!
SO...
HM?
...NOW WHAT DO I DO?

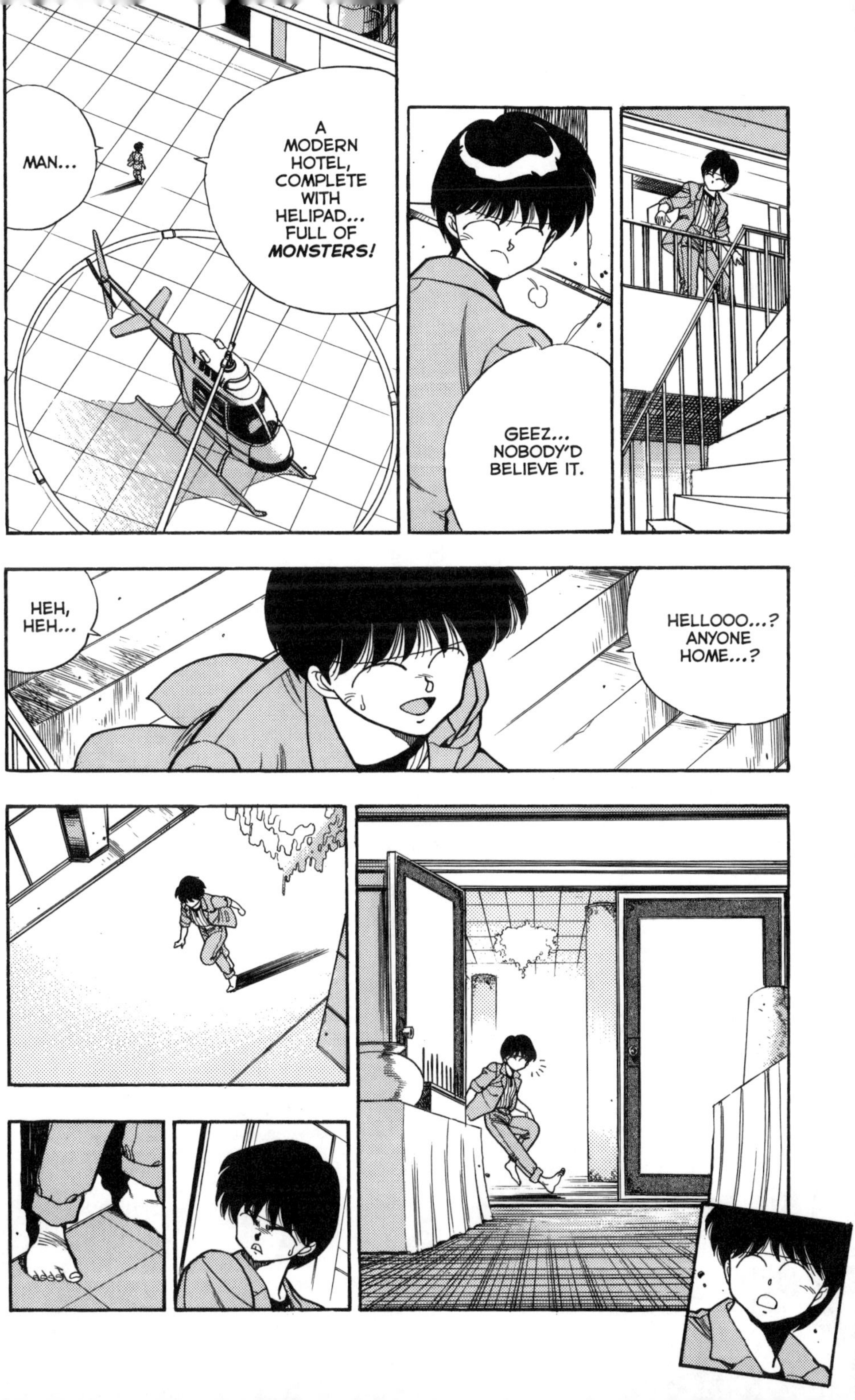
MAN...
A MODERN HOTEL, COMPLETE WITH HELIPAD... FULL OF *MONSTERS!*
GEEZ... NOBODY'D BELIEVE IT.
HEH, HEH...
HELLOOO...? ANYONE HOME...?

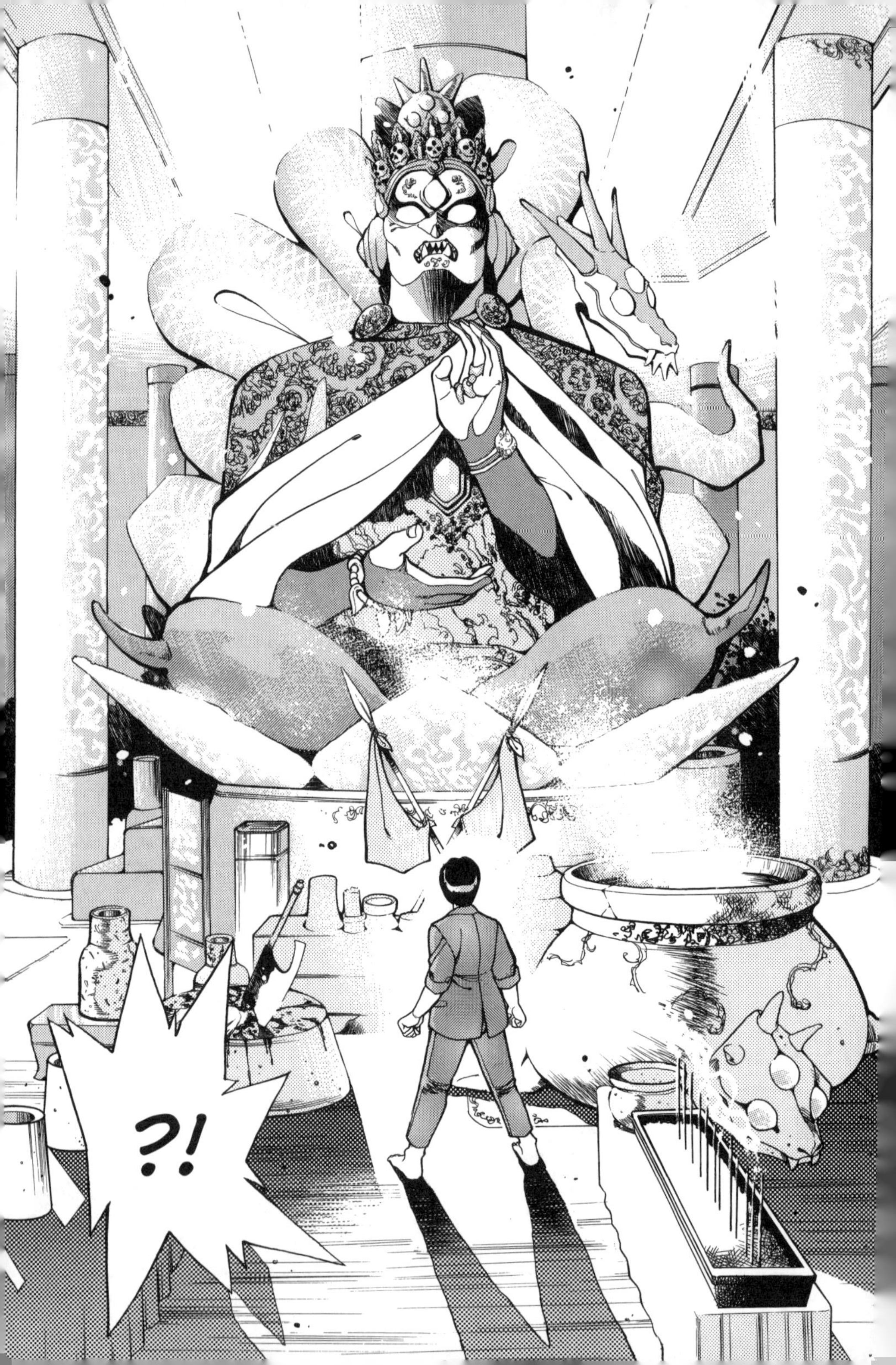
?!

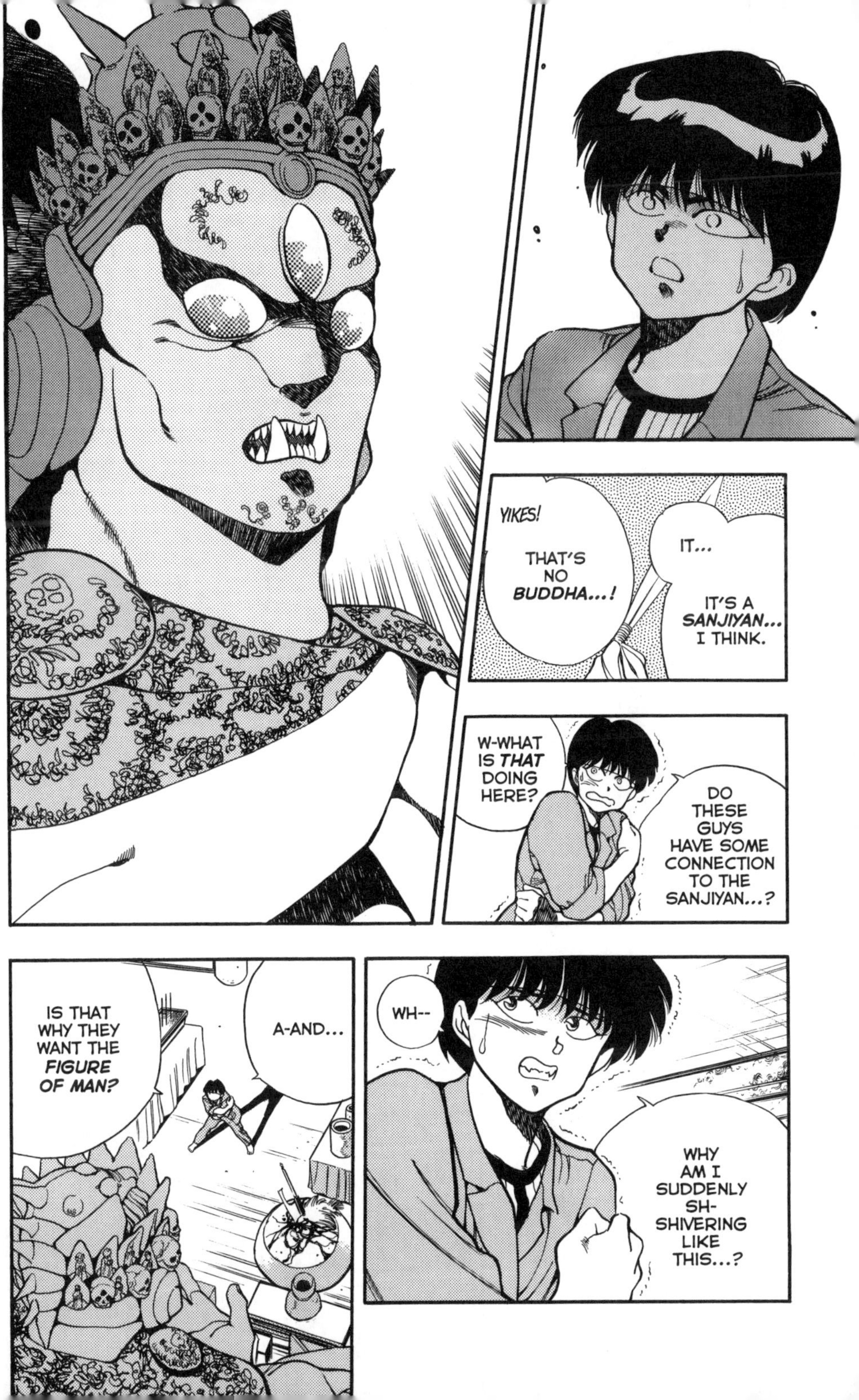
YIKES!
THAT'S NO BUDDHA...!
IT...
IT'S A SANJIYAN... I THINK.
W-WHAT IS THAT DOING HERE?
DO THESE GUYS HAVE SOME CONNECTION TO THE SANJIYAN...?
IS THAT WHY THEY WANT THE FIGURE OF MAN?
A-AND...
WH--
WHY AM I SUDDENLY SH-SHIVERING LIKE THIS...?

WHAT *IS* THIS STATUE ...?!

IT'S KAIYAN-WANG--THE *DEMON EYE KING.*

?!

THOSE EVIL MONSTERS ARE SACRIFICING VIRGIN GIRLS TO THE *TRICLOPS...* THE SANJIYAN.

THAT STATUE REPRESENTS *HIM*-- THE MONSTER THE BELIEVERS CALL "KAIYAN-WANG."

WH--

WHO'S THERE?

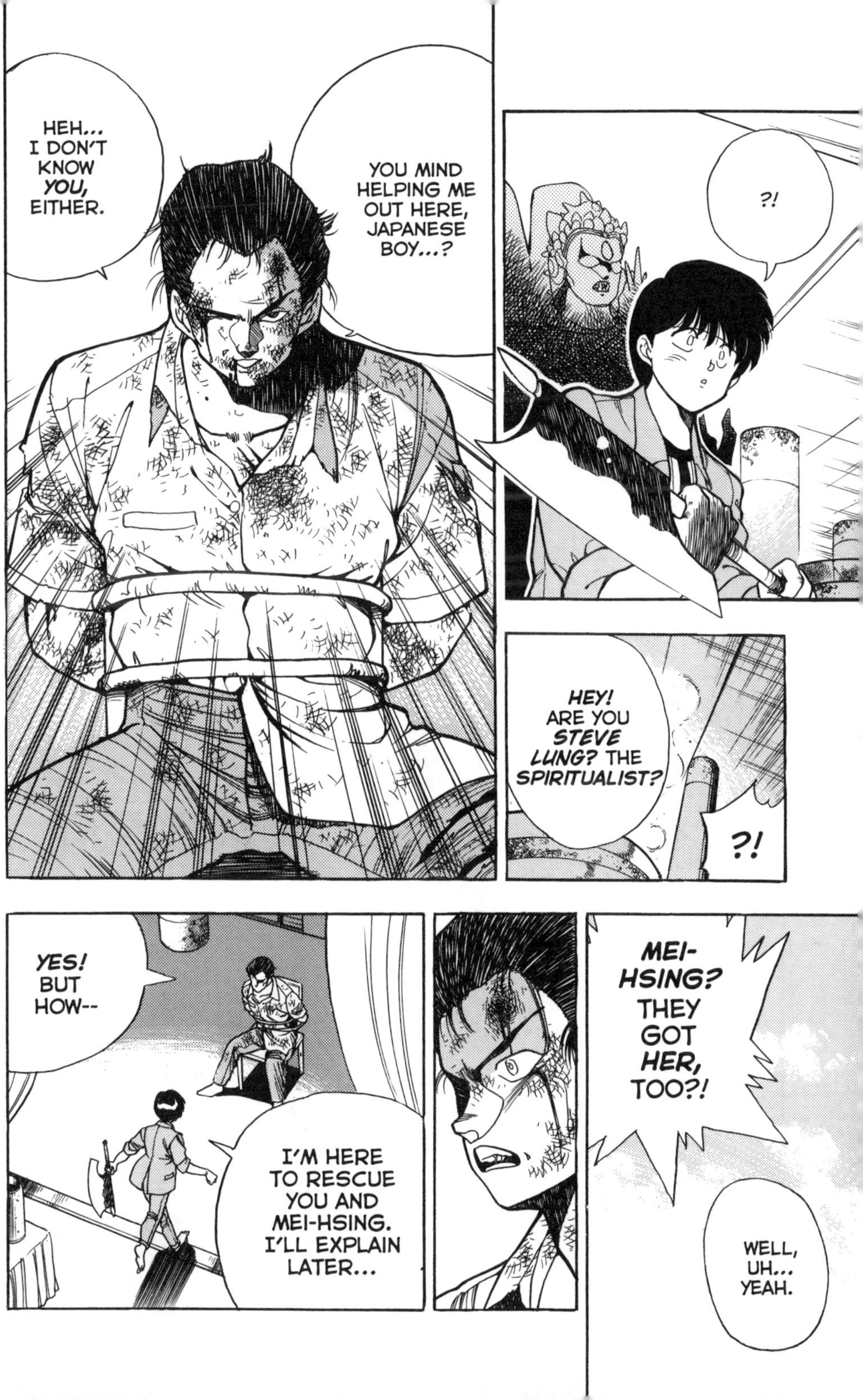
HEH... I DON'T KNOW *YOU,* EITHER.
YOU MIND HELPING ME OUT HERE, JAPANESE BOY...?
?!
HEY! ARE YOU *STEVE LUNG?* THE *SPIRITUALIST?*
?!
YES! BUT HOW--
I'M HERE TO RESCUE YOU AND MEI-HSING. I'LL EXPLAIN LATER...
MEI-HSING? THEY GOT *HER,* TOO?!
WELL, UH... YEAH.

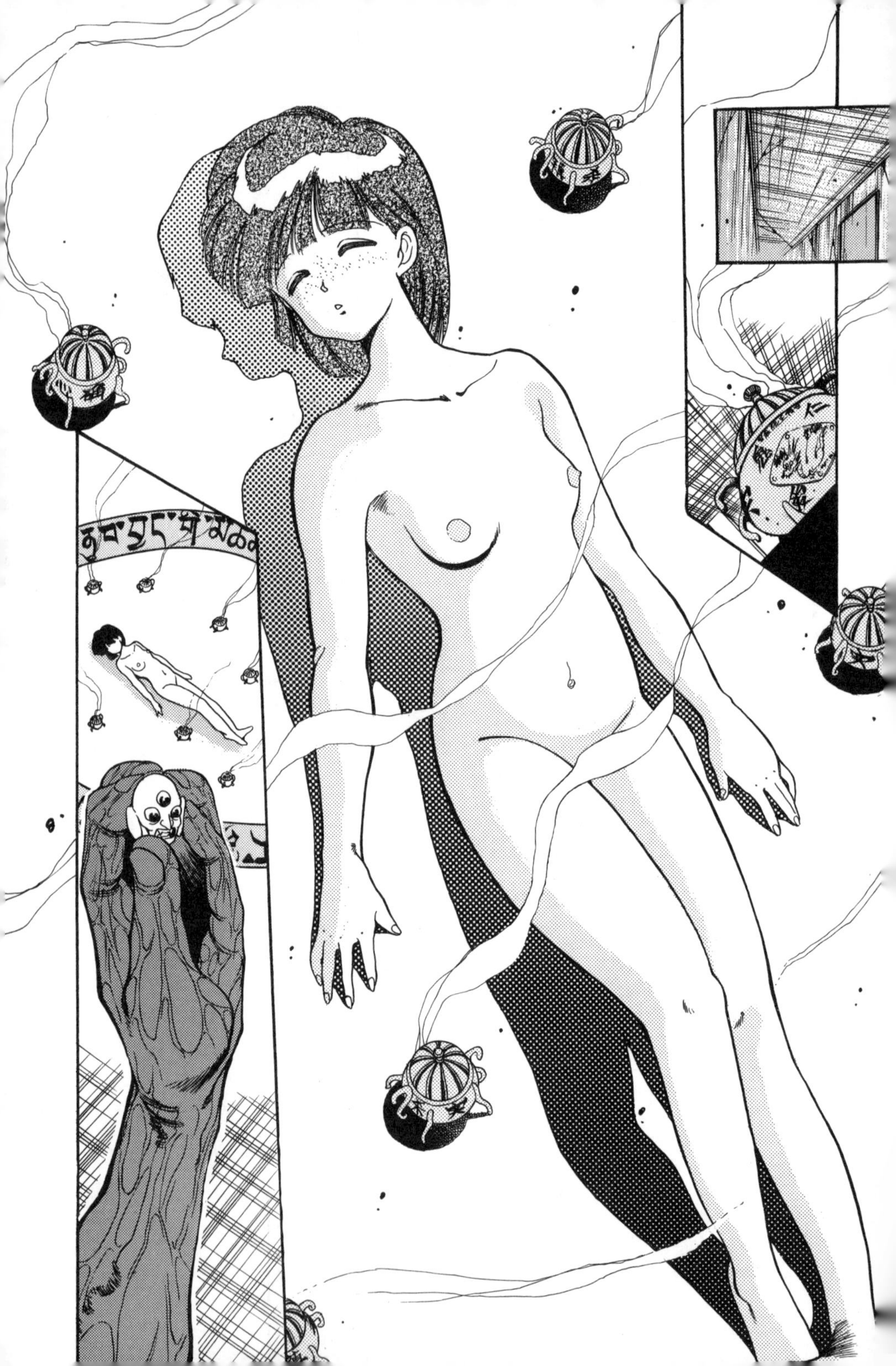

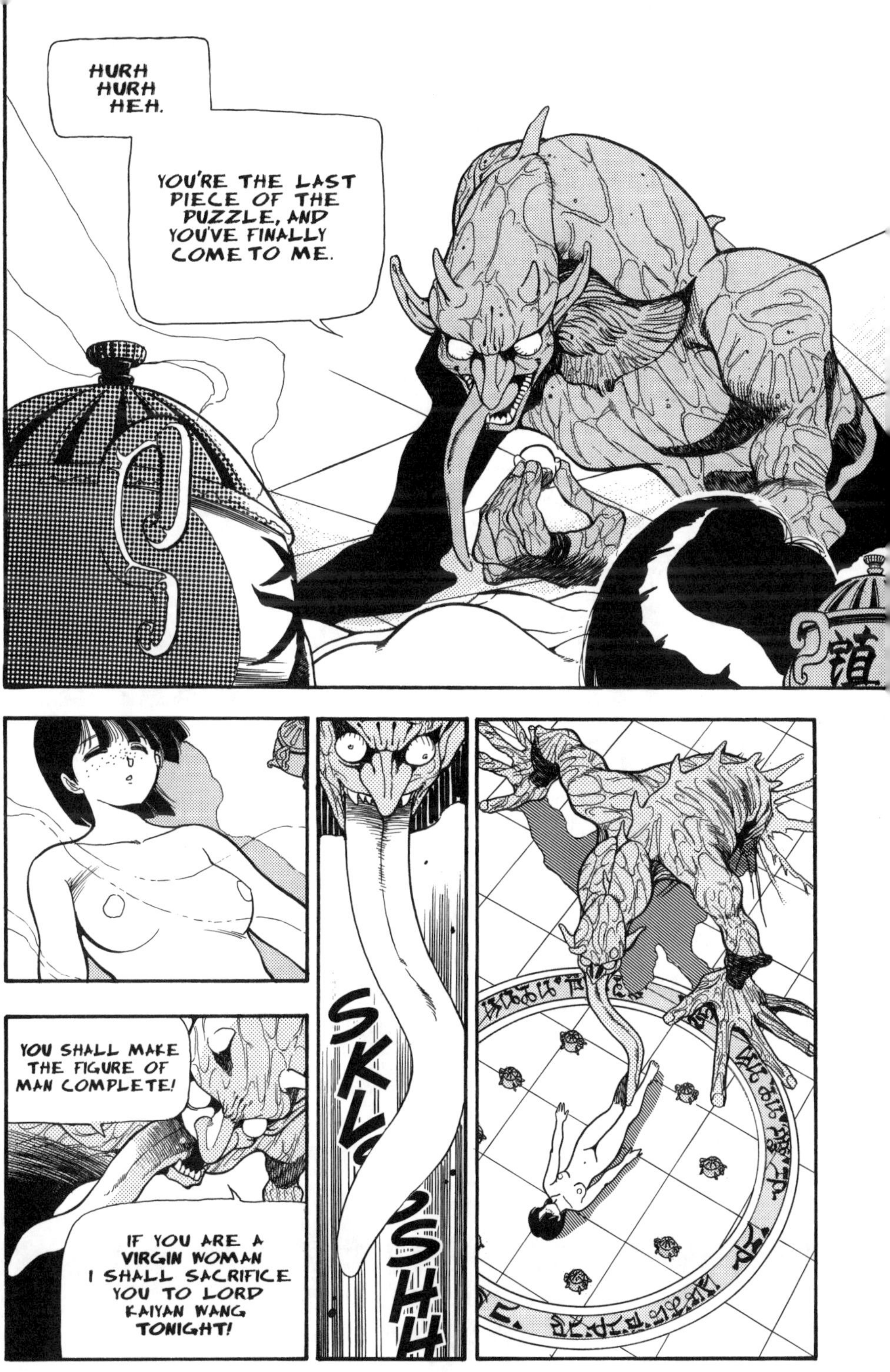
HURH HURH HEH.
YOU'RE THE LAST PIECE OF THE PUZZLE, AND YOU'VE FINALLY COME TO ME.
YOU SHALL MAKE THE FIGURE OF MAN COMPLETE!
IF YOU ARE A VIRGIN WOMAN I SHALL SACRIFICE YOU TO LORD KAIYAN WANG TONIGHT!
SKL SHH

DON'T LOOK!

HURH
HURH
HURH

UH...

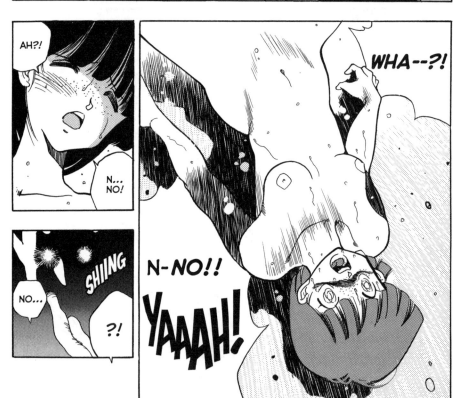

AH?!

N...
NO!

WHA--?!

SHIING

NO...

?!

N-NO!!

YAAAH!

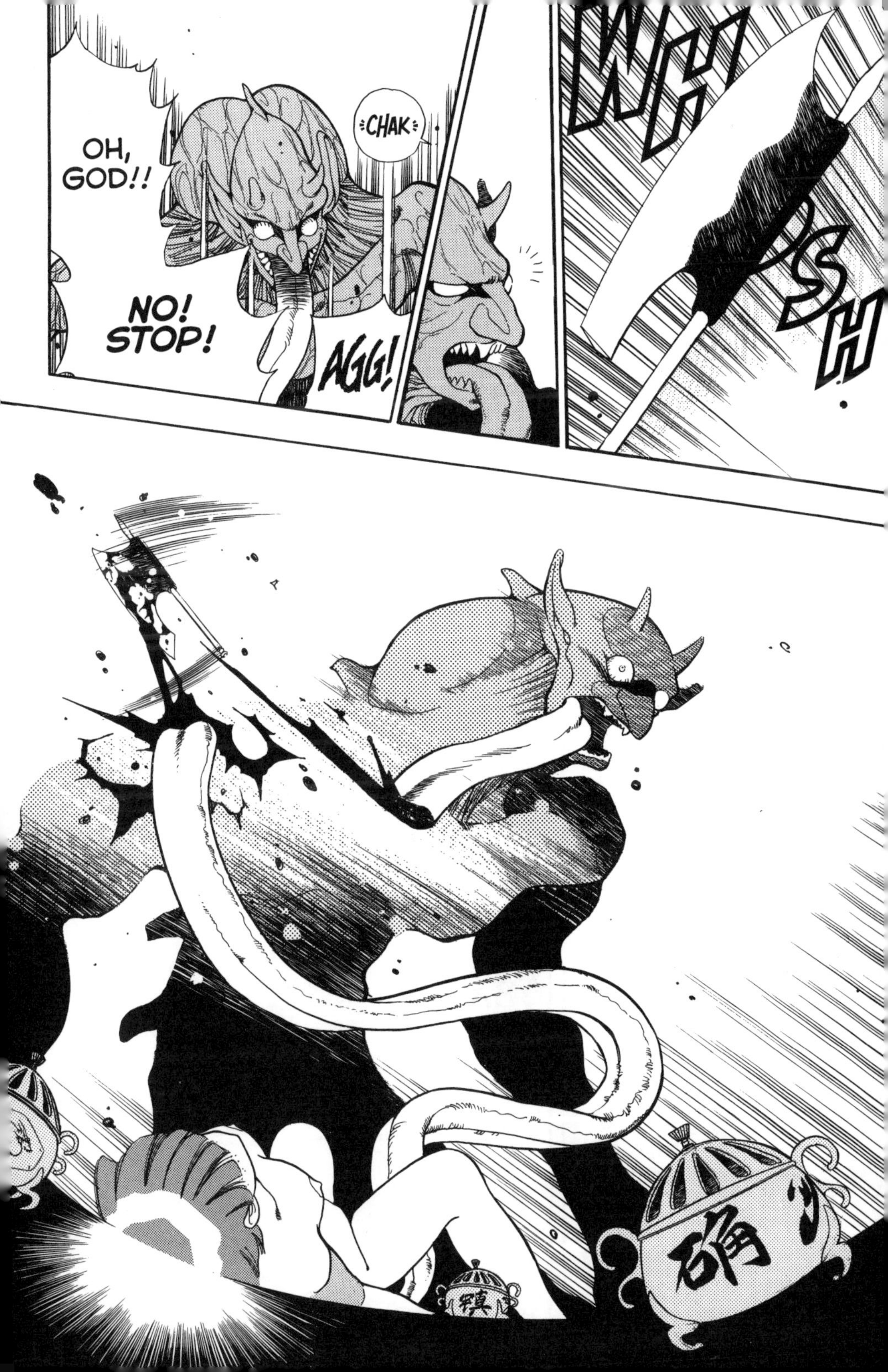
OH, GOD!!
CHAK
NO! STOP!
AGG!

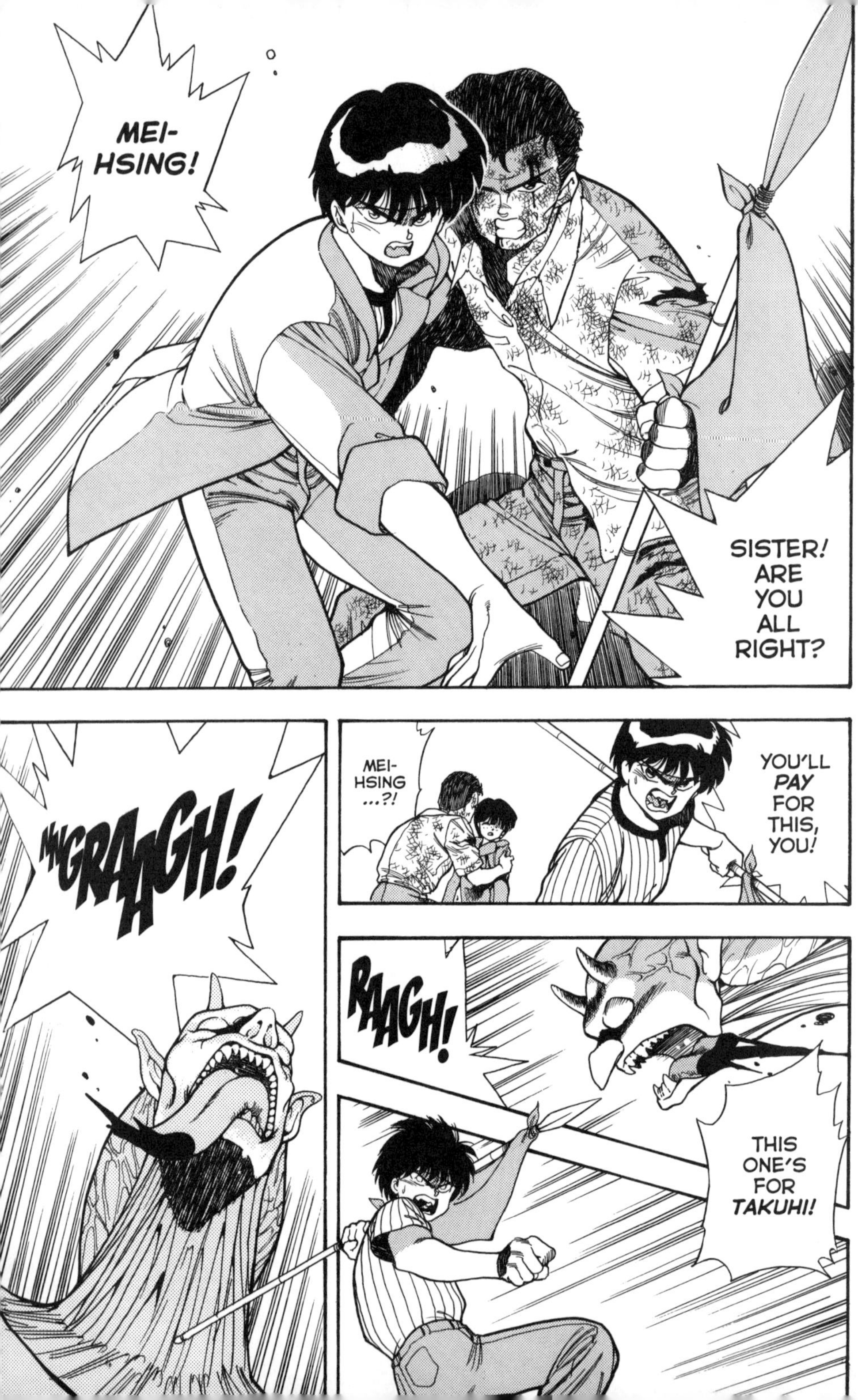
MEI-HSING!
SISTER! ARE YOU ALL RIGHT?
MNGRAAAGH!
MEI-HSING ...?!
YOU'LL PAY FOR THIS, YOU!
RAAGH!
THIS ONE'S FOR TAKUHI!

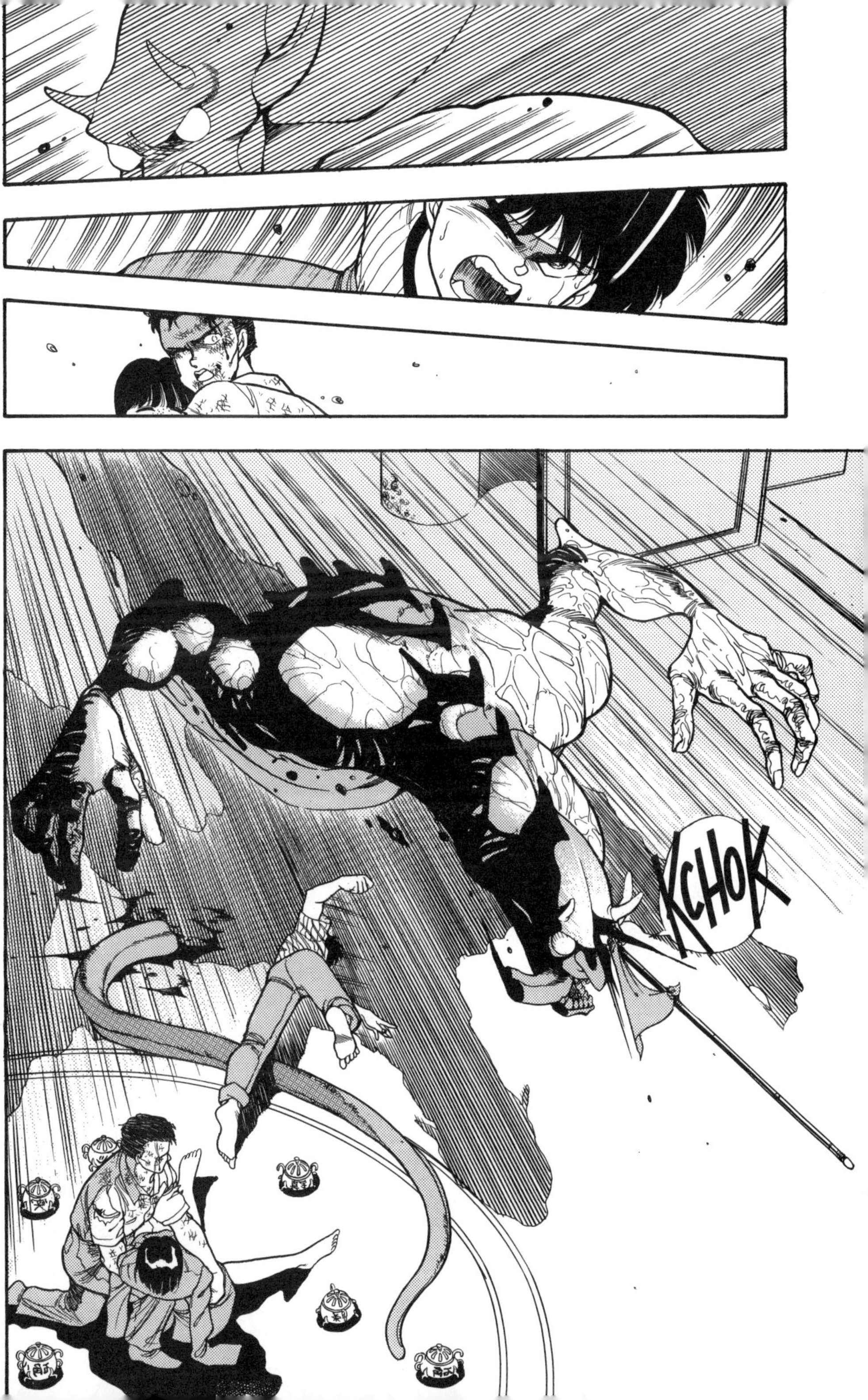
KCHOK

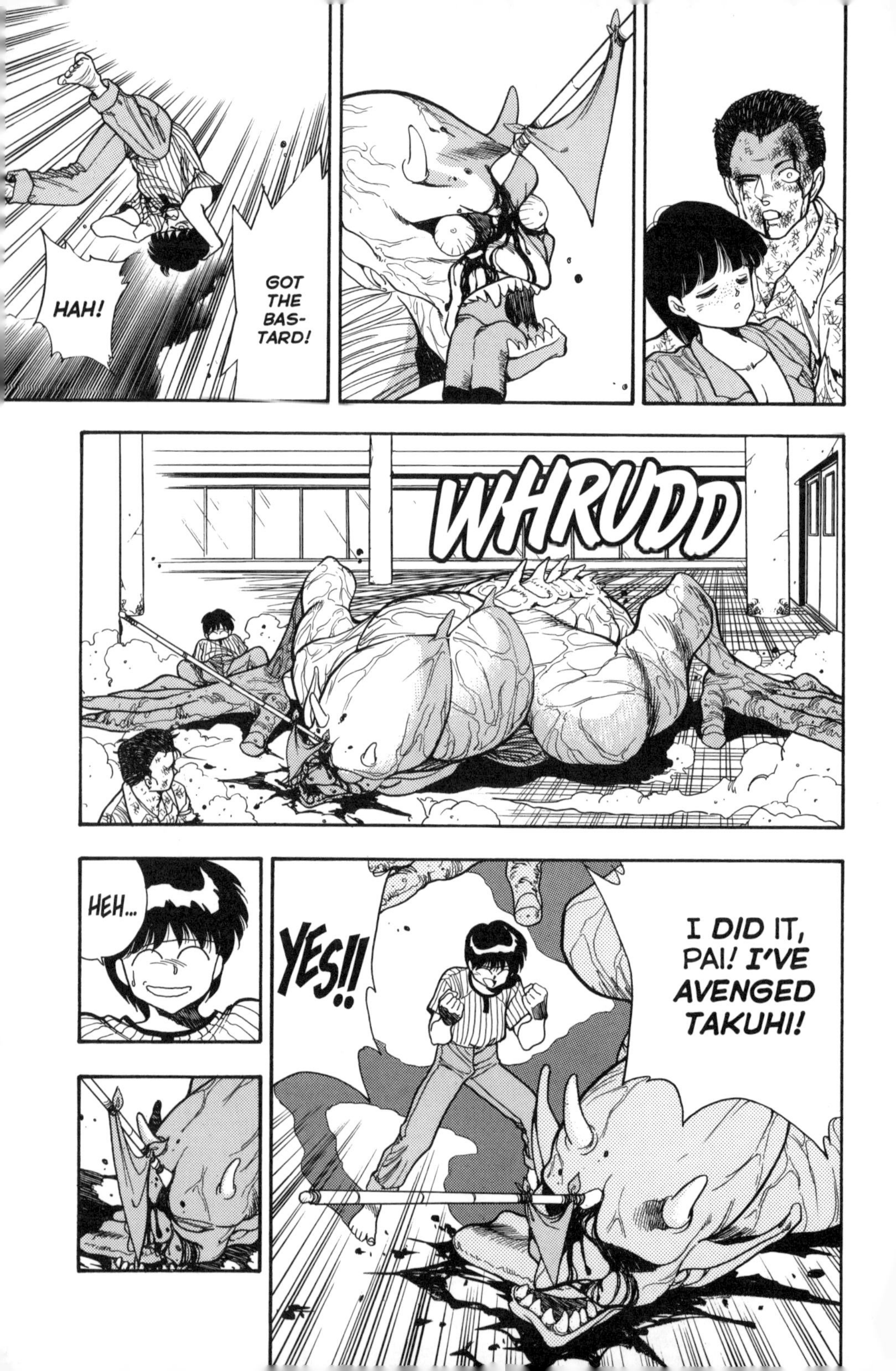
HAH!
GOT THE BAS-TARD!
WHRUDD
HEH...
YES!!
I DID IT, PAI! I'VE AVENGED TAKUHI!

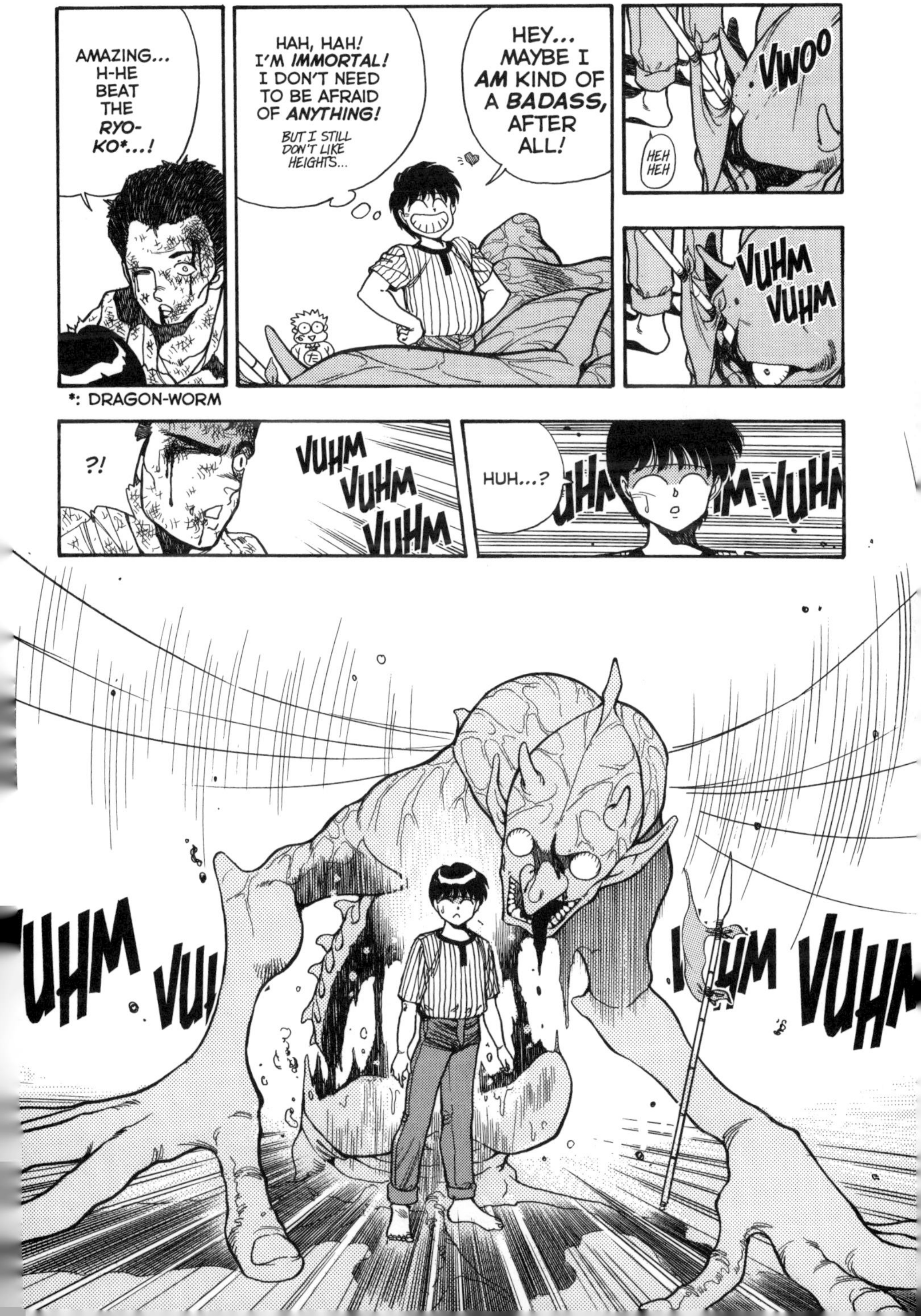
AMAZING... H-HE BEAT THE RYO-KO*...!
HAH, HAH! I'M IMMORTAL! I DON'T NEED TO BE AFRAID OF ANYTHING!
BUT I STILL DON'T LIKE HEIGHTS...
HEY... MAYBE I AM KIND OF A BADASS, AFTER ALL!
VWOO
HEH HEH
VUHM VUHM
*: DRAGON-WORM
?!
VUHM VUHM VUHM
HUH...?
VUHM
VUHM
VUHM
VUHM

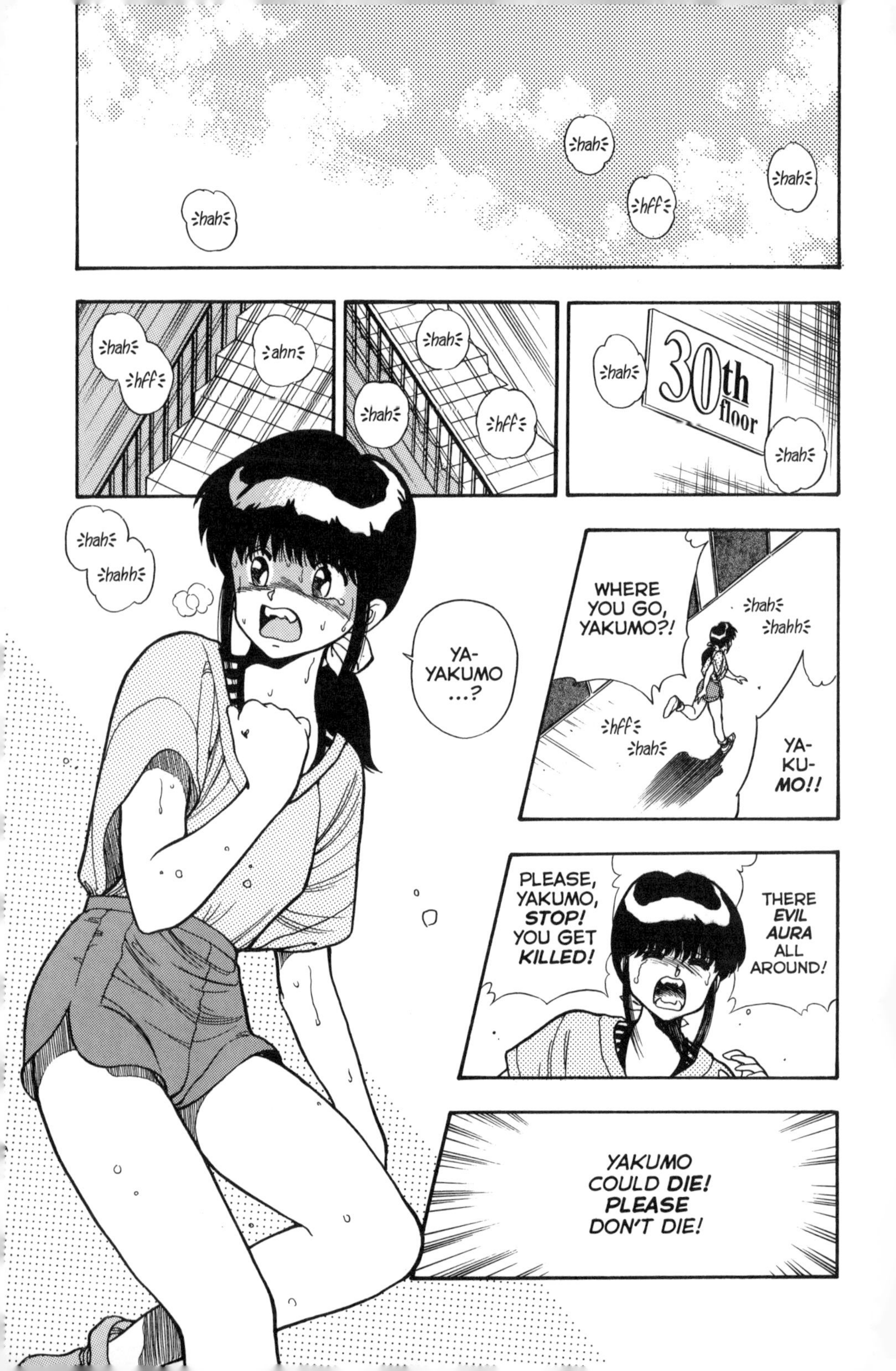
hah
hah
hff
hah
hah
hff
ahn
hah
hah
hff
hah
30th floor
hah
hah
hahh
YA-YAKUMO...?
WHERE YOU GO, YAKUMO?!
hah
hahh
hff
hah
YA-KU-MO!!
PLEASE, YAKUMO, STOP! YOU GET KILLED!
THERE EVIL AURA ALL AROUND!
YAKUMO COULD DIE! PLEASE DON'T DIE!

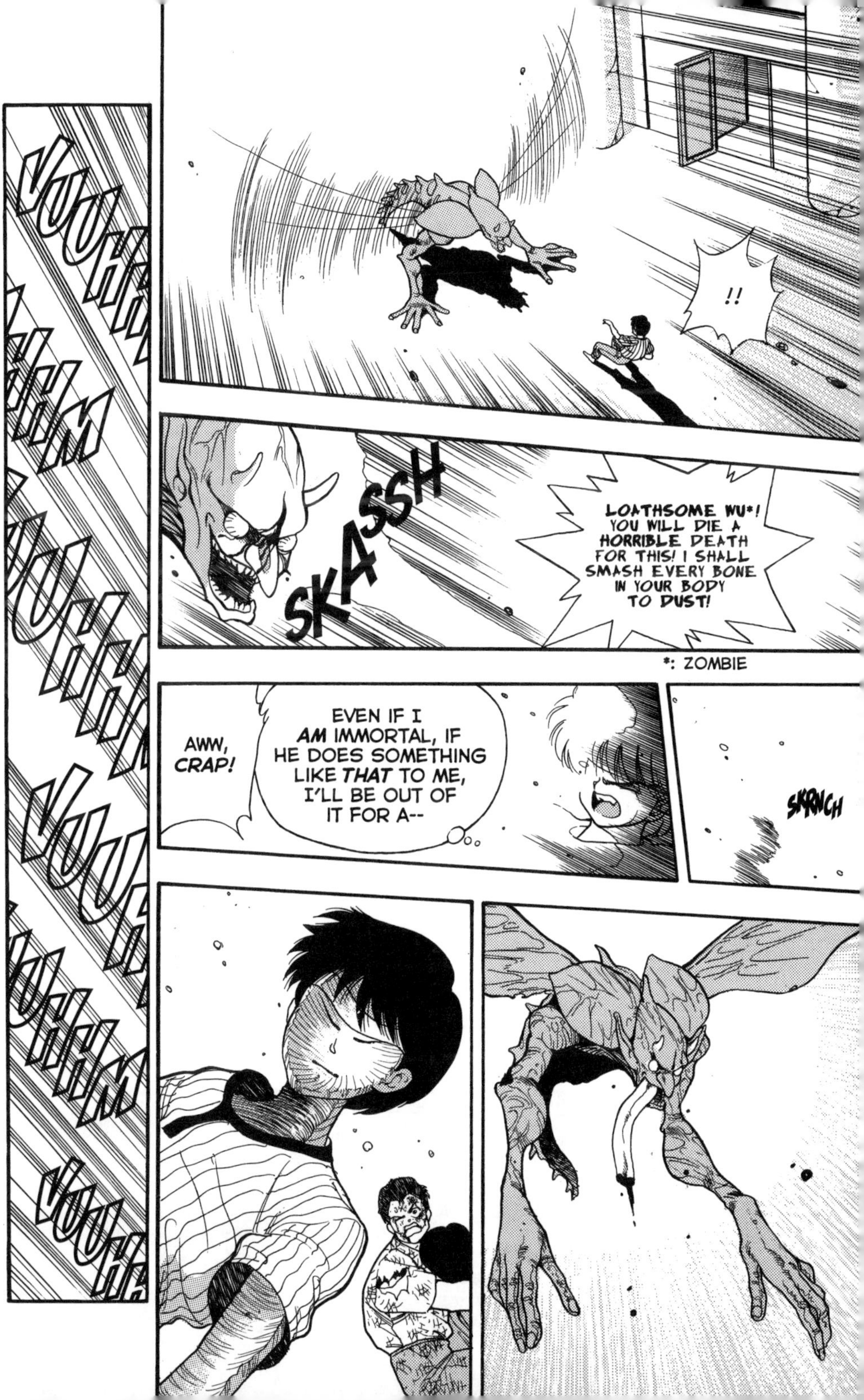
!!
SKASSH
LOATHSOME WU*! YOU WILL DIE A HORRIBLE DEATH FOR THIS! I SHALL SMASH EVERY BONE IN YOUR BODY TO DUST!
*: ZOMBIE
AWW, CRAP!
EVEN IF I AM IMMORTAL, IF HE DOES SOMETHING LIKE THAT TO ME, I'LL BE OUT OF IT FOR A--
SKRNCH

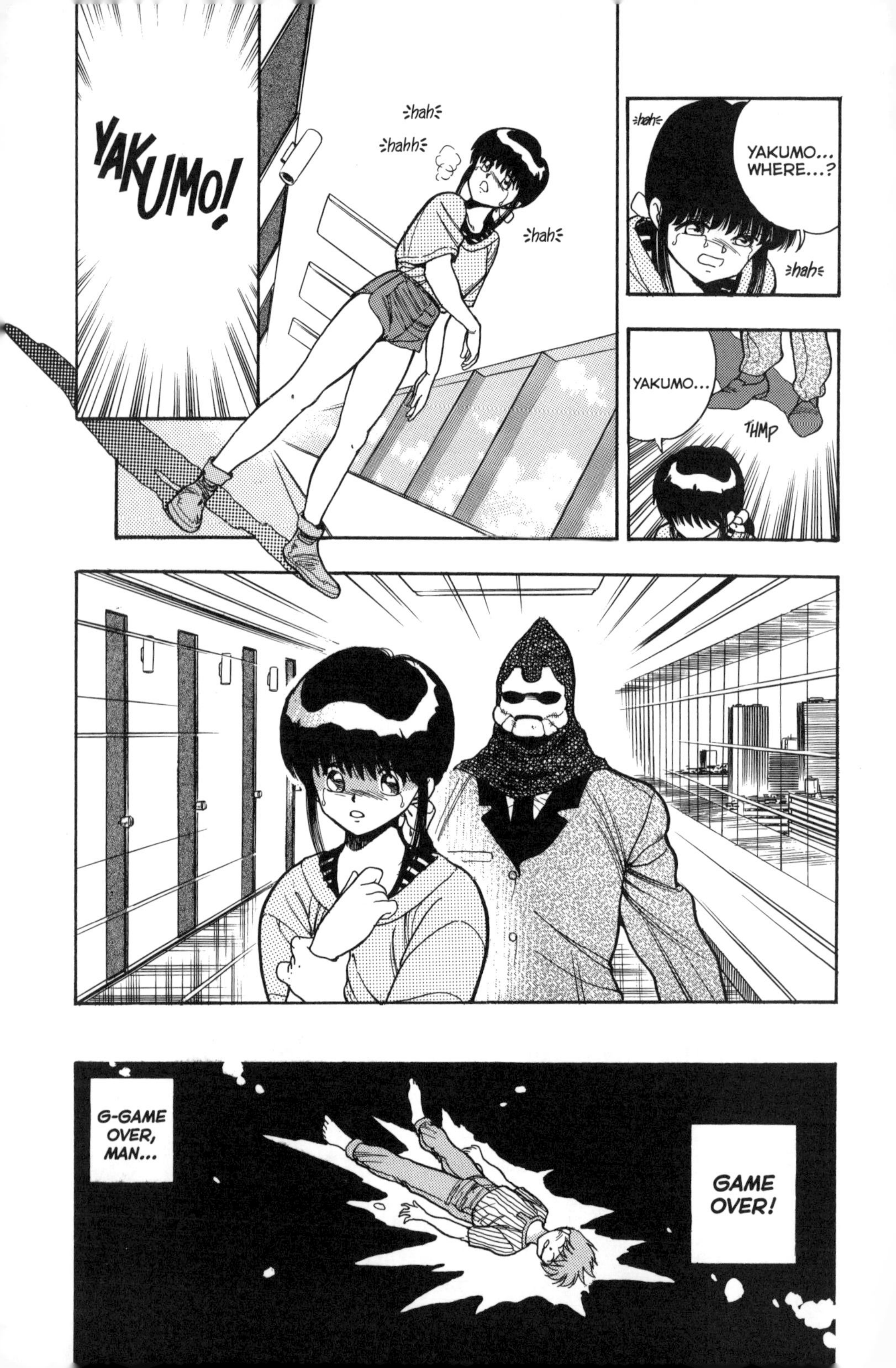
YAKUMO!
hah
hahh
hah
hah
YAKUMO... WHERE...?
hah
YAKUMO...
THMP
G-GAME OVER, MAN...
GAME OVER!

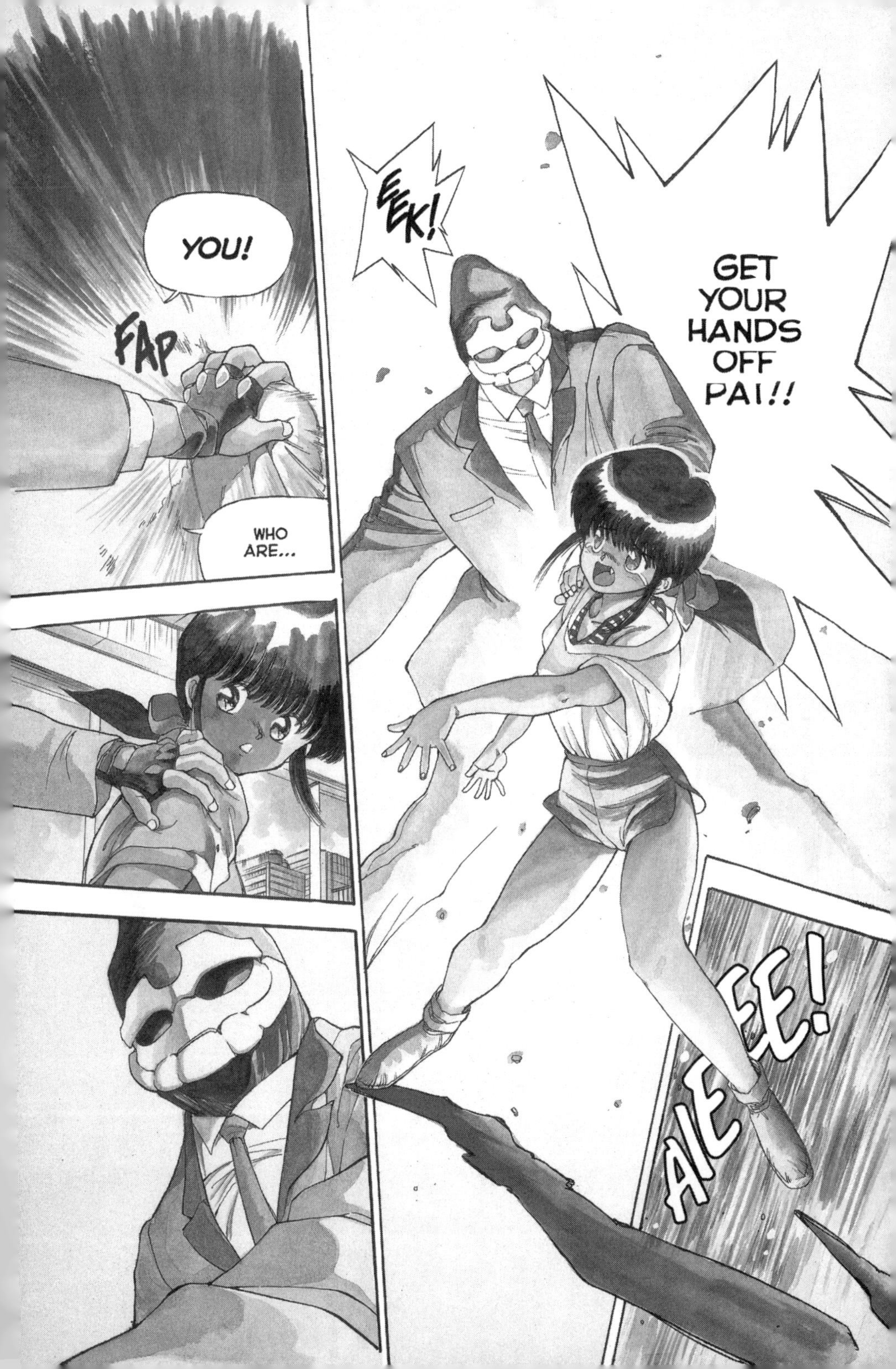

YOU!
FAP
WHO ARE...
EEK!
GET YOUR HANDS OFF PAI!!
AIEEE!

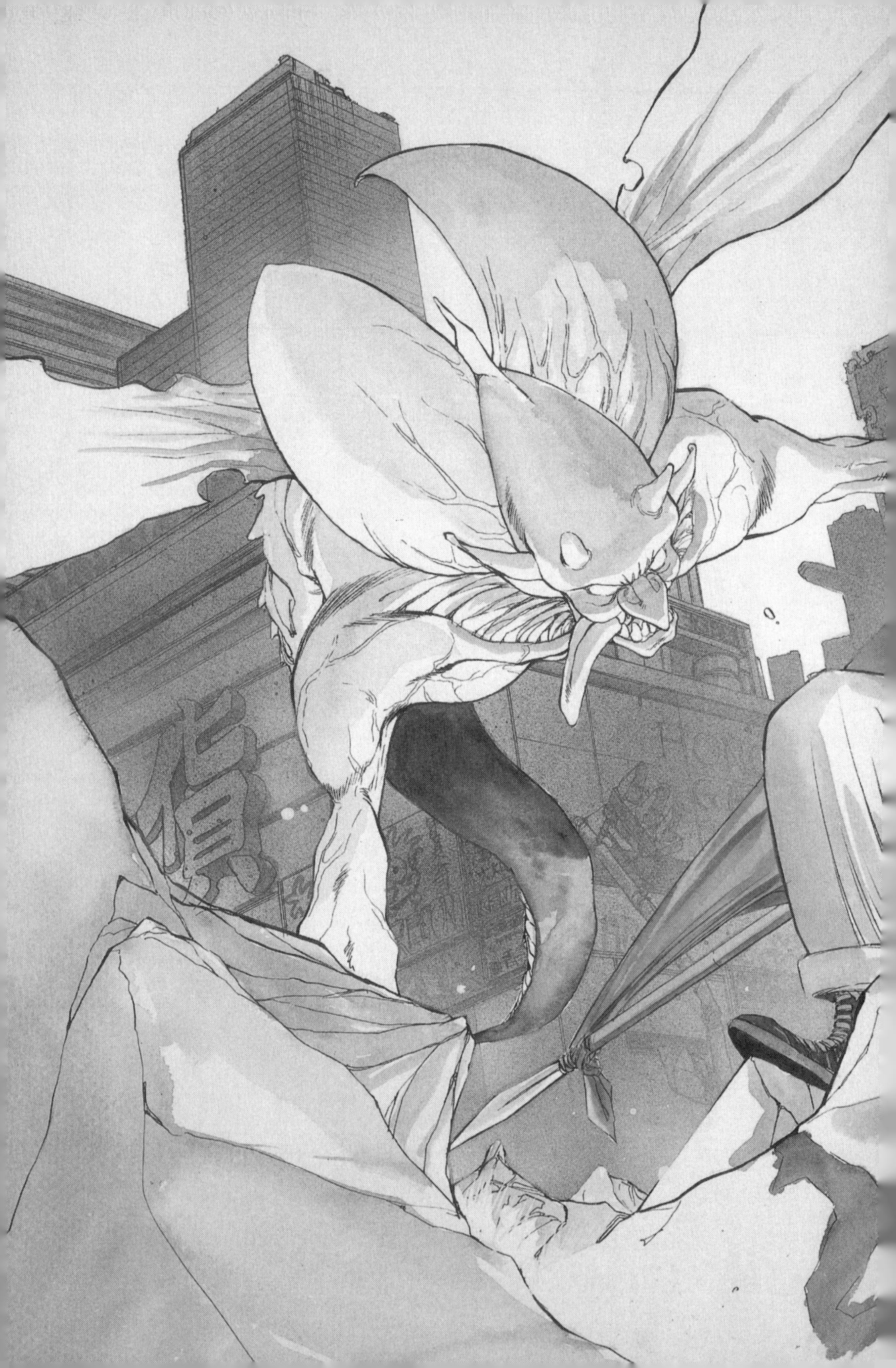

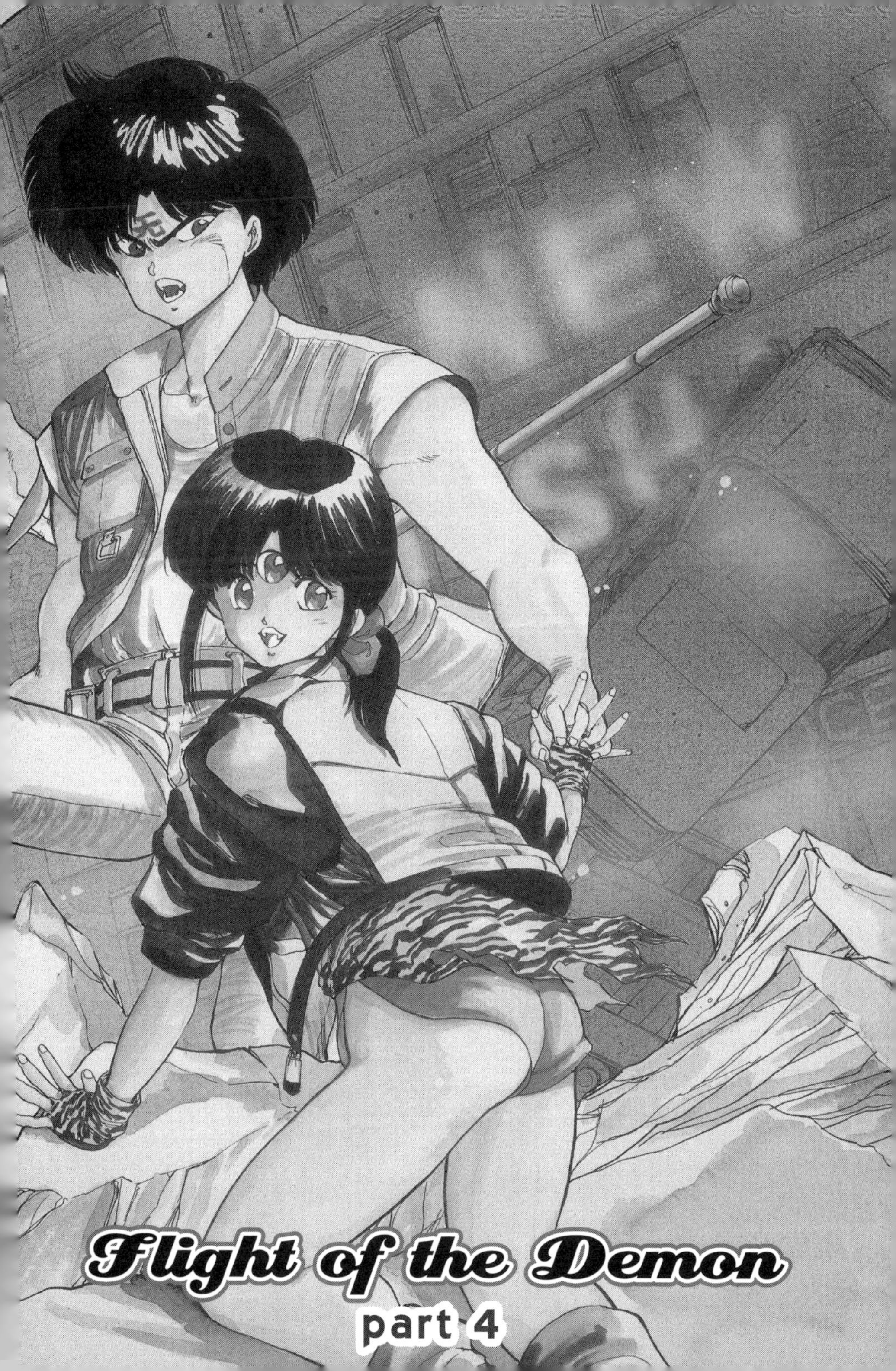

Flight of the Demon
part 4

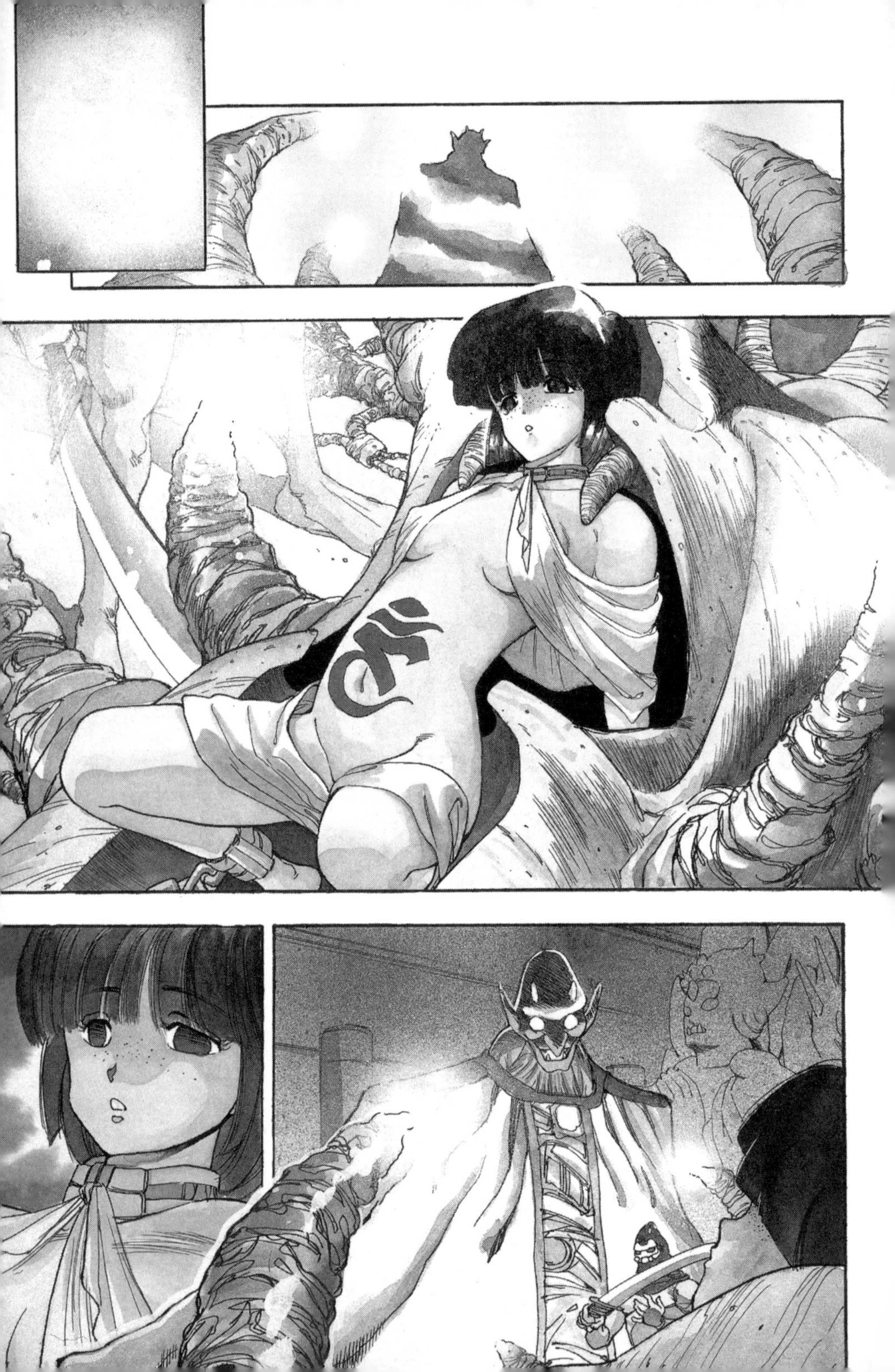

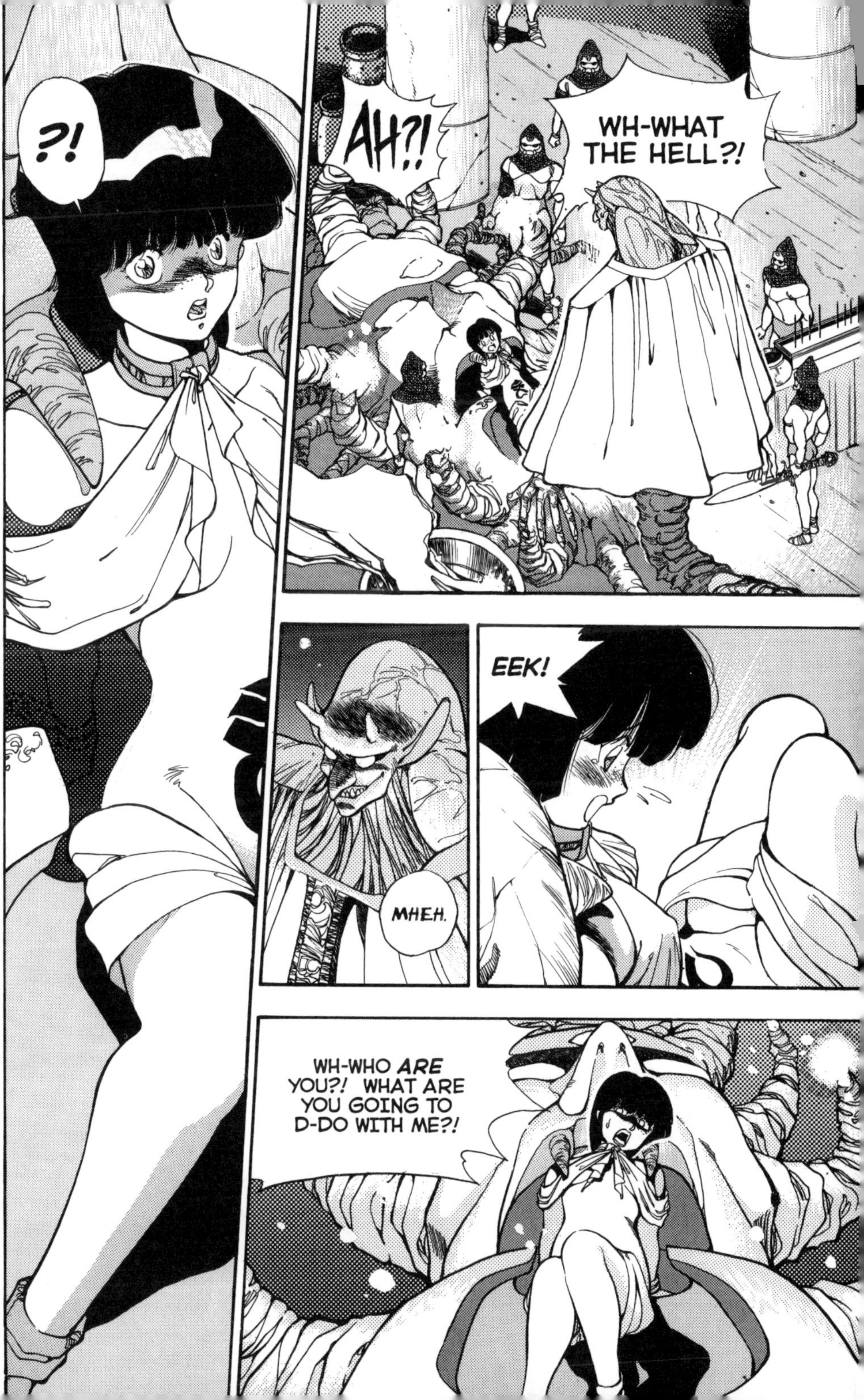
?!
AH?!
WH-WHAT THE HELL?!
MHEH.
EEK!
WH-WHO *ARE* YOU?! WHAT ARE YOU GOING TO D-DO WITH ME?!

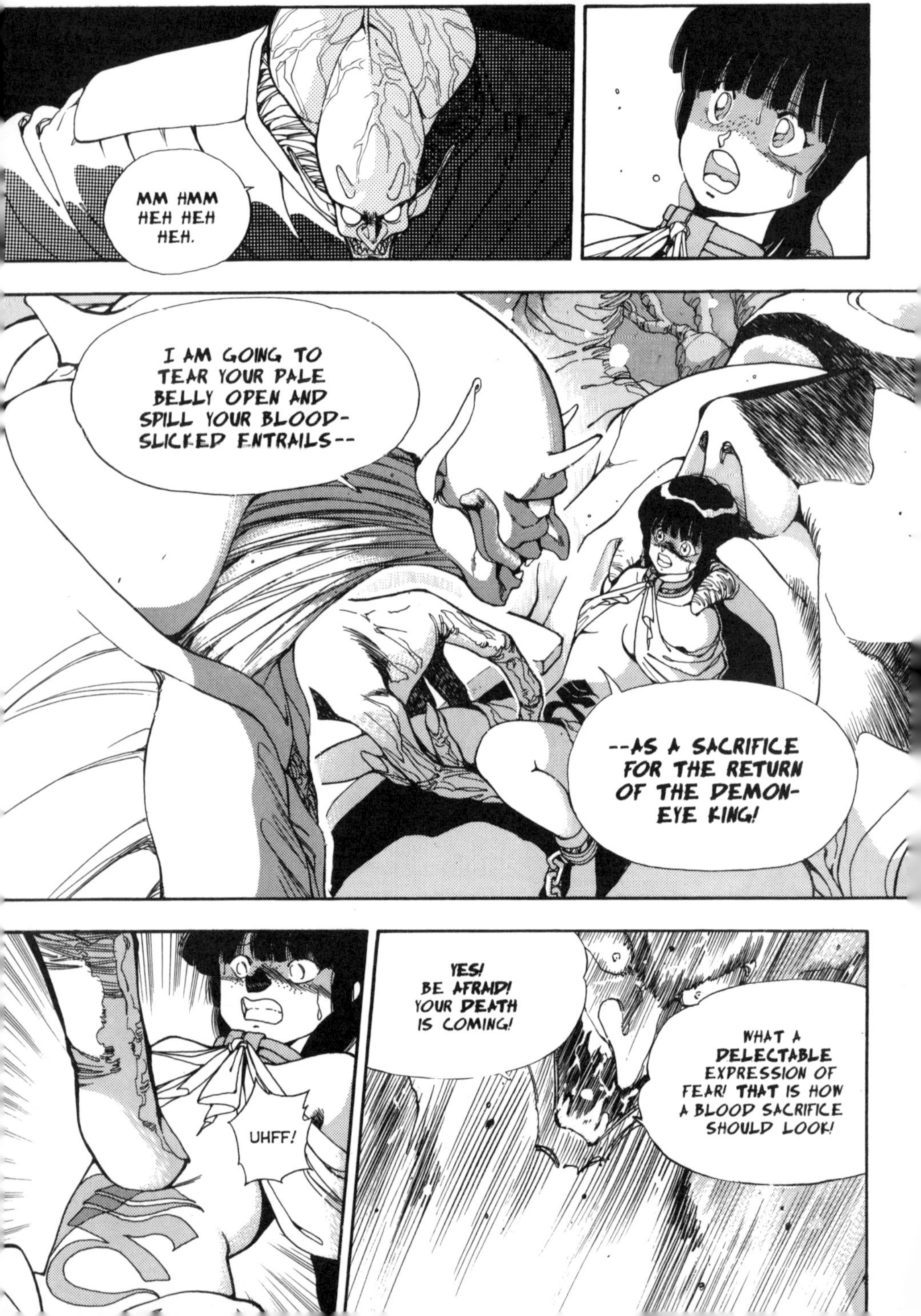
MM HMM HEH HEH HEH.
I AM GOING TO TEAR YOUR PALE BELLY OPEN AND SPILL YOUR BLOOD-SLICKED ENTRAILS--
--AS A SACRIFICE FOR THE RETURN OF THE DEMON-EYE KING!
UHFF!
YES! BE AFRAID! YOUR DEATH IS COMING!
WHAT A DELECTABLE EXPRESSION OF FEAR! THAT IS HOW A BLOOD SACRIFICE SHOULD LOOK!

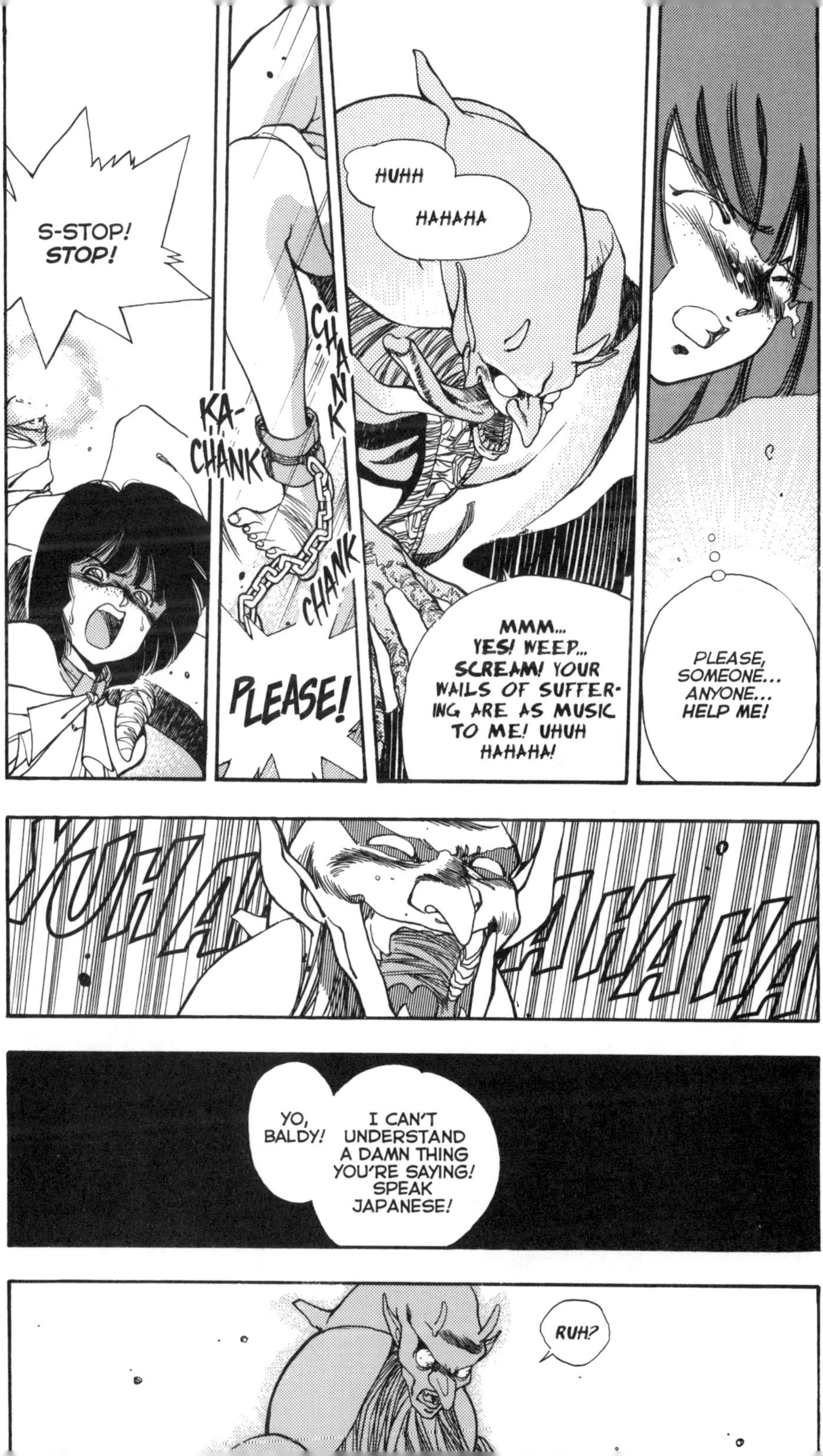
S-STOP! STOP!
KA-CHANK
CHANK
CHANK
PLEASE!
HUHH HAHAHA
MMM... YES! WEEP... SCREAM! YOUR WAILS OF SUFFERING ARE AS MUSIC TO ME! UHUH HAHAHA!
PLEASE, SOMEONE... ANYONE... HELP ME!
YO, BALDY!
I CAN'T UNDERSTAND A DAMN THING YOU'RE SAYING! SPEAK JAPANESE!
RUH?

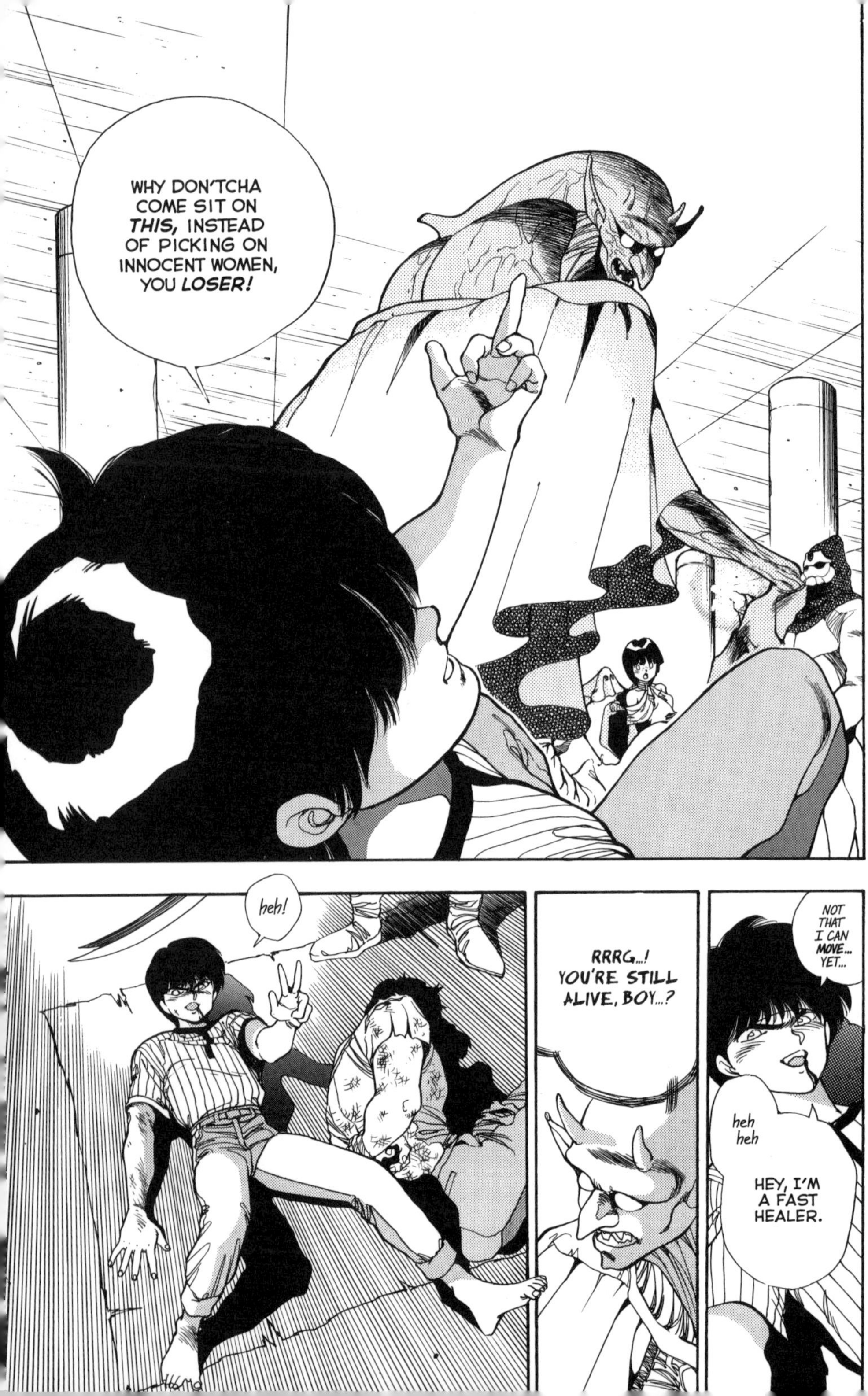
WHY DON'TCHA COME SIT ON THIS, INSTEAD OF PICKING ON INNOCENT WOMEN, YOU LOSER!
heh!
RRRG...! YOU'RE STILL ALIVE, BOY...?
NOT THAT I CAN MOVE... YET...
heh heh
HEY, I'M A FAST HEALER.

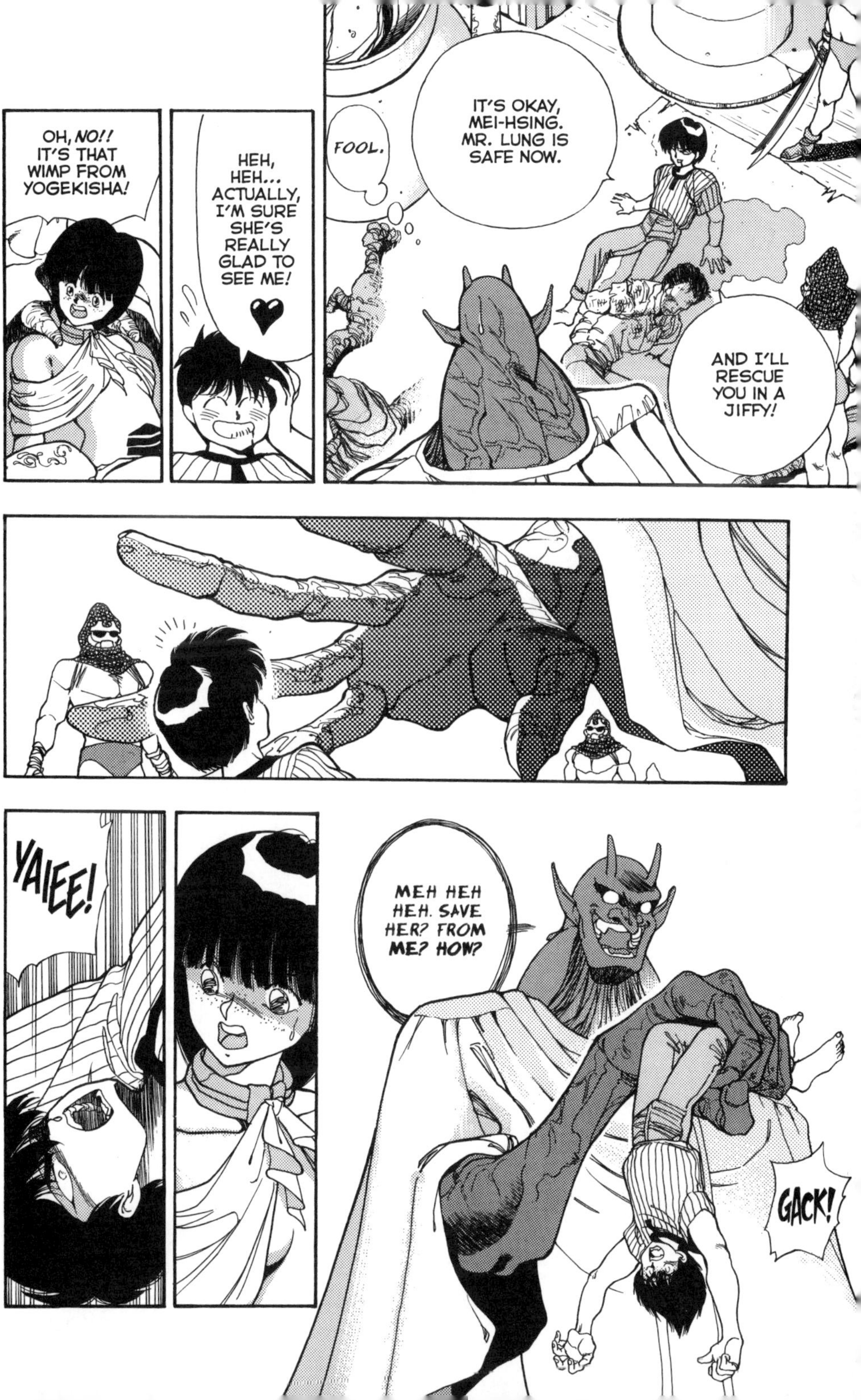
OH, NO!! IT'S THAT WIMP FROM YOGEKISHA!
HEH, HEH... ACTUALLY, I'M SURE SHE'S REALLY GLAD TO SEE ME!
FOOL.
IT'S OKAY, MEI-HSING. MR. LUNG IS SAFE NOW.
AND I'LL RESCUE YOU IN A JIFFY!
YAIEE!
MEH HEH HEH. SAVE HER? FROM ME? HOW?
GACK!

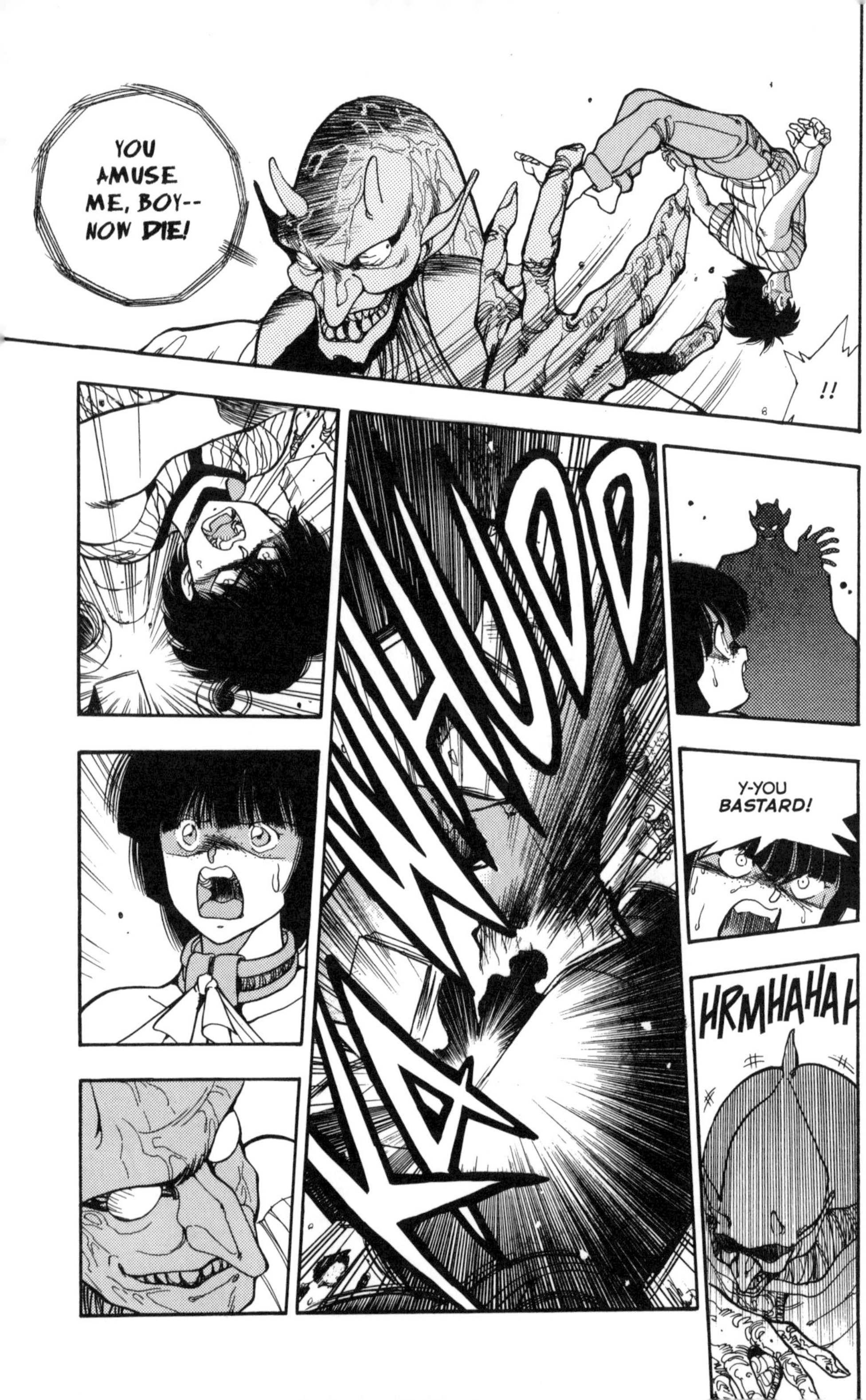
YOU AMUSE ME, BOY-- NOW DIE!
!!
Y-YOU BASTARD!
HRMHAHAH

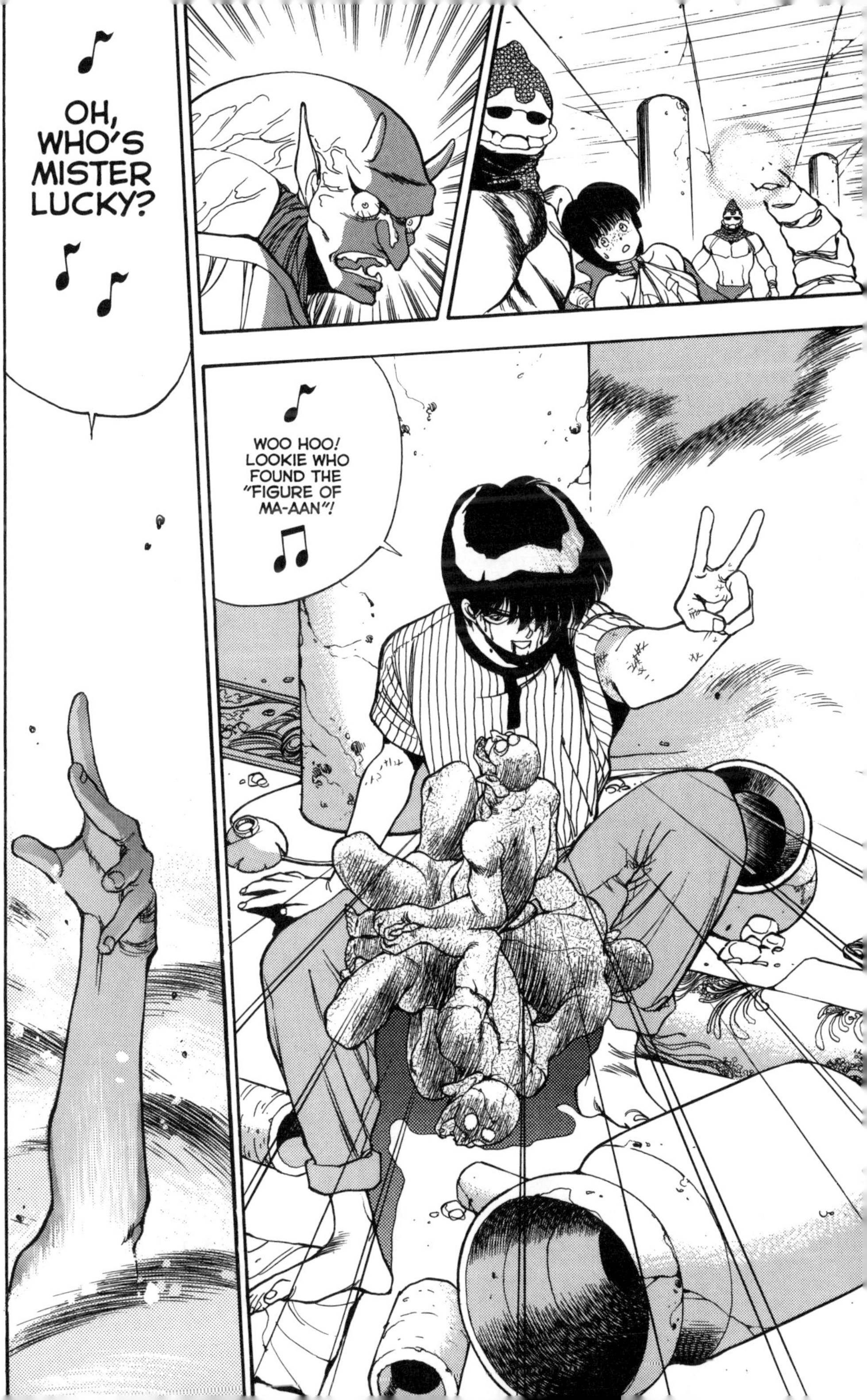
OH, WHO'S MISTER LUCKY?
WOO HOO! LOOKIE WHO FOUND THE "FIGURE OF MA-AAN"!

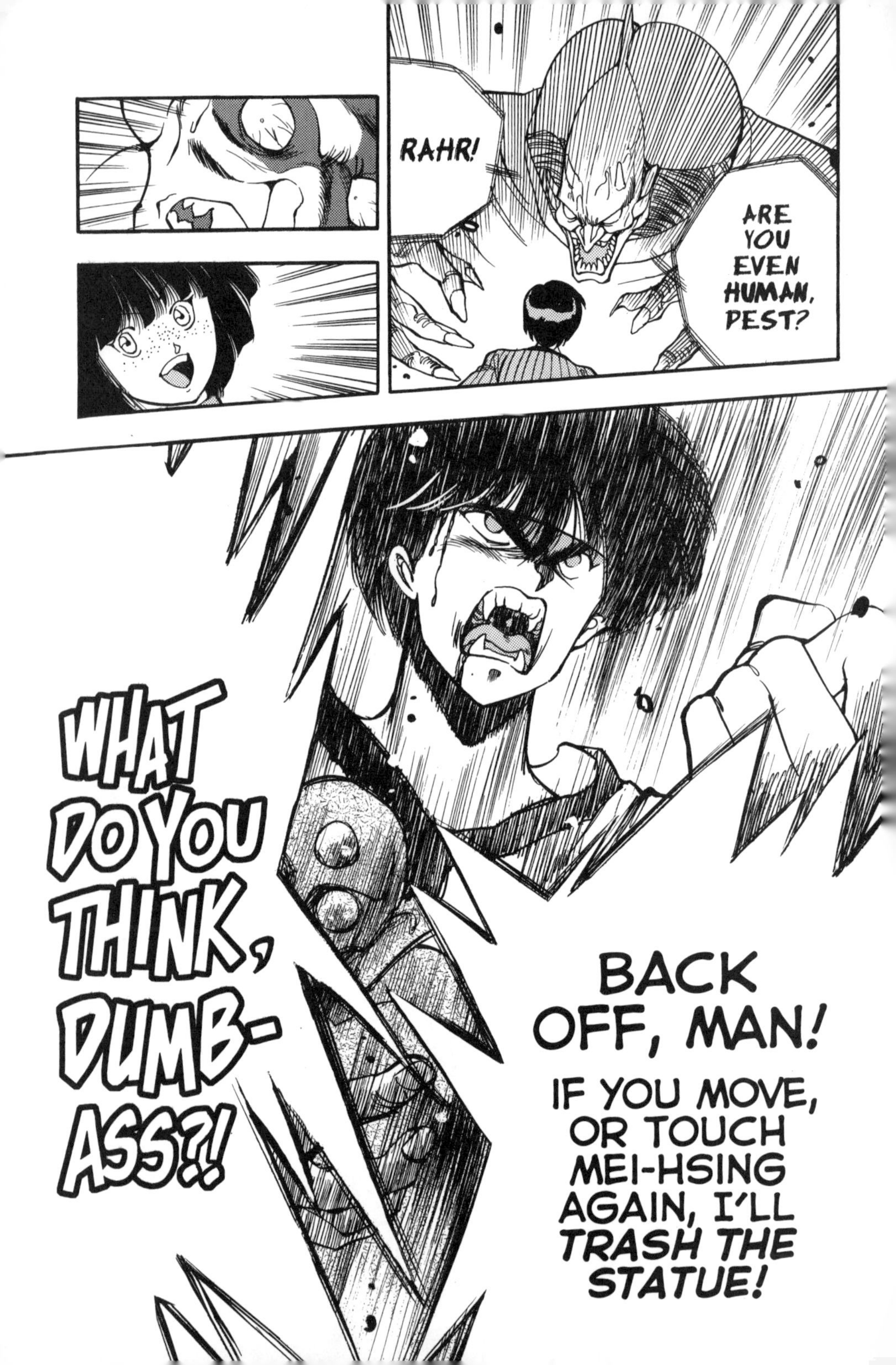
RAHR!
ARE YOU EVEN HUMAN, PEST?
WHAT DO YOU THINK, DUMB-ASS?!
BACK OFF, MAN!
IF YOU MOVE, OR TOUCH MEI-HSING AGAIN, I'LL *TRASH THE STATUE!*

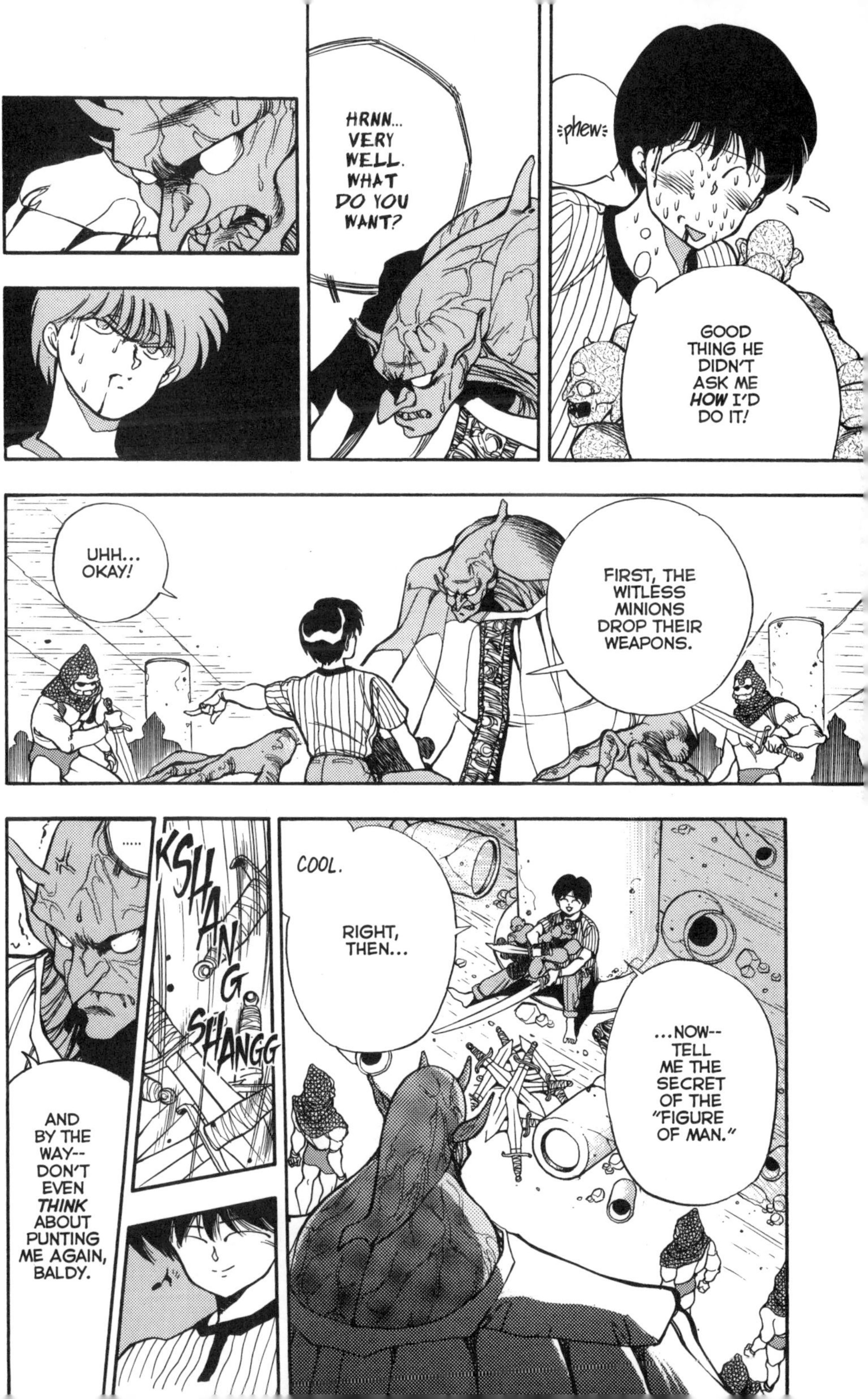
HRNN... VERY WELL. WHAT DO YOU WANT?
phew
GOOD THING HE DIDN'T ASK ME *HOW* I'D DO IT!
UHH... OKAY!
FIRST, THE WITLESS MINIONS DROP THEIR WEAPONS.
.....
KSHANG
SHANGG
AND BY THE WAY-- DON'T EVEN *THINK* ABOUT PUNTING ME AGAIN, BALDY.
COOL.
RIGHT, THEN...
...NOW-- TELL ME THE SECRET OF THE "FIGURE OF MAN."

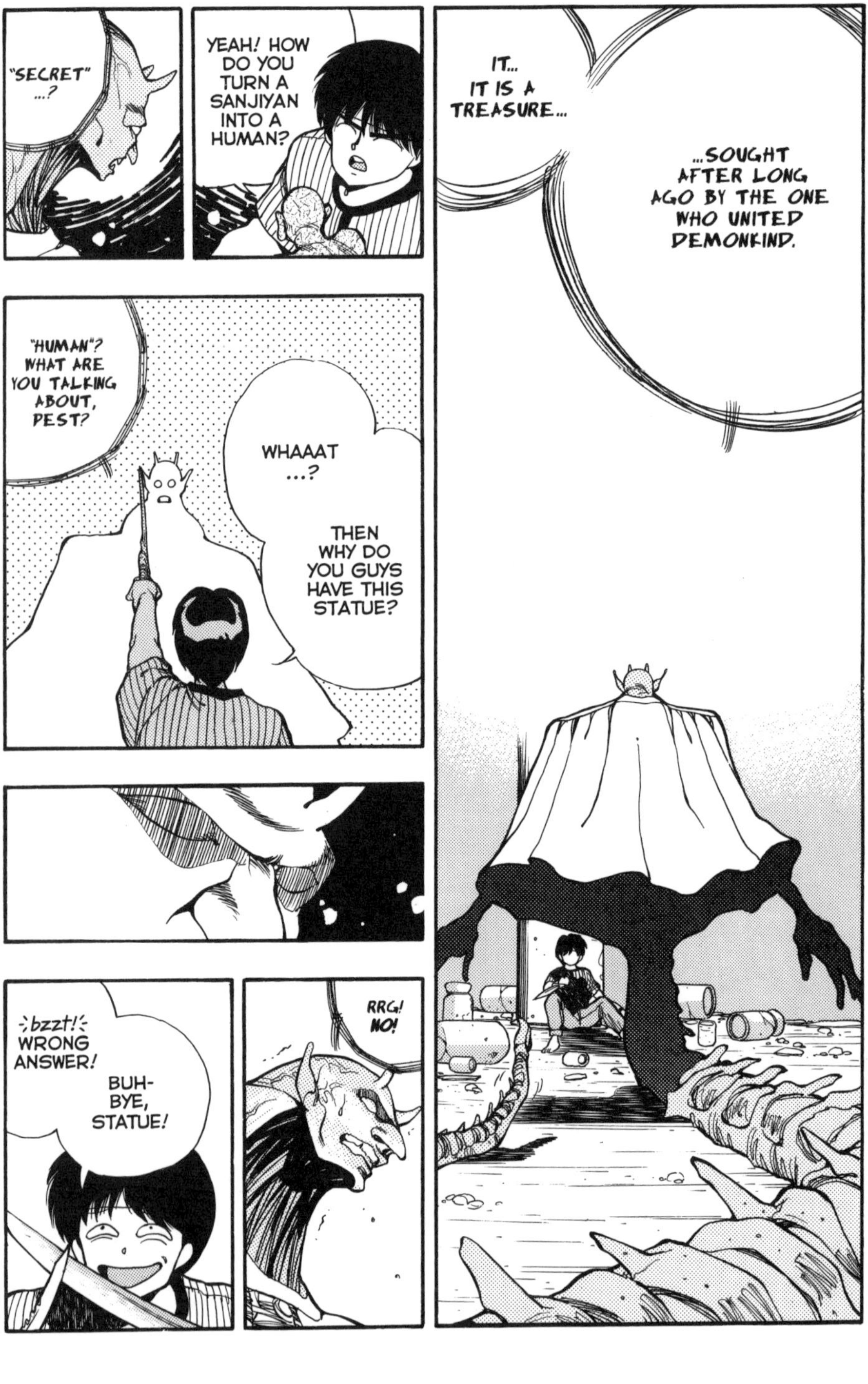
"SECRET" ...?
YEAH! HOW DO YOU TURN A SANJIYAN INTO A HUMAN?
"HUMAN"? WHAT ARE YOU TALKING ABOUT, PEST?
WHAAAT ...?
THEN WHY DO YOU GUYS HAVE THIS STATUE?
bzzt! WRONG ANSWER!
BUH-BYE, STATUE!
RRG! NO!
IT... IT IS A TREASURE...
...SOUGHT AFTER LONG AGO BY THE ONE WHO UNITED DEMONKIND.

KAIYAN WANG.

RIGHT?

YES.

HE PROMISED ETERNAL LIFE TO THE ONE WHO BROUGHT HIM THE STATUE.

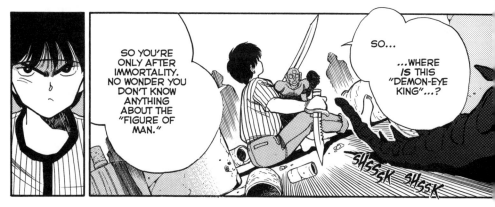

SO YOU'RE ONLY AFTER IMMORTALITY. NO WONDER YOU DON'T KNOW ANYTHING ABOUT THE "FIGURE OF MAN."

SO...

...WHERE IS THIS "DEMON-EYE KING"...?

SHSSK SHSSK

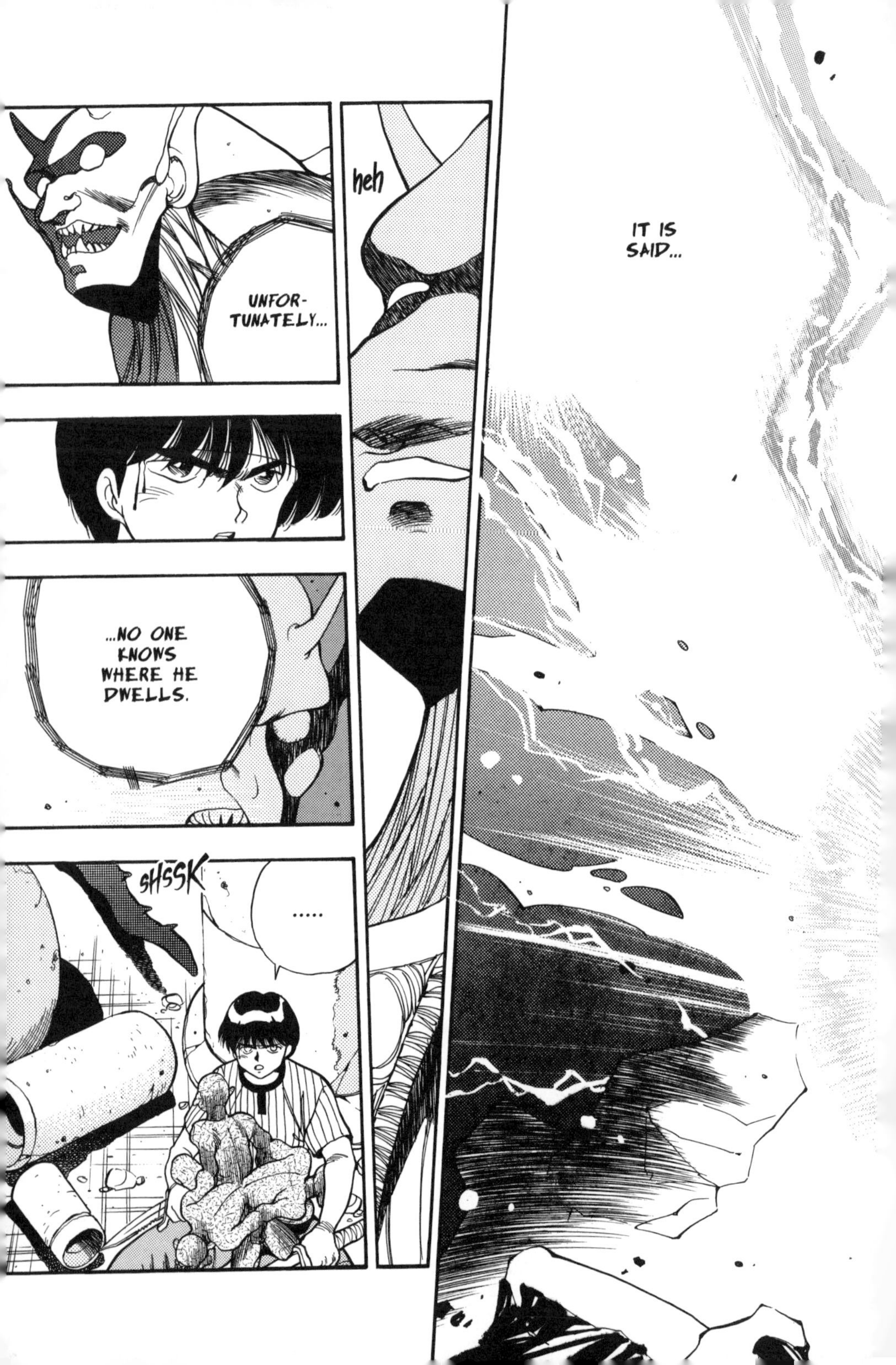
UNFOR-TUNATELY...
...NO ONE KNOWS WHERE HE DWELLS.
SHSSK
.....
heh
IT IS SAID...

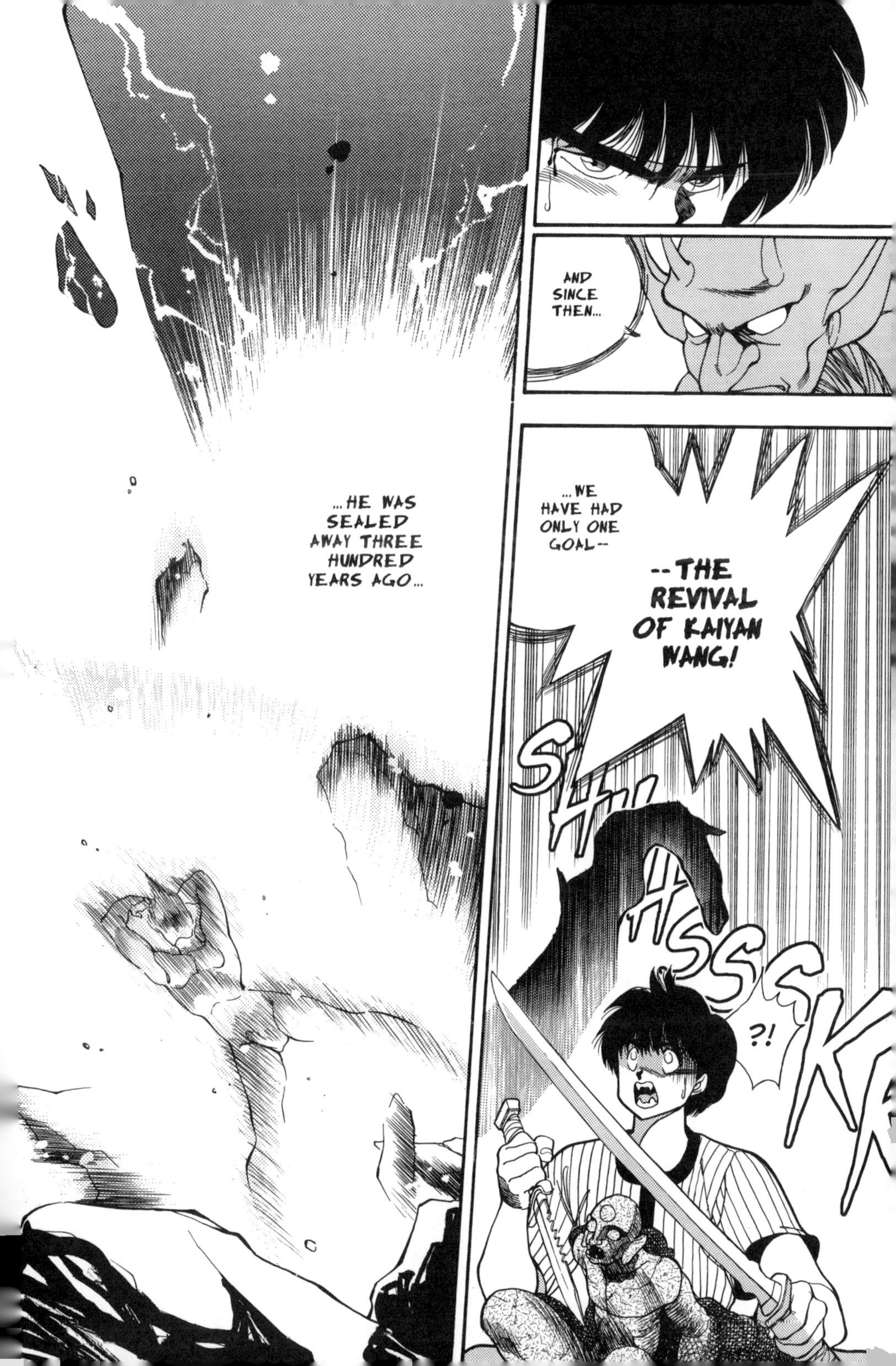
...HE WAS SEALED AWAY THREE HUNDRED YEARS AGO...
AND SINCE THEN...
...WE HAVE HAD ONLY ONE GOAL--
--THE REVIVAL OF KAIYAN WANG!
SHHSSSK
?!

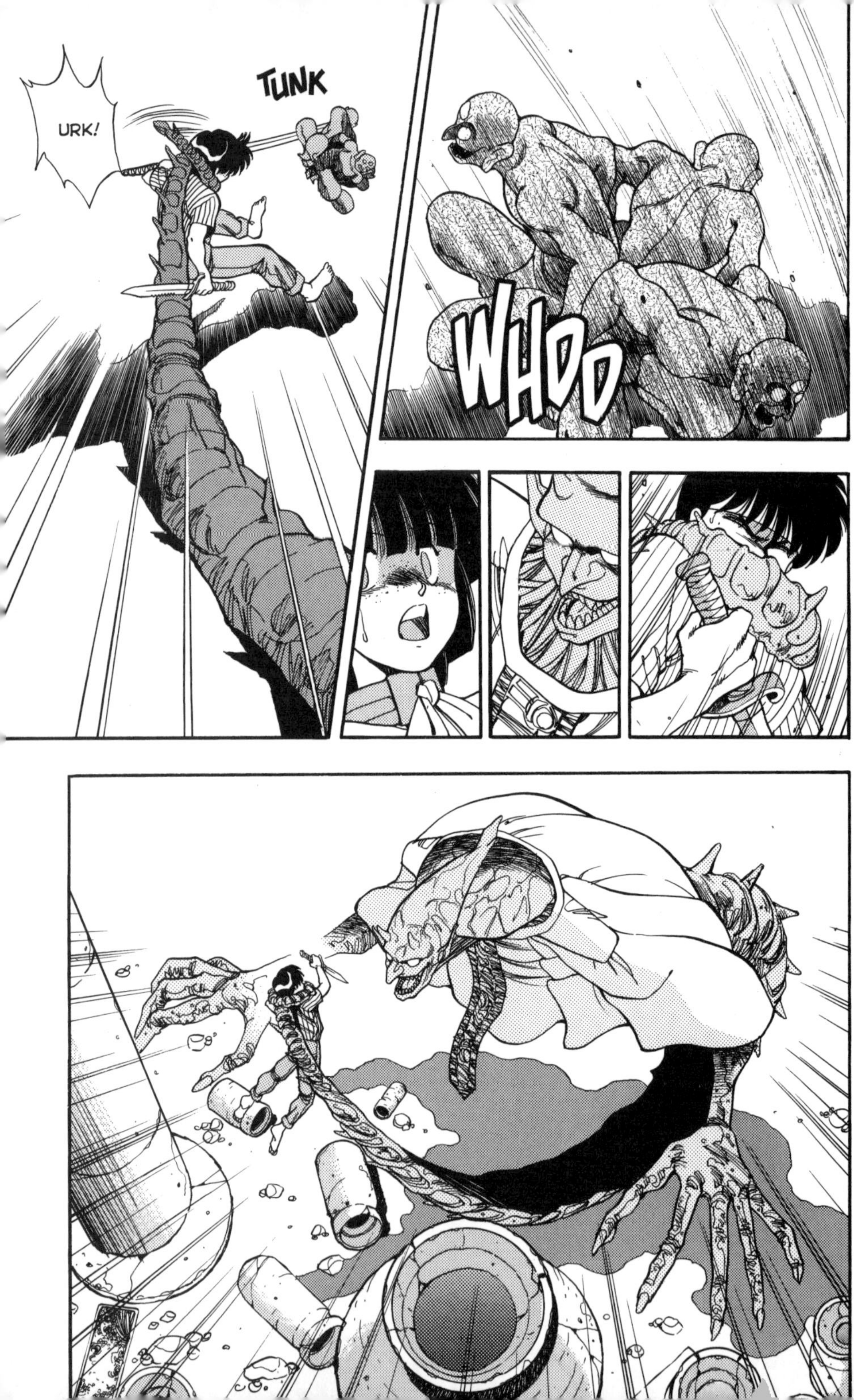
URK!
TUNK
WHOO

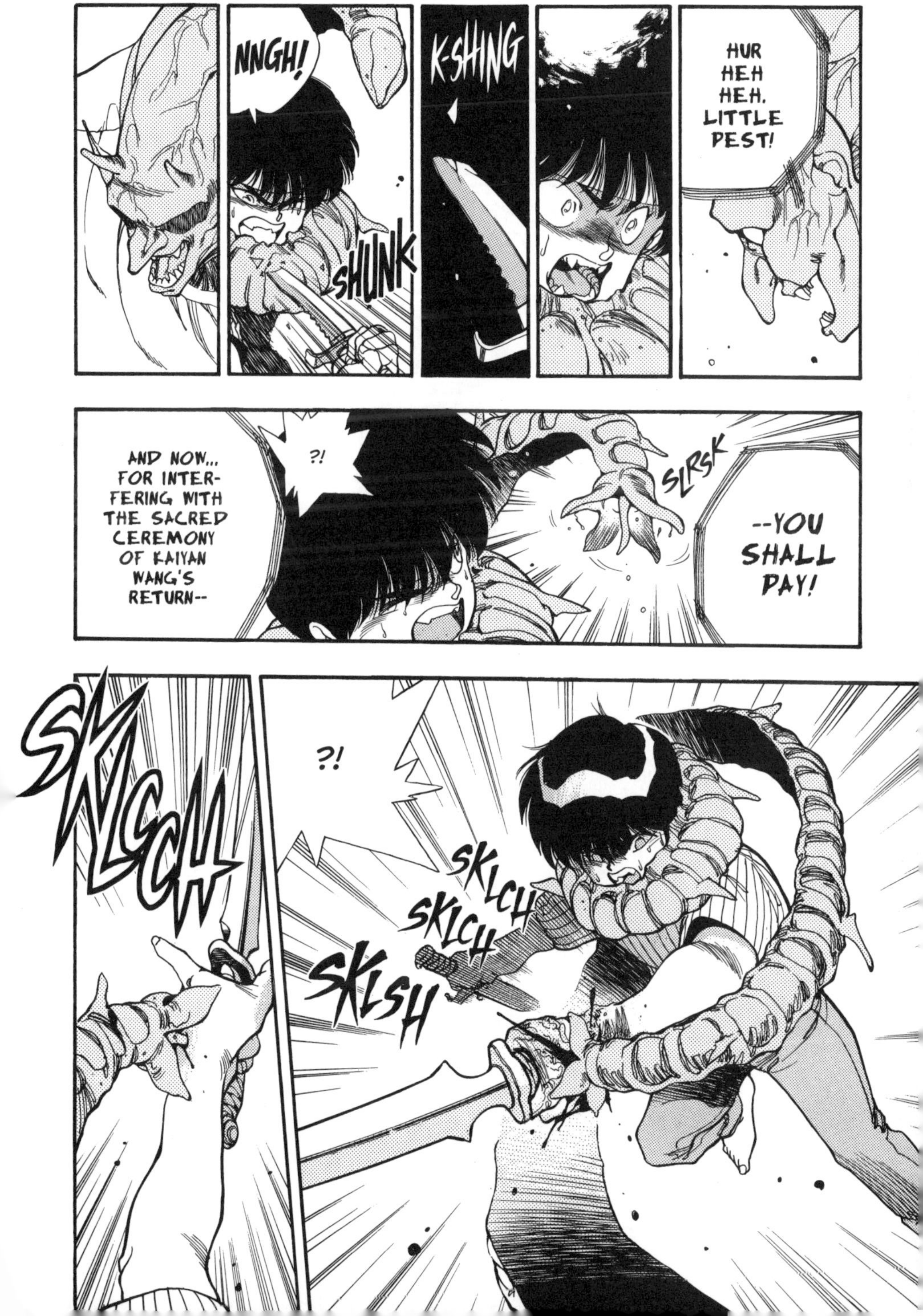
NNGH!
SHUNK
K-SHING
HUR HEH HEH. LITTLE PEST!
AND NOW... FOR INTER-FERING WITH THE SACRED CEREMONY OF KAIYAN WANG'S RETURN--
?!
SLRSK
--YOU SHALL PAY!
SKLCCH
?!
SKLCH
SKLCH
SKLSH

HEH!

HEH HEH HEH

SKLCH

SKLCH

YOU SHALL HAVE THE HONOR OF MAKING THE SACRIFICE!

WHAT?!

YOUR HAND WILL OPEN HER BELLY! YOUR HAND WILL REND HER BOWELS!

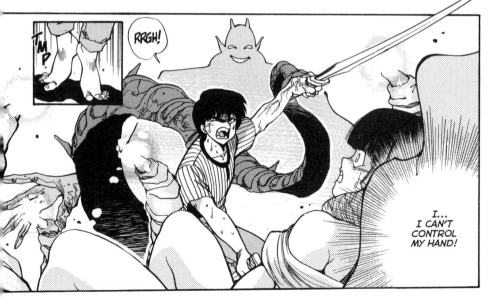

RRGH!

TMP

I... I CAN'T CONTROL MY HAND!

IT'S MOVING ON ITS OWN!

IT HURTS!

WHSSK

AND MY BODY... IS GOING NUMB...

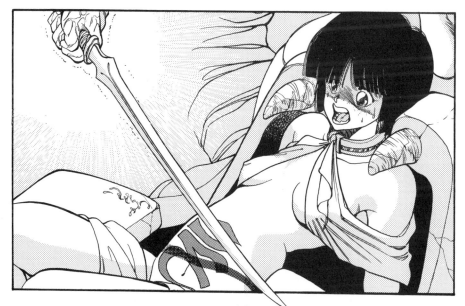

NO... NO!

SKTCH

YAA!

SLLTCH

STOP!

DON'T MAKE ME DO THIS!

HURHUR
RUHAHA
HAHAHA!

SUFFER,
BOY!

WSST

NO! NO!!
I WILL NOT
DO THIS!

NOW, BOY...
SPILL HER
BLOOD!

NO!

SOME-
ONE...
PLEASE
HELP
ME!

NOOOO!

SOME-
ONE...
PLEASE!

PAI...!

GIVE ME
STRENGTH,
PAI!

YAKUMO!

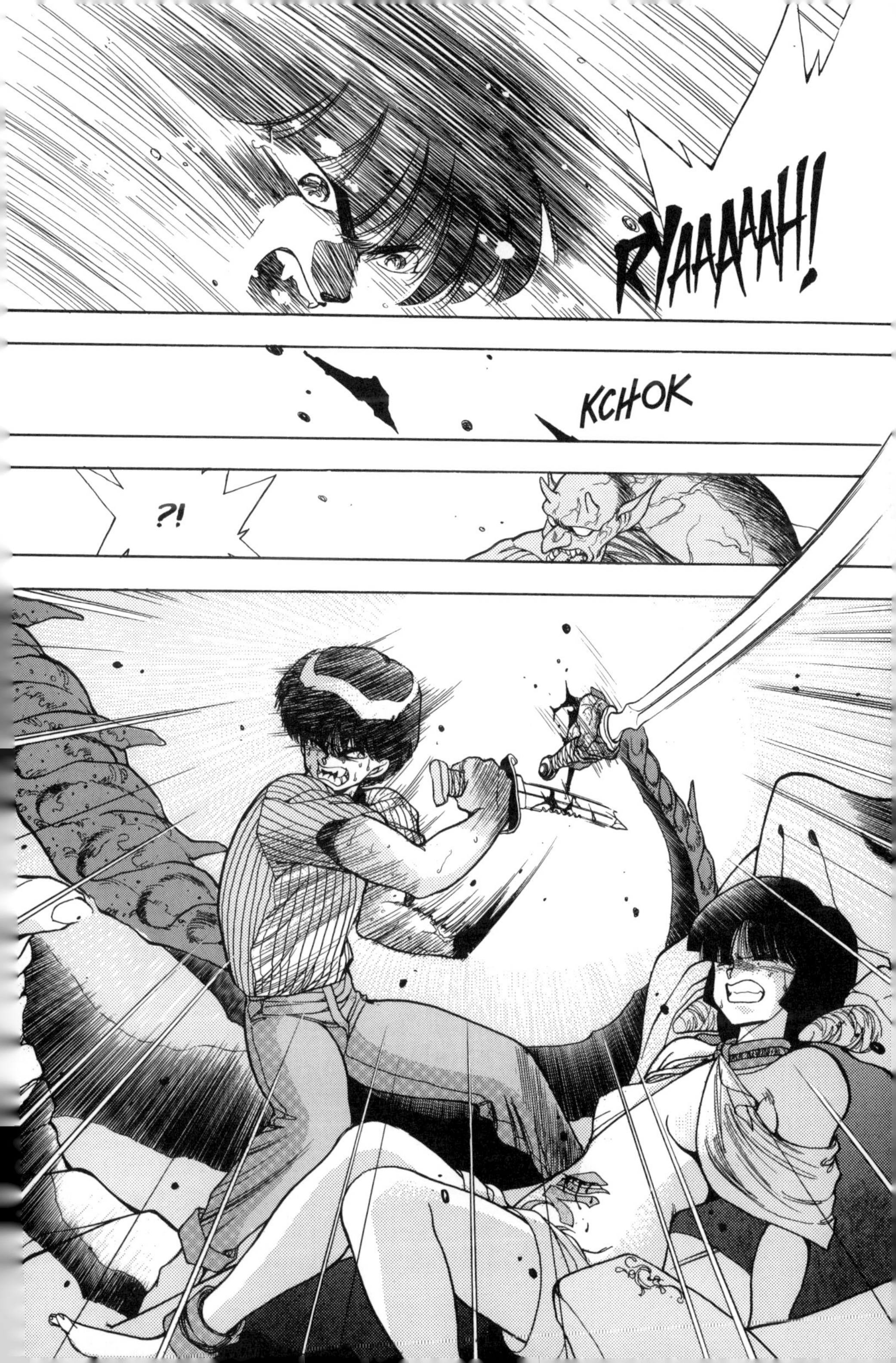
RYAAAAAH!
KCHOK
?!

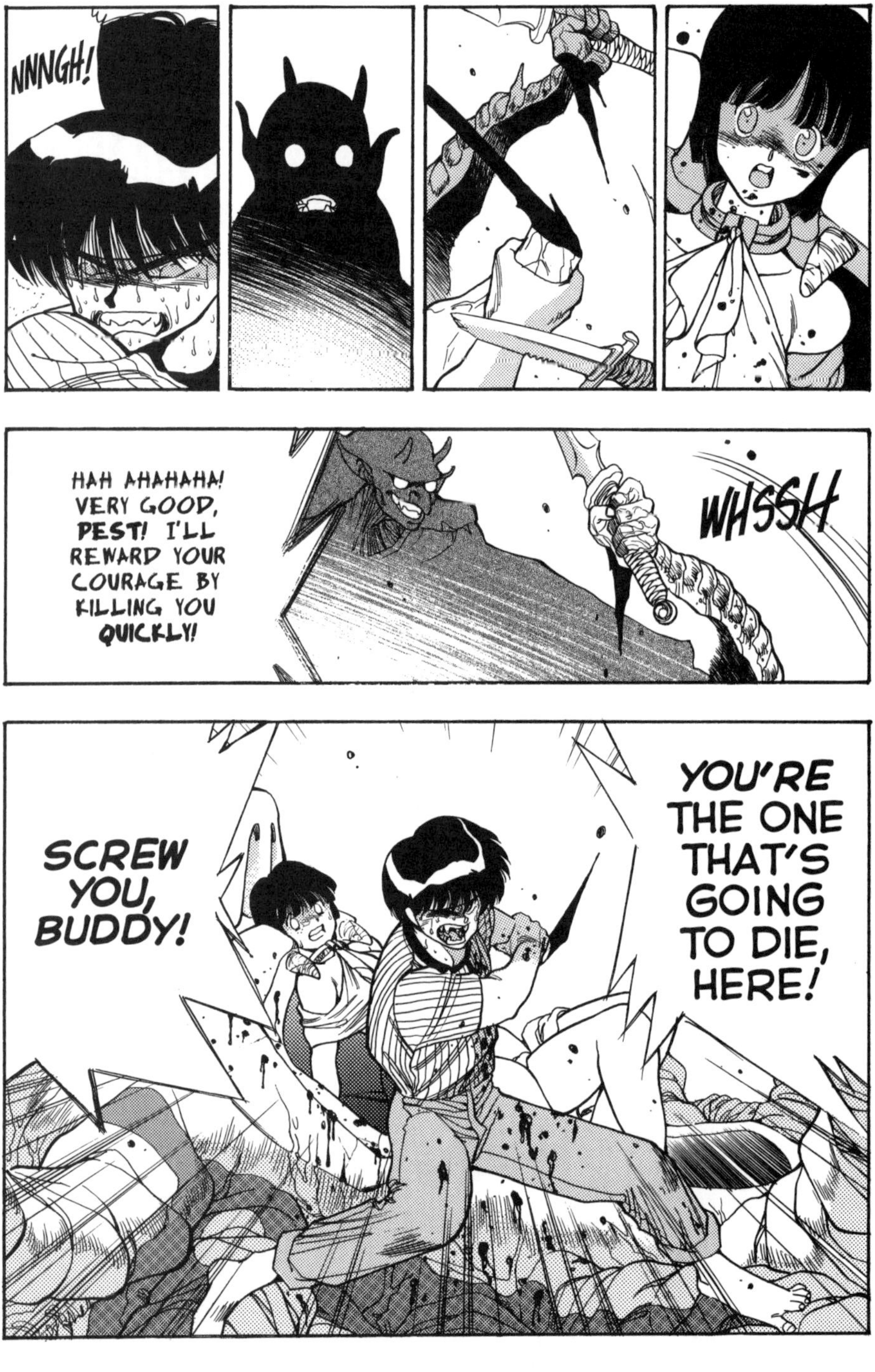
NNNGH!
HAH AHAHAHA! VERY GOOD, PEST! I'LL REWARD YOUR COURAGE BY KILLING YOU QUICKLY!
WHSSH
SCREW YOU, BUDDY!
YOU'RE THE ONE THAT'S GOING TO DIE, HERE!

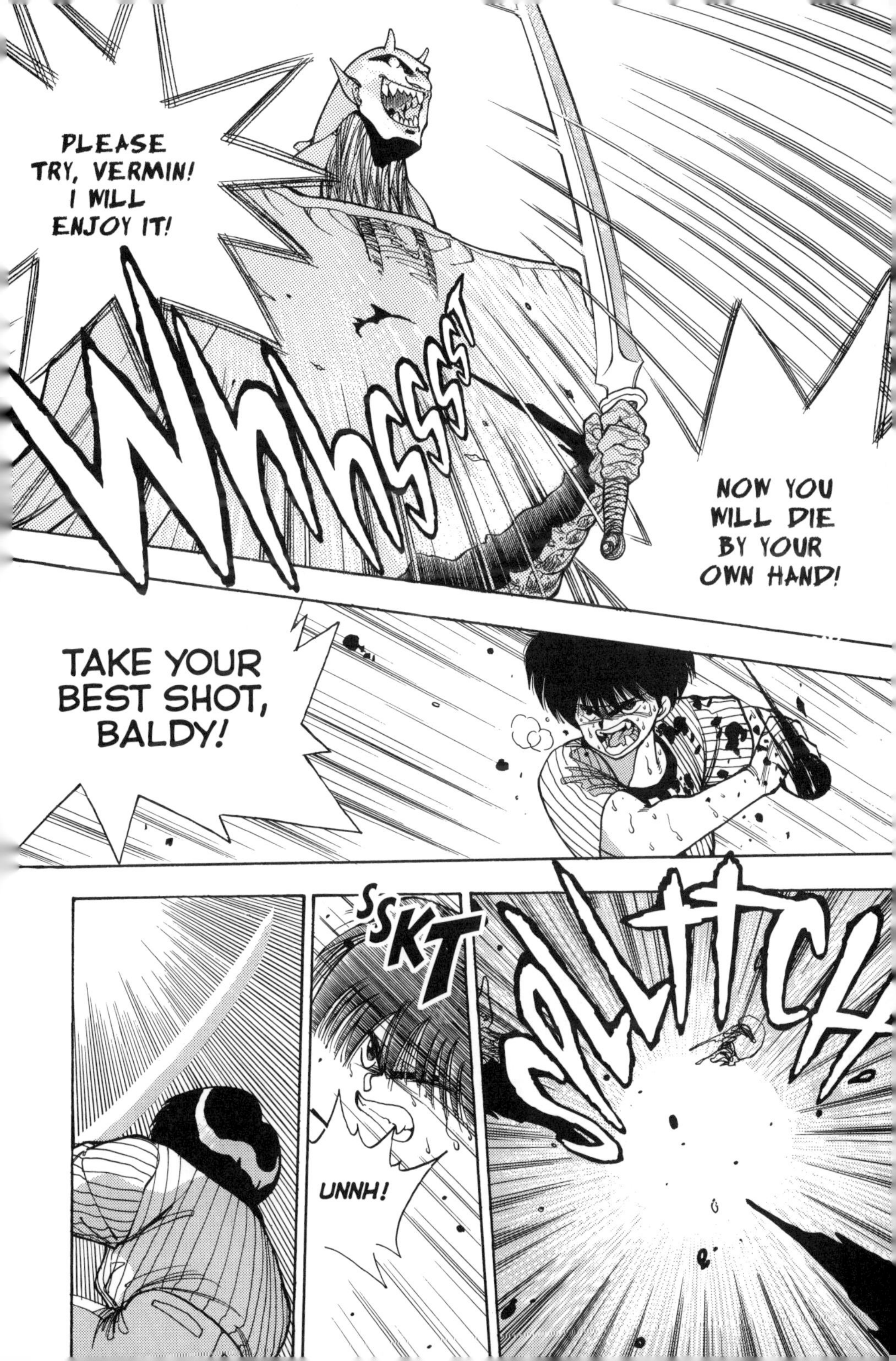
PLEASE TRY, VERMIN! I WILL ENJOY IT!
WHISSSST
NOW YOU WILL DIE BY YOUR OWN HAND!
TAKE YOUR BEST SHOT, BALDY!
SSKT
UNNH!
SPLTTCH

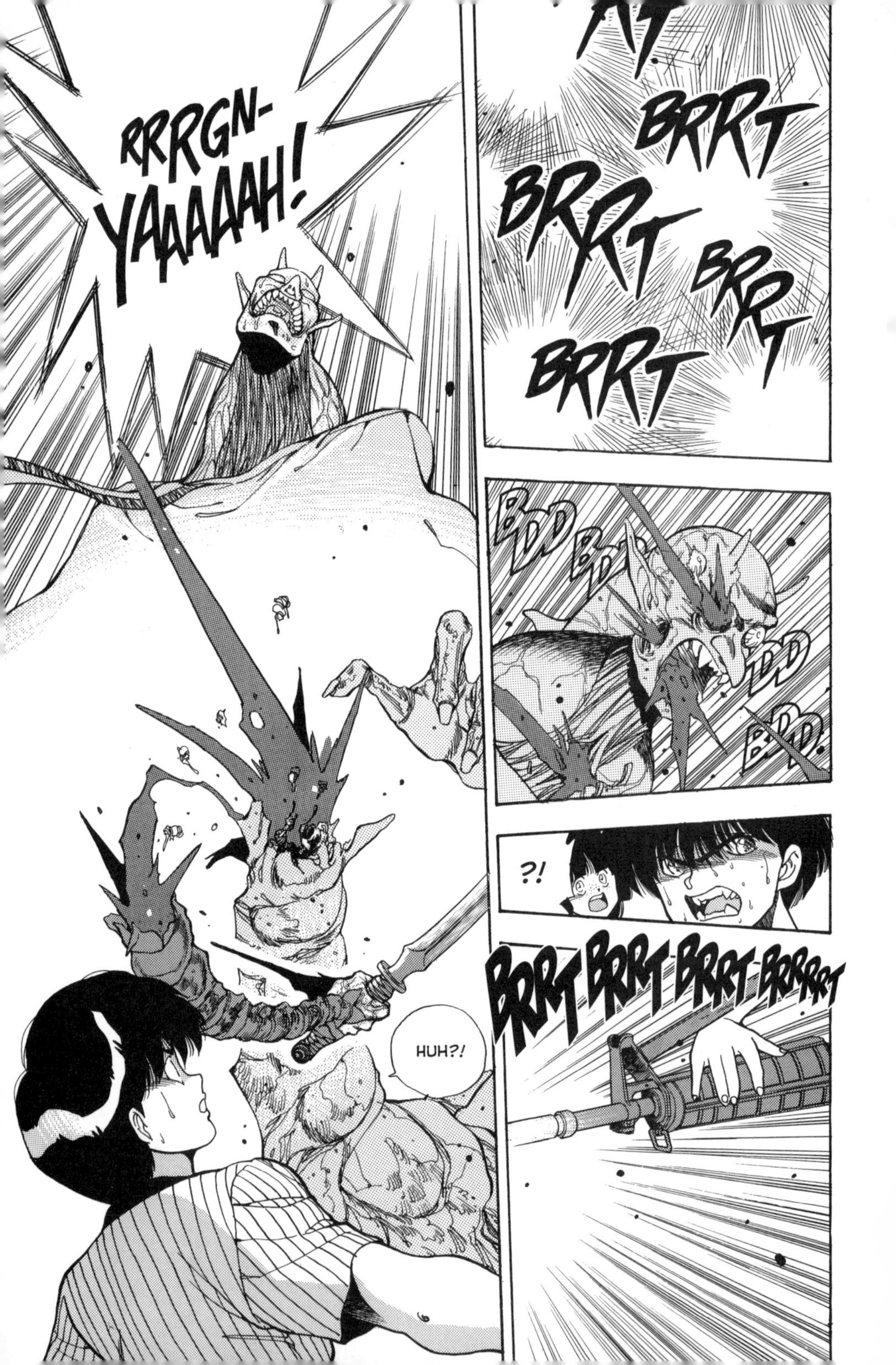
RRRGN-
YAAAAAH!
HUH?!
AT. BRRT BRRT BRRT BRRT BRRT
BDD BDD BDD BDD
?!
BRRT BRRT BRRT BRRRRT

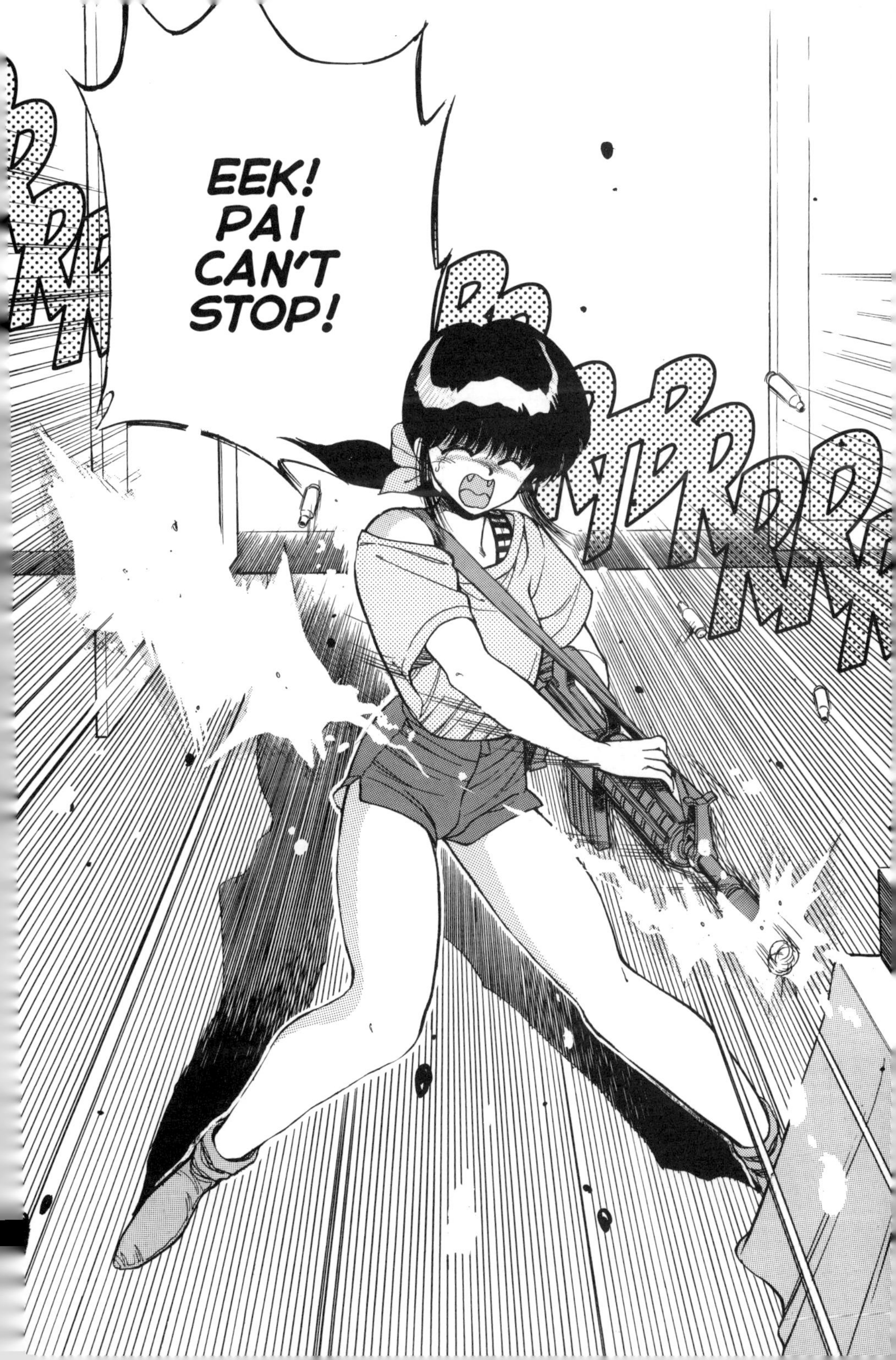
EEK! PAI CAN'T STOP!

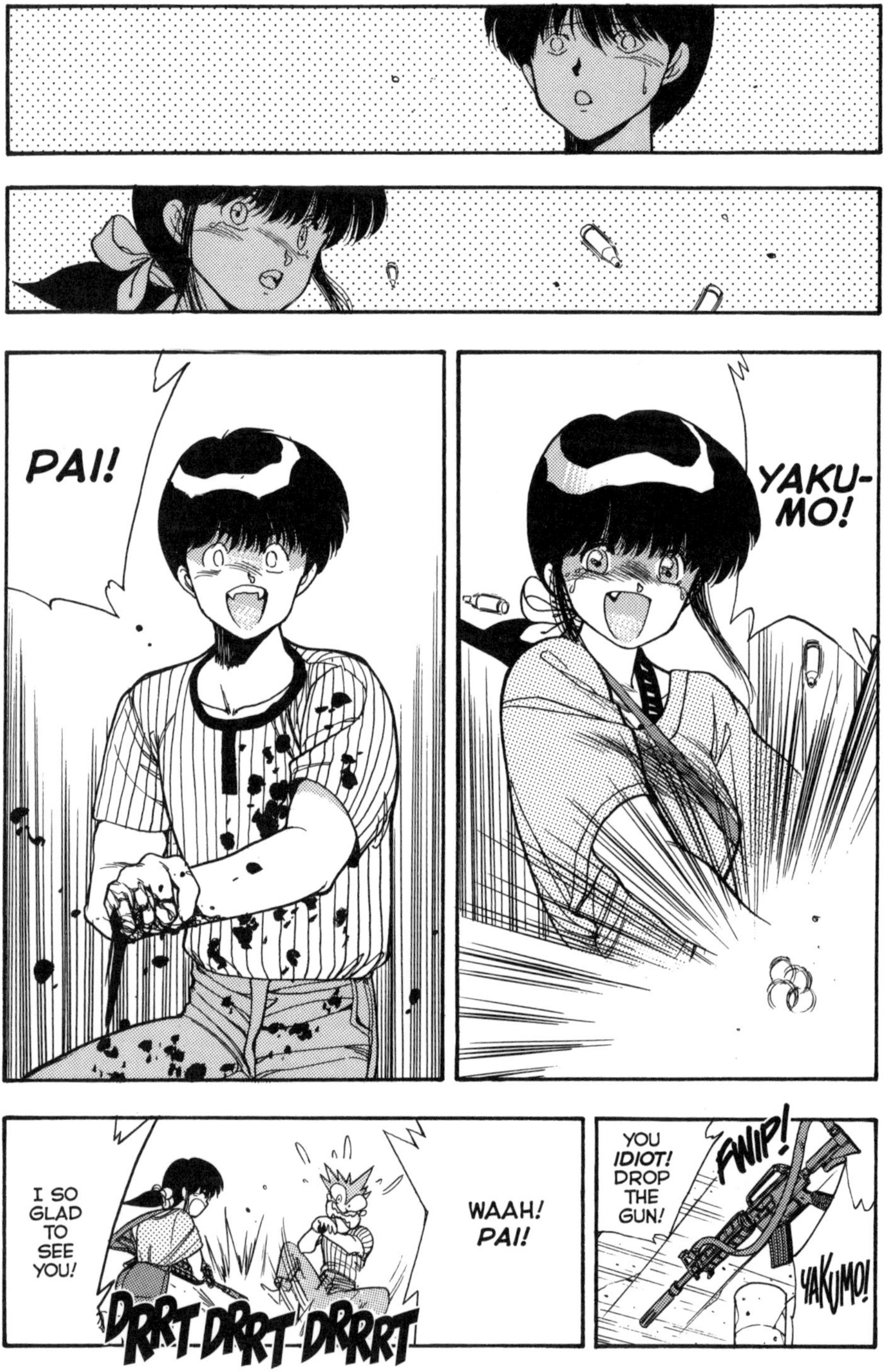

PAI!
YAKU-
MO!
I SO
GLAD
TO
SEE
YOU!
WAAH!
PAI!
DRRRT DRRRT DRRRT
YOU
IDIOT!
DROP
THE
GUN!
FWIP!
YAKUMO!

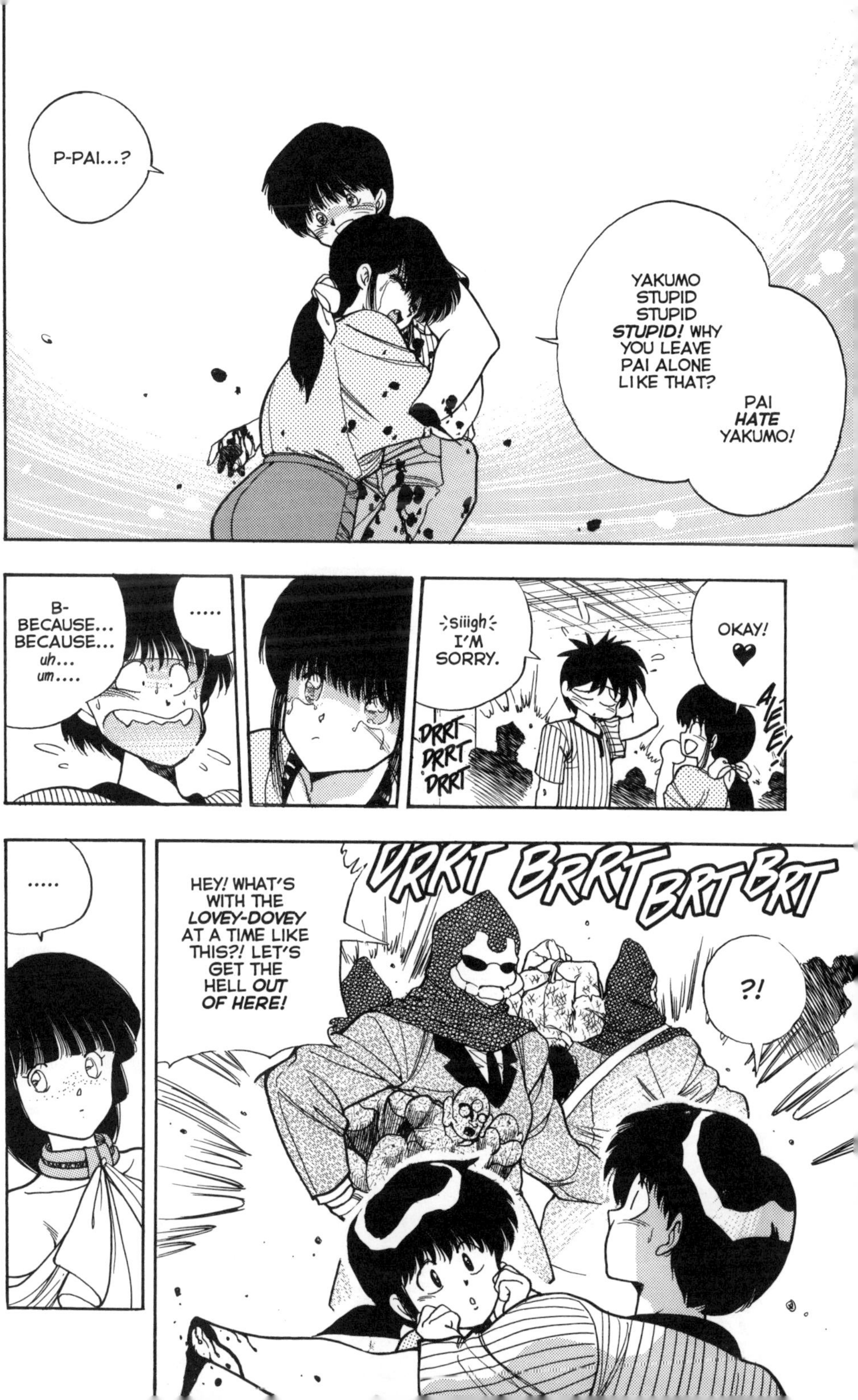
P-PAI...?
YAKUMO STUPID STUPID STUPID! WHY YOU LEAVE PAI ALONE LIKE THAT?
PAI HATE YAKUMO!
B- BECAUSE... BECAUSE... uh... um....
.....
siiigh I'M SORRY.
DRRT DRRT DRRT
OKAY!
AIEEE!
.....
DRRT BRRT BRRT BRRT
HEY! WHAT'S WITH THE LOVEY-DOVEY AT A TIME LIKE THIS?! LET'S GET THE HELL OUT OF HERE!
?!

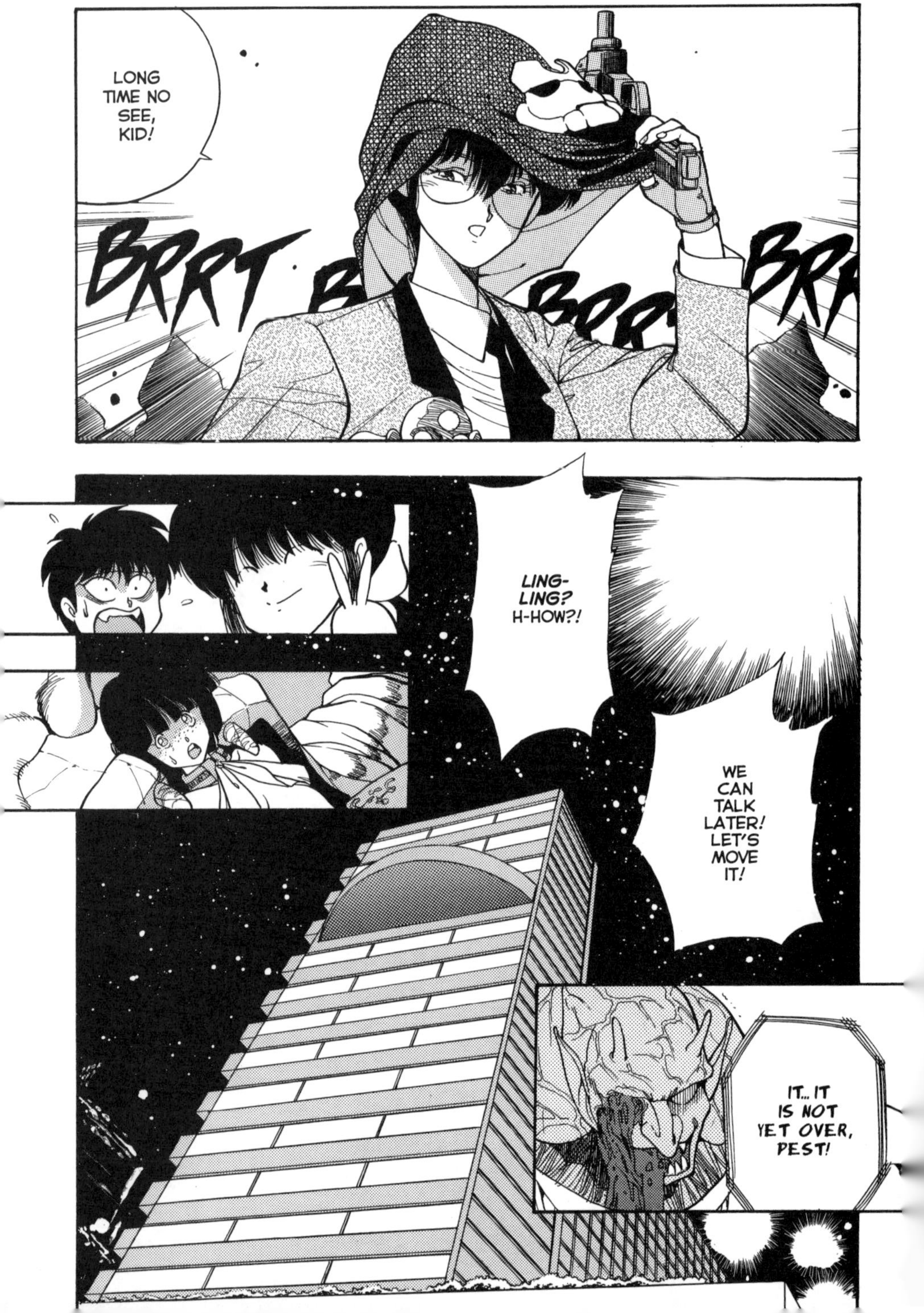
LONG TIME NO SEE, KID!
BRRT
BRRT
BRR
LING-LING? H-HOW?!
WE CAN TALK LATER! LET'S MOVE IT!
IT... IT IS NOT YET OVER, PEST!

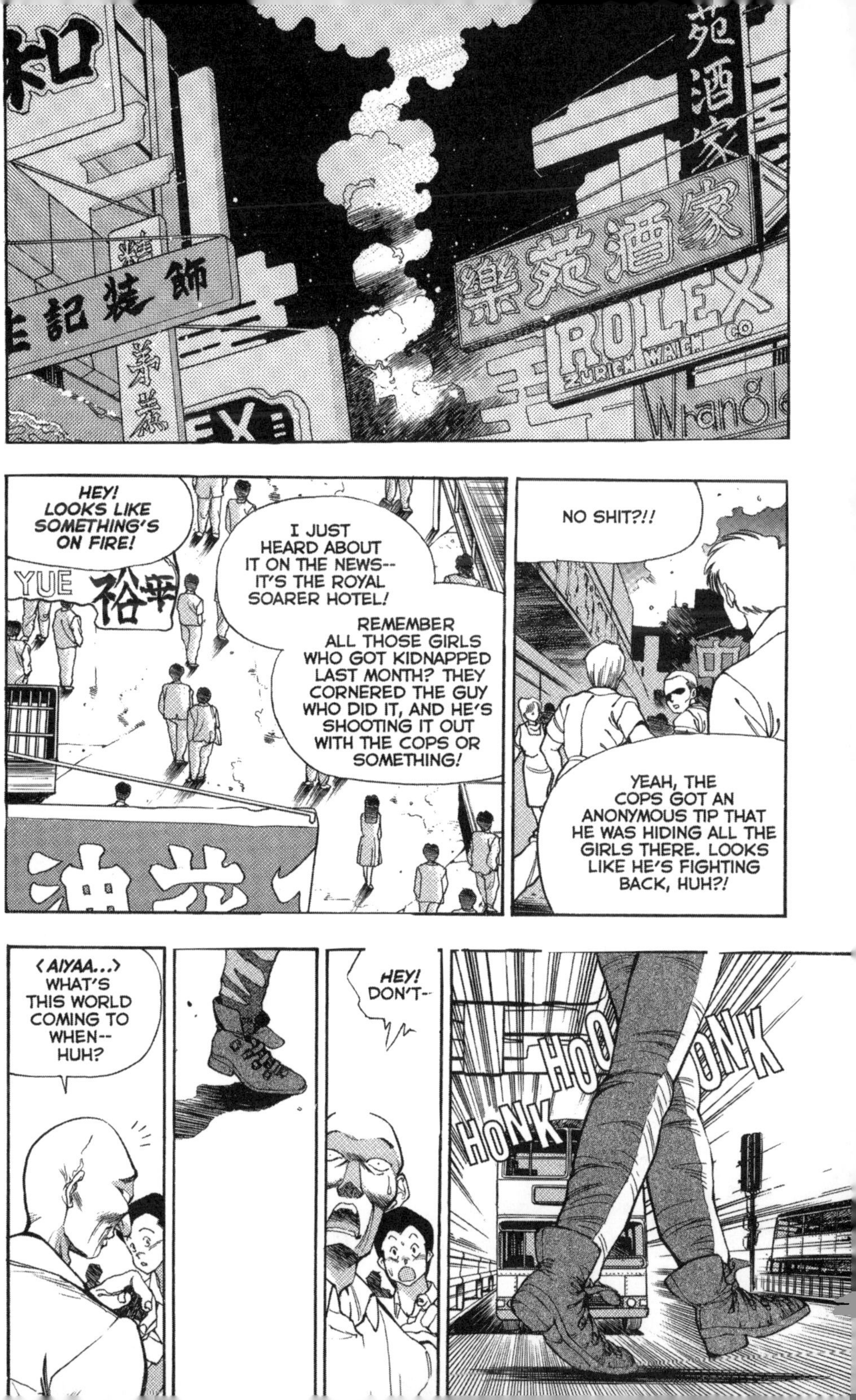
苑酒家
樂苑酒家
ROLEX
ZURICH WATCH CO
記裝飾
HEY! LOOKS LIKE SOMETHING'S ON FIRE!
YUE
I JUST HEARD ABOUT IT ON THE NEWS-- IT'S THE ROYAL SOARER HOTEL!
REMEMBER ALL THOSE GIRLS WHO GOT KIDNAPPED LAST MONTH? THEY CORNERED THE GUY WHO DID IT, AND HE'S SHOOTING IT OUT WITH THE COPS OR SOMETHING!
NO SHIT?!!
YEAH, THE COPS GOT AN ANONYMOUS TIP THAT HE WAS HIDING ALL THE GIRLS THERE. LOOKS LIKE HE'S FIGHTING BACK, HUH?!
‹AIYAA...› WHAT'S THIS WORLD COMING TO WHEN-- HUH?
HEY! DON'T--
HONK HOO ONK

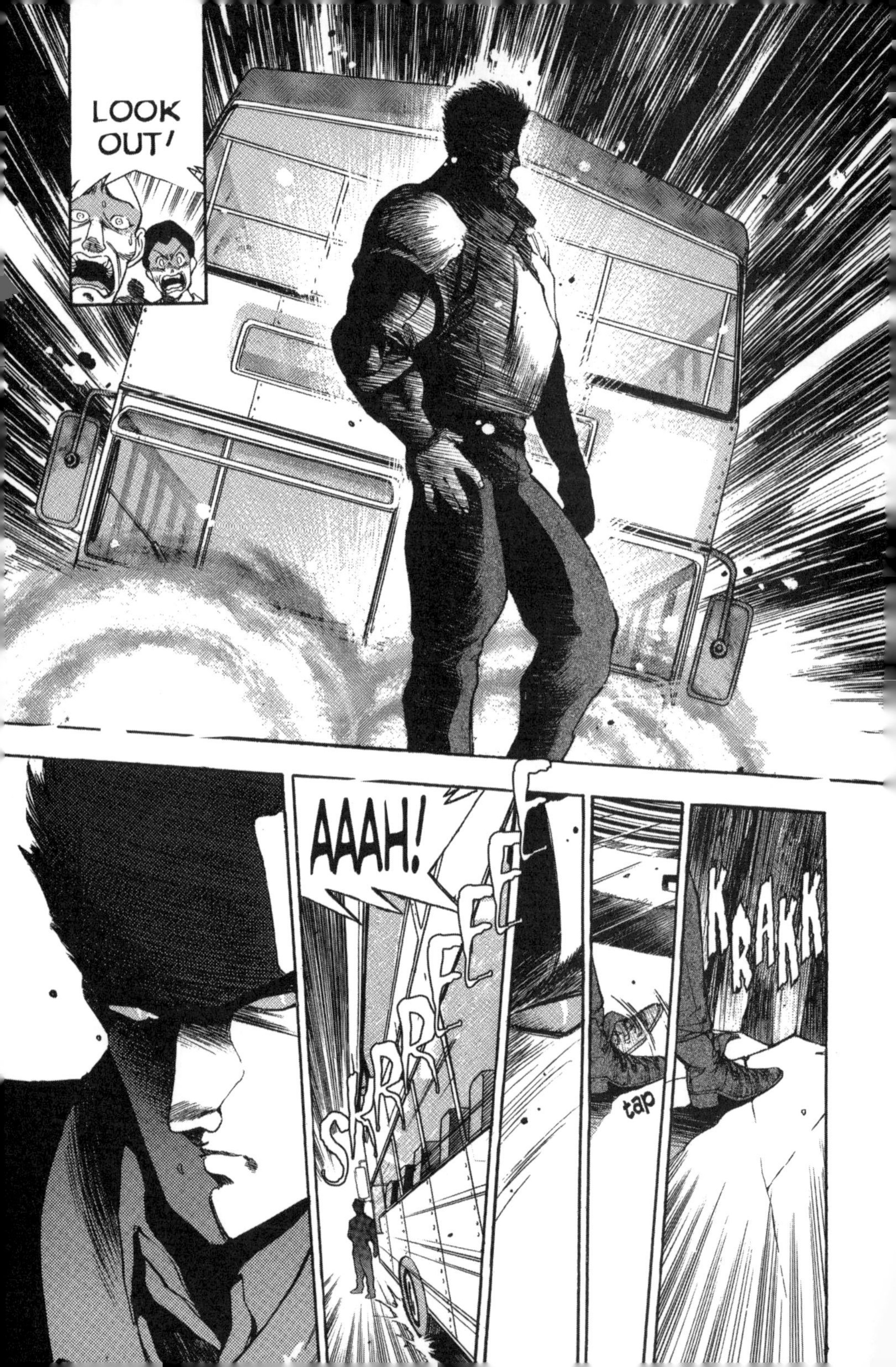
LOOK OUT!
AAAH!
SKRREEEE
tap
KRAKK

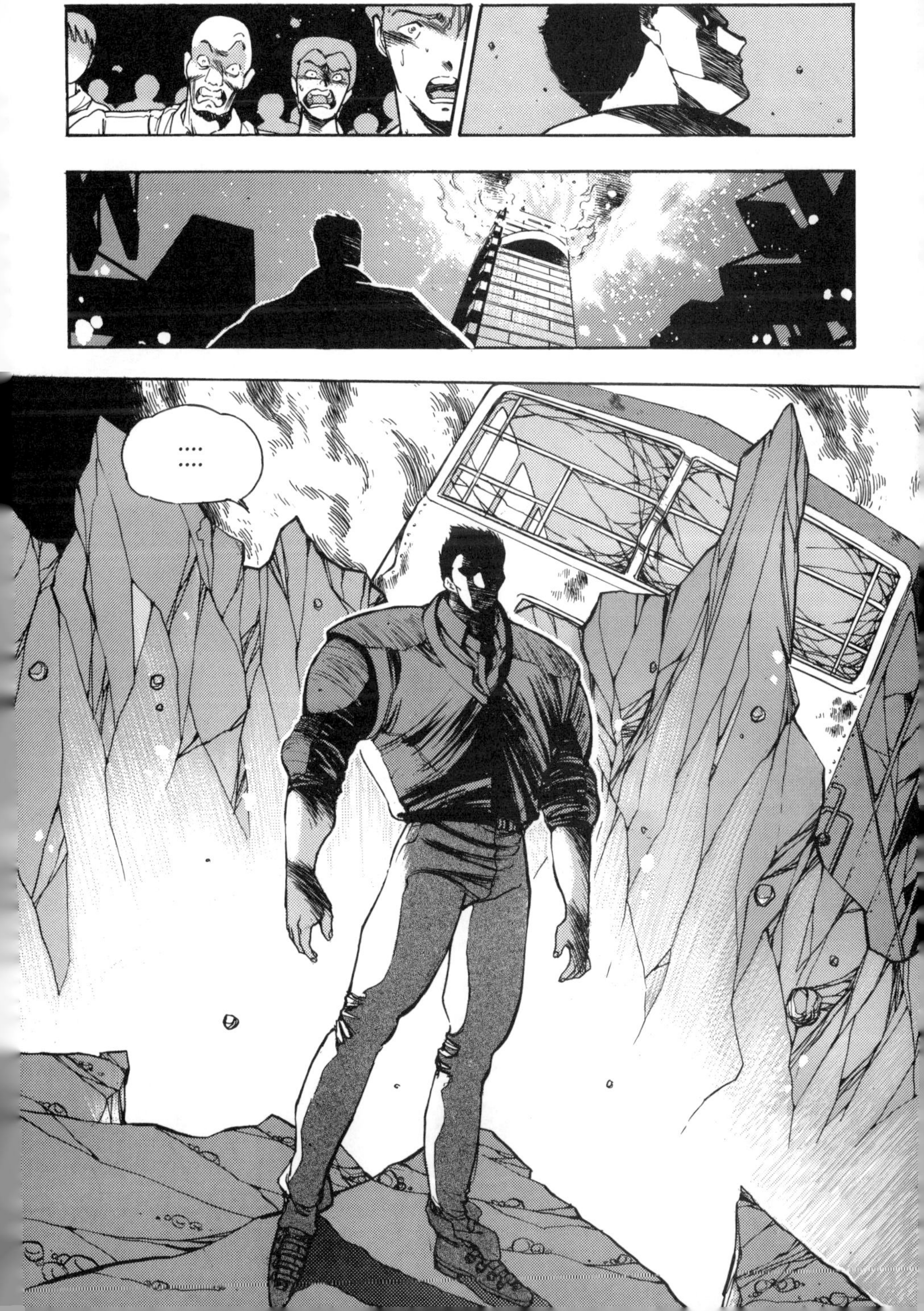
....
....

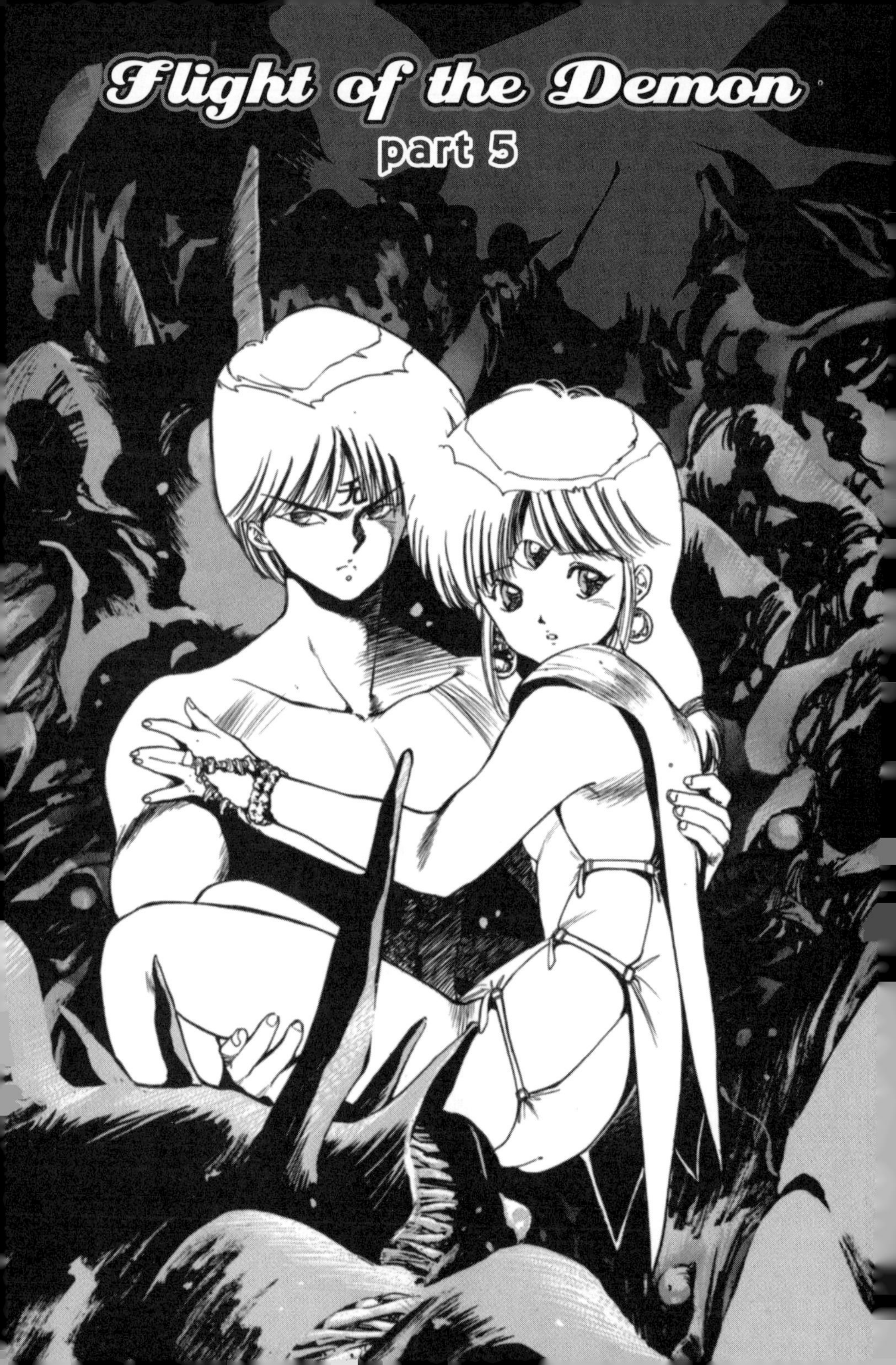
Flight of the Demon
part 5

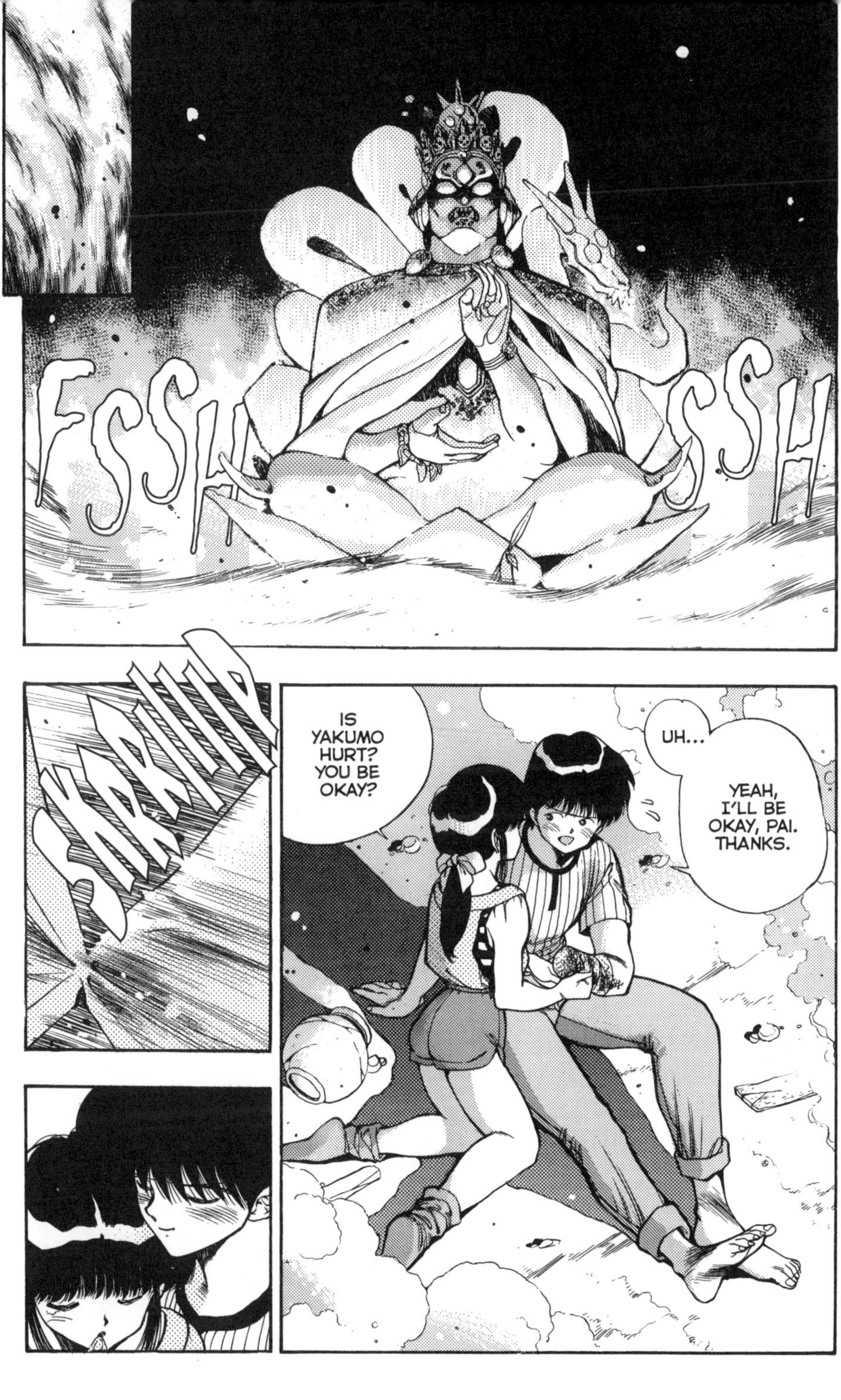
FSSH
SSH
SKRIIIP
IS YAKUMO HURT? YOU BE OKAY?
UH...
YEAH, I'LL BE OKAY, PAI. THANKS.

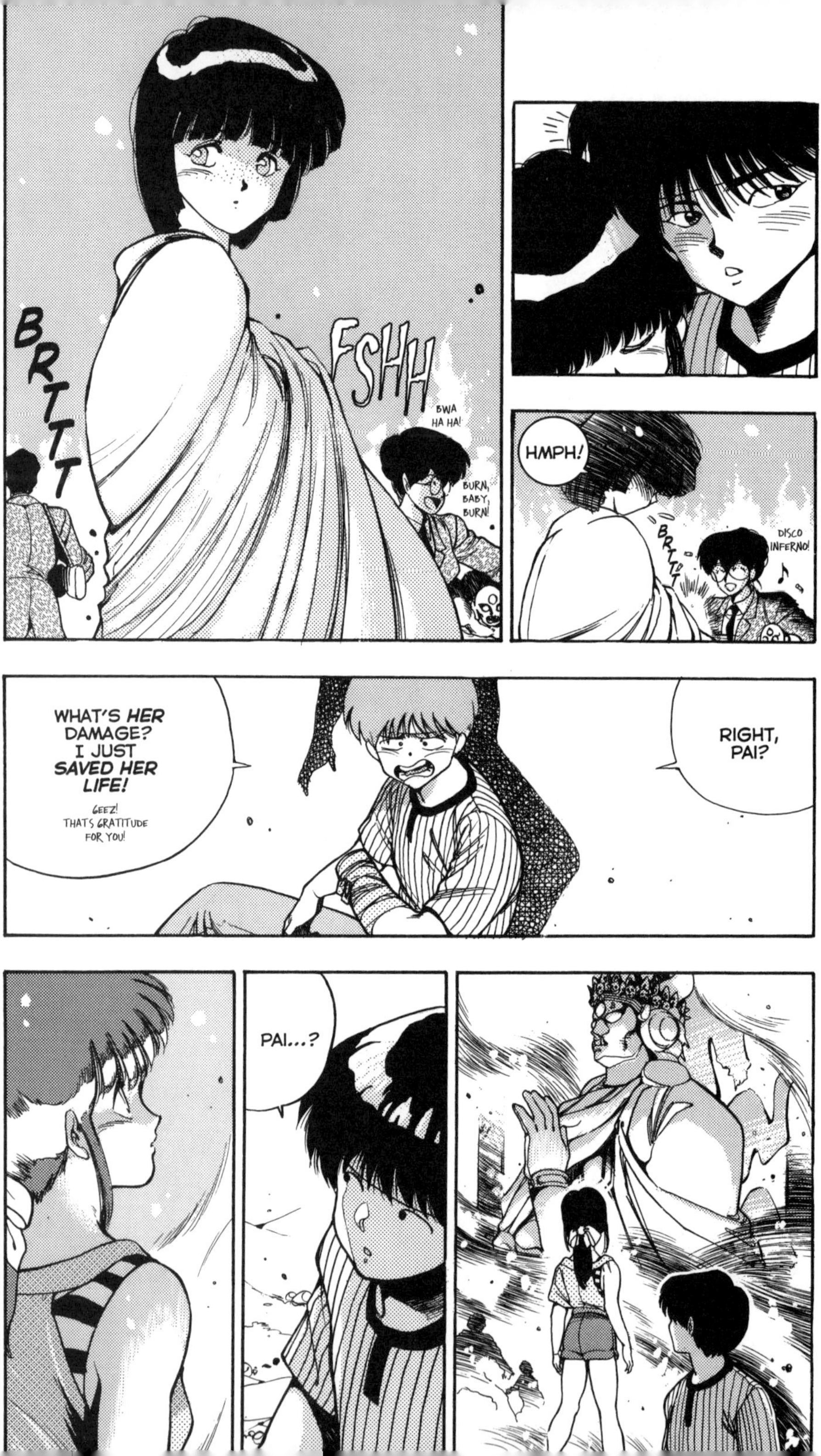
BRTTTT
FSHH
BWA HA HA!
BURN, BABY, BURN!
HMPH!
BRTTT
DISCO INFERNO!
WHAT'S HER DAMAGE? I JUST SAVED HER LIFE!
GEEZ! THATS GRATITUDE FOR YOU!
RIGHT, PAI?
PAI...?

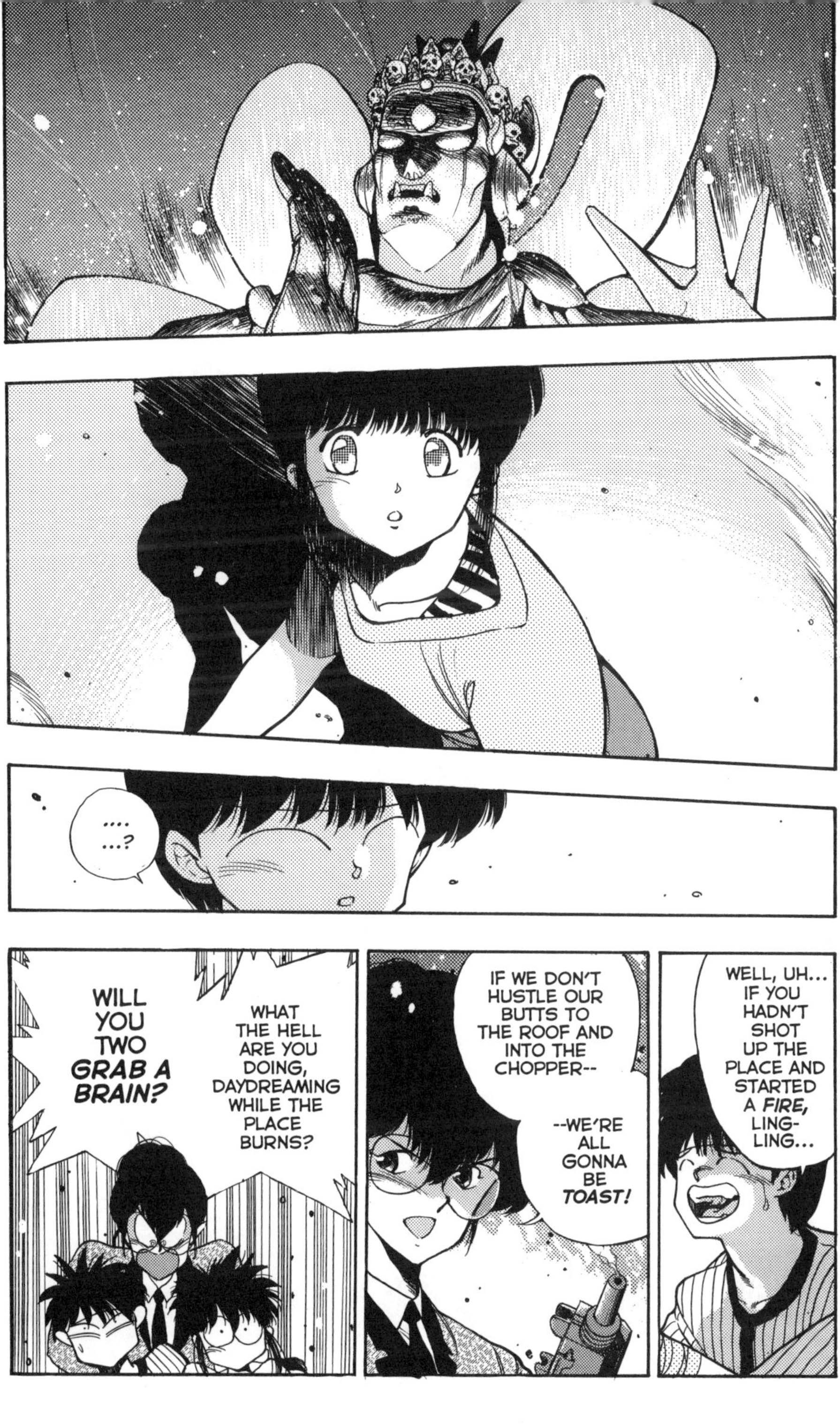
....
...?
WILL YOU TWO GRAB A BRAIN?
WHAT THE HELL ARE YOU DOING, DAYDREAMING WHILE THE PLACE BURNS?
IF WE DON'T HUSTLE OUR BUTTS TO THE ROOF AND INTO THE CHOPPER--
--WE'RE ALL GONNA BE TOAST!
WELL, UH... IF YOU HADN'T SHOT UP THE PLACE AND STARTED A FIRE, LING-LING...

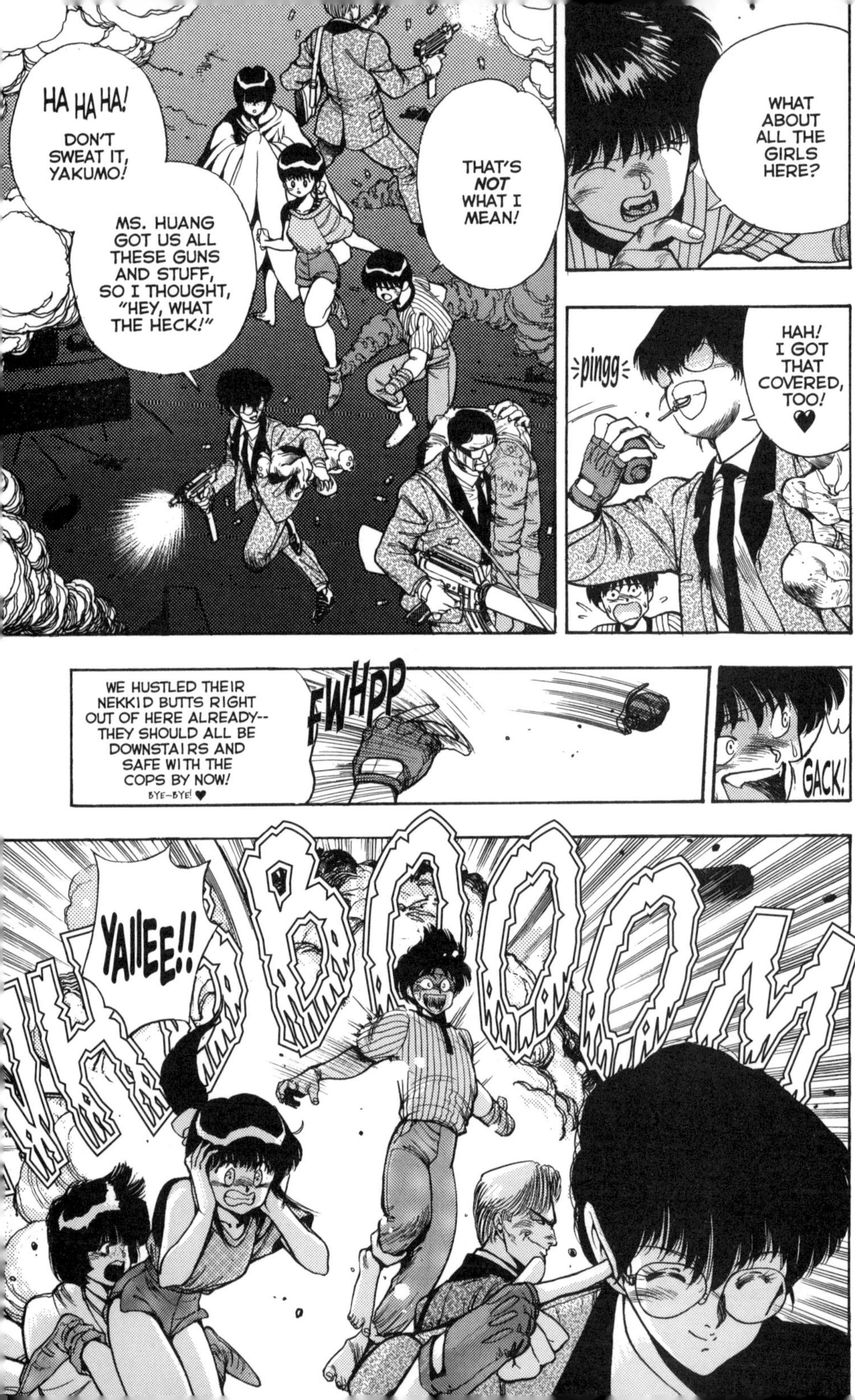
HA HA HA!
DON'T SWEAT IT, YAKUMO!
MS. HUANG GOT US ALL THESE GUNS AND STUFF, SO I THOUGHT, "HEY, WHAT THE HECK!"
THAT'S *NOT* WHAT I MEAN!
WHAT ABOUT ALL THE GIRLS HERE?
pingg
HAH! I GOT THAT COVERED, TOO! ♥
WE HUSTLED THEIR NEKKID BUTTS RIGHT OUT OF HERE ALREADY-- THEY SHOULD ALL BE DOWNSTAIRS AND SAFE WITH THE COPS BY NOW!
BYE-BYE! ♥
FWHPP
GACK!
YAIIEE!!
BOOOM

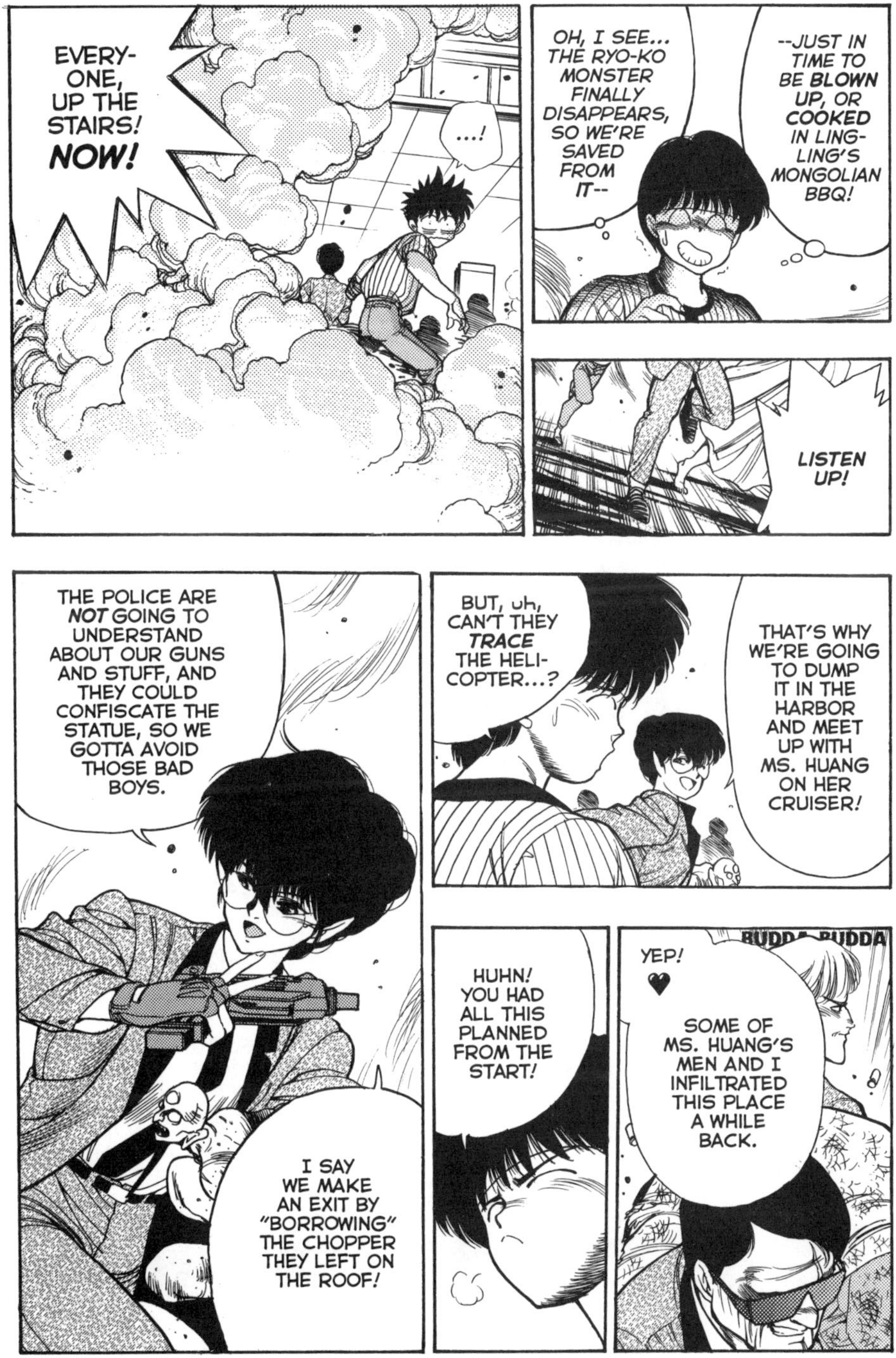

EVERY-ONE, UP THE STAIRS! NOW!
...!
OH, I SEE... THE RYO-KO MONSTER FINALLY DISAPPEARS, SO WE'RE SAVED FROM IT--
--JUST IN TIME TO BE BLOWN UP, OR COOKED IN LING-LING'S MONGOLIAN BBQ!
LISTEN UP!
THE POLICE ARE NOT GOING TO UNDERSTAND ABOUT OUR GUNS AND STUFF, AND THEY COULD CONFISCATE THE STATUE, SO WE GOTTA AVOID THOSE BAD BOYS.
I SAY WE MAKE AN EXIT BY "BORROWING" THE CHOPPER THEY LEFT ON THE ROOF!
BUT, uh, CAN'T THEY TRACE THE HELI-COPTER...?
THAT'S WHY WE'RE GOING TO DUMP IT IN THE HARBOR AND MEET UP WITH MS. HUANG ON HER CRUISER!
HUHN! YOU HAD ALL THIS PLANNED FROM THE START!
YEP! ♥
BUDDA BUDDA
SOME OF MS. HUANG'S MEN AND I INFILTRATED THIS PLACE A WHILE BACK.

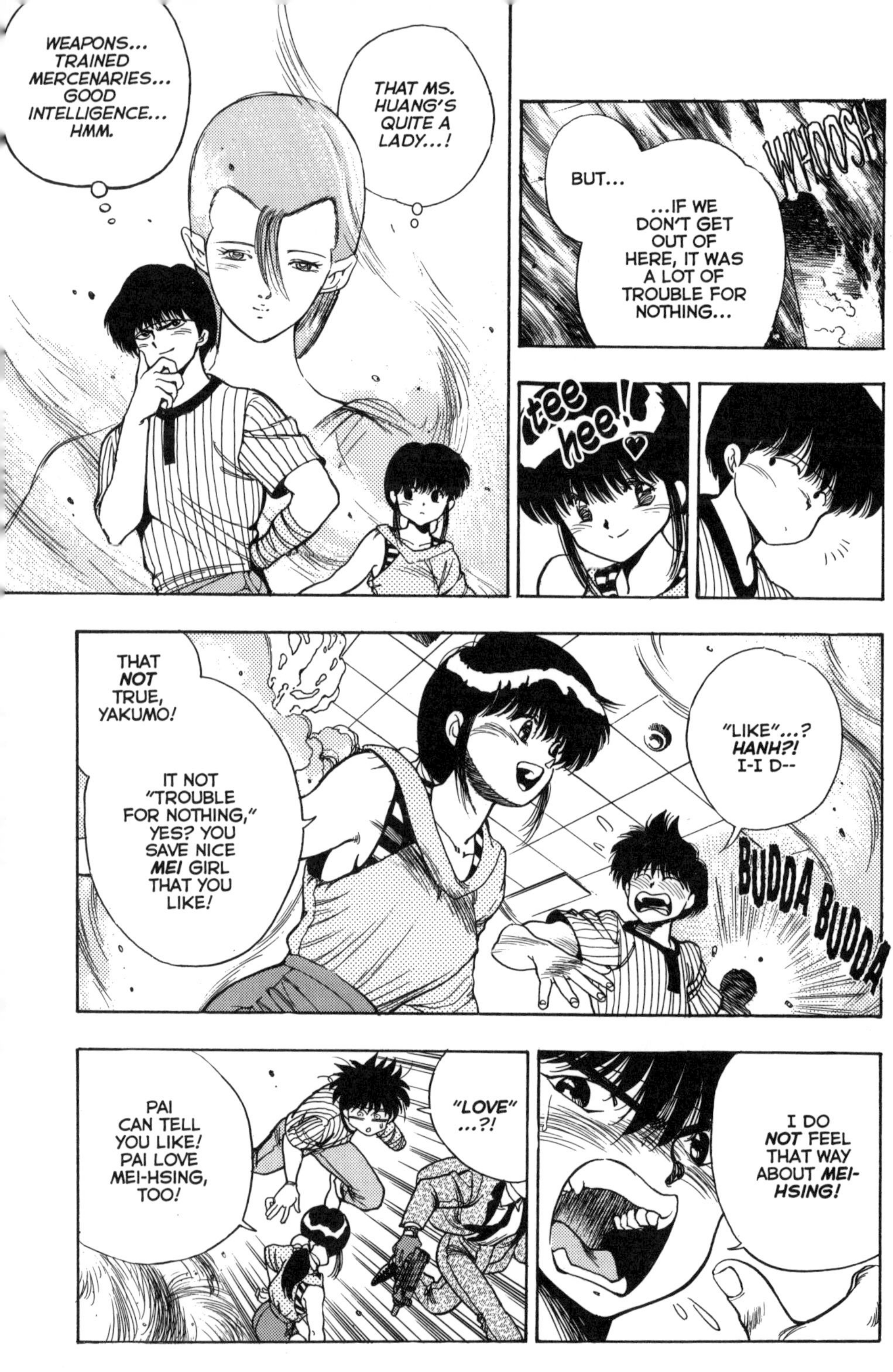
WEAPONS... TRAINED MERCENARIES... GOOD INTELLIGENCE... HMM.
THAT MS. HUANG'S QUITE A LADY...!
BUT...
...IF WE DON'T GET OUT OF HERE, IT WAS A LOT OF TROUBLE FOR NOTHING...
WHOOSH
tee hee!!
THAT NOT TRUE, YAKUMO!
IT NOT "TROUBLE FOR NOTHING," YES? YOU SAVE NICE MEI GIRL THAT YOU LIKE!
"LIKE"...? HANH?! I-I D--
BUDDA BUDDA
PAI CAN TELL YOU LIKE! PAI LOVE MEI-HSING, TOO!
"LOVE" ...?!
I DO NOT FEEL THAT WAY ABOUT MEI-HSING!

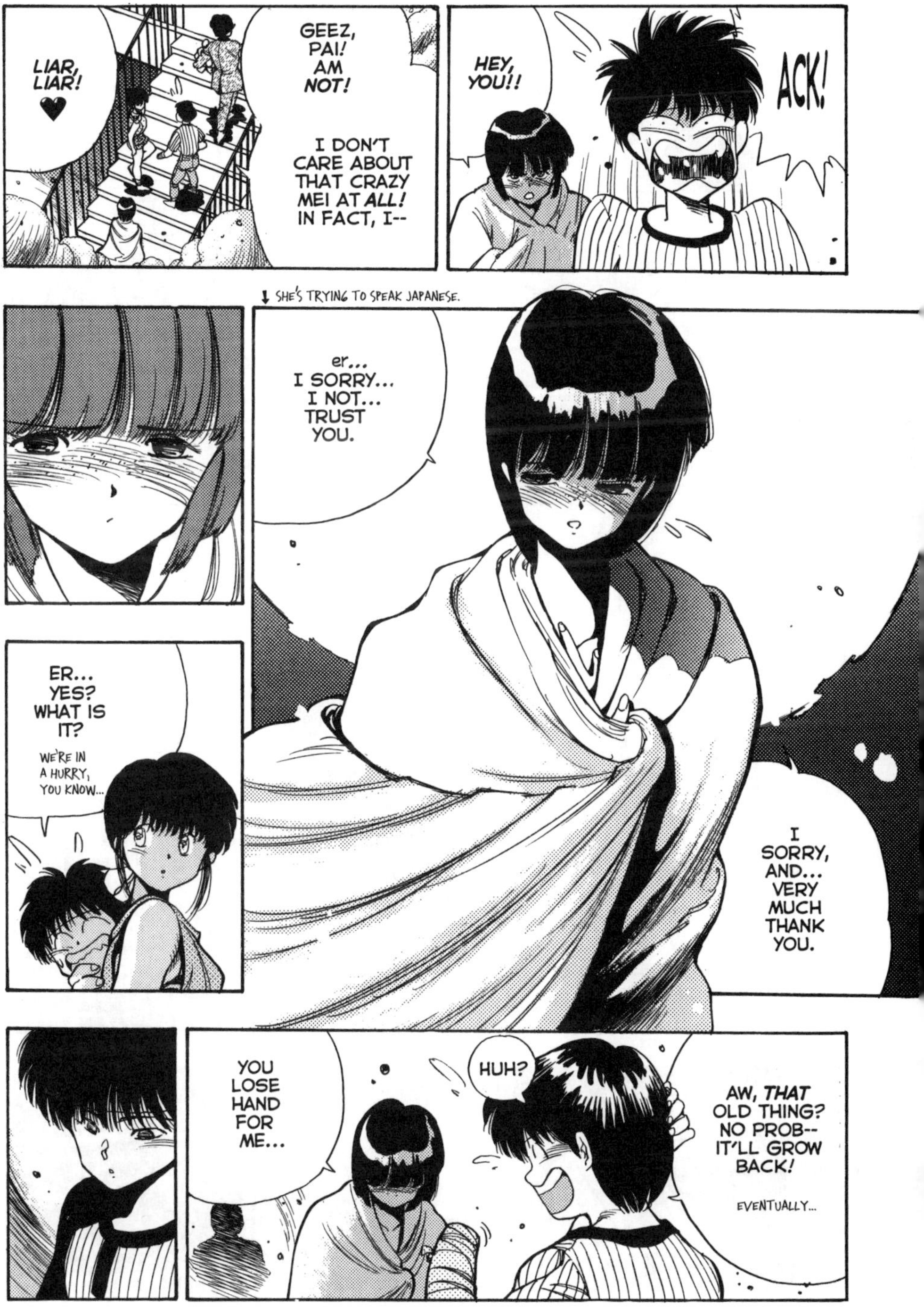
LIAR, LIAR! ♥
GEEZ, PAI! AM NOT!
I DON'T CARE ABOUT THAT CRAZY MEI AT ALL! IN FACT, I--
HEY, YOU!!
ACK!
SHE'S TRYING TO SPEAK JAPANESE.
ER... YES? WHAT IS IT?
WE'RE IN A HURRY, YOU KNOW...
er... I SORRY... I NOT... TRUST YOU.
I SORRY, AND... VERY MUCH THANK YOU.
YOU LOSE HAND FOR ME...
HUH?
AW, THAT OLD THING? NO PROB-- IT'LL GROW BACK!
EVENTUALLY...

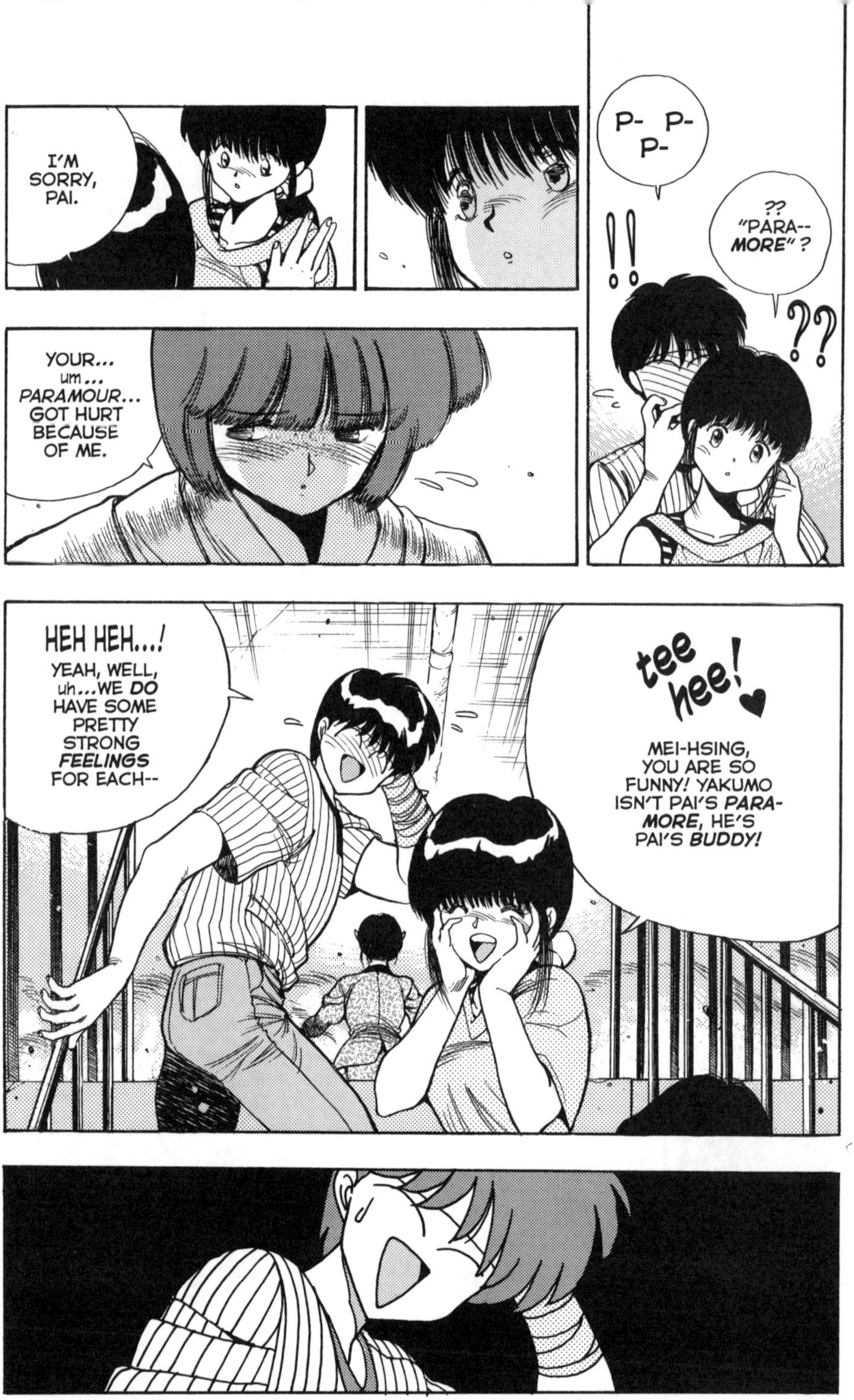
I'M SORRY, PAI.
P- P- P-
?? "PARA--MORE"?
YOUR... um... PARAMOUR... GOT HURT BECAUSE OF ME.
HEH HEH...! YEAH, WELL, uh...WE DO HAVE SOME PRETTY STRONG FEELINGS FOR EACH--
tee hee!
MEI-HSING, YOU ARE SO FUNNY! YAKUMO ISN'T PAI'S PARA-MORE, HE'S PAI'S BUDDY!

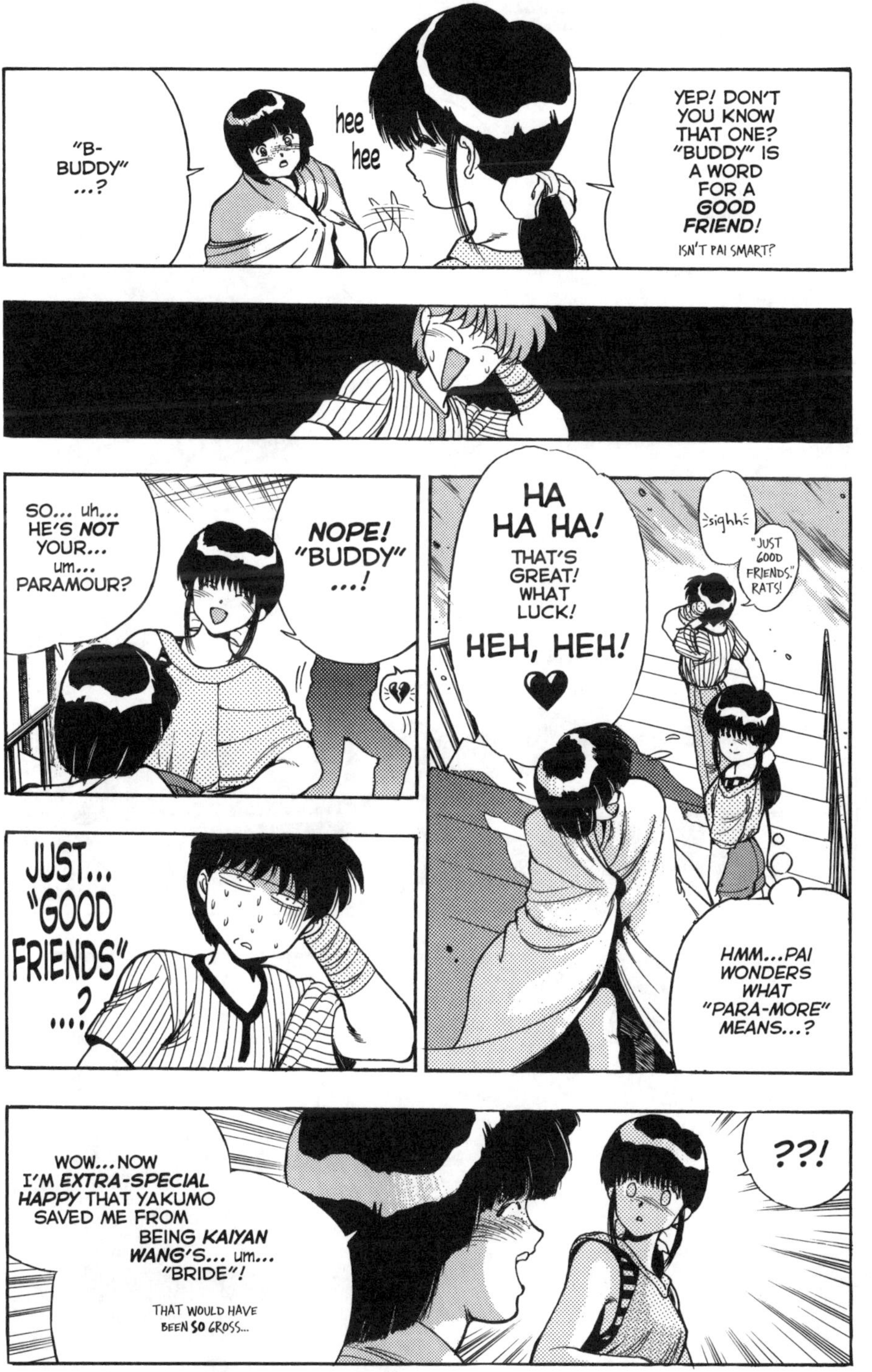
"B-
BUDDY"
...?
hee
hee
YEP! DON'T YOU KNOW THAT ONE? "BUDDY" IS A WORD FOR A GOOD FRIEND!
ISN'T PAI SMART?
SO... uh... HE'S NOT YOUR... um... PARAMOUR?
NOPE! "BUDDY" ...!
HA HA HA! THAT'S GREAT! WHAT LUCK! HEH, HEH!
sighh
"JUST GOOD FRIENDS." RATS!
JUST... "GOOD FRIENDS" ...?
HMM...PAI WONDERS WHAT "PARA-MORE" MEANS...?
WOW...NOW I'M EXTRA-SPECIAL HAPPY THAT YAKUMO SAVED ME FROM BEING KAIYAN WANG'S... um... "BRIDE"!
THAT WOULD HAVE BEEN SO GROSS...
??!

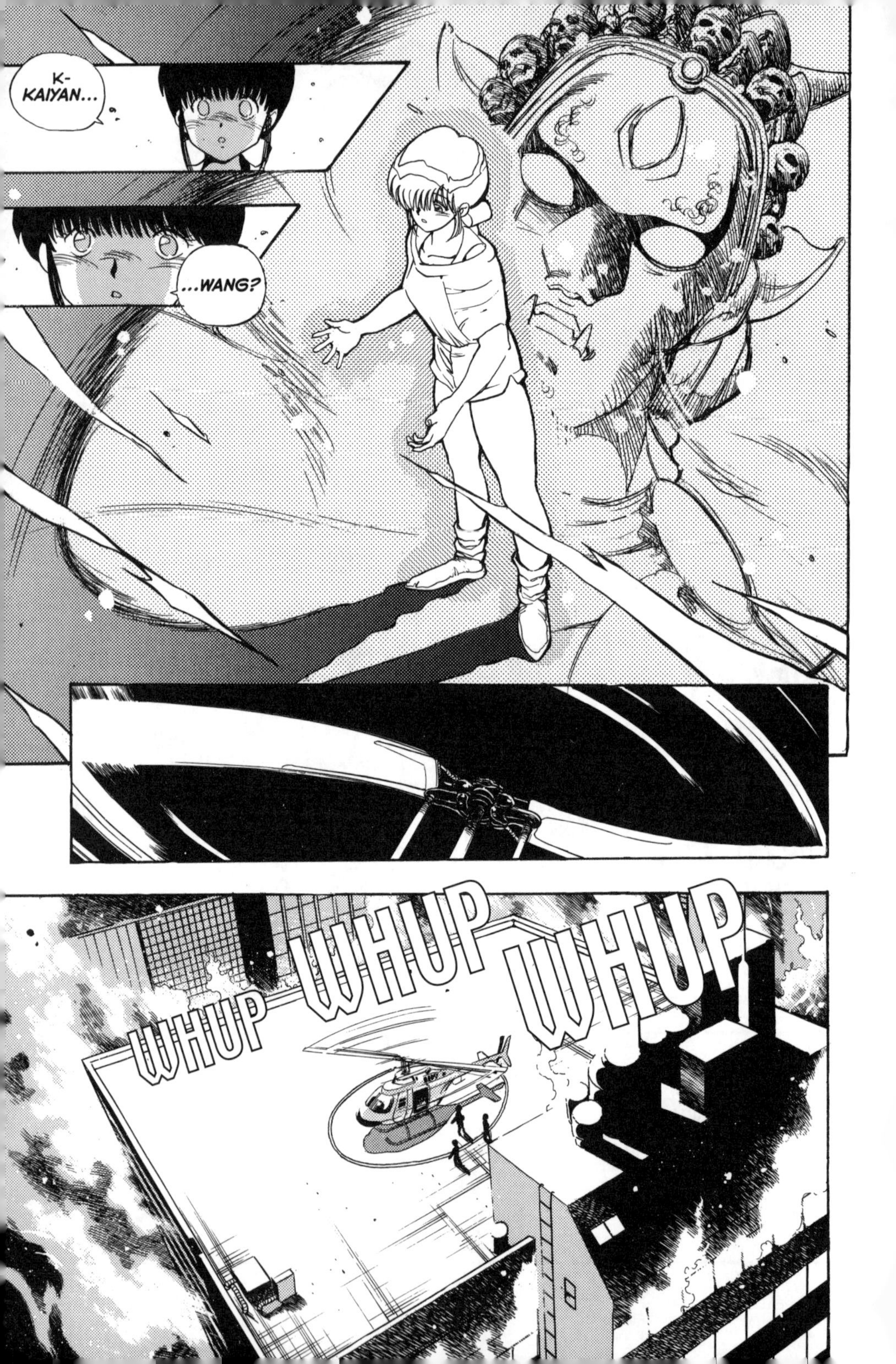
K-KAIYAN...
...WANG?
WHUP
WHUP
WHUP

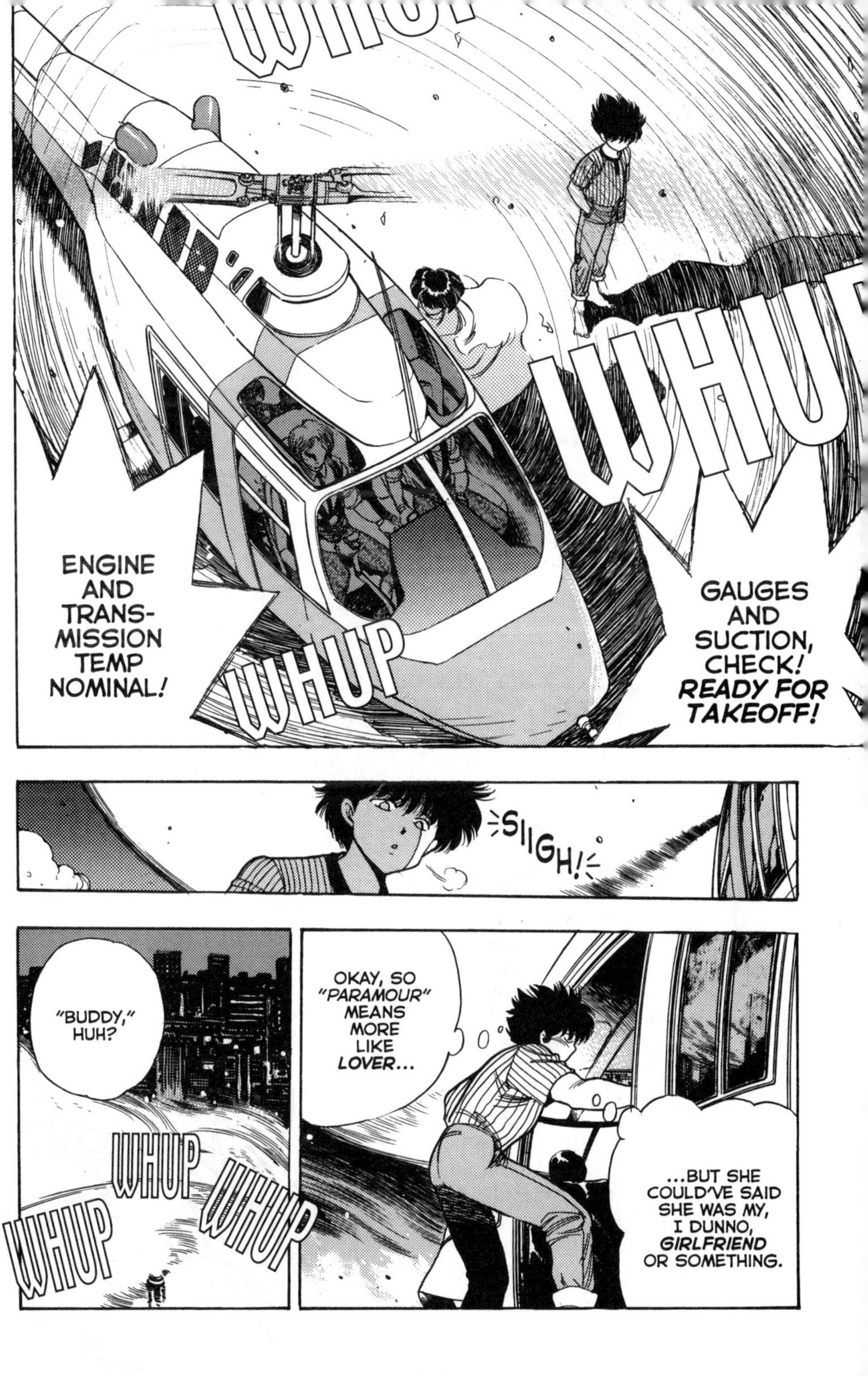
WHUP
WHUP
ENGINE AND TRANS-MISSION TEMP NOMINAL!
WHUP
GAUGES AND SUCTION, CHECK! READY FOR TAKEOFF!
SIIGH!
"BUDDY," HUH?
WHUP
WHUP
WHUP
OKAY, SO "PARAMOUR" MEANS MORE LIKE LOVER...
...BUT SHE COULD'VE SAID SHE WAS MY, I DUNNO, GIRLFRIEND OR SOMETHING.

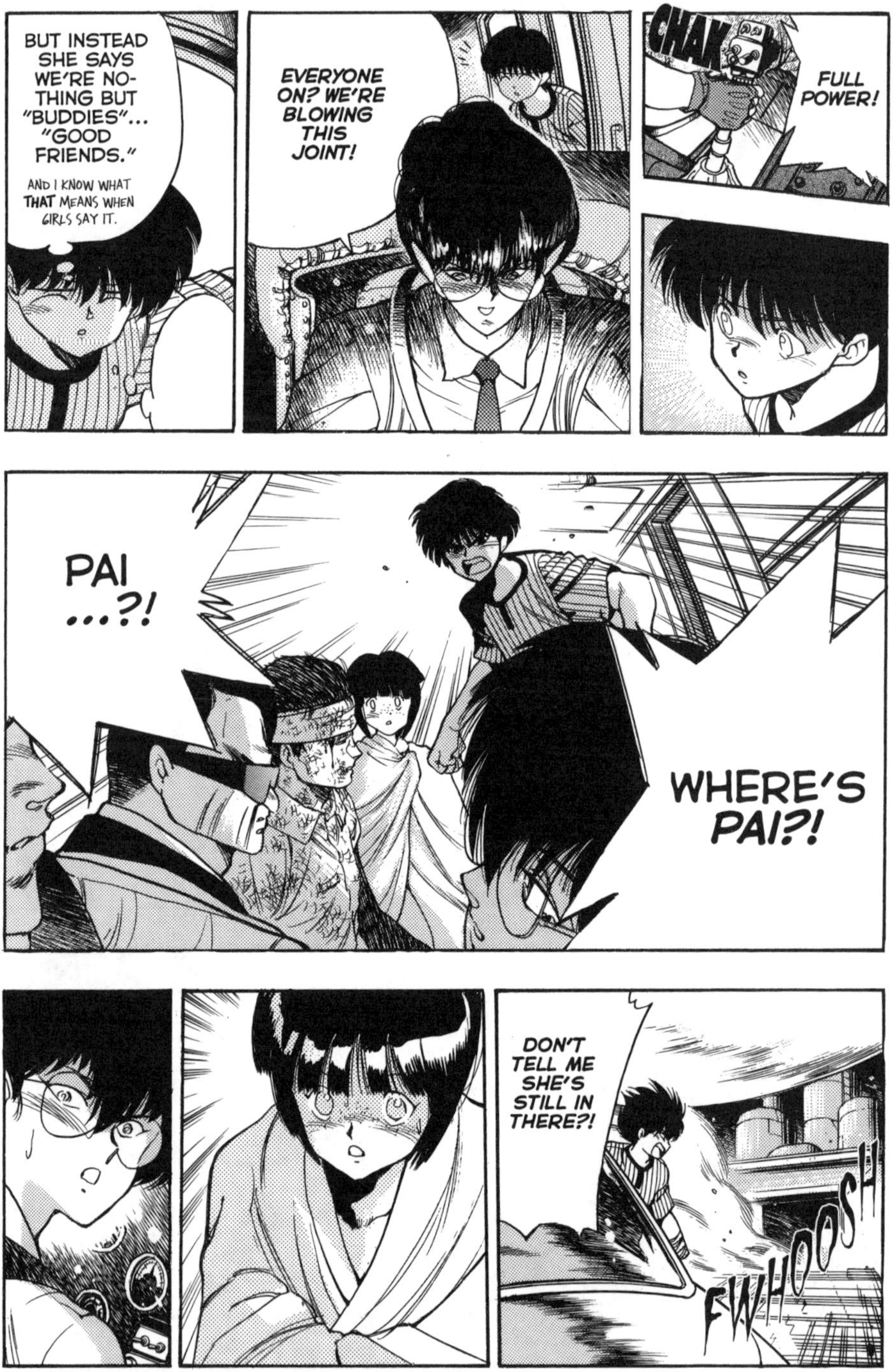
BUT INSTEAD SHE SAYS WE'RE NOTHING BUT "BUDDIES"... "GOOD FRIENDS."
AND I KNOW WHAT **THAT** MEANS WHEN GIRLS SAY IT.
EVERYONE ON? WE'RE BLOWING THIS JOINT!
CHAK
FULL POWER!
PAI ...?!
WHERE'S PAI?!
DON'T TELL ME SHE'S STILL IN THERE?!
FWHOOSH

PAI!!

IT'S TOO LATE, YAKUMO! THE FIRE'S BREAKING THROUGH THE ROOF!

DON'T WORRY-- I SHOWED HER THE WAY DOWN WHEN WE MET ON THE 30TH FLOOR! SHE'LL BE FINE!

YEAH, *RIGHT!* THIS IS *PAI* WE'RE TALKING ABOUT, LING-LING!

SHE'S A DITZ!

GLRCCH

YOU GUYS JUST LEAVE, I'LL--

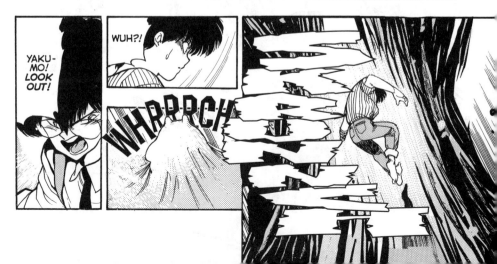

YAKU-MO! LOOK OUT!

WUH?!

WHRRRCH

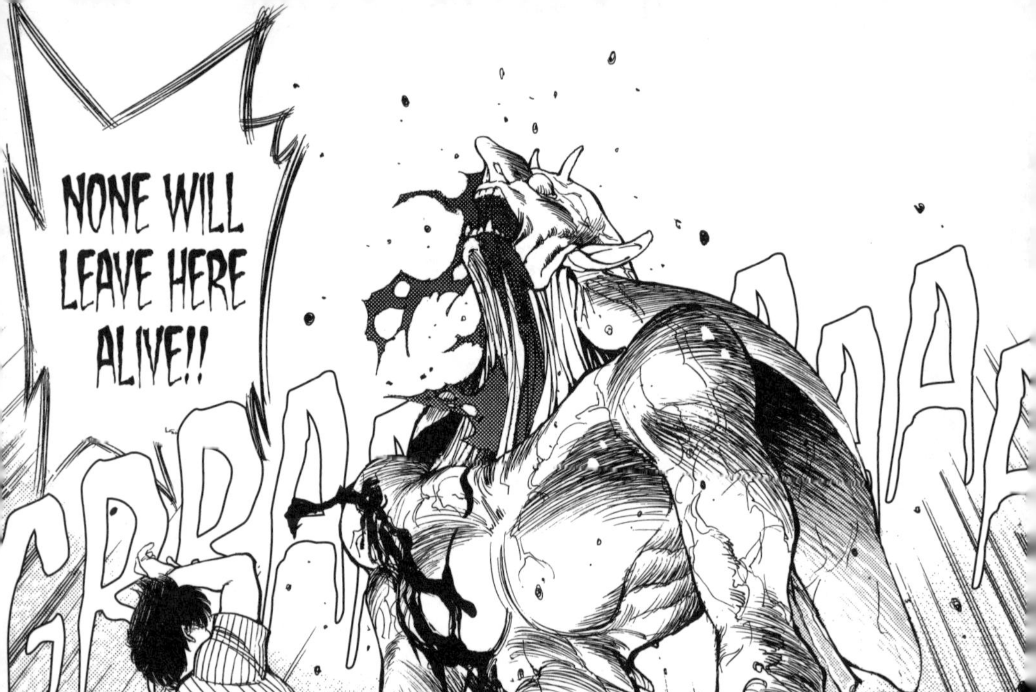
NONE WILL LEAVE HERE ALIVE!!

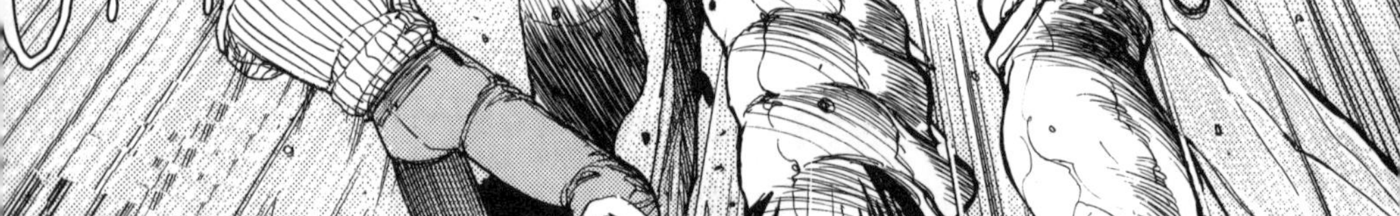
RYO-KO?!
DAMN! WHAT DOES IT TAKE TO *KILL* YOU?!

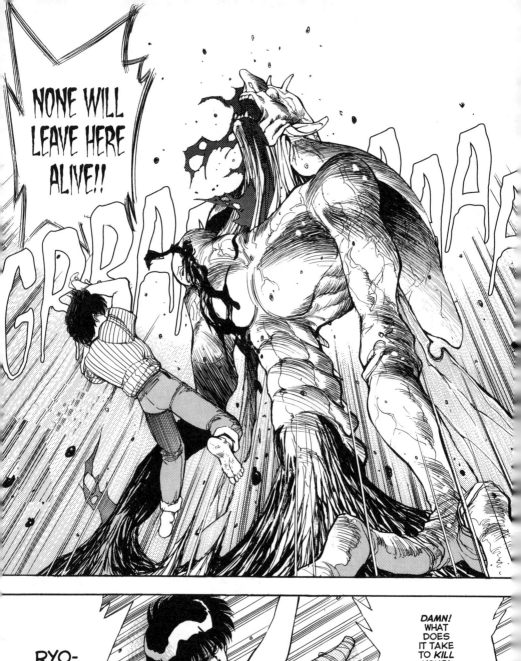

YAKUMO!

BRRRT
BRRRT
DRTDRT
DRT

VRREEEEEEEN

SPAK
SPAK
SPAK
SPAKK

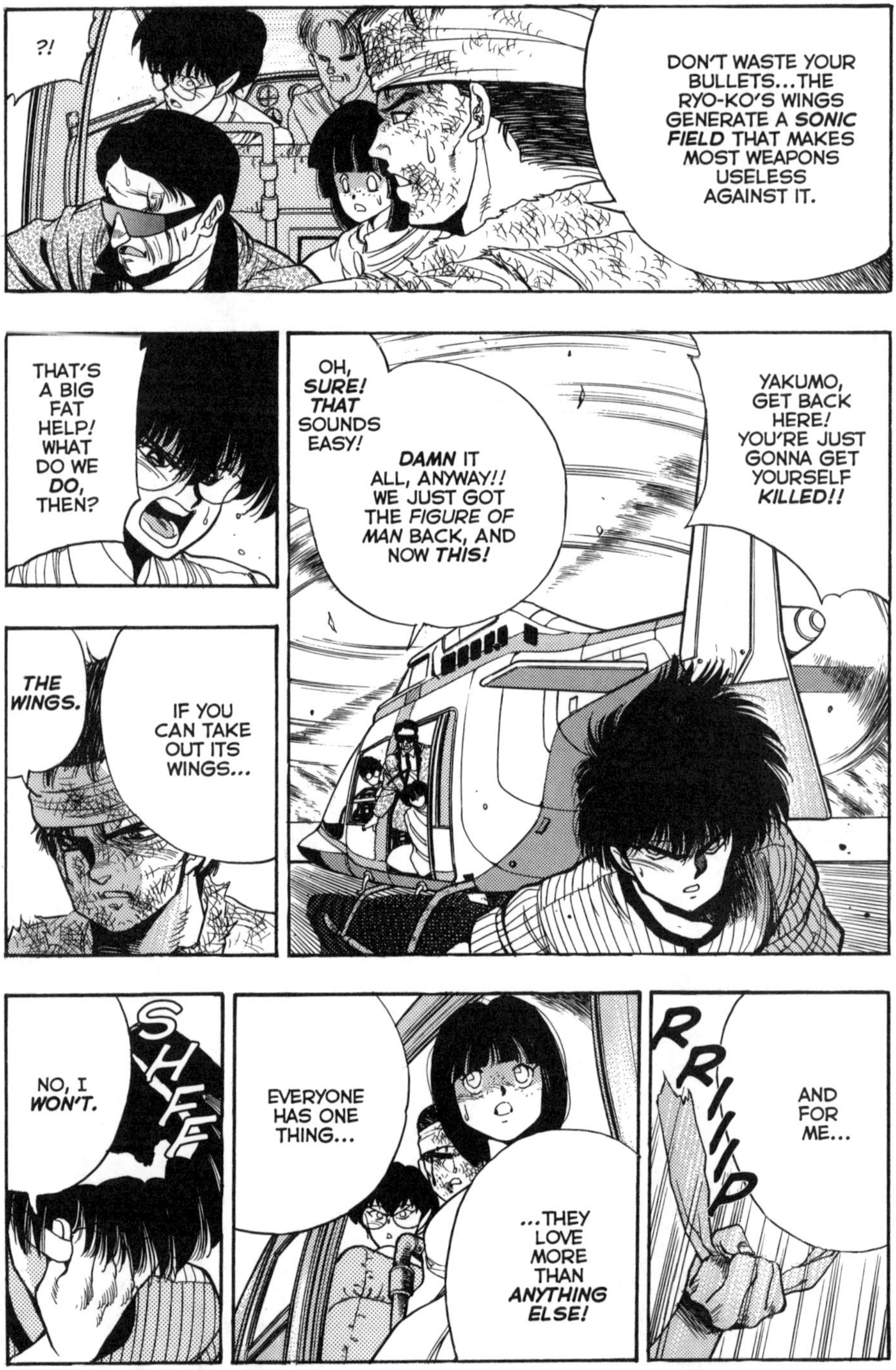
?!
DON'T WASTE YOUR BULLETS...THE RYO-KO'S WINGS GENERATE A ***SONIC FIELD*** THAT MAKES MOST WEAPONS USELESS AGAINST IT.
THAT'S A BIG FAT HELP*!* WHAT DO WE ***DO***, THEN?
THE WINGS.
IF YOU CAN TAKE OUT ITS WINGS...
OH, ***SURE! THAT*** SOUNDS EASY*!*
DAMN IT ALL, ANYWAY*!!* WE JUST GOT THE ***FIGURE*** OF ***MAN*** BACK, AND NOW ***THIS!***
YAKUMO, GET BACK HERE*!* YOU'RE JUST GONNA GET YOURSELF ***KILLED!!***
SHFF
NO, I ***WON'T.***
EVERYONE HAS ONE THING...
...THEY LOVE MORE THAN ***ANYTHING ELSE!***
RRIIIP
AND FOR ME...

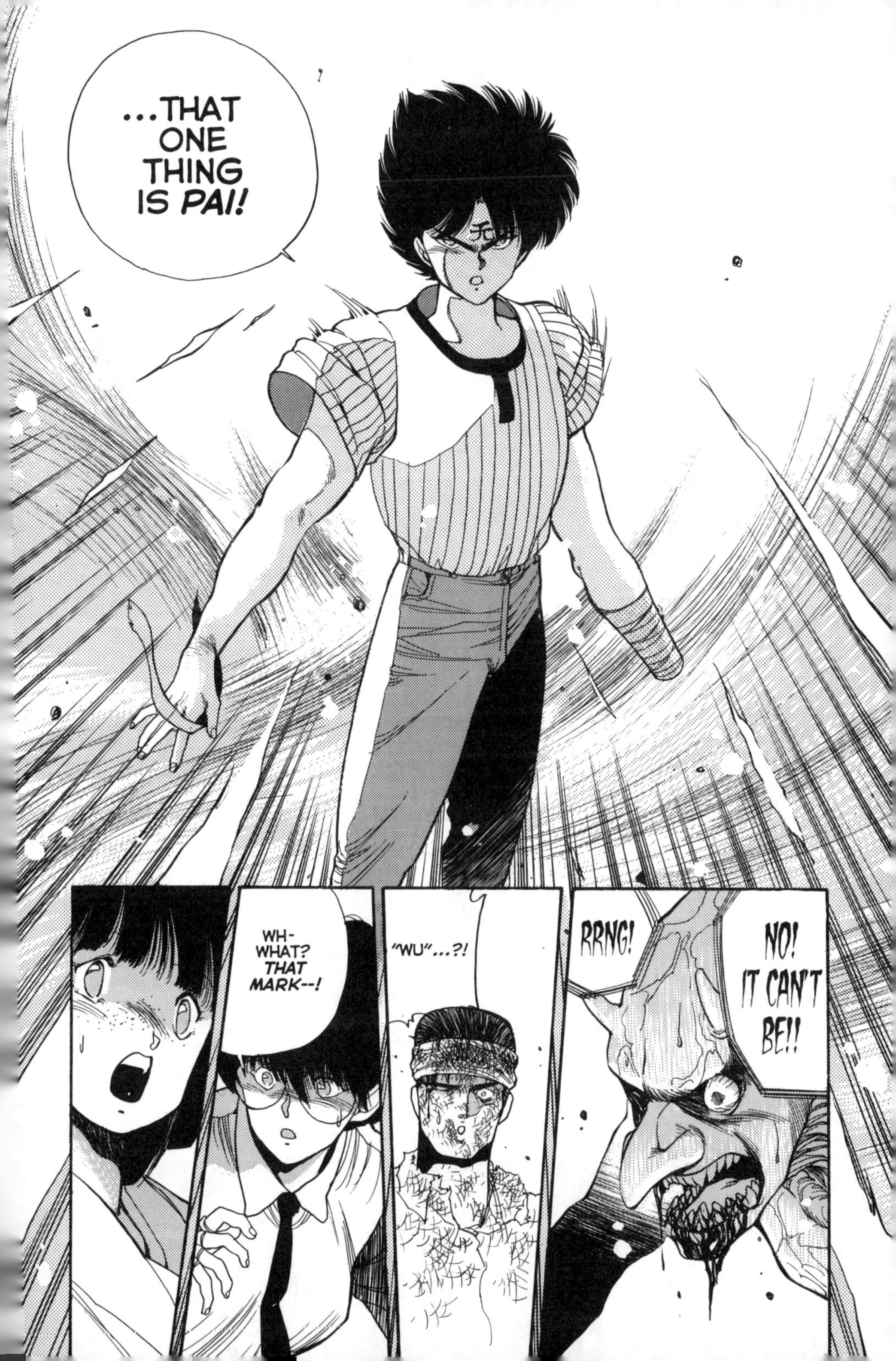
...THAT ONE THING IS *PAI!*
WH- WHAT? *THAT MARK--!*
"WU"...?!
RRNG!
NO! IT CAN'T BE!!

NOW YOU SEE?! I *WON'T* DIE, BECAUSE I *CAN'T* BE KILLED!

THIS... THIS IS IMPOSSIBLE!!

ANOTHER SANJIYAN STILL WALKS THIS WORLD?

LING-LING, GO ON WITHOUT ME!

AND THIS PEST IS THAT SANJIYAN'S WU?! I CANNOT--?!?

hur-HEH!

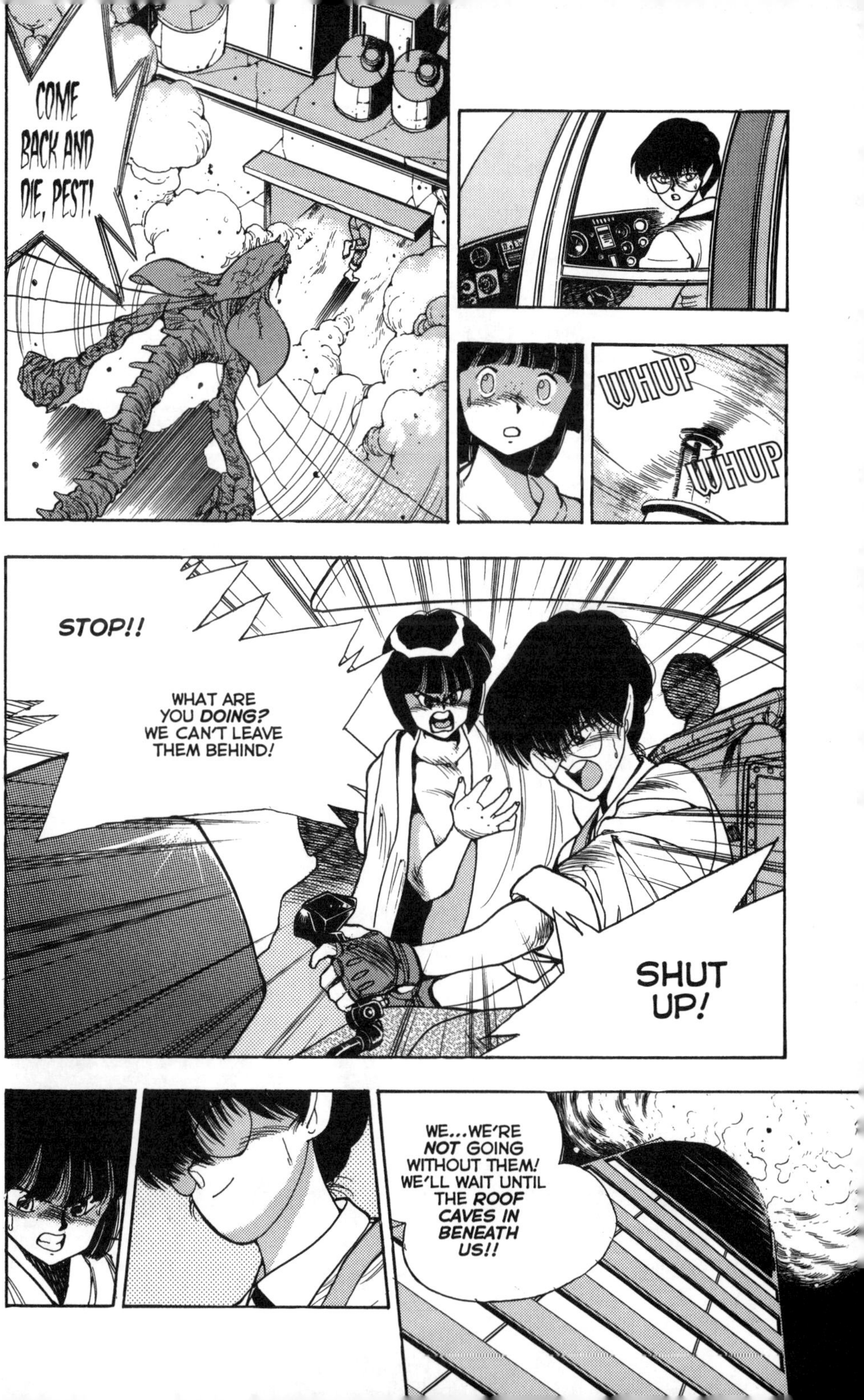
COME BACK AND DIE, PEST!
WHUP
WHUP
STOP!!
WHAT ARE YOU DOING? WE CAN'T LEAVE THEM BEHIND!
SHUT UP!
WE...WE'RE NOT GOING WITHOUT THEM! WE'LL WAIT UNTIL THE ROOF CAVES IN BENEATH US!!

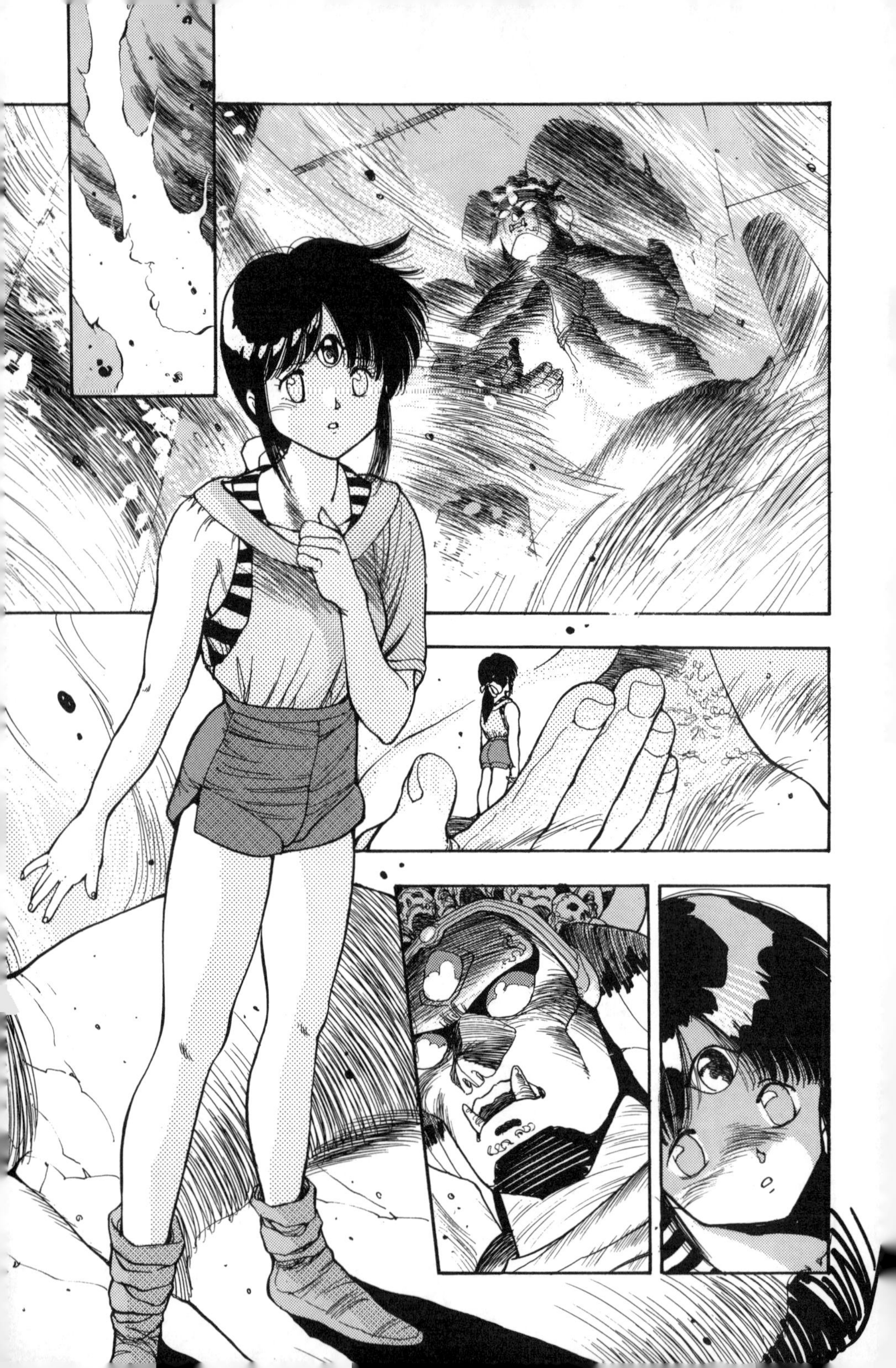

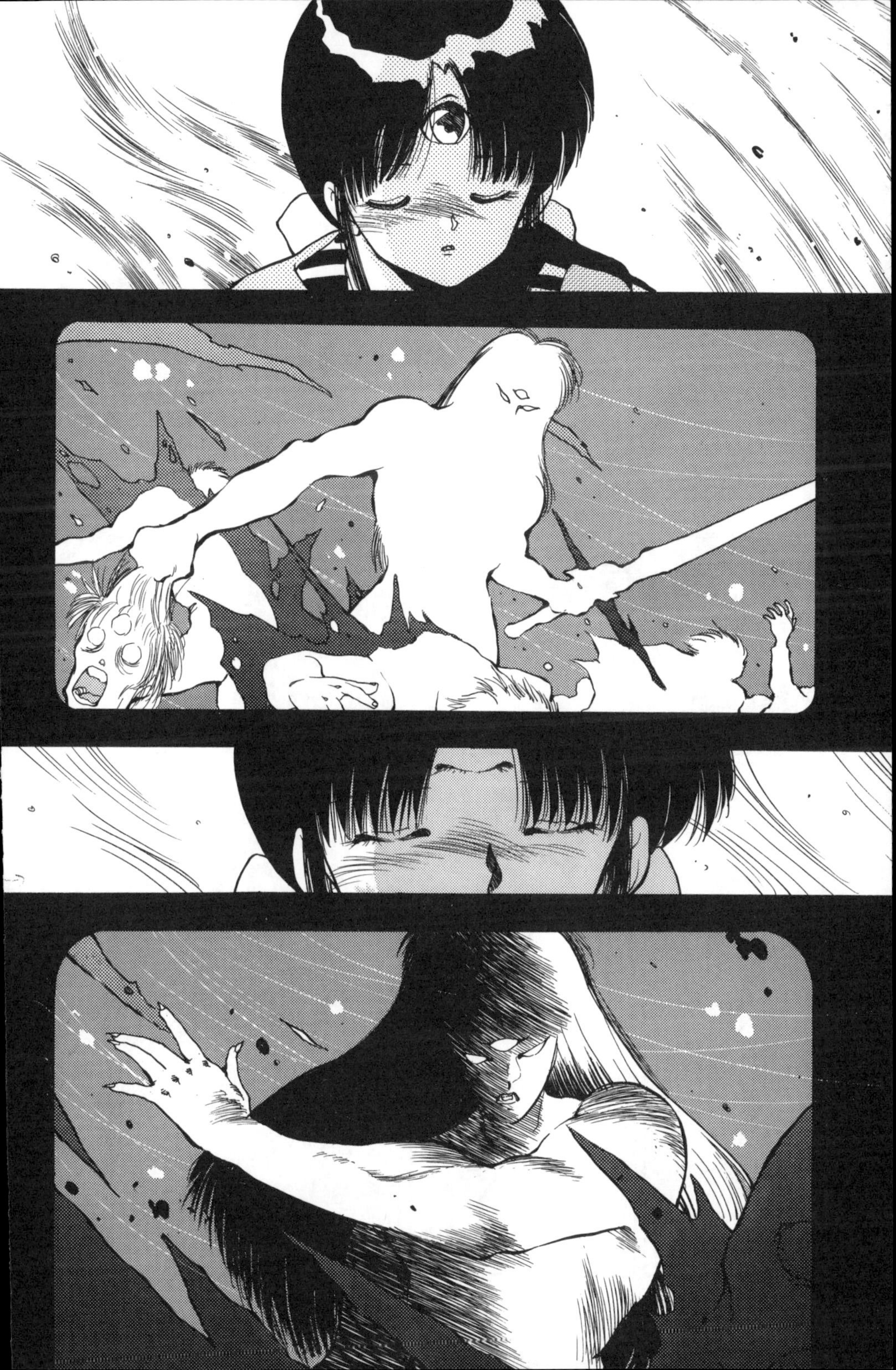

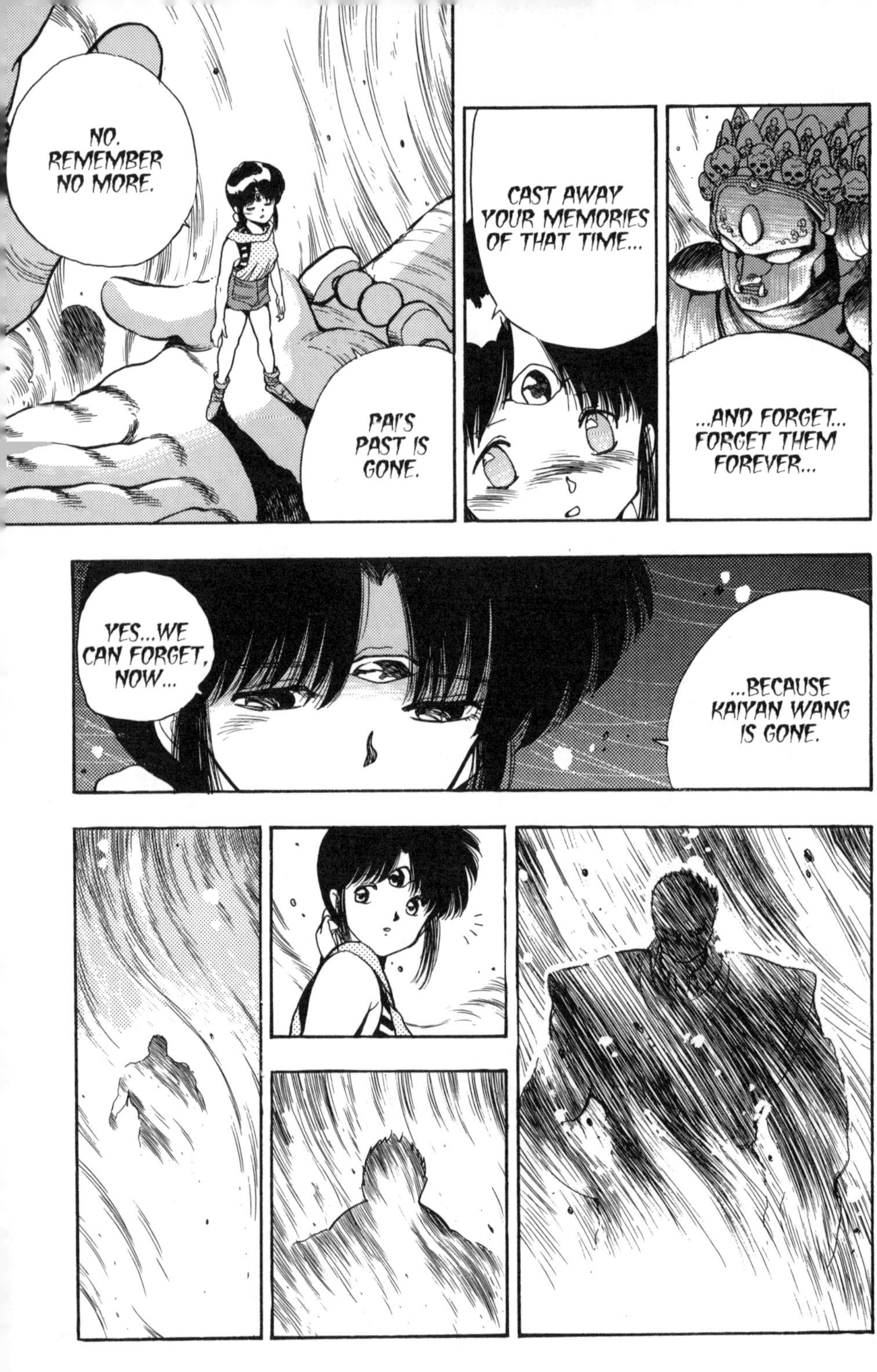
NO. REMEMBER NO MORE.
PAI'S PAST IS GONE.
CAST AWAY YOUR MEMORIES OF THAT TIME...
...AND FORGET... FORGET THEM FOREVER...
YES...WE CAN FORGET, NOW...
...BECAUSE KAIYAN WANG IS GONE.

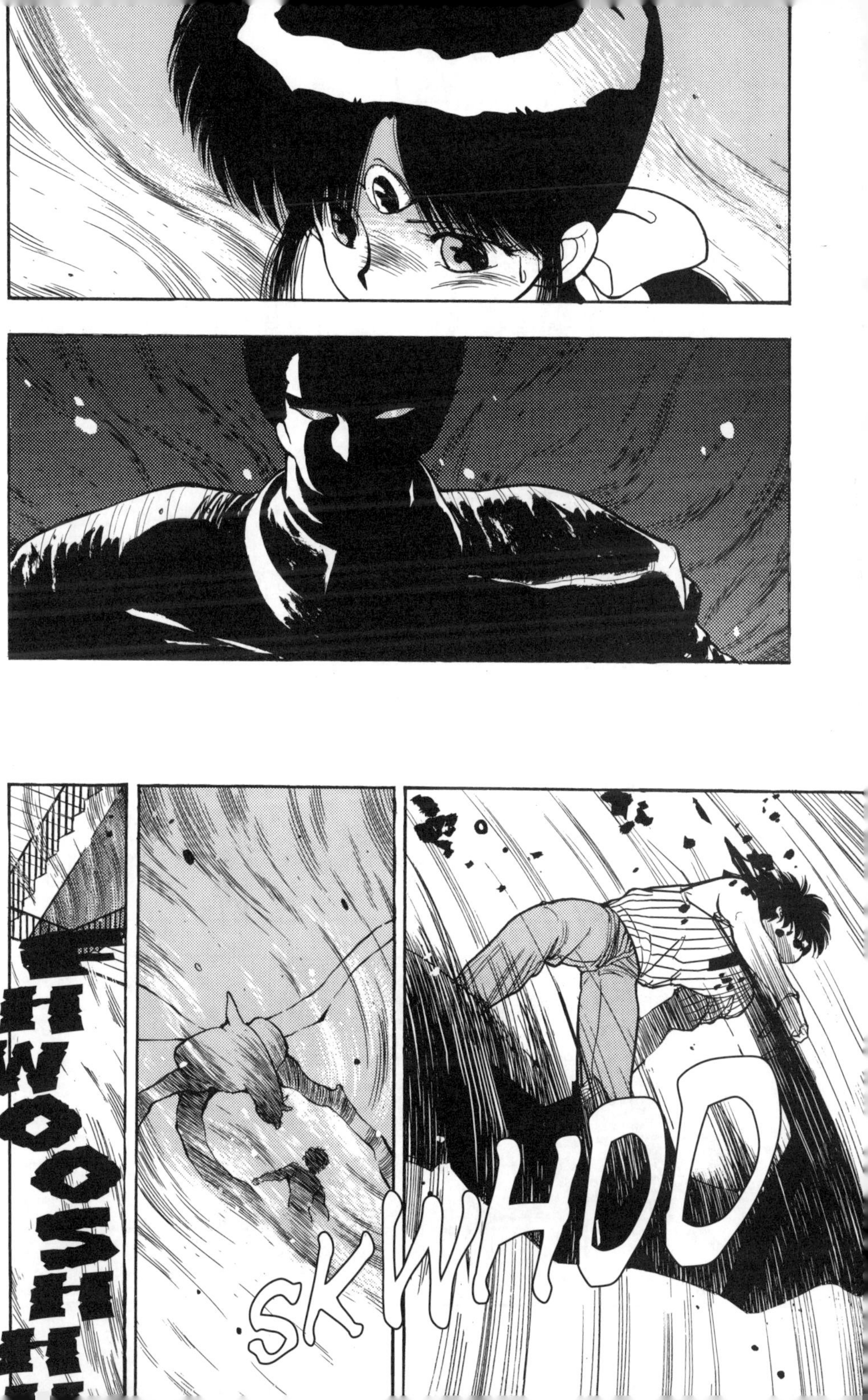
HWOOSHH
SKWHOO

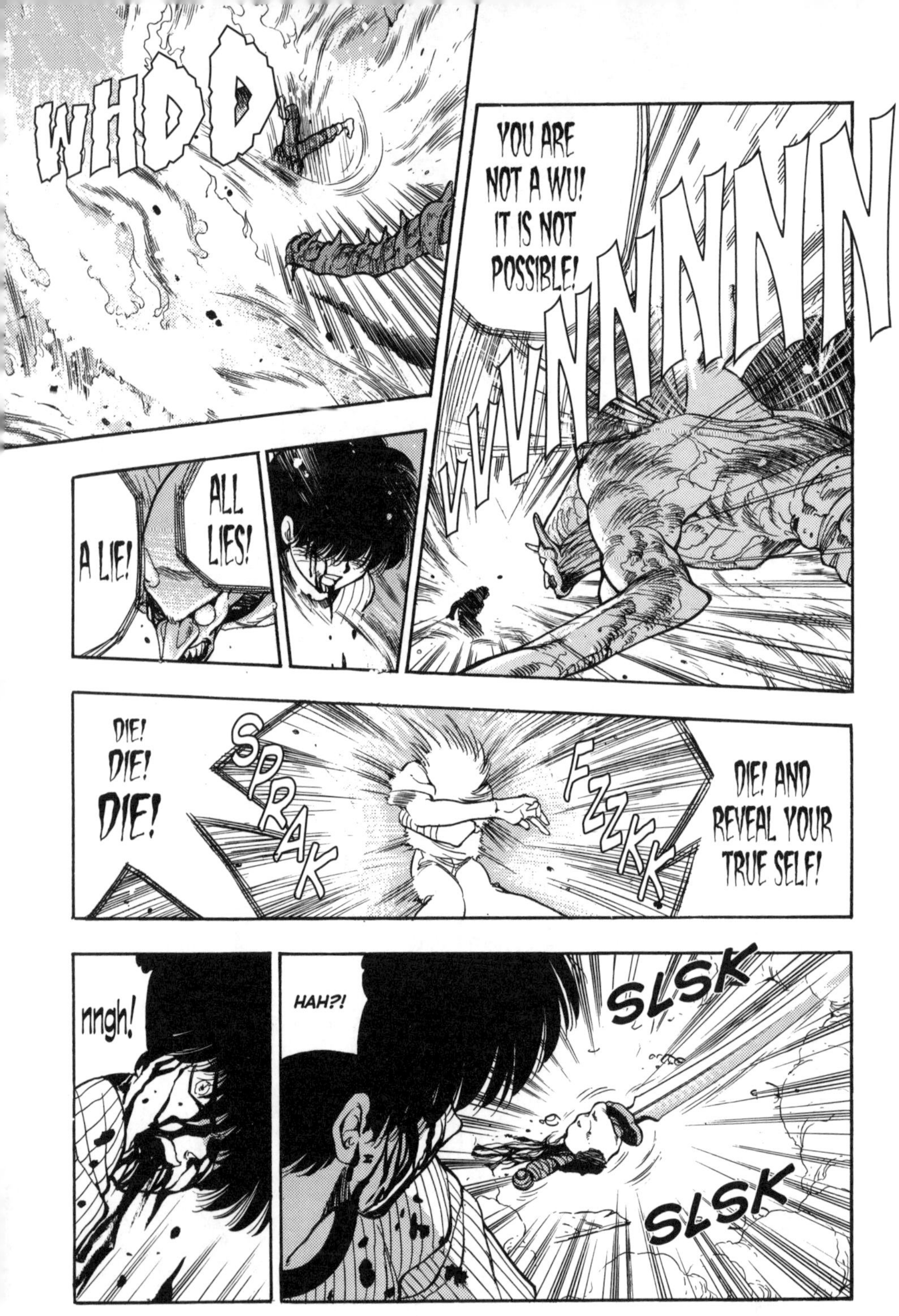
WHDD
YOU ARE NOT A WU! IT IS NOT POSSIBLE!
VVVVNNNNNNNNN
A LIE!
ALL LIES!
DIE! DIE! DIE!
SPRAK
FZZKKK
DIE! AND REVEAL YOUR TRUE SELF!
nngh!
HAH?!
SLSK
SLSK

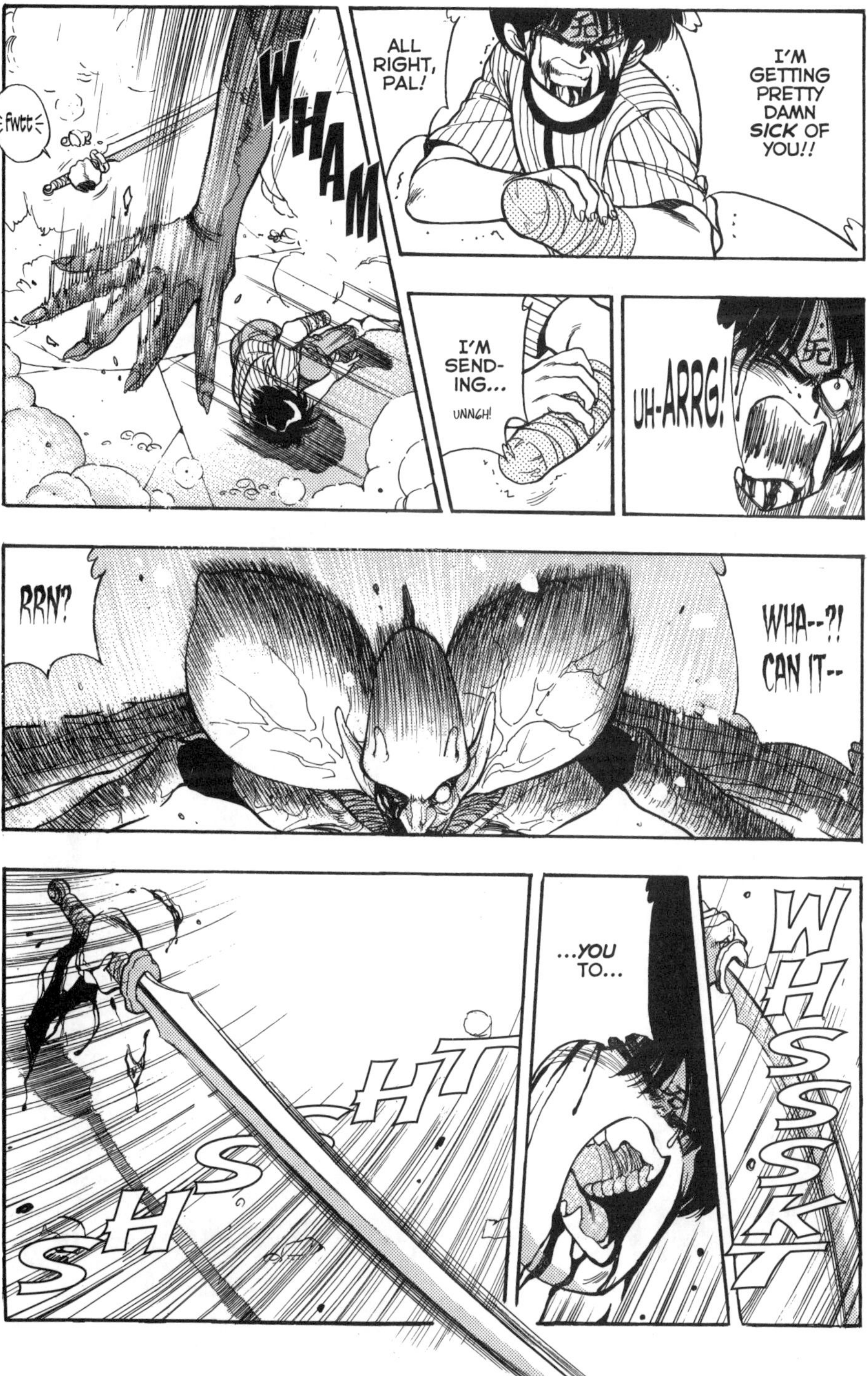
fwtt
WHAM
ALL RIGHT, PAL!
I'M GETTING PRETTY DAMN SICK OF YOU!!
I'M SEND-ING...
UNNGH!
UH-ARRG!
RRN?
WHA--?! CAN IT--
SHSS-HT
...YOU TO...
WHSSSKT

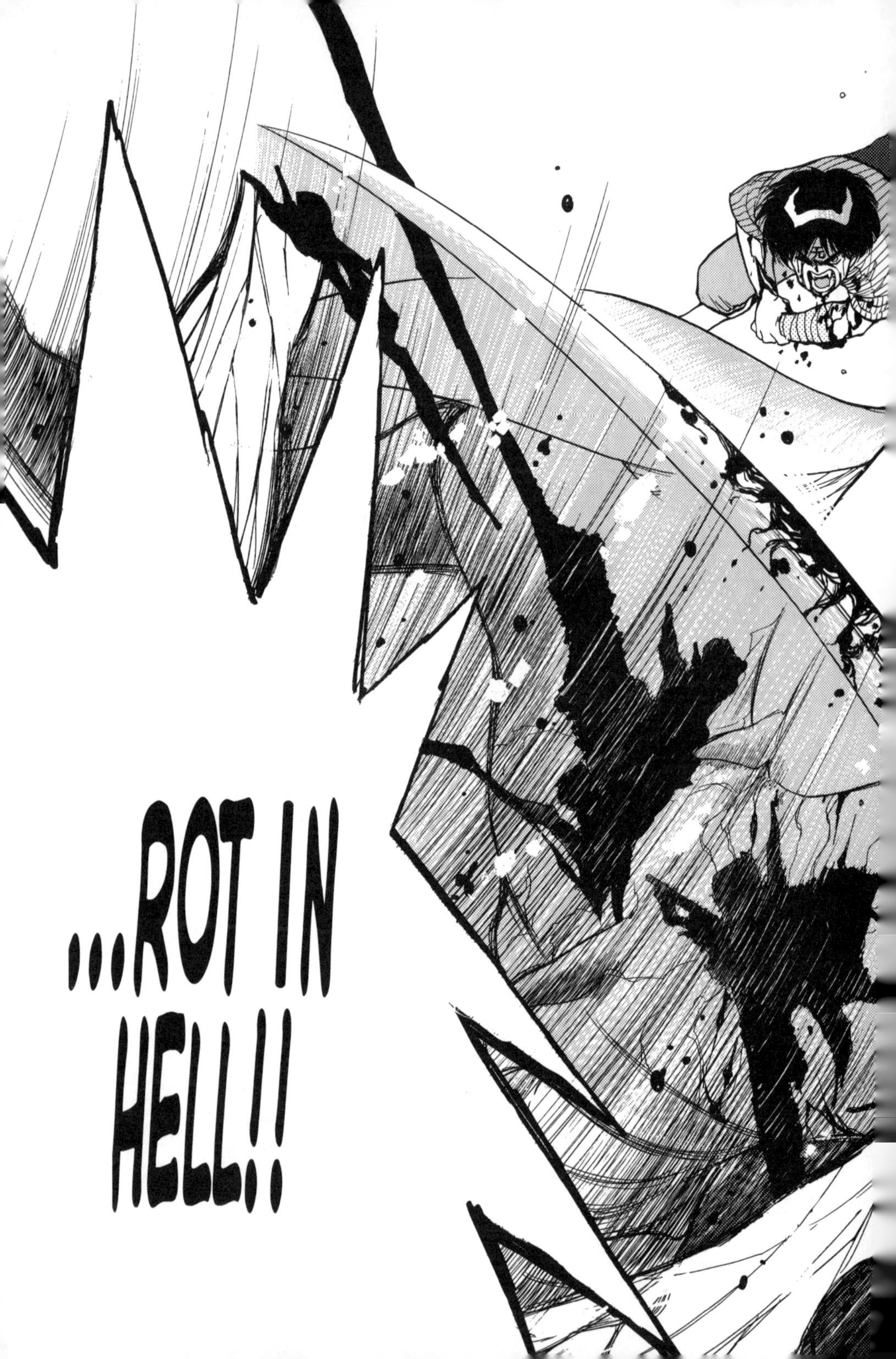
...ROT IN HELL!!

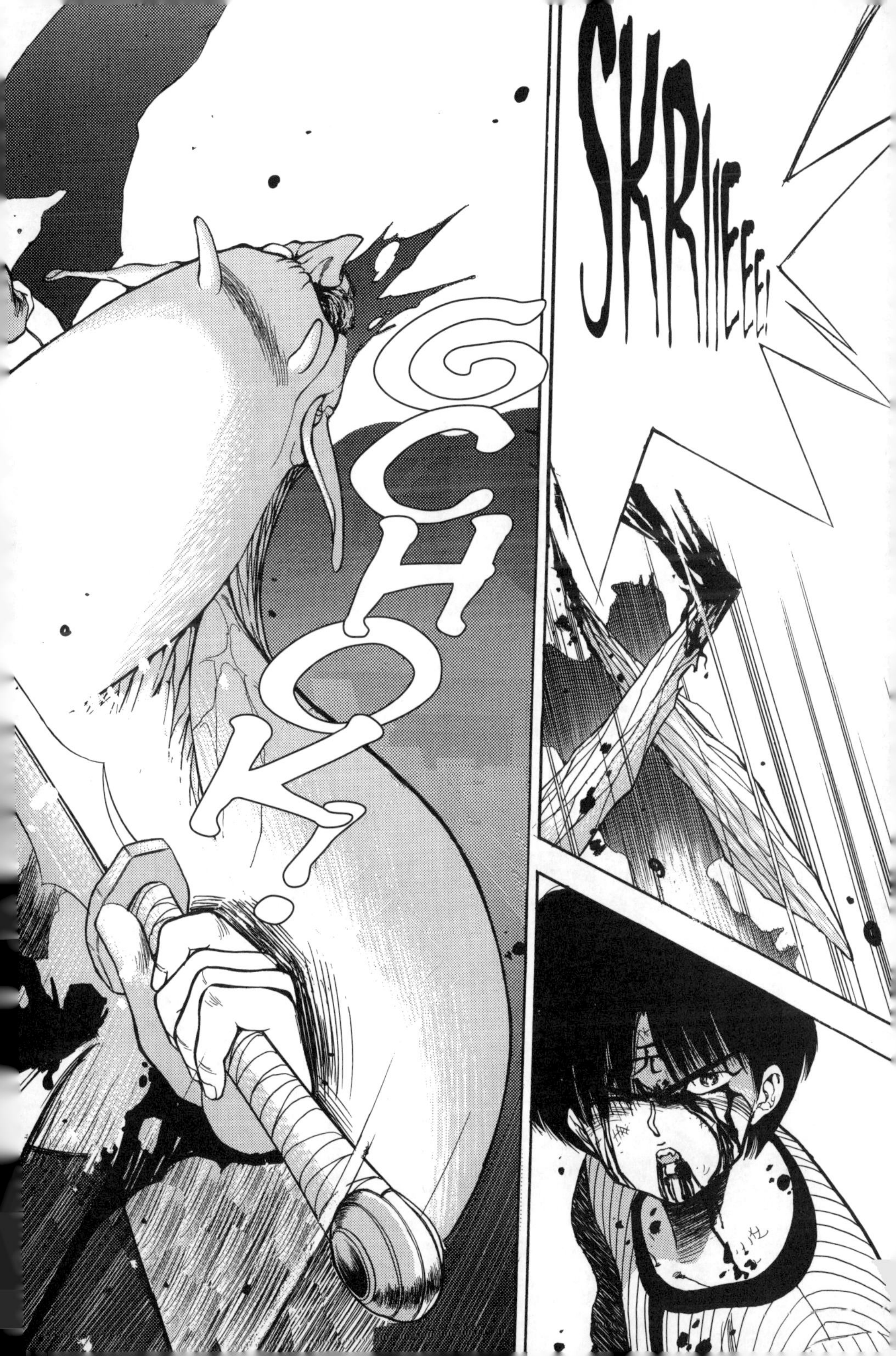
GCHOK!
SKRIIIEEE!

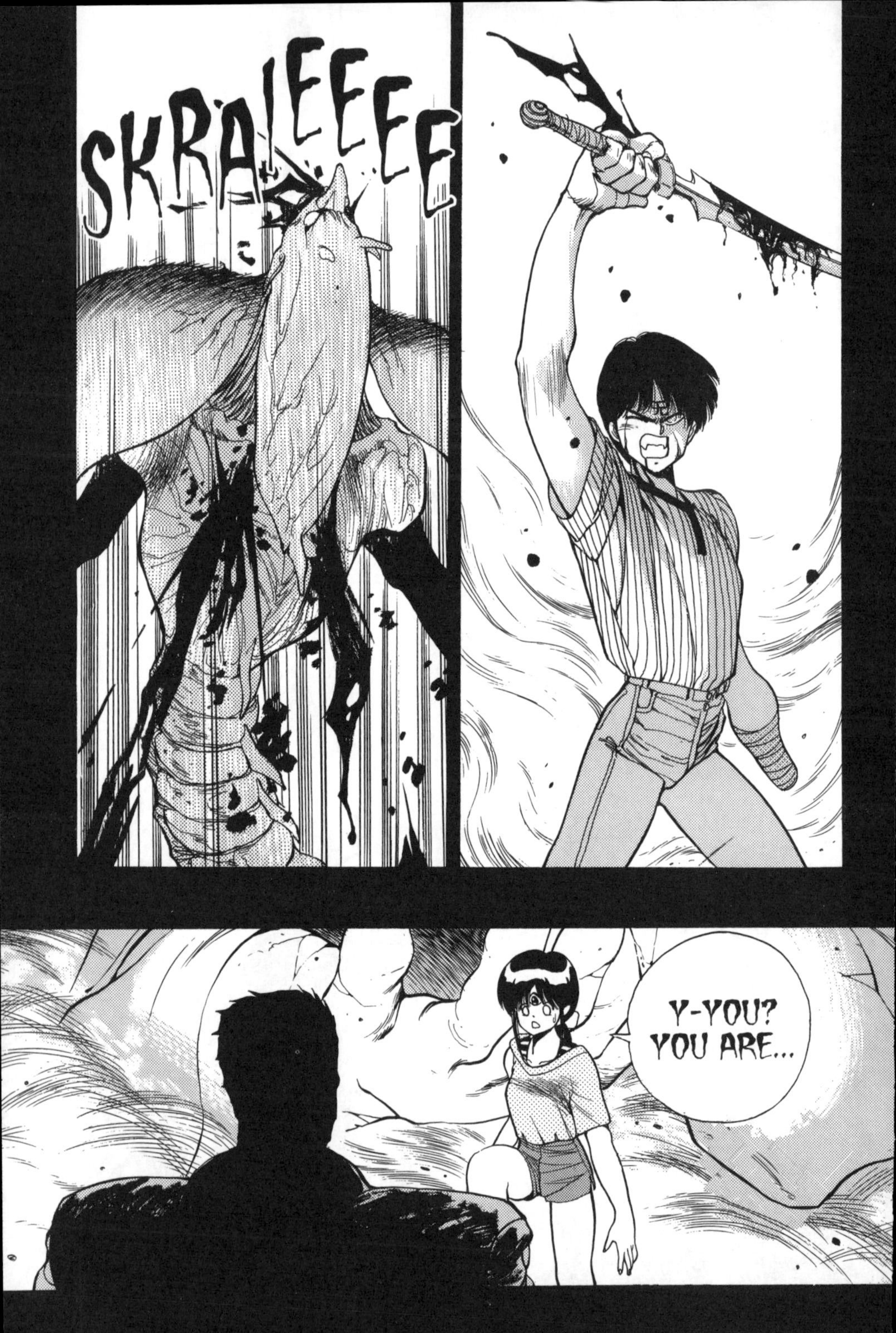
SKRAIEEEEE
Y-YOU? YOU ARE...

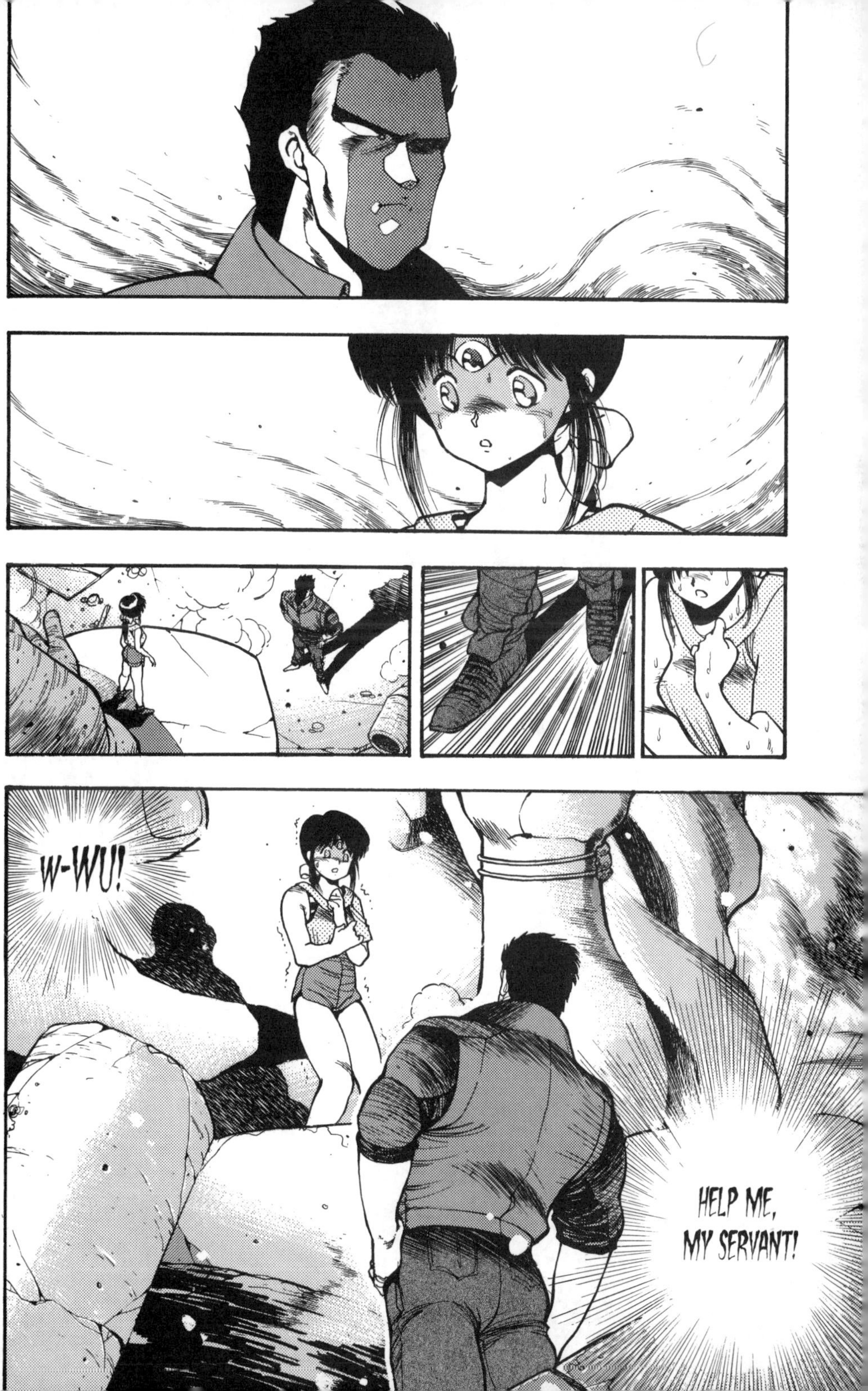
W-WU!
HELP ME,
MY SERVANT!

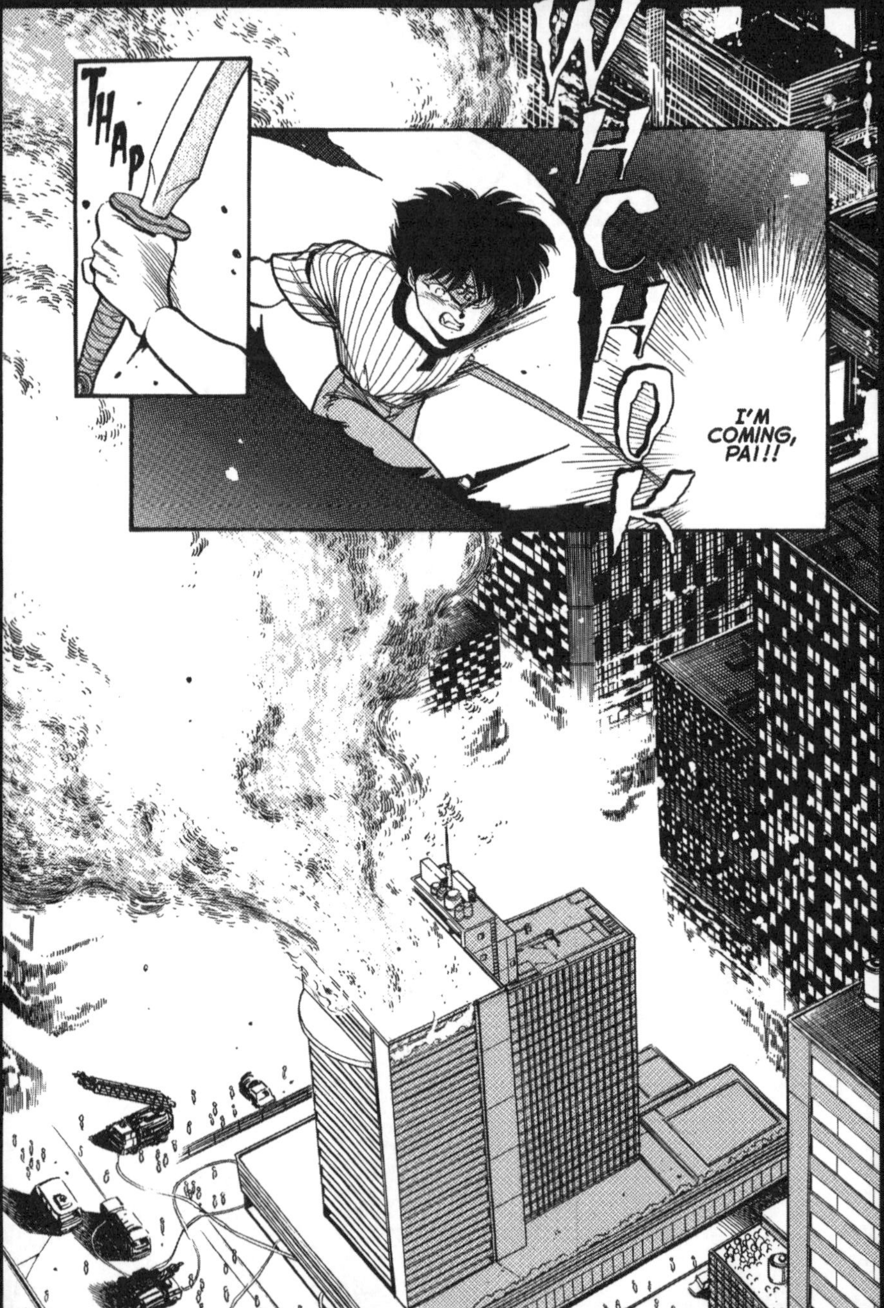
WHCHOK
I'M COMING, PAI!!
THAP

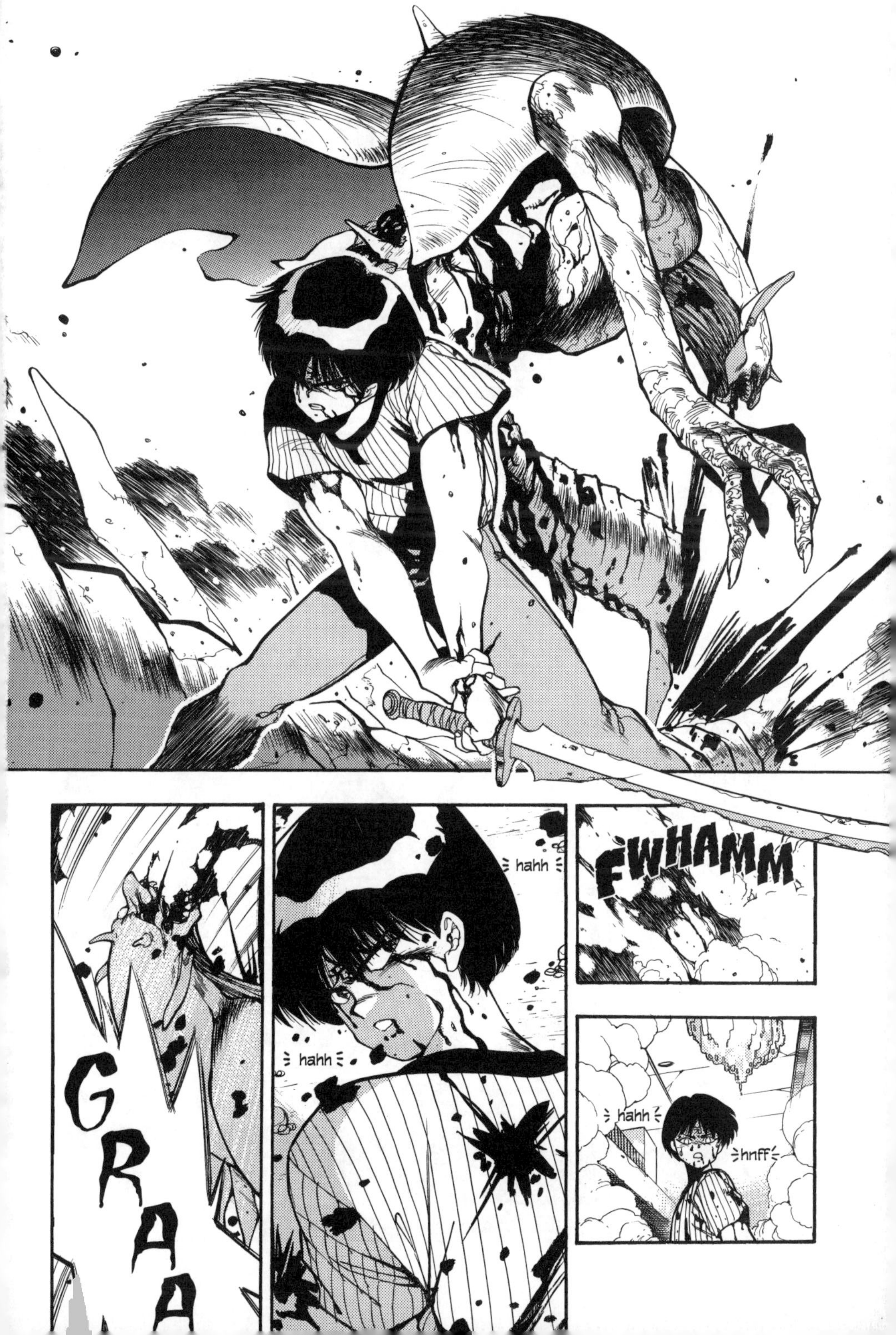
GRAA
hahh
hahh
FWHAMM
hahh
hnff

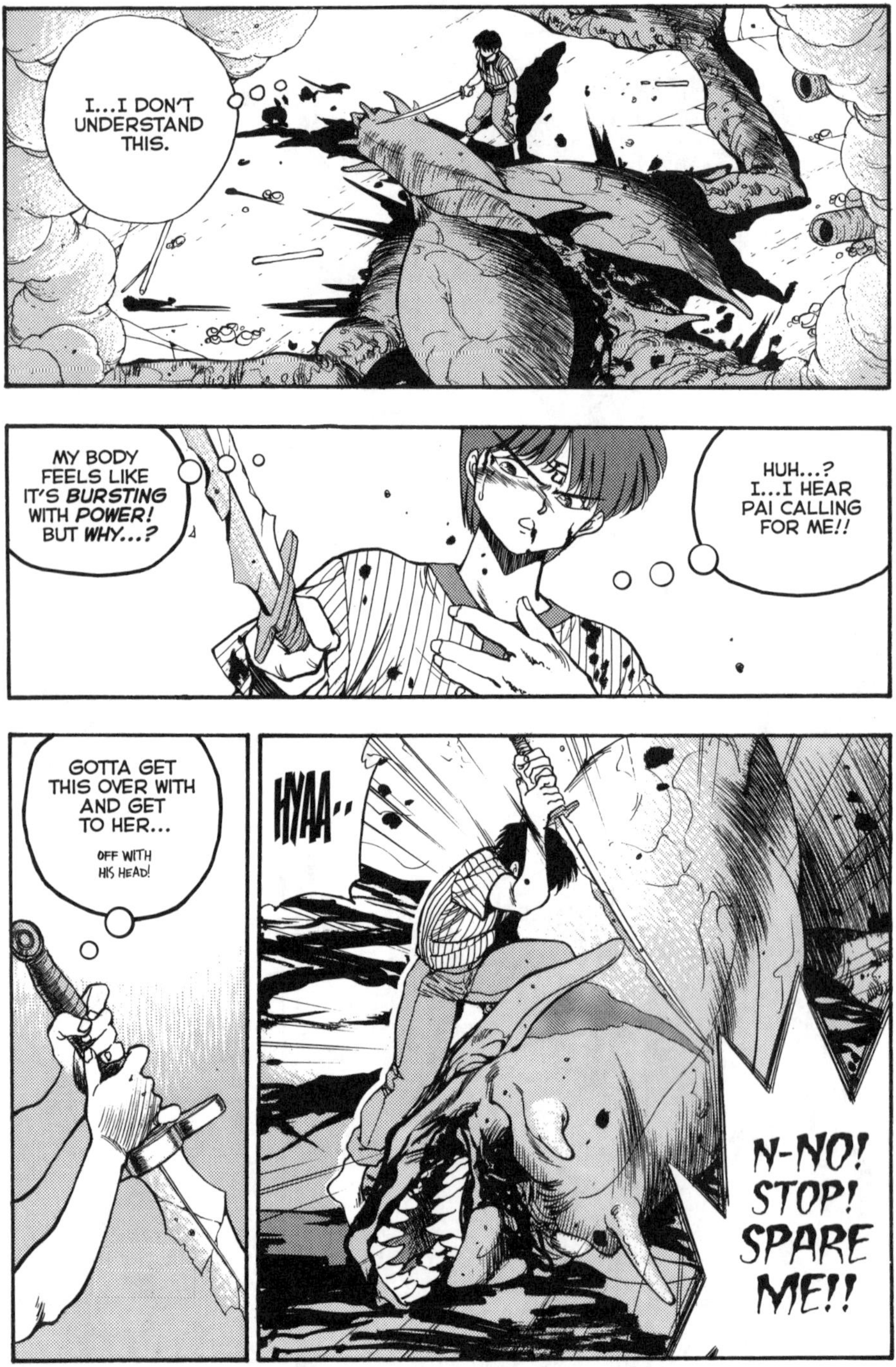
I...I DON'T UNDERSTAND THIS.
MY BODY FEELS LIKE IT'S BURSTING WITH POWER! BUT WHY...?
HUH...? I...I HEAR PAI CALLING FOR ME!!
GOTTA GET THIS OVER WITH AND GET TO HER...
OFF WITH HIS HEAD!
HYAA..
N-NO! STOP! SPARE ME!!

YOU GOTTA BE KIDDING-- BEGGING FOR FORGIVENESS AFTER SACRIFICING ALL THOSE GIRLS?!

I WAS ORDERED TO DO SO BY OUR MASTER.

IT WAS NOT SOMETHING I CHOSE TO DO.

I...

I HAD NO CHOICE.

OUR MASTER IS SEARCHING FOR THE MEANS TO REVIVE THE LORD KAIYAN WANG.

AND SO, HE IS ORDERING ALL DWELLERS OF THE DARK TO TRY OUT VARIOUS POSSIBLE RITUALS.

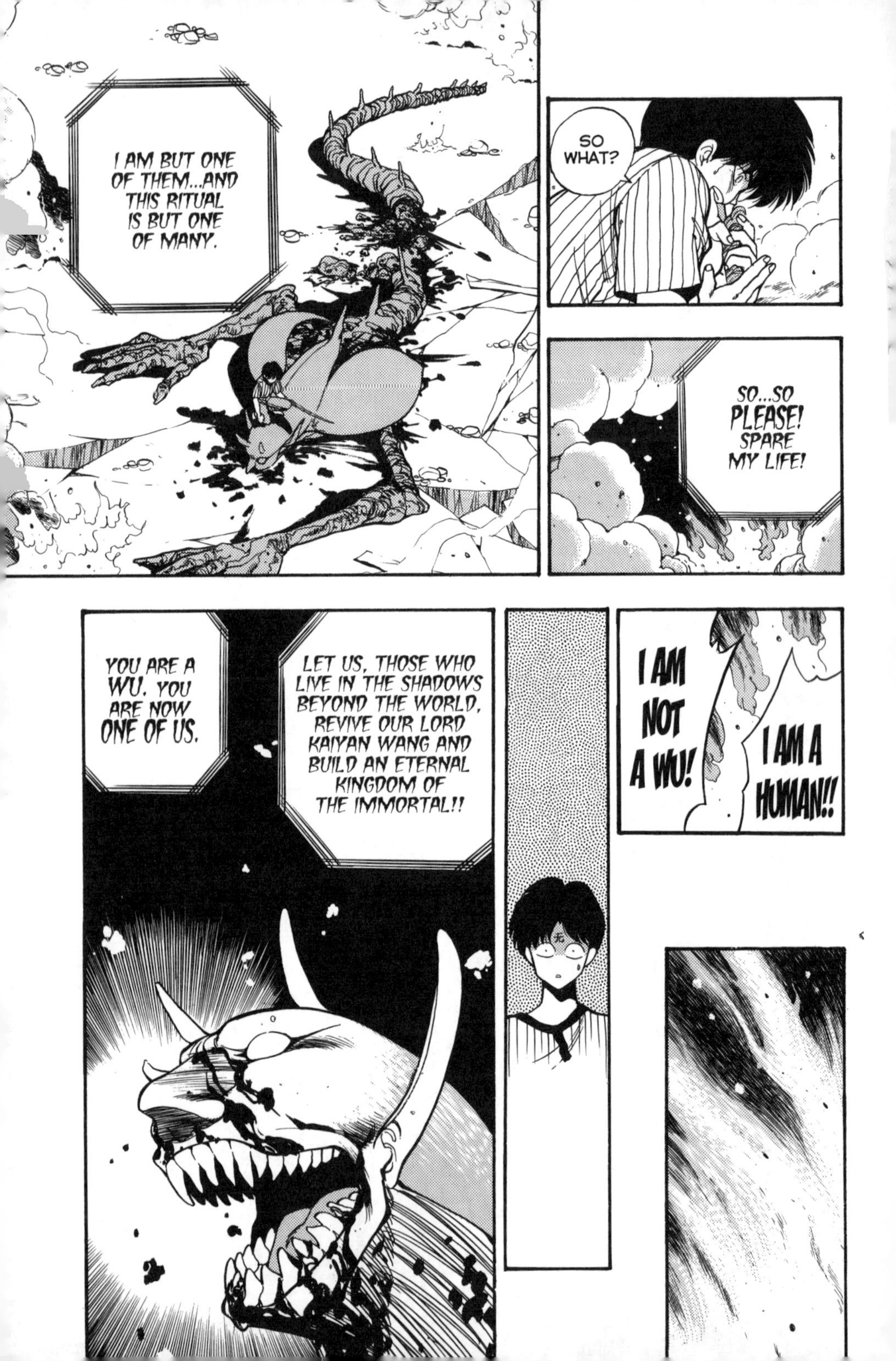
I AM BUT ONE OF THEM...AND THIS RITUAL IS BUT ONE OF MANY.
SO WHAT?
SO...SO PLEASE! SPARE MY LIFE!
YOU ARE A WU. YOU ARE NOW ONE OF US.
LET US, THOSE WHO LIVE IN THE SHADOWS BEYOND THE WORLD, REVIVE OUR LORD KAIYAN WANG AND BUILD AN ETERNAL KINGDOM OF THE IMMORTAL!!
I AM NOT A WU!
I AM A HUMAN!!

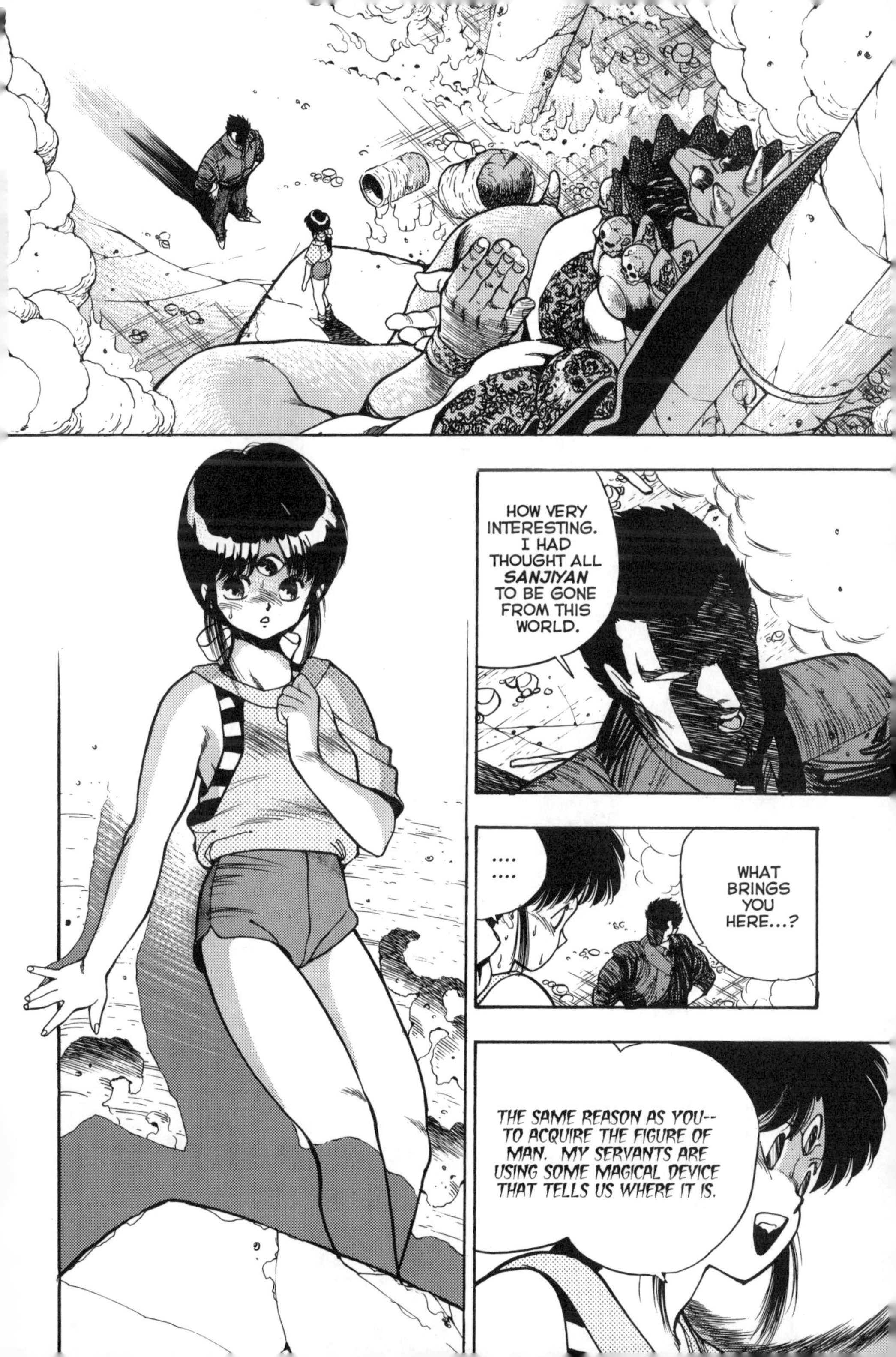
HOW VERY INTERESTING. I HAD THOUGHT ALL SANJIYAN TO BE GONE FROM THIS WORLD.
....
....
WHAT BRINGS YOU HERE...?
THE SAME REASON AS YOU-- TO ACQUIRE THE FIGURE OF MAN. MY SERVANTS ARE USING SOME MAGICAL DEVICE THAT TELLS US WHERE IT IS.

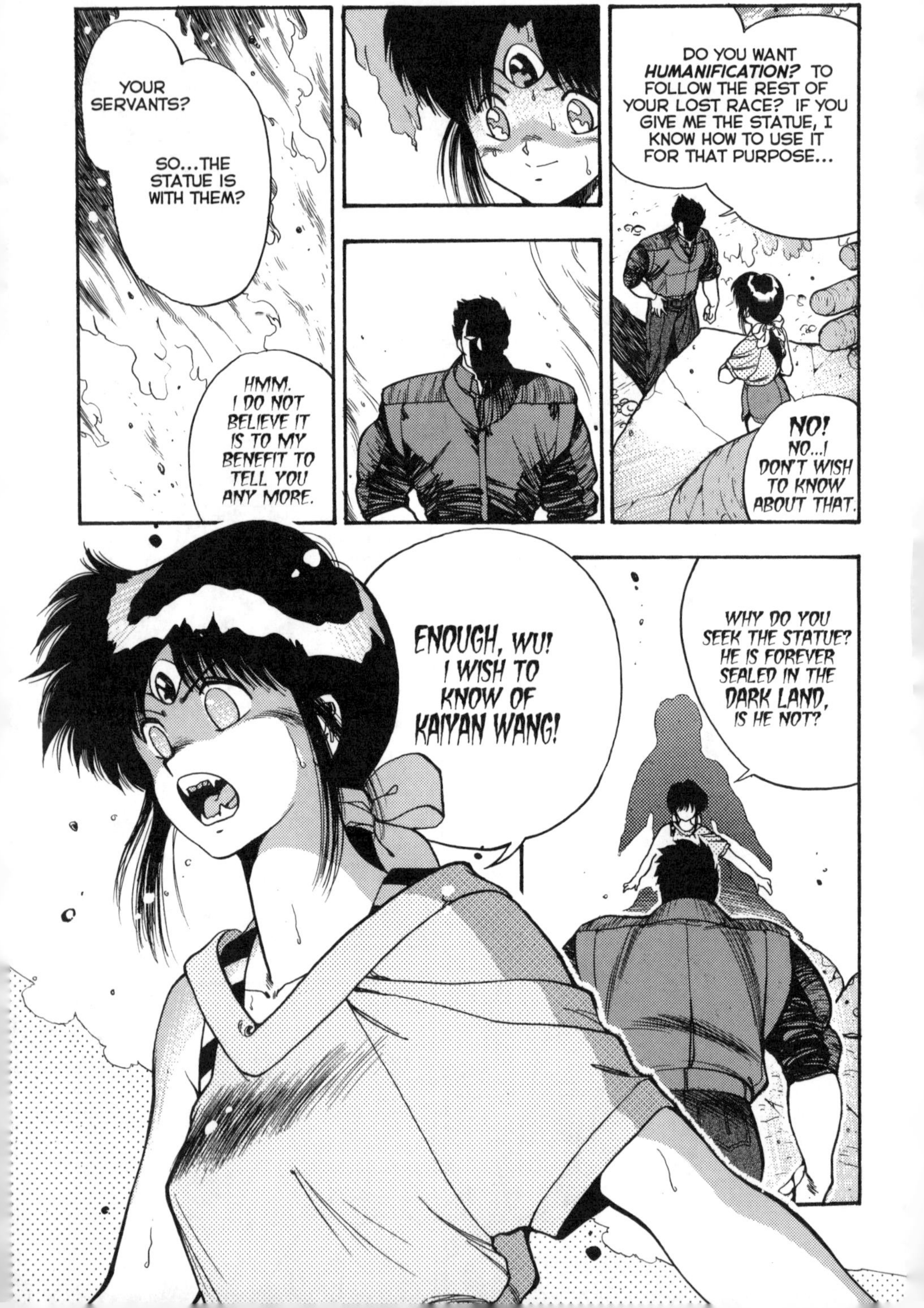
YOUR SERVANTS?
SO...THE STATUE IS WITH THEM?
HMM. I DO NOT BELIEVE IT IS TO MY BENEFIT TO TELL YOU ANY MORE.
DO YOU WANT HUMANIFICATION? TO FOLLOW THE REST OF YOUR LOST RACE? IF YOU GIVE ME THE STATUE, I KNOW HOW TO USE IT FOR THAT PURPOSE...
NO! NO...I DON'T WISH TO KNOW ABOUT THAT.
ENOUGH, WU! I WISH TO KNOW OF KAIYAN WANG!
WHY DO YOU SEEK THE STATUE? HE IS FOREVER SEALED IN THE DARK LAND, IS HE NOT?

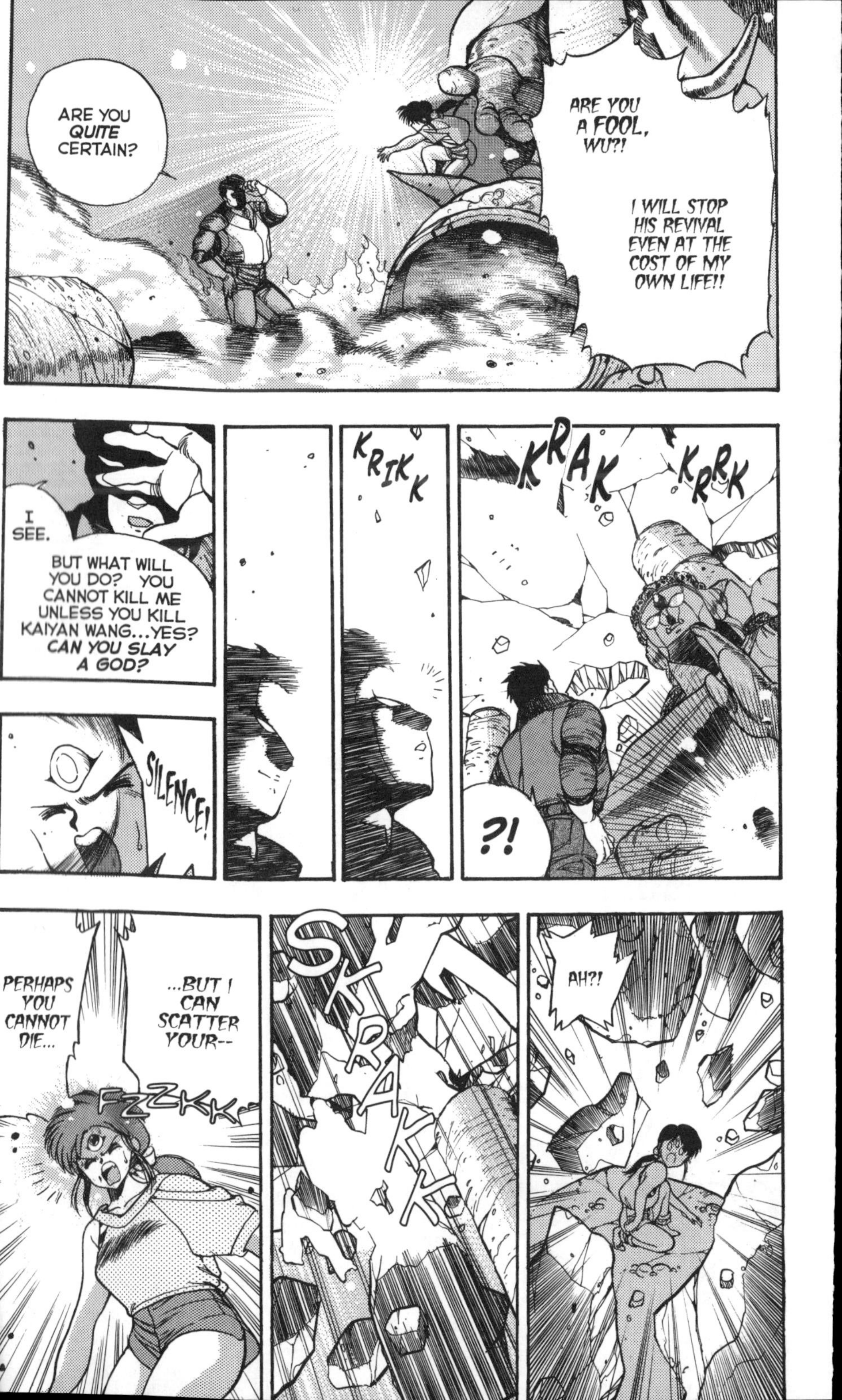
ARE YOU QUITE CERTAIN?
ARE YOU A FOOL, WU?!
I WILL STOP HIS REVIVAL EVEN AT THE COST OF MY OWN LIFE!!
I SEE.
BUT WHAT WILL YOU DO? YOU CANNOT KILL ME UNLESS YOU KILL KAIYAN WANG...YES? CAN YOU SLAY A GOD?
SILENCE!
KRIKK
KRAK
KRRK
?!
PERHAPS YOU CANNOT DIE...
...BUT I CAN SCATTER YOUR--
FZZKK
SKRAKK
AH?!

THE SEAL HAS WEAKENED WITH THE PASSING OF THE AGES.

THE REVIVAL OF MY LORD KAIYAN WANG IS NOW ONLY A MATTER OF TIME.

AH!

SO THAT IS WHY YOU WANT THE STATUE!!

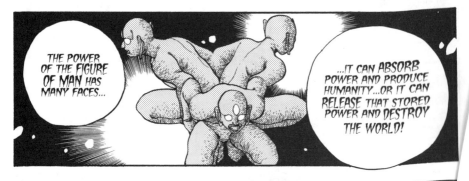

THE POWER OF THE FIGURE OF MAN HAS MANY FACES...

...IT CAN ABSORB POWER AND PRODUCE HUMANITY...OR IT CAN RELEASE THAT STORED POWER AND DESTROY THE WORLD!

HOWEVER, I WISH TO LIVE IN THIS WORLD!

I AM NOT ABOUT TO LET KAIYAN WANG USE THE COLLECTIVE POWER OF MY ENTIRE RACE TO DESTROY IT!!

YOU SHALL NOT HAVE THE STATUE!!

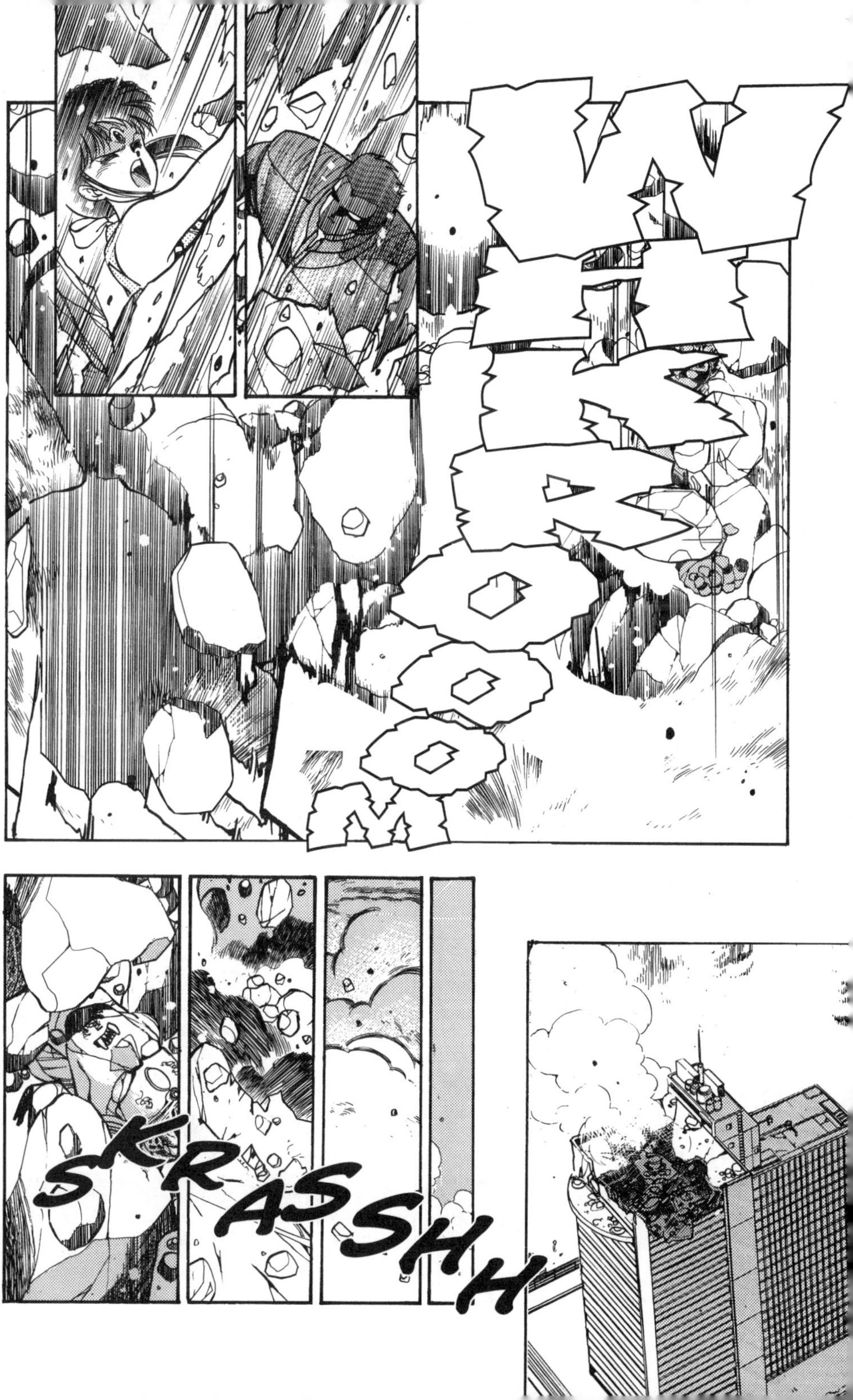
WHKBOOOM
SKRASSHH

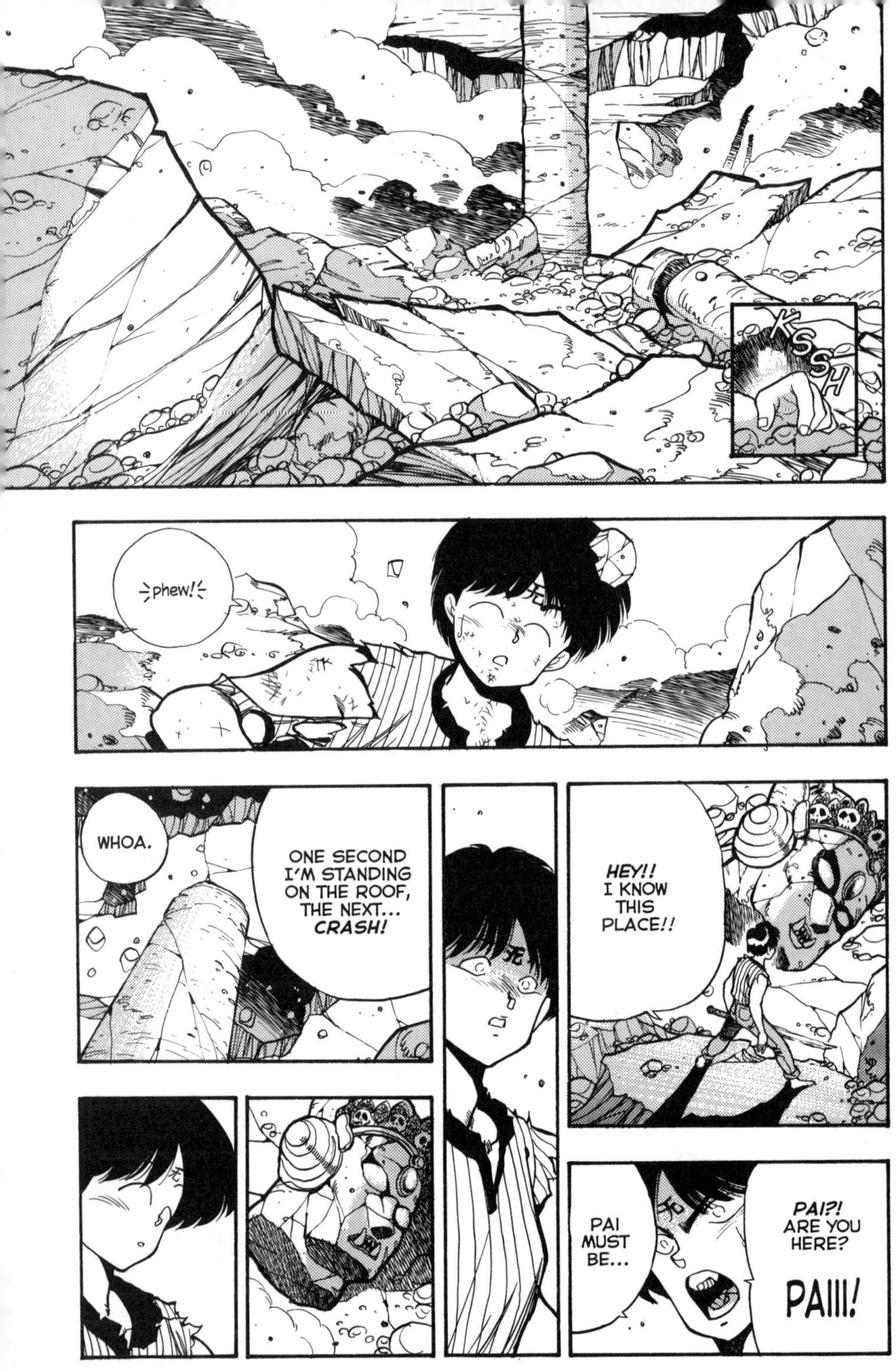
KSSH
phew!
WHOA.
ONE SECOND I'M STANDING ON THE ROOF, THE NEXT... CRASH!
HEY!! I KNOW THIS PLACE!!
PAI MUST BE...
PAI?! ARE YOU HERE?
PAIII!

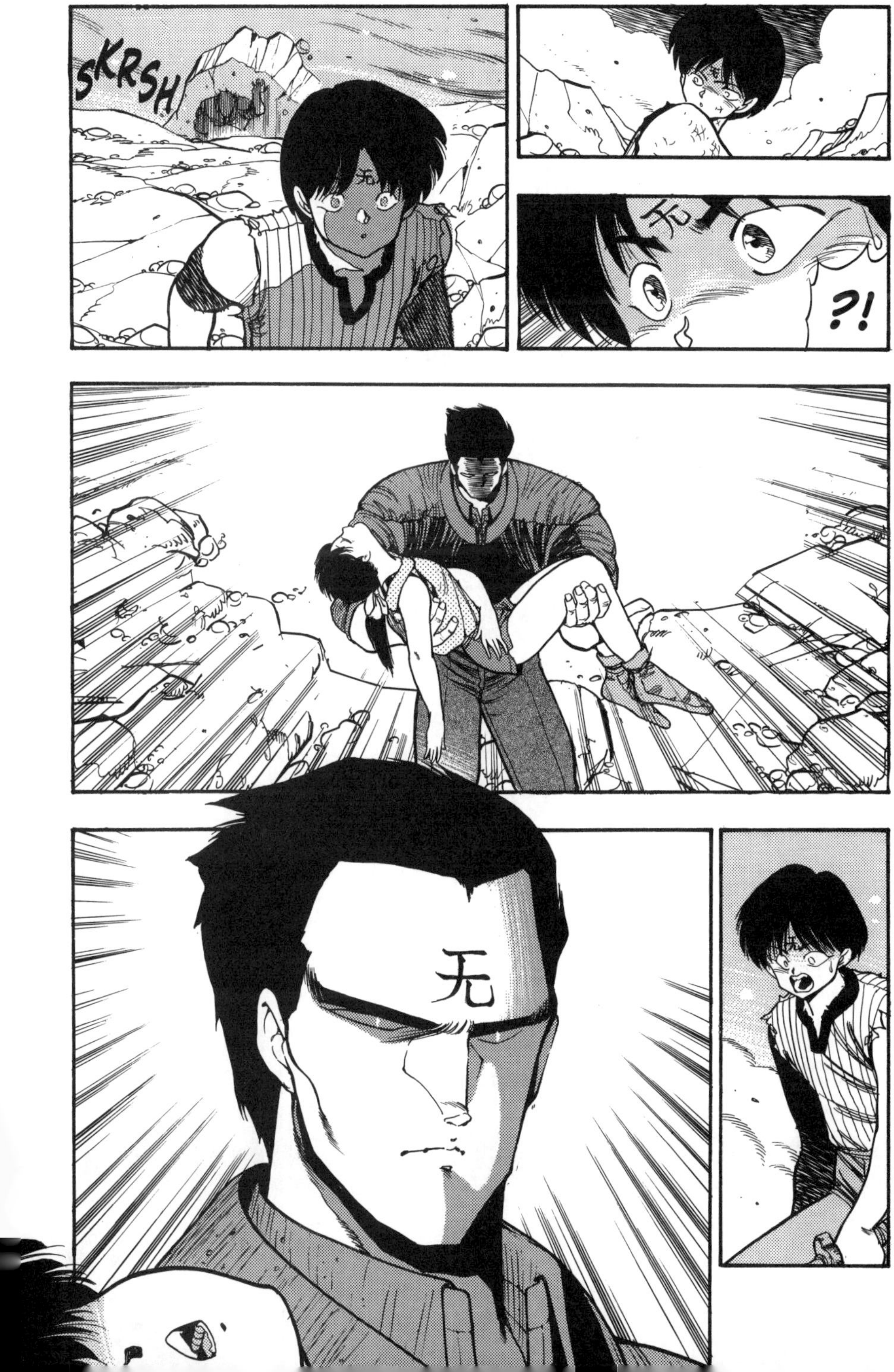
SKRSH
?!
无

H-HEY.
YOU'RE
A--

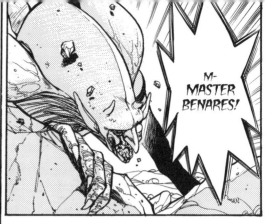

M-MASTER
BENARES!

!!

YES
...?

WHOA...
SO THIS
GUY
IS THE
BOSS
OF THESE
MONSTERS?!

AND NOT
ONLY THAT...
HE MUST BE
KAIYAN
WANG'S
WU?!

HYUH HUR HUR...
I GIVE
YOU A GIFT,
MASTER!
LOOK!
ANOTHER WU!!

A FOOL
WITHOUT
THE WIT
TO
FINISH
OFF
HIS
ENEMY!

THE
ONLY
FOOL
HERE...

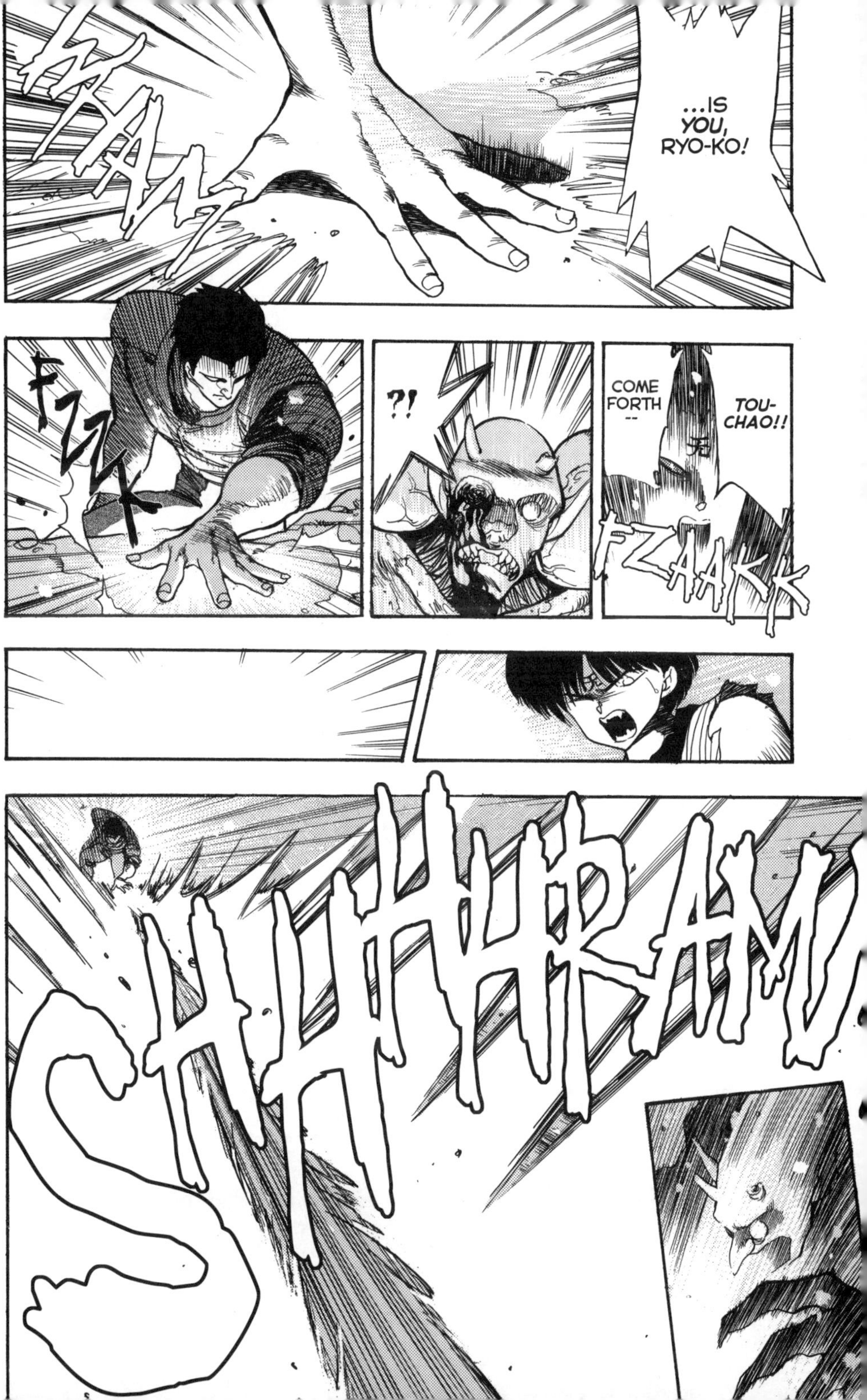
WHAM
...IS YOU, RYO-KO!
FZZZK
?!
COME FORTH --
TOU-CHAO!!
FZAAKK
SHHHRAM

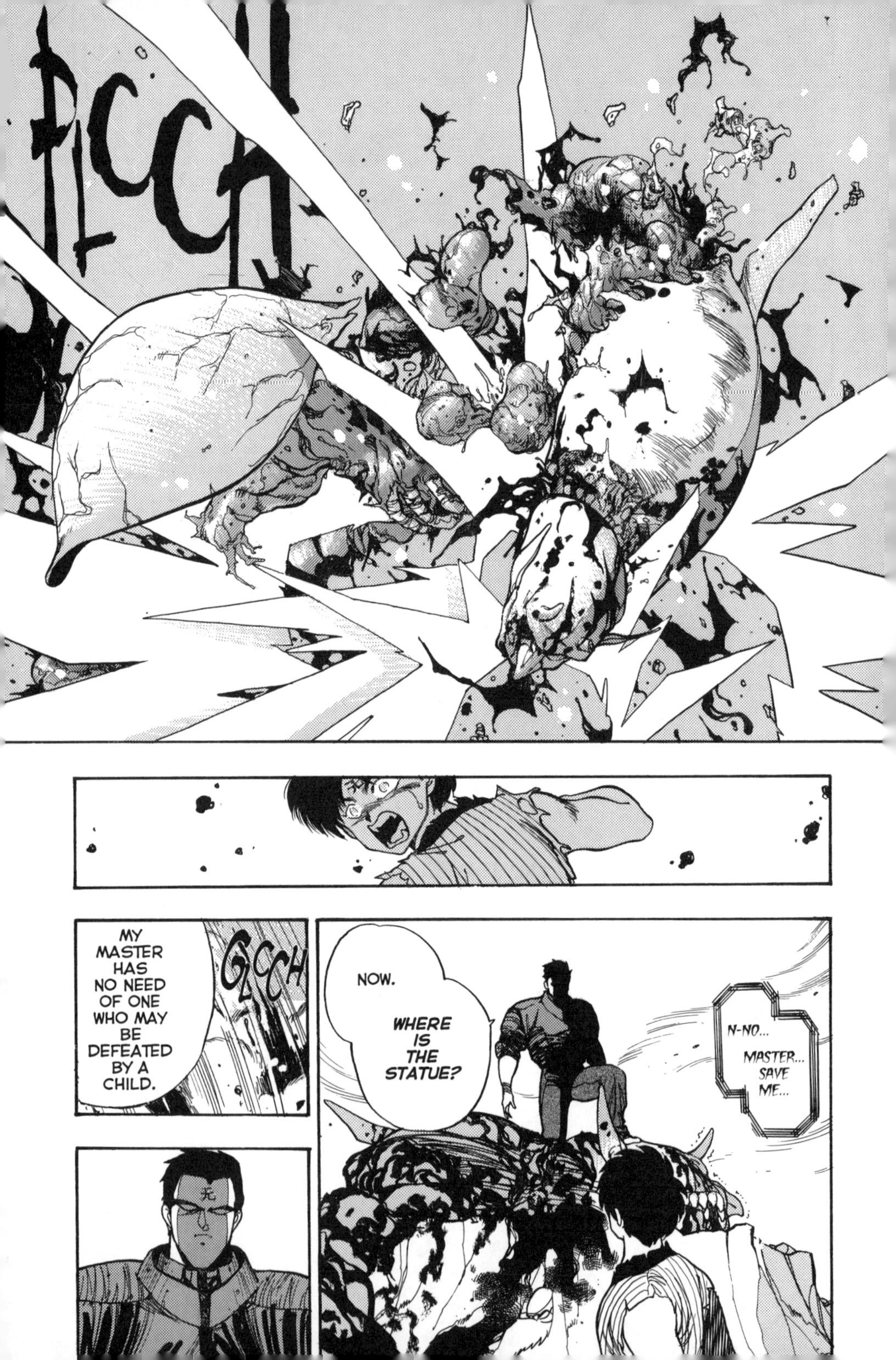
SPLCCH
MY MASTER HAS NO NEED OF ONE WHO MAY BE DEFEATED BY A CHILD.
GZCCH
NOW.
WHERE IS THE STATUE?
N-NO... MASTER... SAVE ME...

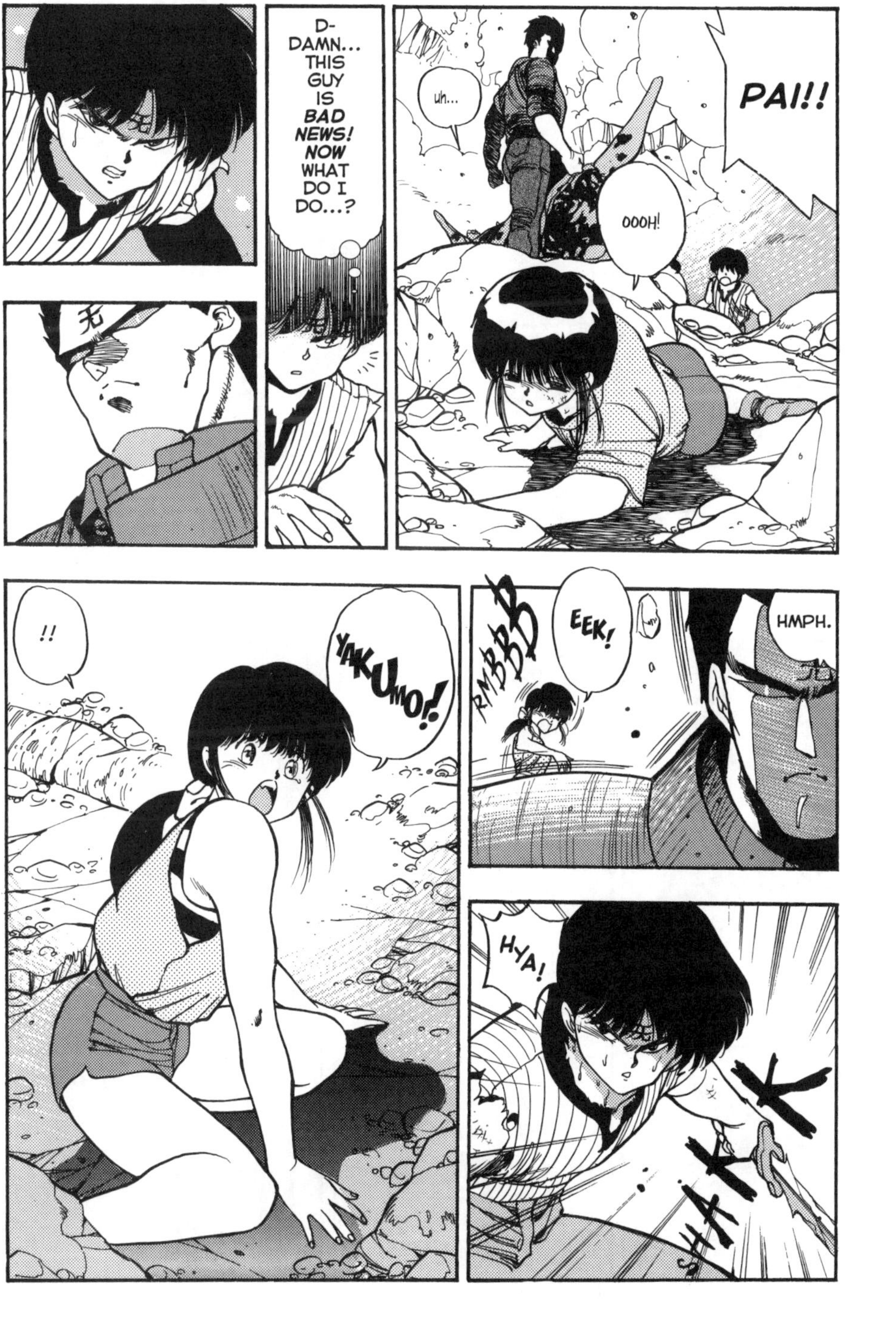
D-DAMN... THIS GUY IS BAD NEWS! NOW WHAT DO I DO...?
uh...
OOOH!
PAI!!
!!
YAKUMO!!
RMBBBB
EEK!
HMPH.
HYA!
HAKK

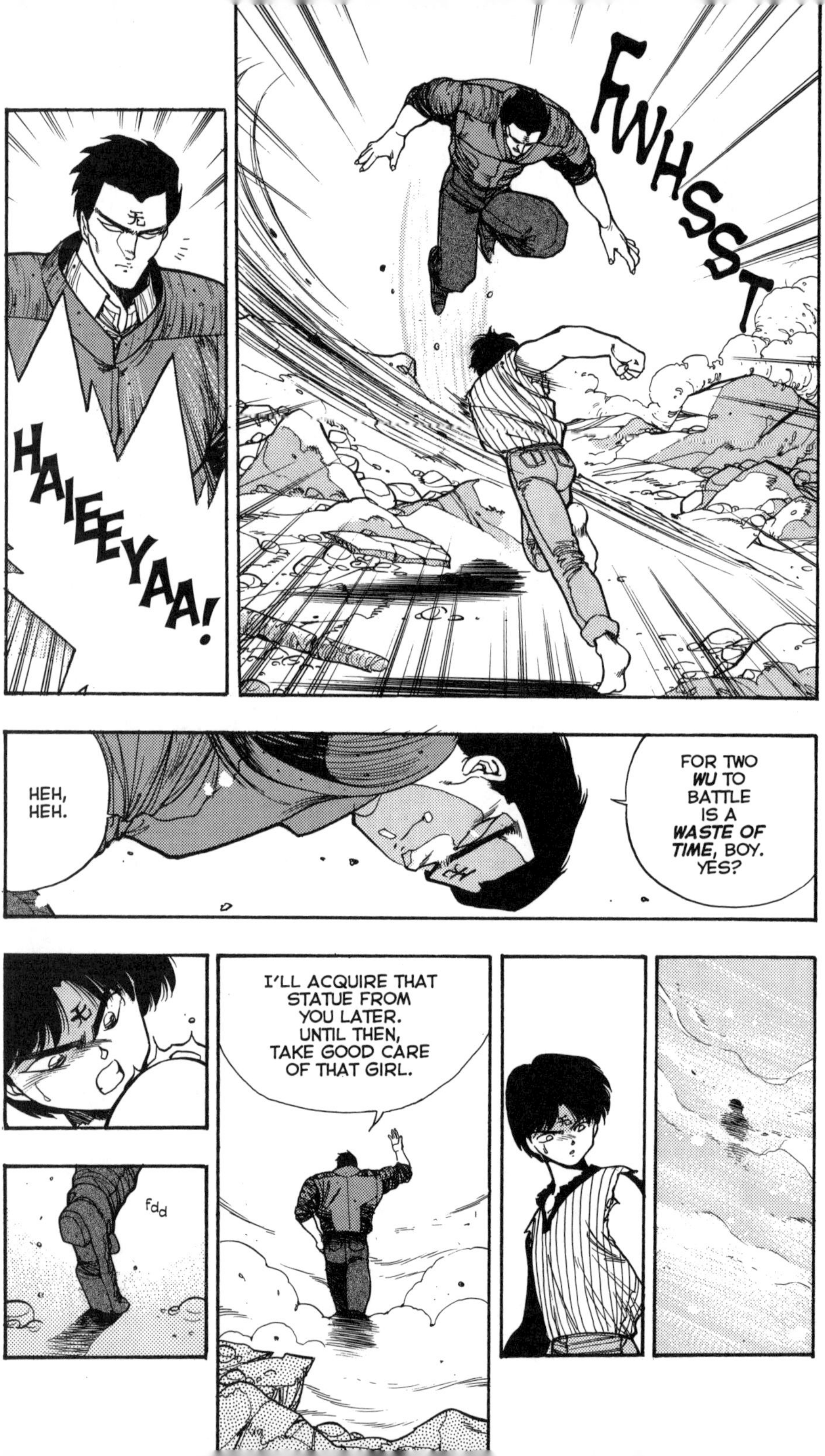
HAIEEEYAA!
FWHSSST
HEH, HEH.
FOR TWO WU TO BATTLE IS A WASTE OF TIME, BOY. YES?
I'LL ACQUIRE THAT STATUE FROM YOU LATER. UNTIL THEN, TAKE GOOD CARE OF THAT GIRL.
fdd

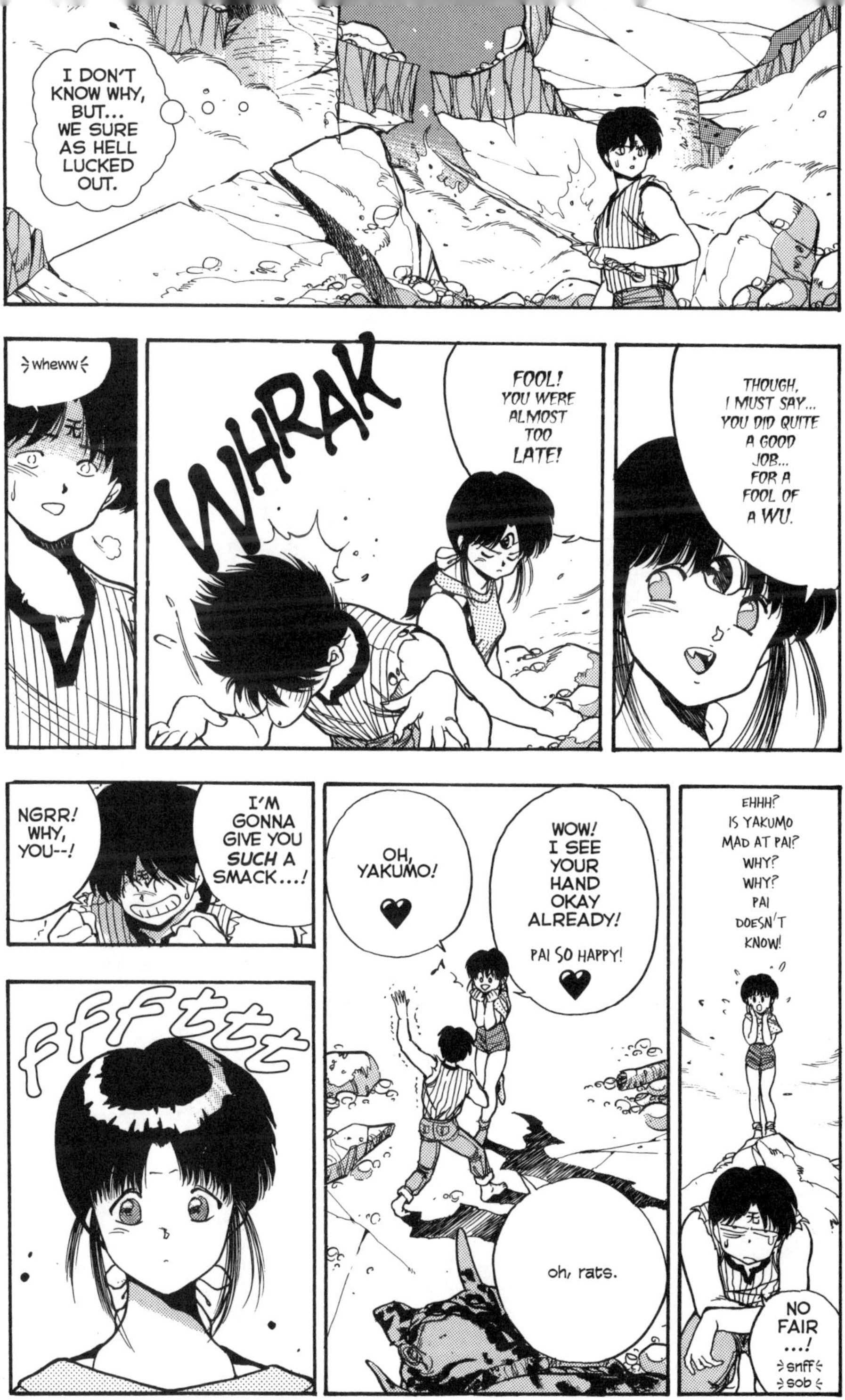
I DON'T KNOW WHY, BUT... WE SURE AS HELL LUCKED OUT.
wheww
WHRAK
FOOL! YOU WERE ALMOST TOO LATE!
THOUGH, I MUST SAY... YOU DID QUITE A GOOD JOB... FOR A FOOL OF A WU.
NGRR! WHY, YOU--!
I'M GONNA GIVE YOU SUCH A SMACK...!
ffftttt
OH, YAKUMO!
WOW! I SEE YOUR HAND OKAY ALREADY!
PAI SO HAPPY!
oh, rats.
EHHH? IS YAKUMO MAD AT PAI? WHY? WHY? PAI DOESN'T KNOW!
NO FAIR ...!
snff
sob

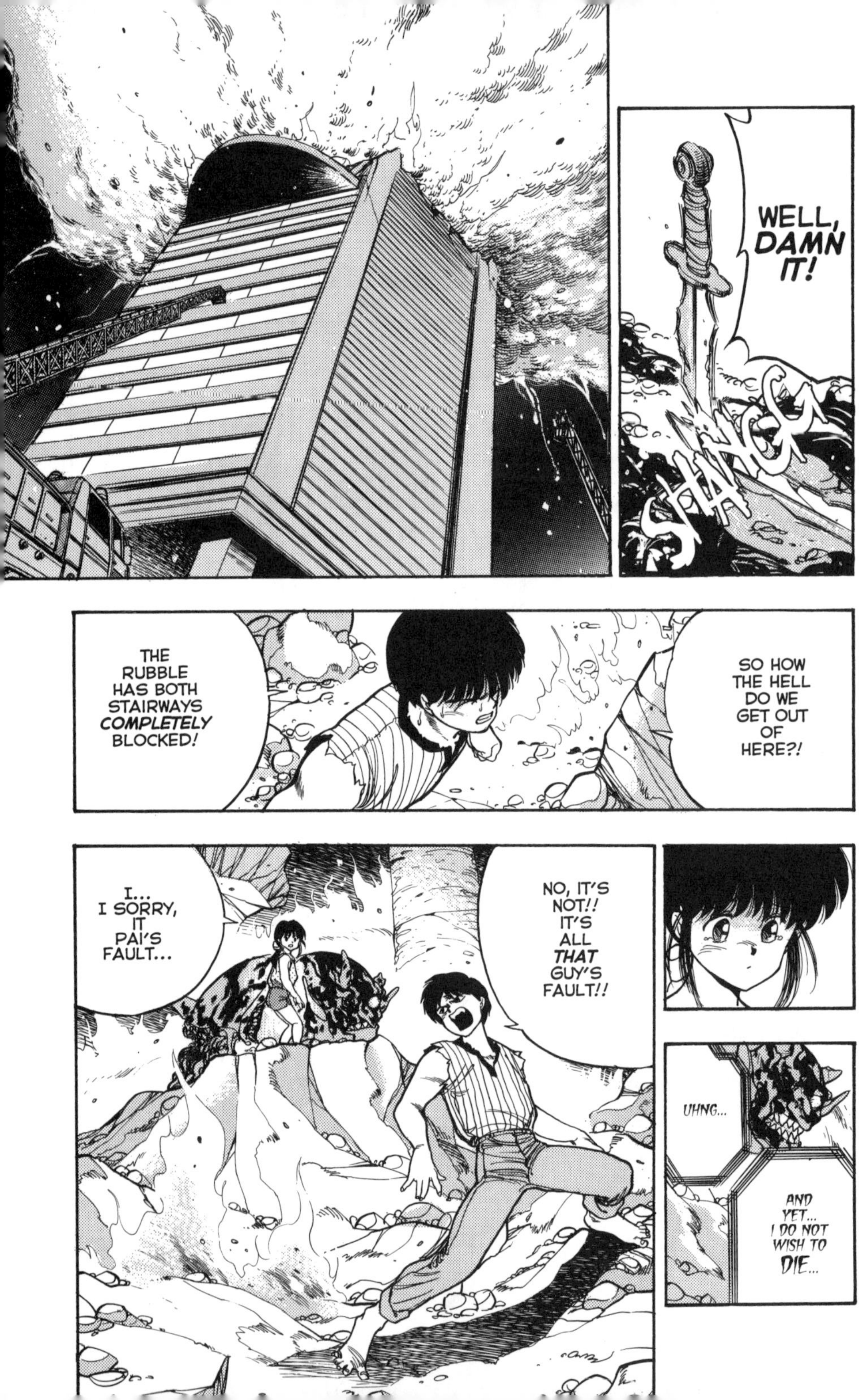
WELL, DAMN IT!
SHAKO
THE RUBBLE HAS BOTH STAIRWAYS COMPLETELY BLOCKED!
SO HOW THE HELL DO WE GET OUT OF HERE?!
I... I SORRY, IT PAI'S FAULT...
NO, IT'S NOT!! IT'S ALL THAT GUY'S FAULT!!
UHNG...
AND YET... I DO NOT WISH TO DIE...

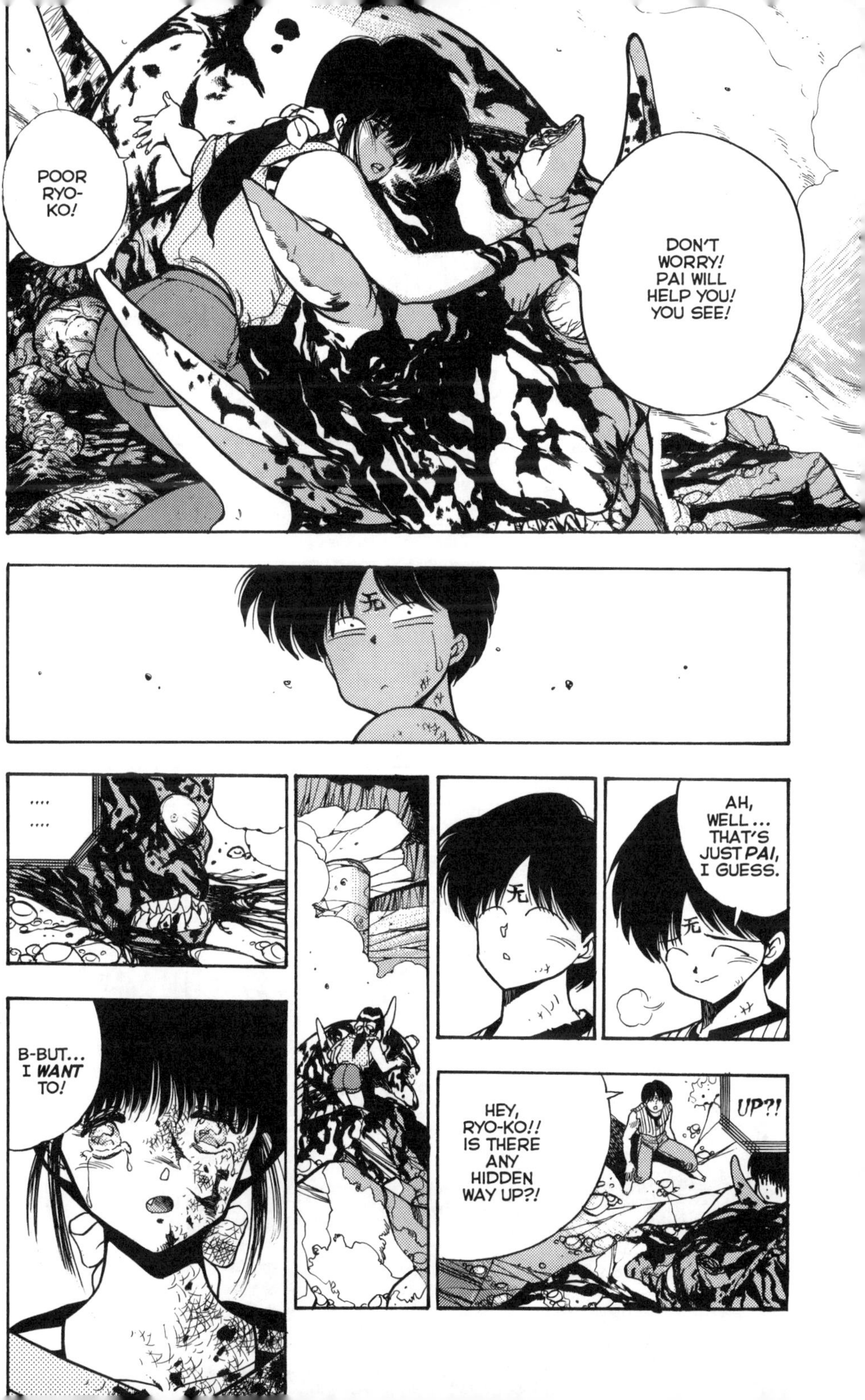

POOR RYO-KO!
DON'T WORRY! PAI WILL HELP YOU! YOU SEE!
....
B-BUT... I *WANT* TO!
AH, WELL... THAT'S JUST *PAI*, I GUESS.
HEY, RYO-KO!! IS THERE ANY HIDDEN WAY UP?!
UP?!

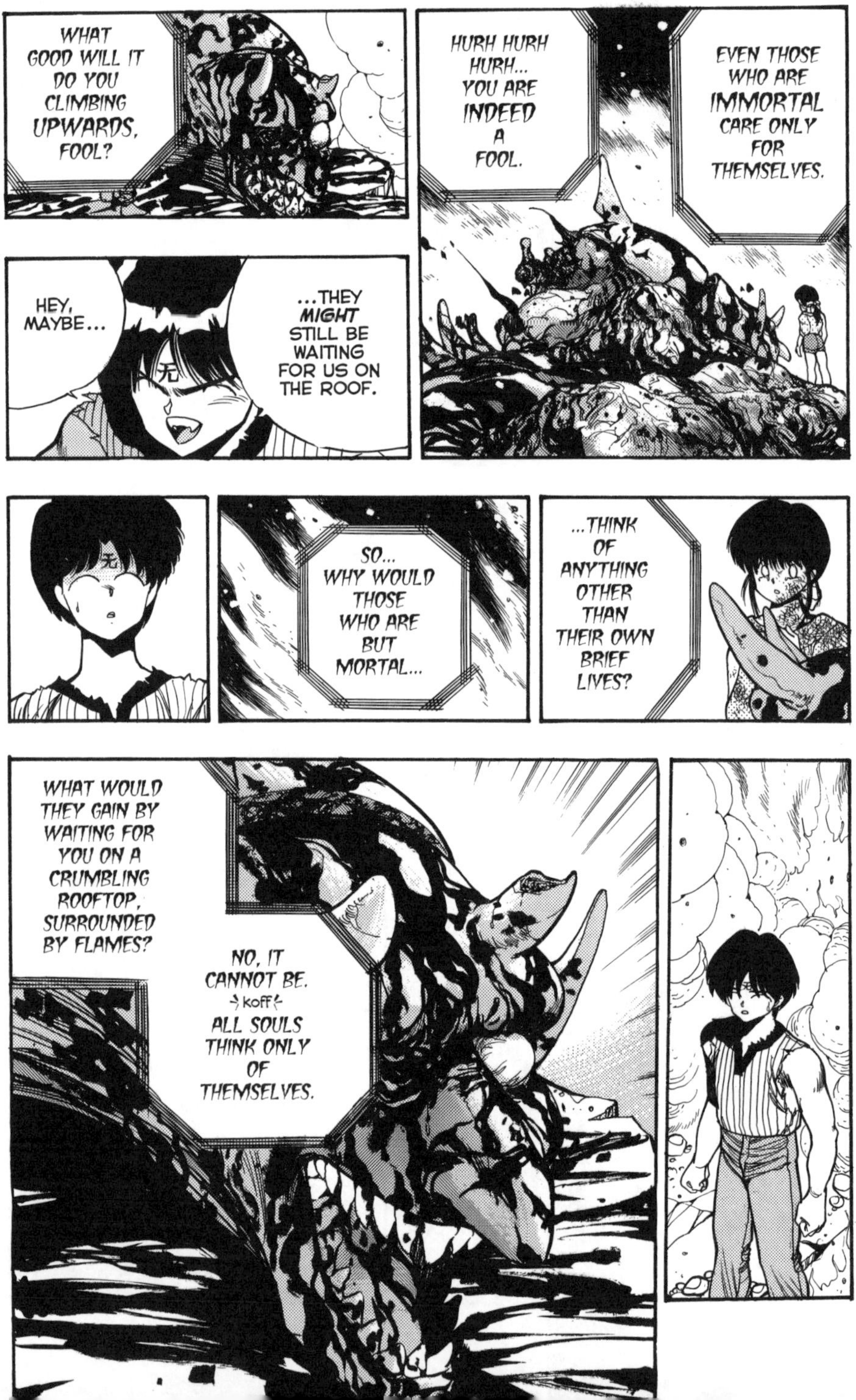
WHAT GOOD WILL IT DO YOU CLIMBING UPWARDS, FOOL?
HURH HURH HURH... YOU ARE INDEED A FOOL.
EVEN THOSE WHO ARE IMMORTAL CARE ONLY FOR THEMSELVES.
HEY, MAYBE...
...THEY MIGHT STILL BE WAITING FOR US ON THE ROOF.
SO... WHY WOULD THOSE WHO ARE BUT MORTAL...
...THINK OF ANYTHING OTHER THAN THEIR OWN BRIEF LIVES?
WHAT WOULD THEY GAIN BY WAITING FOR YOU ON A CRUMBLING ROOFTOP, SURROUNDED BY FLAMES?
NO, IT CANNOT BE.
koff
ALL SOULS THINK ONLY OF THEMSELVES.

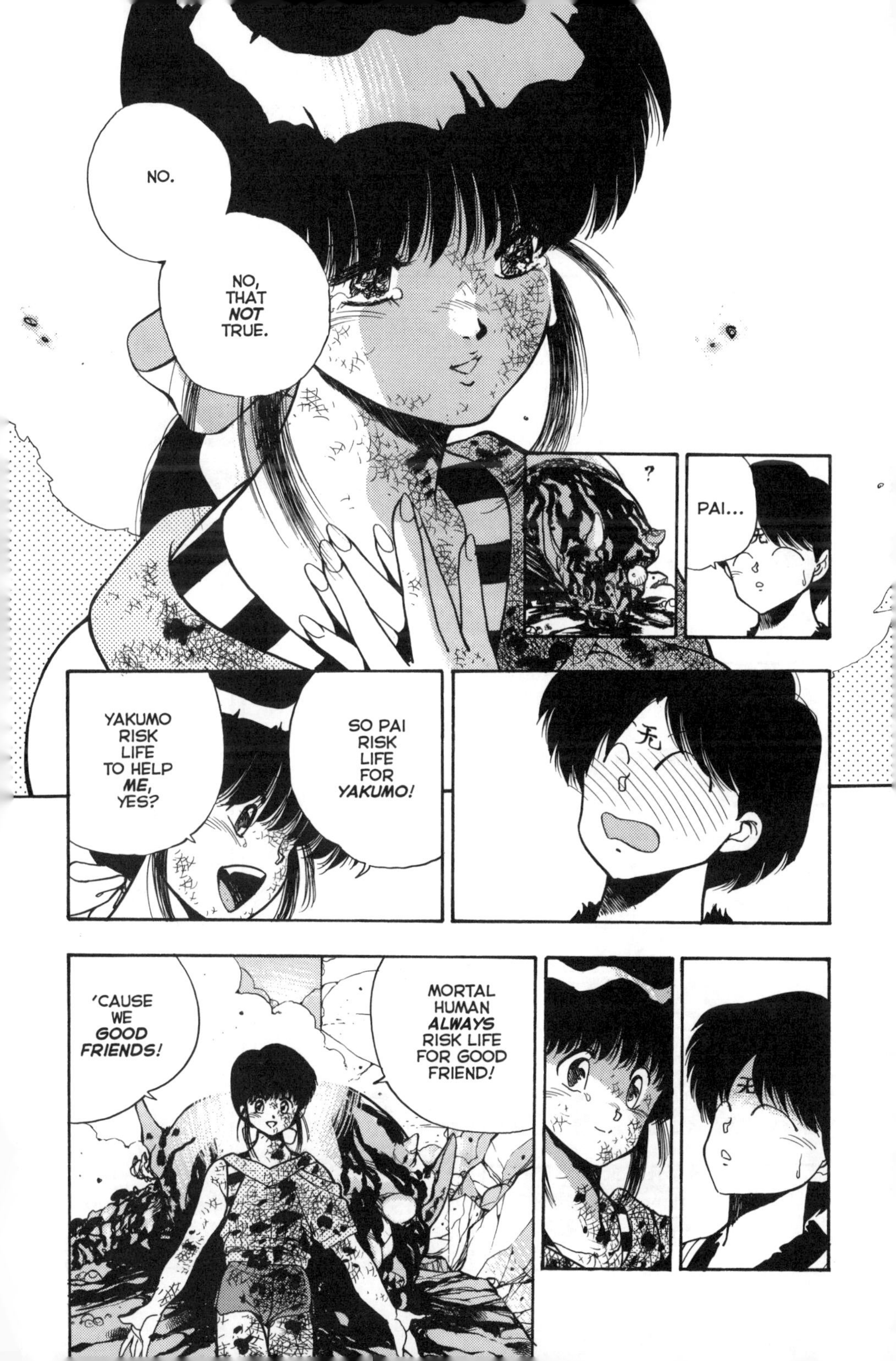
NO.
NO, THAT *NOT* TRUE.
?
PAI...
YAKUMO RISK LIFE TO HELP *ME*, YES?
SO PAI RISK LIFE FOR *YAKUMO!*
'CAUSE WE *GOOD FRIENDS!*
MORTAL HUMAN *ALWAYS* RISK LIFE FOR GOOD FRIEND!

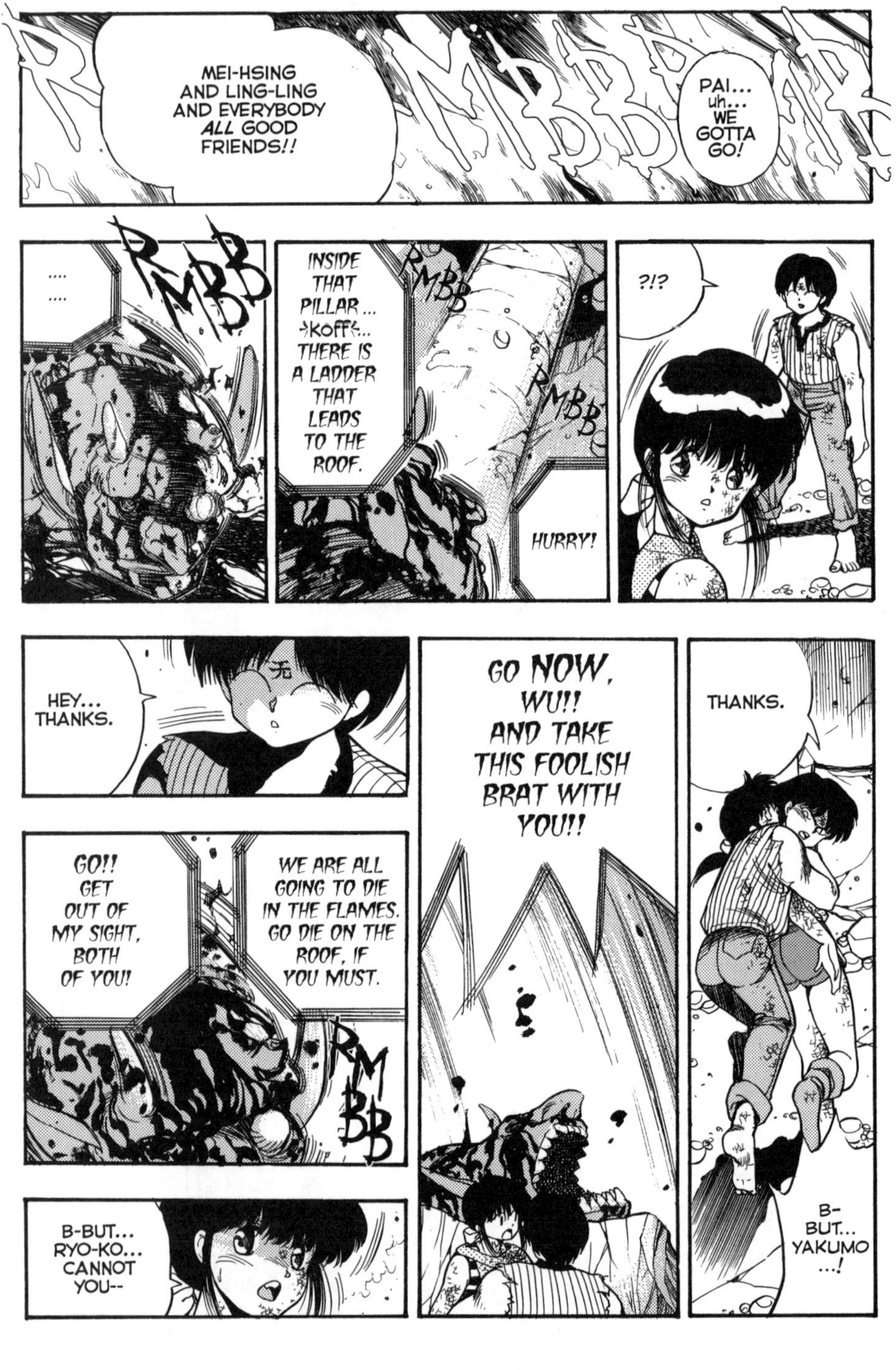
MEI-HSING AND LING-LING AND EVERYBODY *ALL* GOOD FRIENDS!!
PAI... uh... WE GOTTA GO!
....
....
RMBB
INSIDE THAT PILLAR... *koff*... THERE IS A LADDER THAT LEADS TO THE ROOF.
RMBB
RMBB
HURRY!
?!?
HEY... THANKS.
GO!! GET OUT OF MY SIGHT, BOTH OF YOU!
WE ARE ALL GOING TO DIE IN THE FLAMES. GO DIE ON THE ROOF, IF YOU MUST.
RMBB
B-BUT... RYO-KO... CANNOT YOU--
GO NOW, WU!! AND TAKE THIS FOOLISH BRAT WITH YOU!!
THANKS.
B-BUT... YAKUMO...!

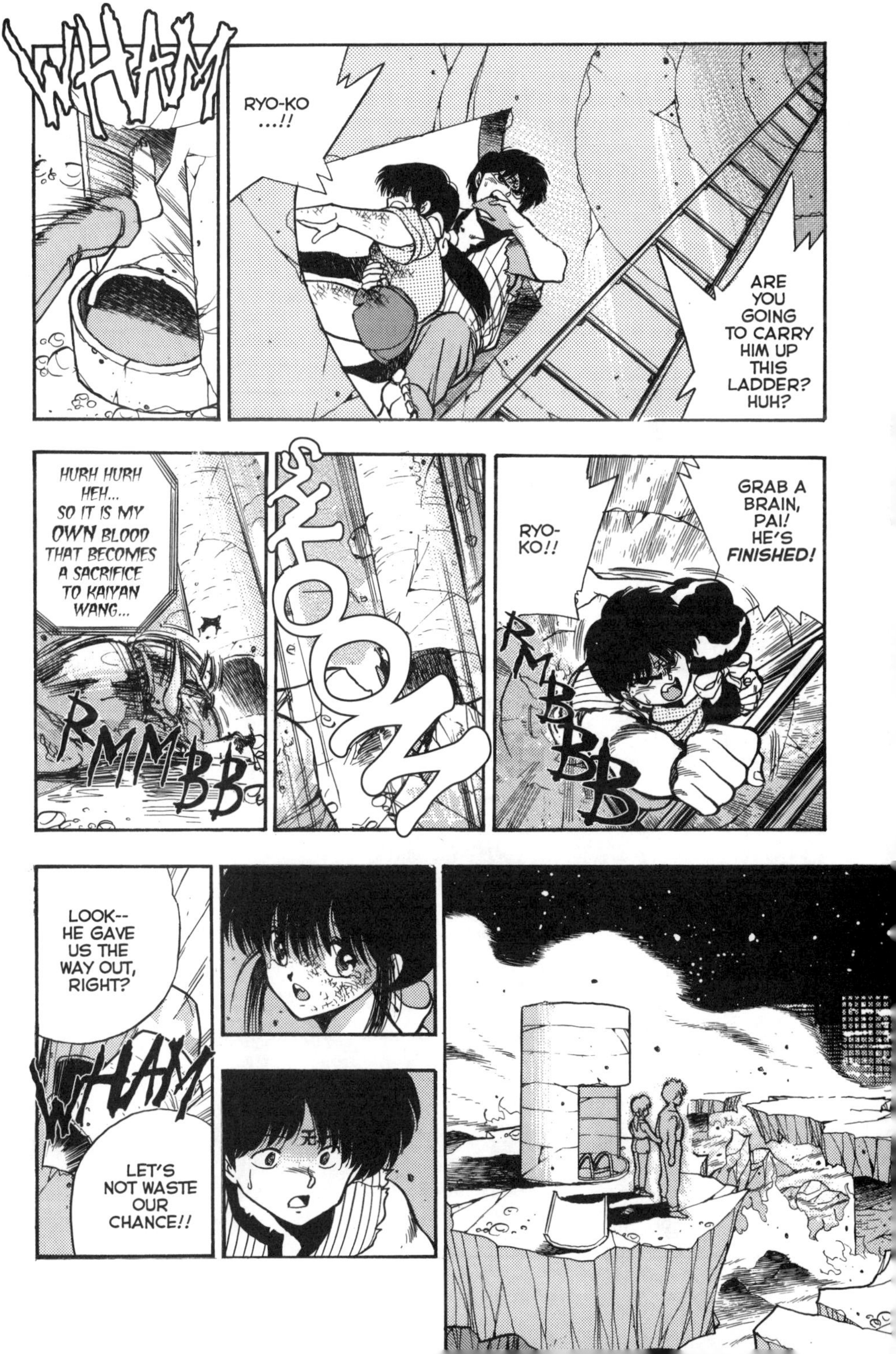
WHAM
RYO-KO ...!!
ARE YOU GOING TO CARRY HIM UP THIS LADDER? HUH?
HURH HURH HEH... SO IT IS MY OWN BLOOD THAT BECOMES A SACRIFICE TO KAIYAN WANG...
RMMBB
SKOOM
RYO-KO!!
GRAB A BRAIN, PAI! HE'S FINISHED!
RMBBBBB
LOOK-- HE GAVE US THE WAY OUT, RIGHT?
WHAM
LET'S NOT WASTE OUR CHANCE!!

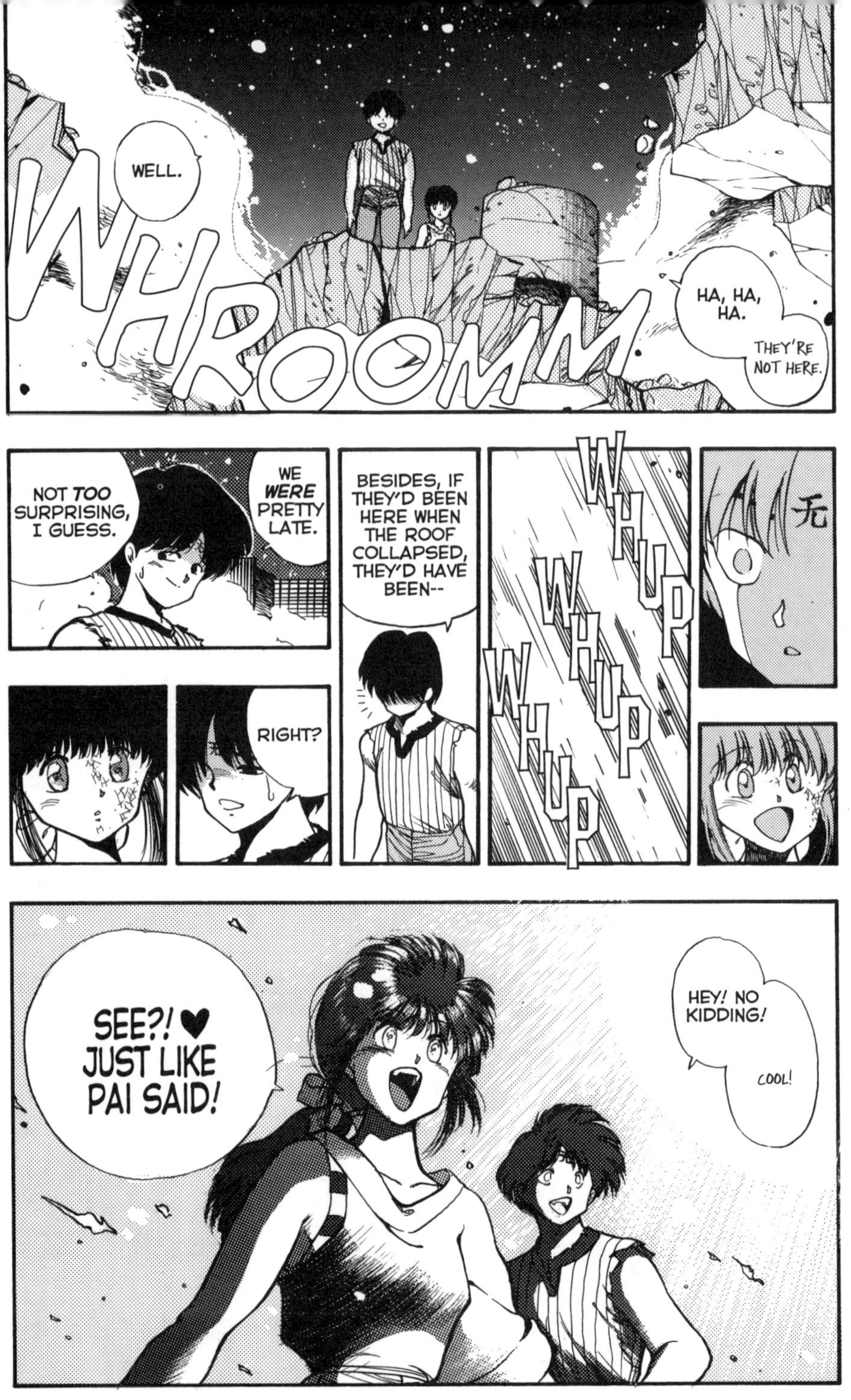
WELL.
WHROOMM
HA, HA, HA.
THEY'RE NOT HERE.
NOT TOO SURPRISING, I GUESS.
WE WERE PRETTY LATE.
RIGHT?
BESIDES, IF THEY'D BEEN HERE WHEN THE ROOF COLLAPSED, THEY'D HAVE BEEN--
WHUP WHUP WHUP
SEE?! ♥ JUST LIKE PAI SAID!
HEY! NO KIDDING!
COOL!

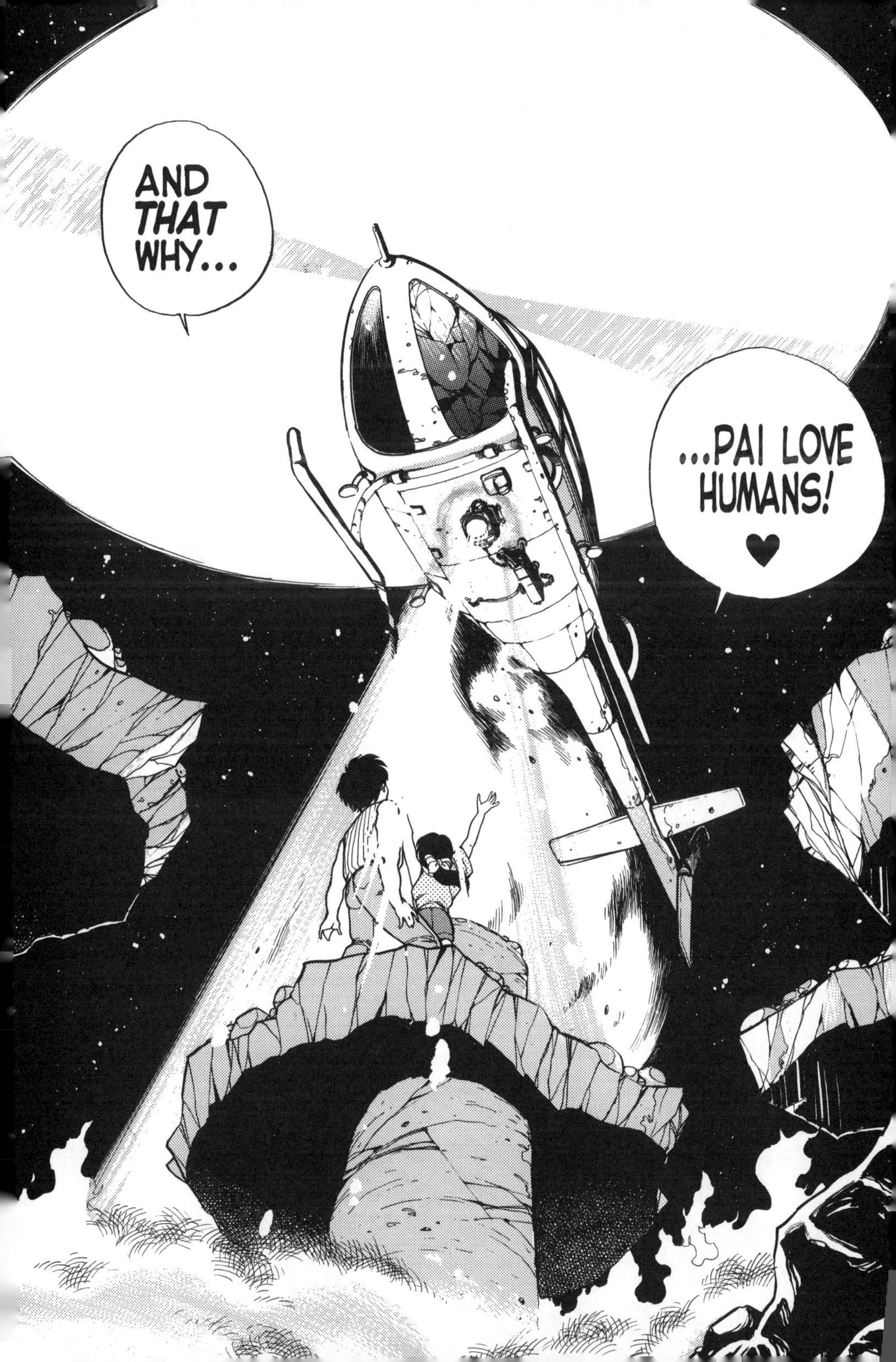
AND THAT WHY...
...PAI LOVE HUMANS! ♥

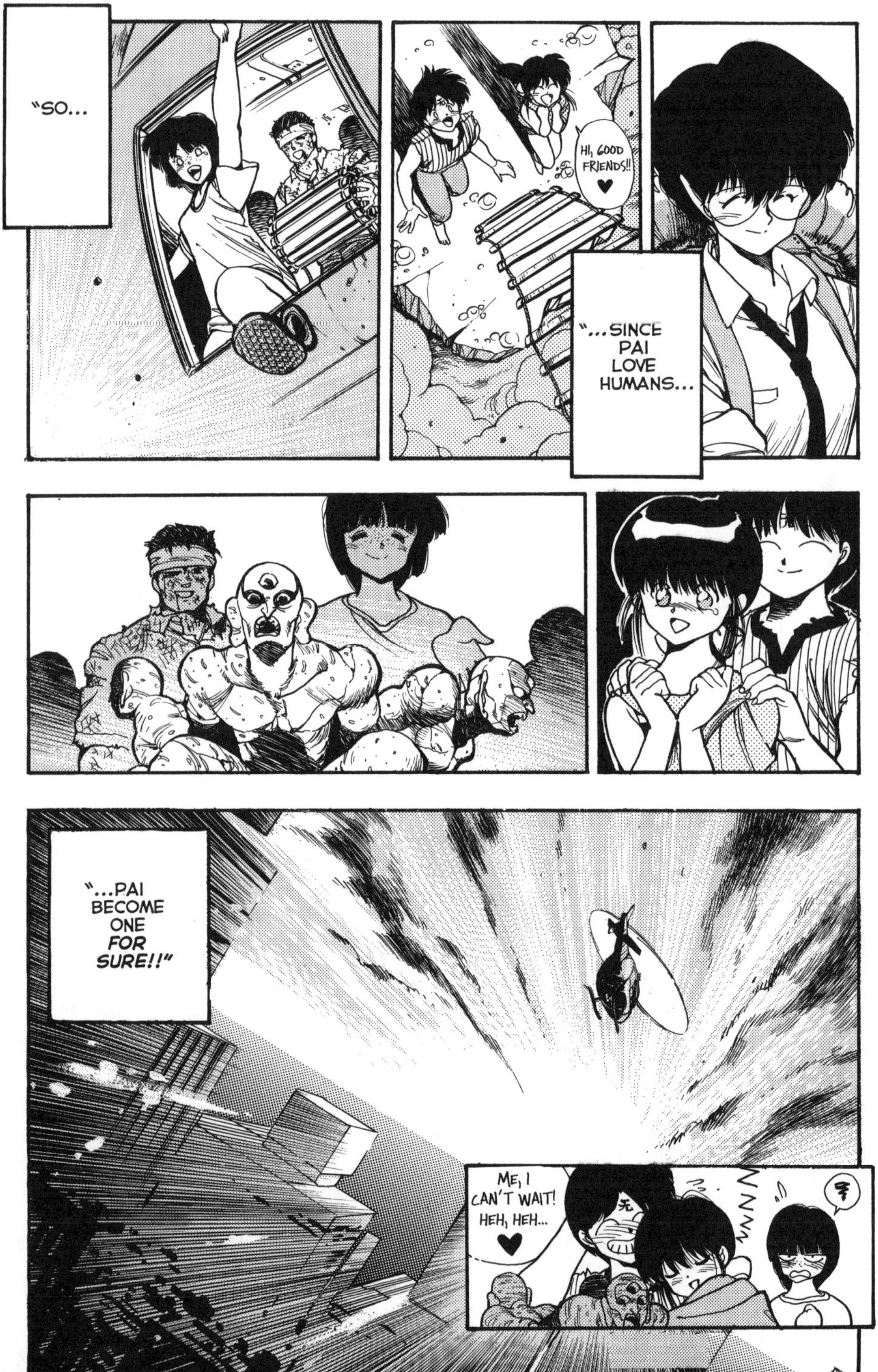
"SO...
HI, GOOD FRIENDS!! ♥
"...SINCE PAI LOVE HUMANS...
"...PAI BECOME ONE FOR SURE!!"
ME, I CAN'T WAIT! HEH, HEH... ♥

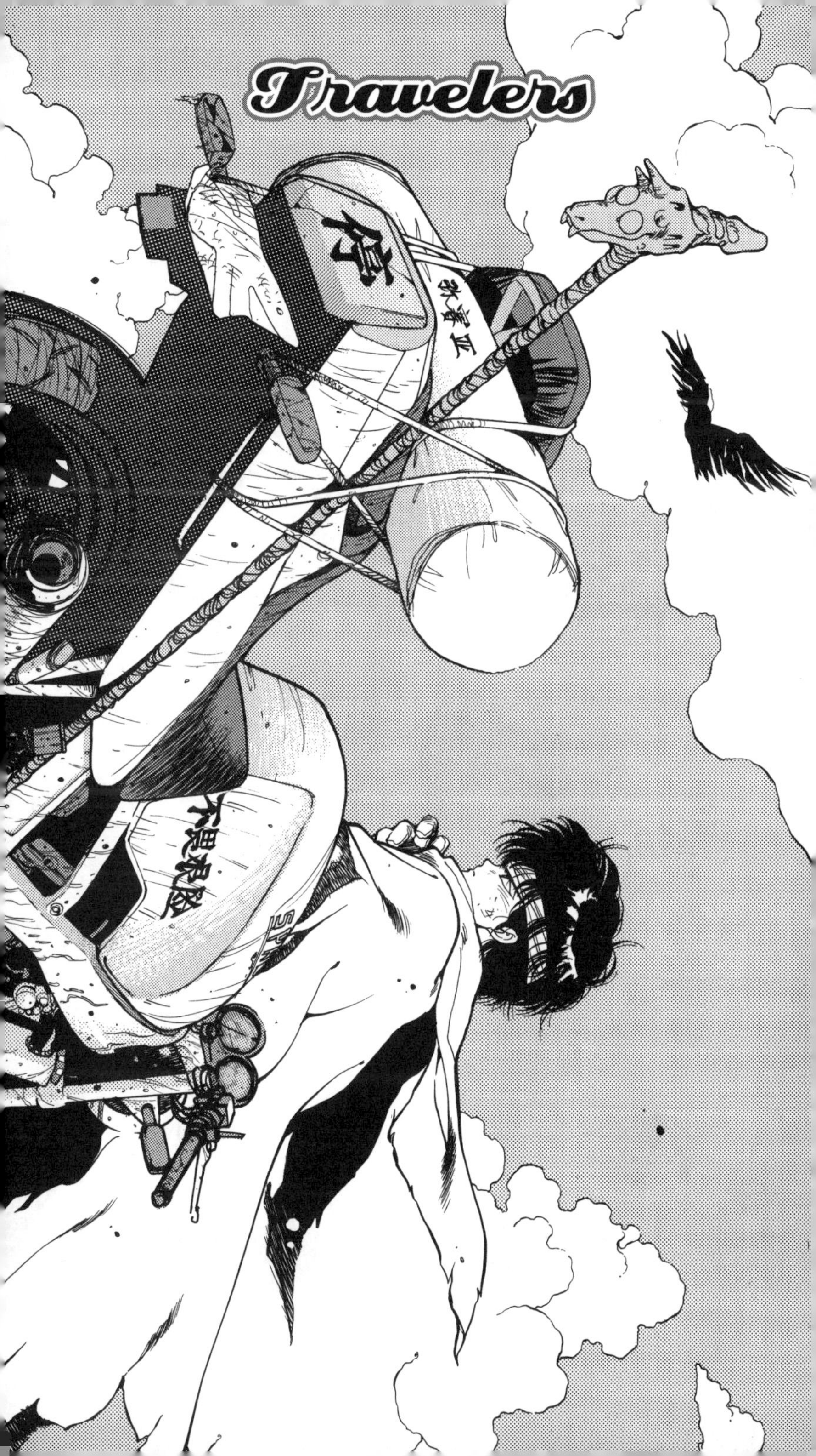
Travelers

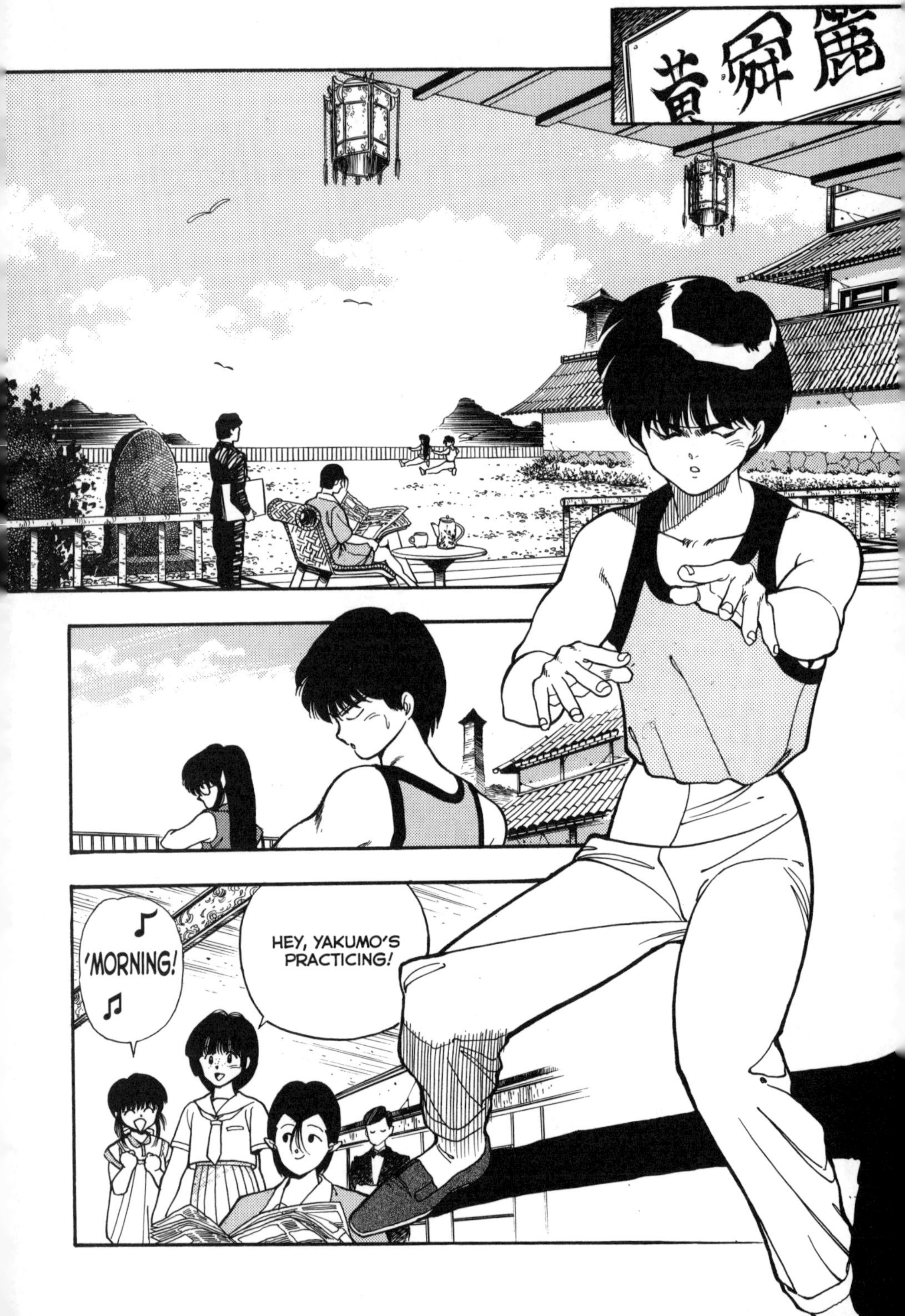

黄舜麗
♪ 'MORNING! ♫
HEY, YAKUMO'S PRACTICING!

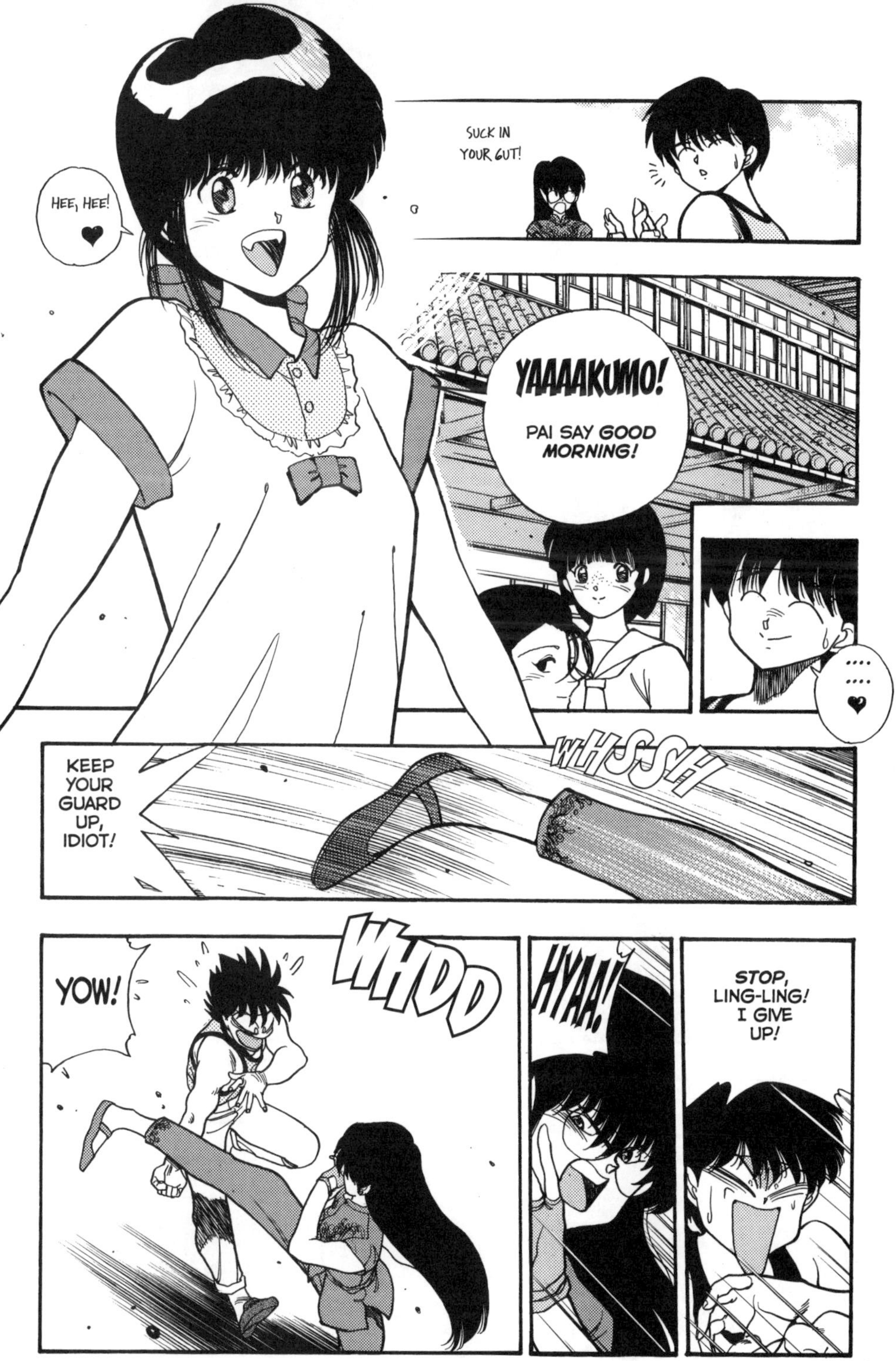
HEE, HEE! ♥
SUCK IN YOUR GUT!
YAAAAKUMO!
PAI SAY GOOD MORNING!
.... ♥
KEEP YOUR GUARD UP, IDIOT!
WHSSH
YOW!
WHDD
HYAA!
STOP, LING-LING! I GIVE UP!

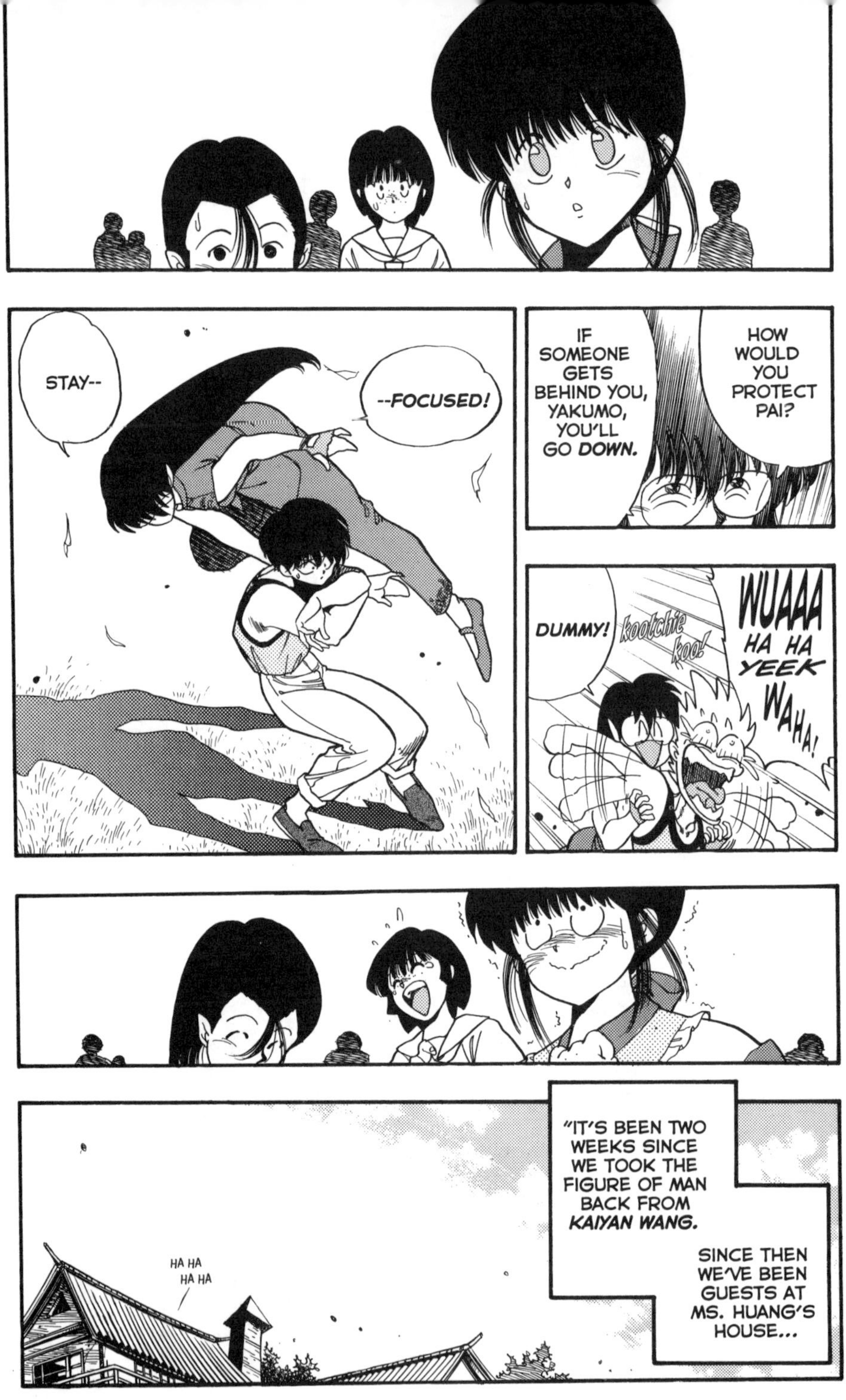
STAY--
--FOCUSED!
IF SOMEONE GETS BEHIND YOU, YAKUMO, YOU'LL GO DOWN.
HOW WOULD YOU PROTECT PAI?
DUMMY!
kootchie koo!
WUAAA HA HA YEEK WAHA!
HA HA HA HA
"IT'S BEEN TWO WEEKS SINCE WE TOOK THE FIGURE OF MAN BACK FROM KAIYAN WANG.
SINCE THEN WE'VE BEEN GUESTS AT MS. HUANG'S HOUSE...

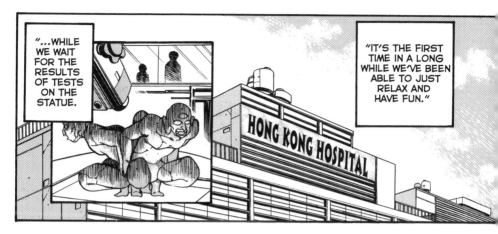

"...WHILE WE WAIT FOR THE RESULTS OF TESTS ON THE STATUE.

"IT'S THE FIRST TIME IN A LONG WHILE WE'VE BEEN ABLE TO JUST RELAX AND HAVE FUN."

MR. STEVE, TOMORROW WE HAVE BIG PARTY AND MUCH FOOD TO CELEBRATE YOU LEAVING HOSPITAL!

HEH HEH, THANKS. THAT SOUNDS NICE!

HMPH! YOU'RE NOT READY TO EAT *TOO* MUCH, BROTHER DEAR.

BUT... DON'T YOU HAVE ANY PLANS TO CELEBRATE BECOMING *HUMAN*, THOUGH?

....

....

"WHEN WE BECOME HUMAN...

≥siiigh≤

"I'D HAVE NEVER BELIEVED BEING HUMAN AGAIN WOULD BE A PROBLEM, BUT...

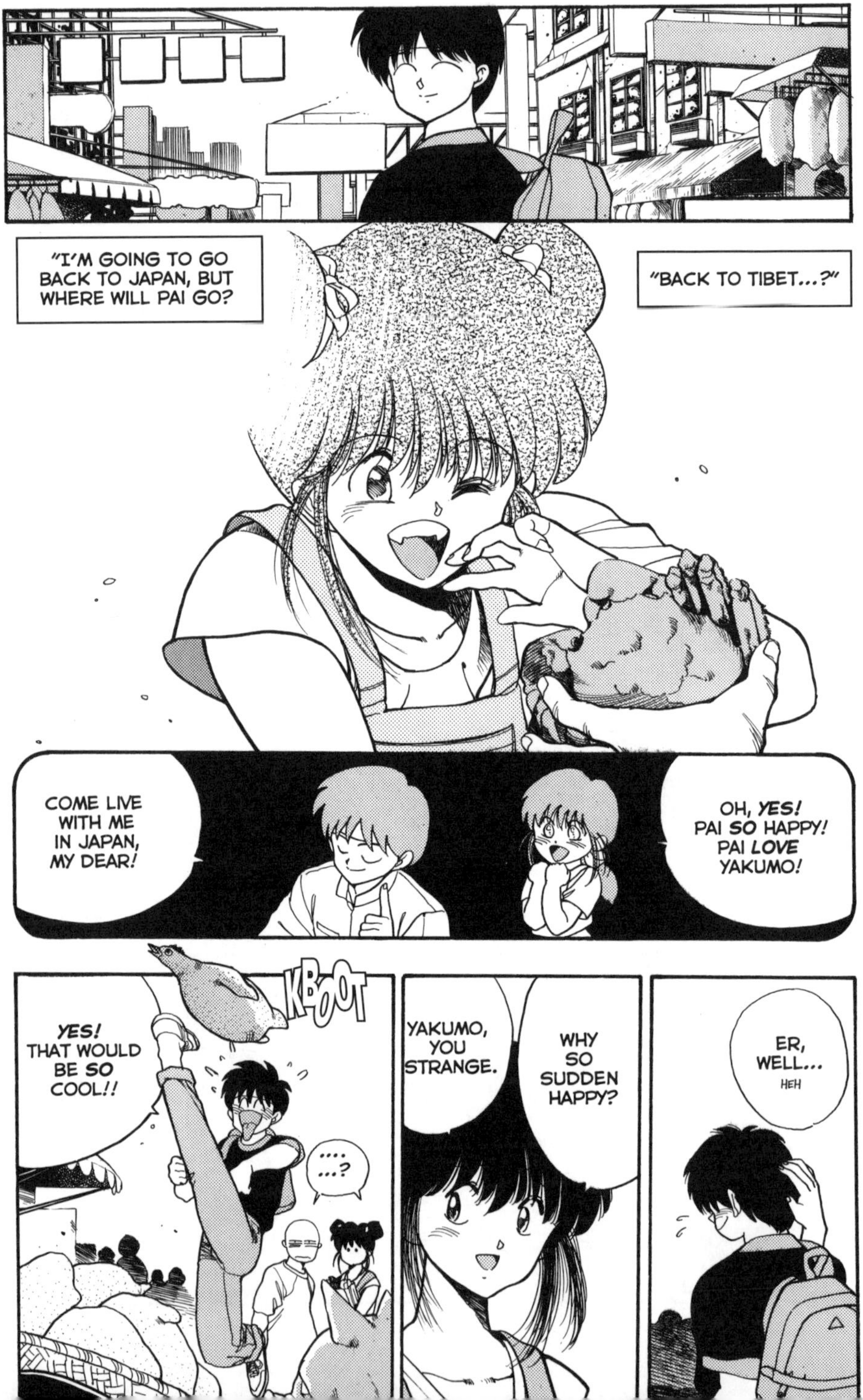
"I'M GOING TO GO BACK TO JAPAN, BUT WHERE WILL PAI GO?
"BACK TO TIBET...?"
COME LIVE WITH ME IN JAPAN, MY DEAR!
OH, YES! PAI SO HAPPY! PAI LOVE YAKUMO!
YES! THAT WOULD BE SO COOL!!
KBOOT
....
...?
YAKUMO, YOU STRANGE.
WHY SO SUDDEN HAPPY?
ER, WELL...
HEH

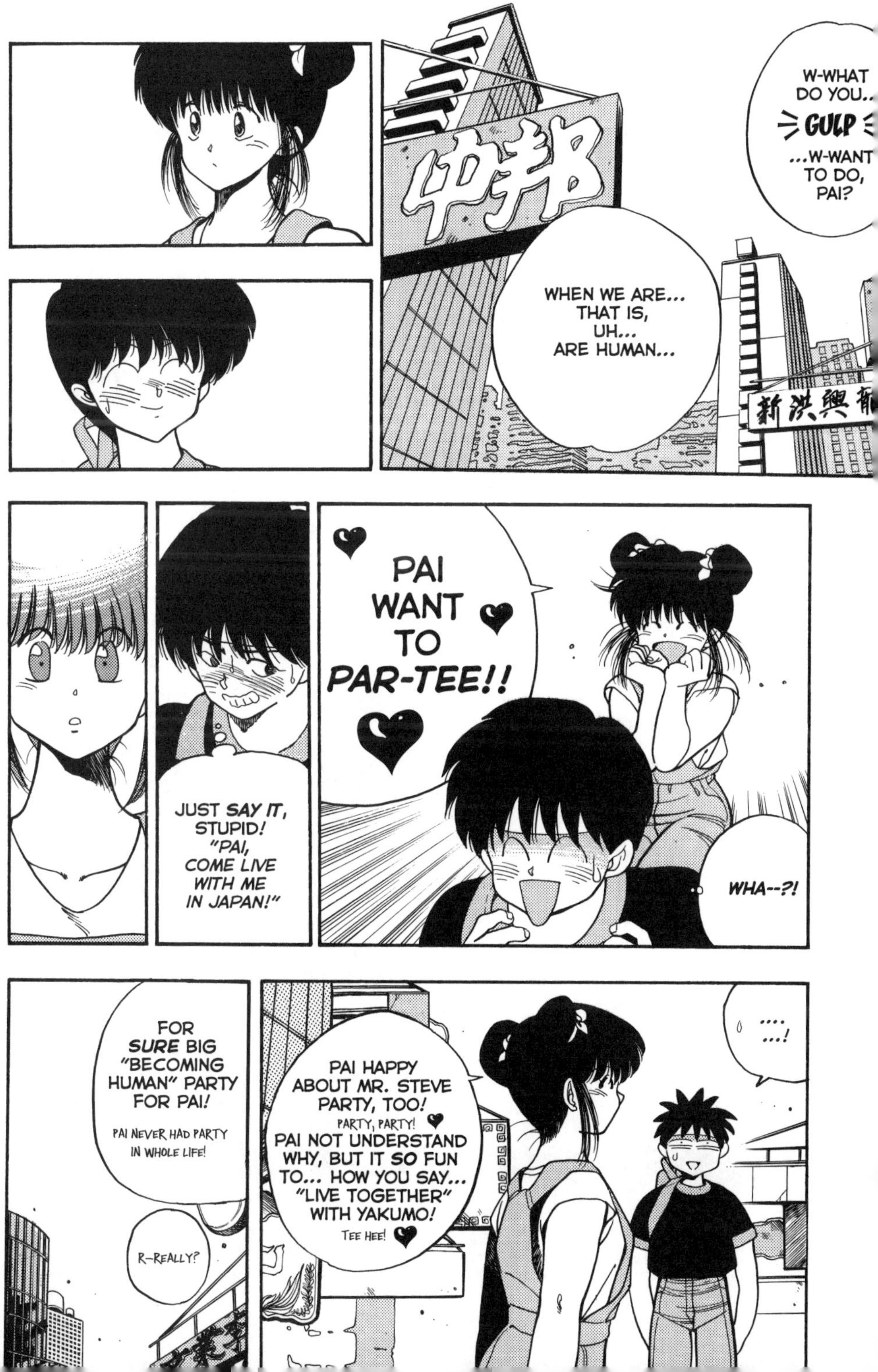

WHEN WE ARE... THAT IS, UH... ARE HUMAN...
W-WHAT DO YOU...
GULP
...W-WANT TO DO, PAI?
新洪興
JUST SAY IT, STUPID! "PAI, COME LIVE WITH ME IN JAPAN!"
PAI WANT TO PAR-TEE!!
WHA--?!
FOR SURE BIG "BECOMING HUMAN" PARTY FOR PAI!
PAI NEVER HAD PARTY IN WHOLE LIFE!
R-REALLY?
PAI HAPPY ABOUT MR. STEVE PARTY, TOO!
PARTY, PARTY!
PAI NOT UNDERSTAND WHY, BUT IT SO FUN TO... HOW YOU SAY... "LIVE TOGETHER" WITH YAKUMO!
TEE HEE!
...., ...!

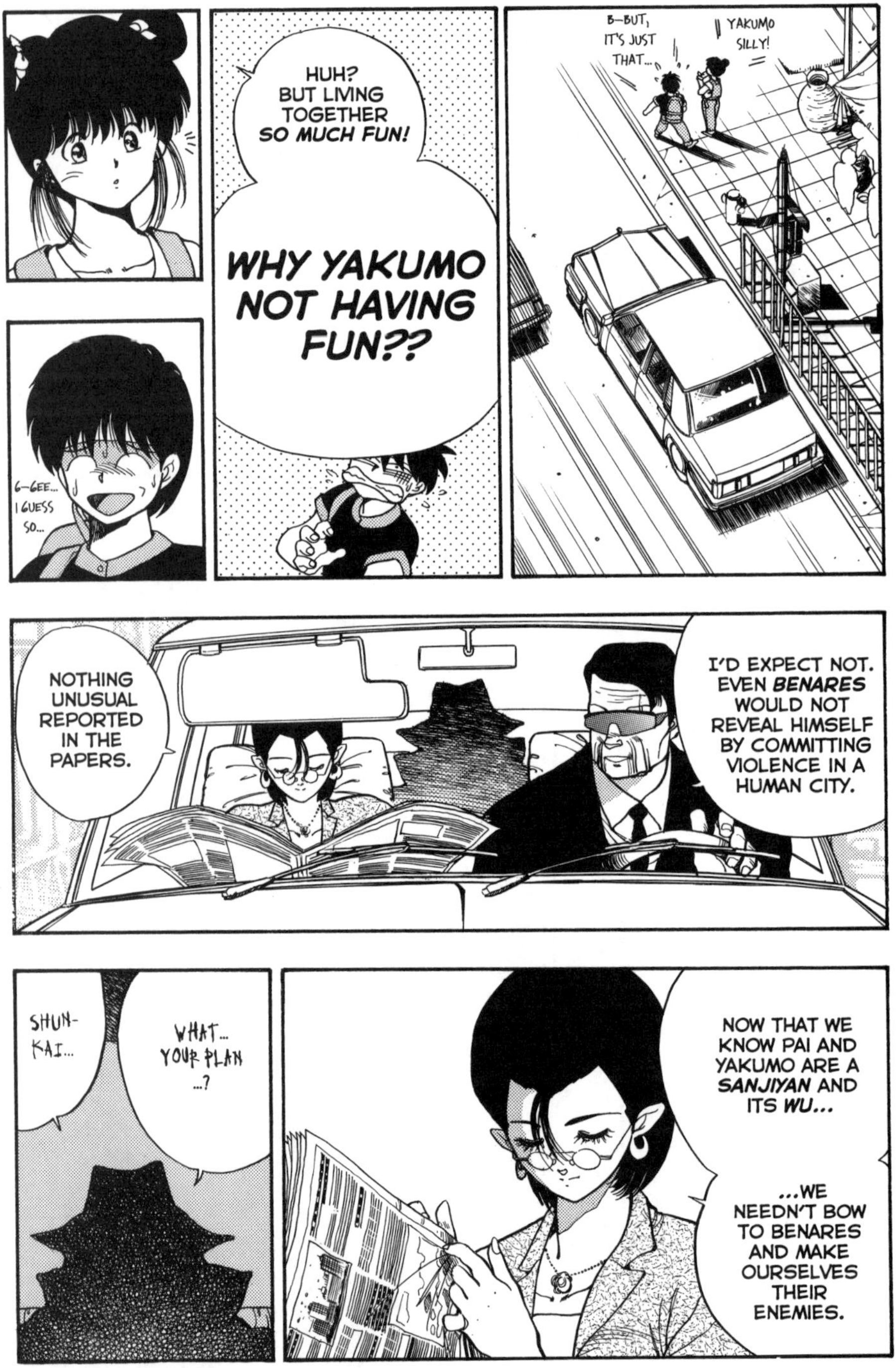
HUH? BUT LIVING TOGETHER SO MUCH FUN!
WHY YAKUMO NOT HAVING FUN??
B-BUT, IT'S JUST THAT...
YAKUMO SILLY!
G-GEE... I GUESS SO...
NOTHING UNUSUAL REPORTED IN THE PAPERS.
I'D EXPECT NOT. EVEN BENARES WOULD NOT REVEAL HIMSELF BY COMMITTING VIOLENCE IN A HUMAN CITY.
SHUN-KAI...
WHAT... YOUR PLAN ...?
NOW THAT WE KNOW PAI AND YAKUMO ARE A SANJIYAN AND ITS WU...
...WE NEEDN'T BOW TO BENARES AND MAKE OURSELVES THEIR ENEMIES.

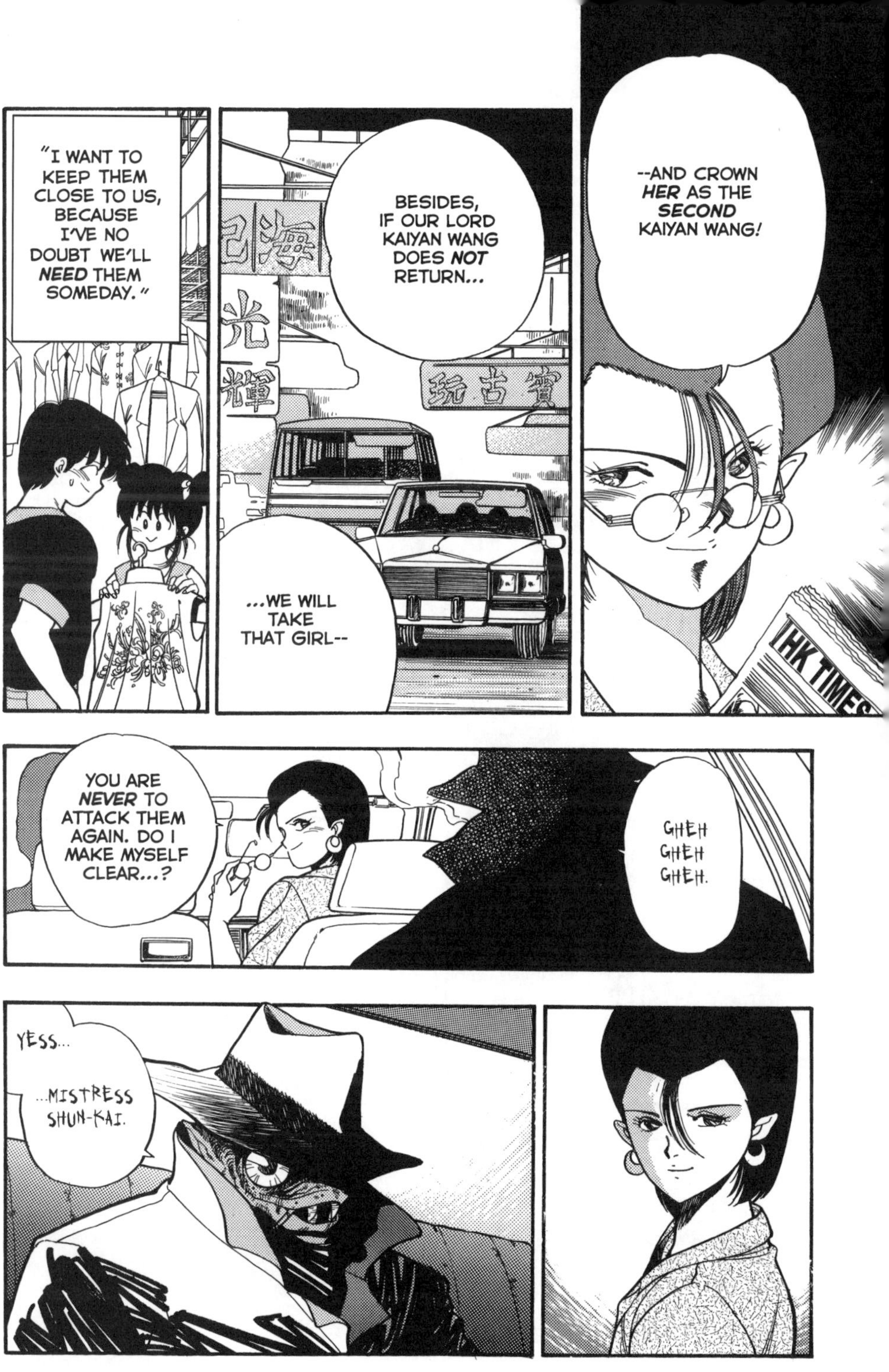
"I WANT TO KEEP THEM CLOSE TO US, BECAUSE I'VE NO DOUBT WE'LL NEED THEM SOMEDAY."
BESIDES, IF OUR LORD KAIYAN WANG DOES NOT RETURN...
...WE WILL TAKE THAT GIRL--
--AND CROWN HER AS THE SECOND KAIYAN WANG!
HK TIMES
YOU ARE NEVER TO ATTACK THEM AGAIN. DO I MAKE MYSELF CLEAR...?
GHEH GHEH GHEH.
YESS...
...MISTRESS SHUN-KAI.

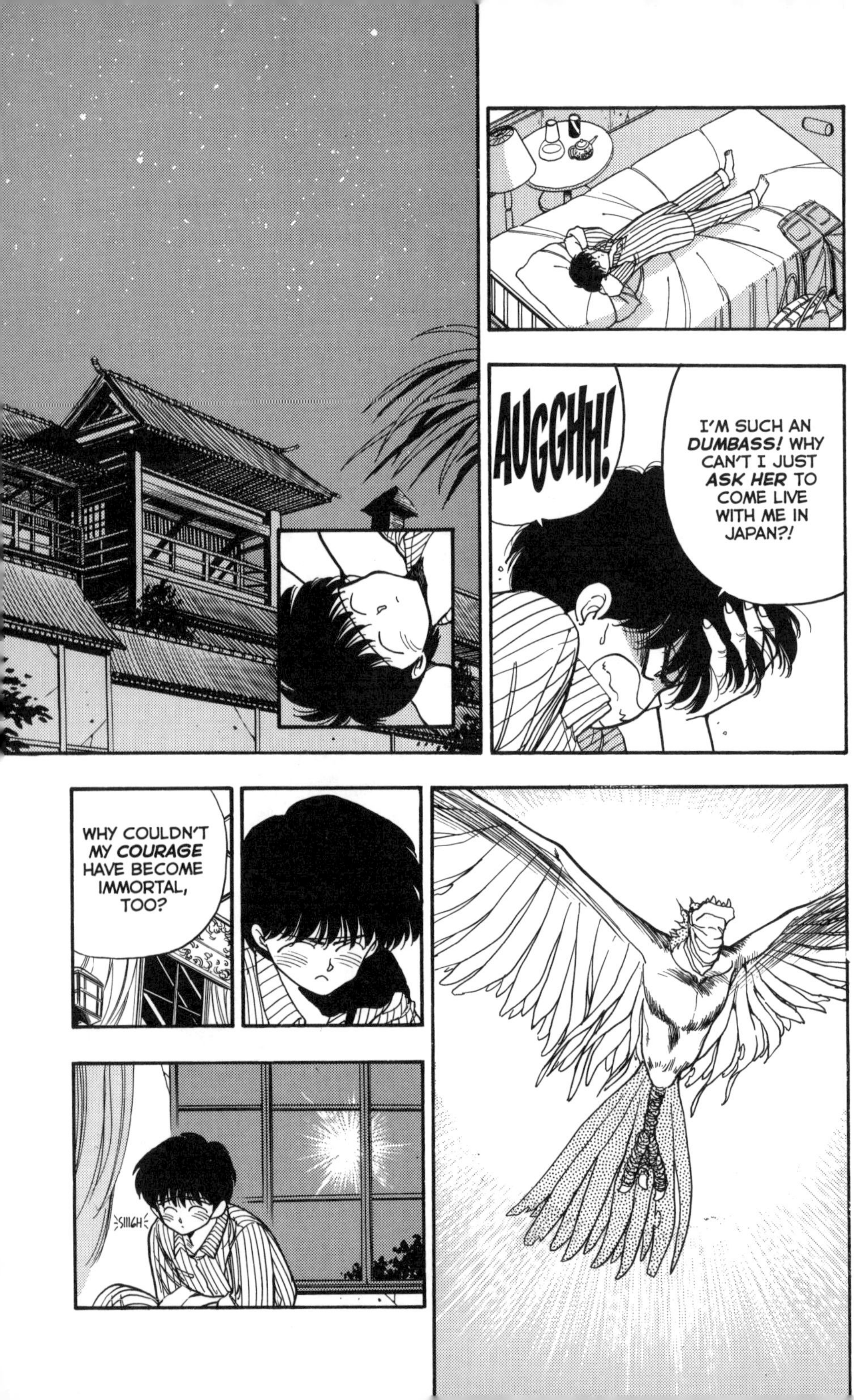
AUGGHH!
I'M SUCH AN DUMBASS! WHY CAN'T I JUST ASK HER TO COME LIVE WITH ME IN JAPAN?!
WHY COULDN'T MY COURAGE HAVE BECOME IMMORTAL, TOO?
SIIIGH

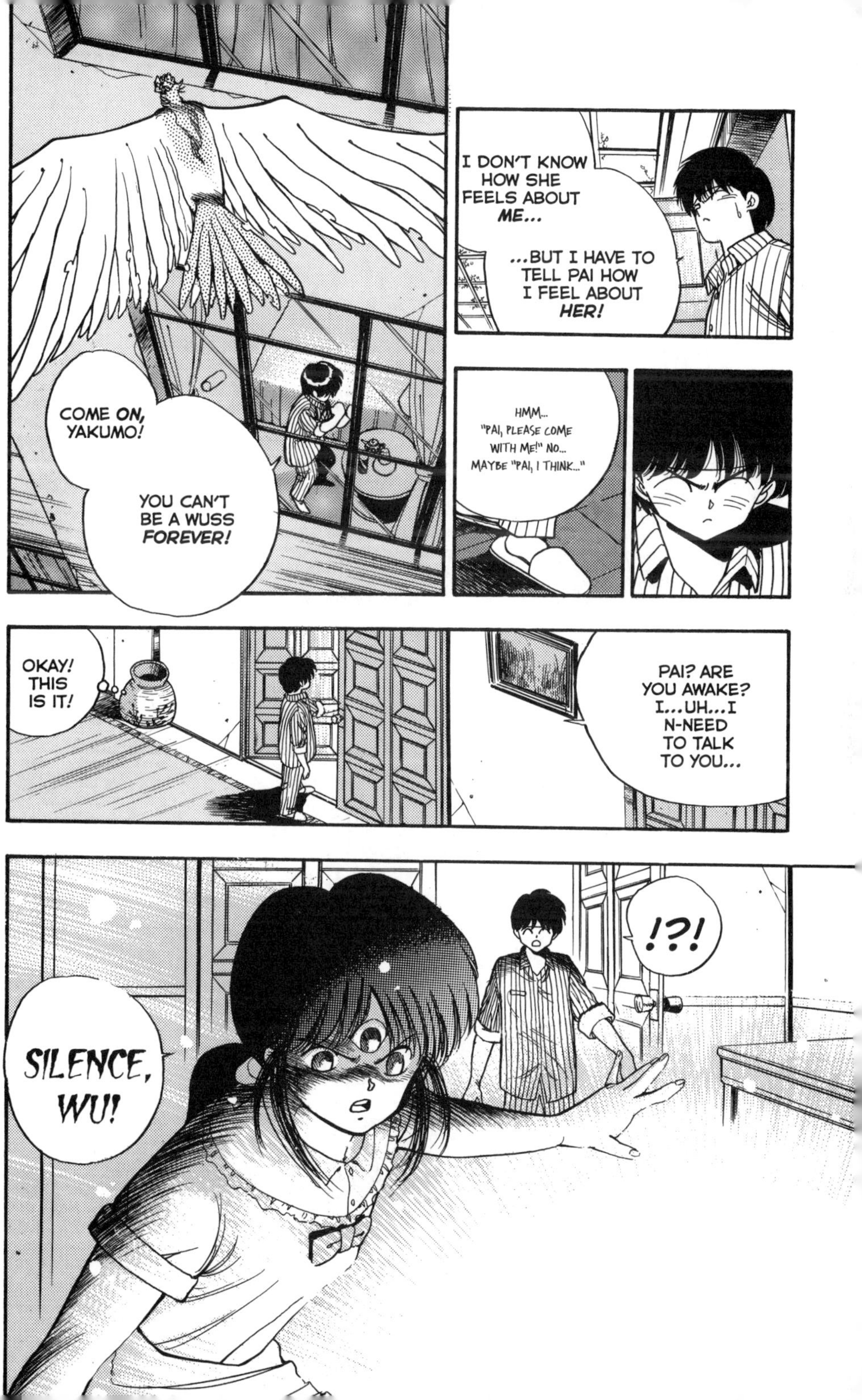
COME ON, YAKUMO!
YOU CAN'T BE A WUSS FOREVER!
I DON'T KNOW HOW SHE FEELS ABOUT ME...
...BUT I HAVE TO TELL PAI HOW I FEEL ABOUT HER!
HMM... "PAI, PLEASE COME WITH ME!" NO... MAYBE "PAI, I THINK..."
OKAY! THIS IS IT!
PAI? ARE YOU AWAKE? I...UH...I N-NEED TO TALK TO YOU...
SILENCE, WU!
!?!

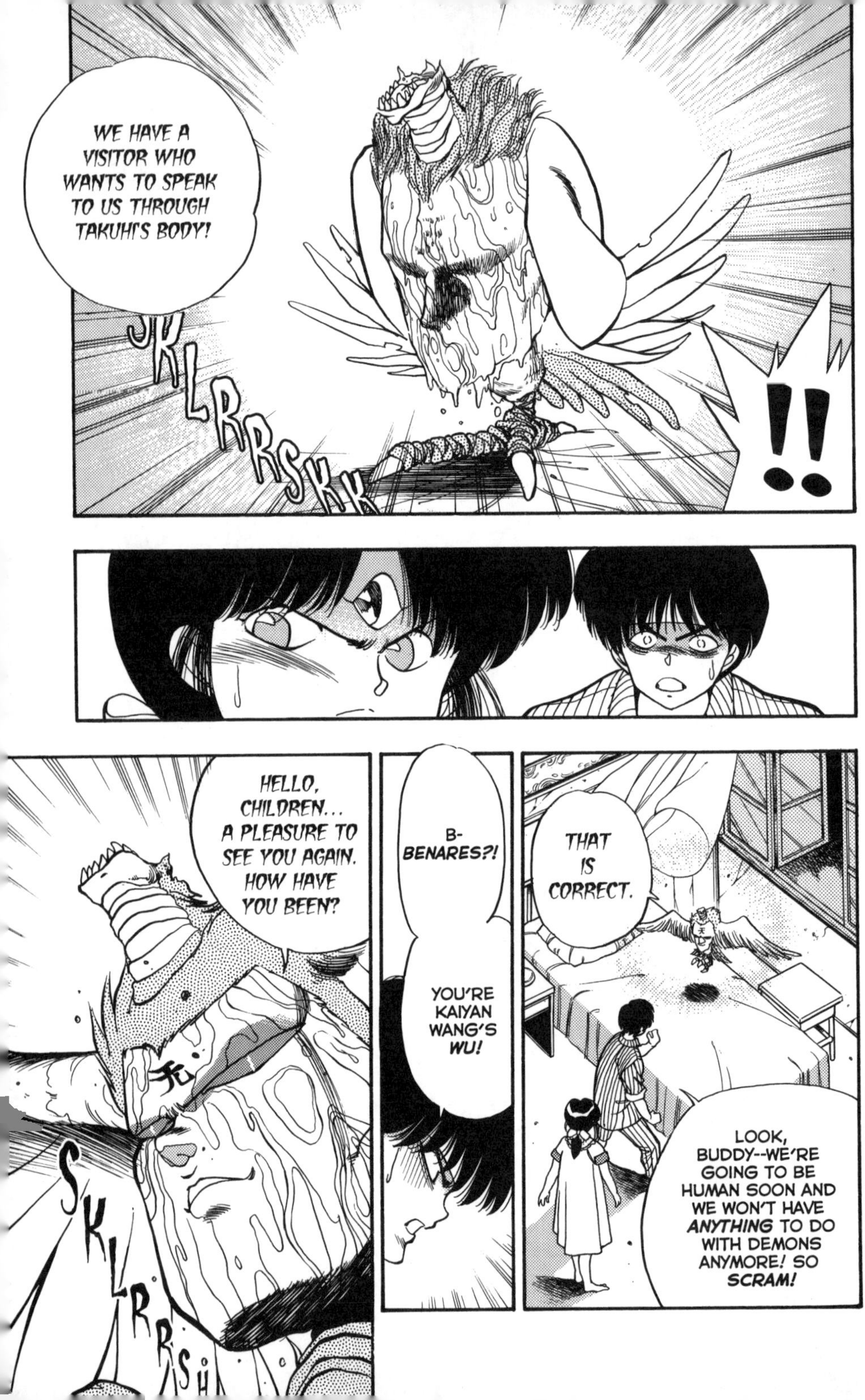
WE HAVE A VISITOR WHO WANTS TO SPEAK TO US THROUGH TAKUHI'S BODY!
SKLRRSKK
!!
HELLO, CHILDREN... A PLEASURE TO SEE YOU AGAIN. HOW HAVE YOU BEEN?
SKLRRSH
B-BENARES?!
YOU'RE KAIYAN WANG'S WU!
THAT IS CORRECT.
LOOK, BUDDY--WE'RE GOING TO BE HUMAN SOON AND WE WON'T HAVE ANYTHING TO DO WITH DEMONS ANYMORE! SO SCRAM!

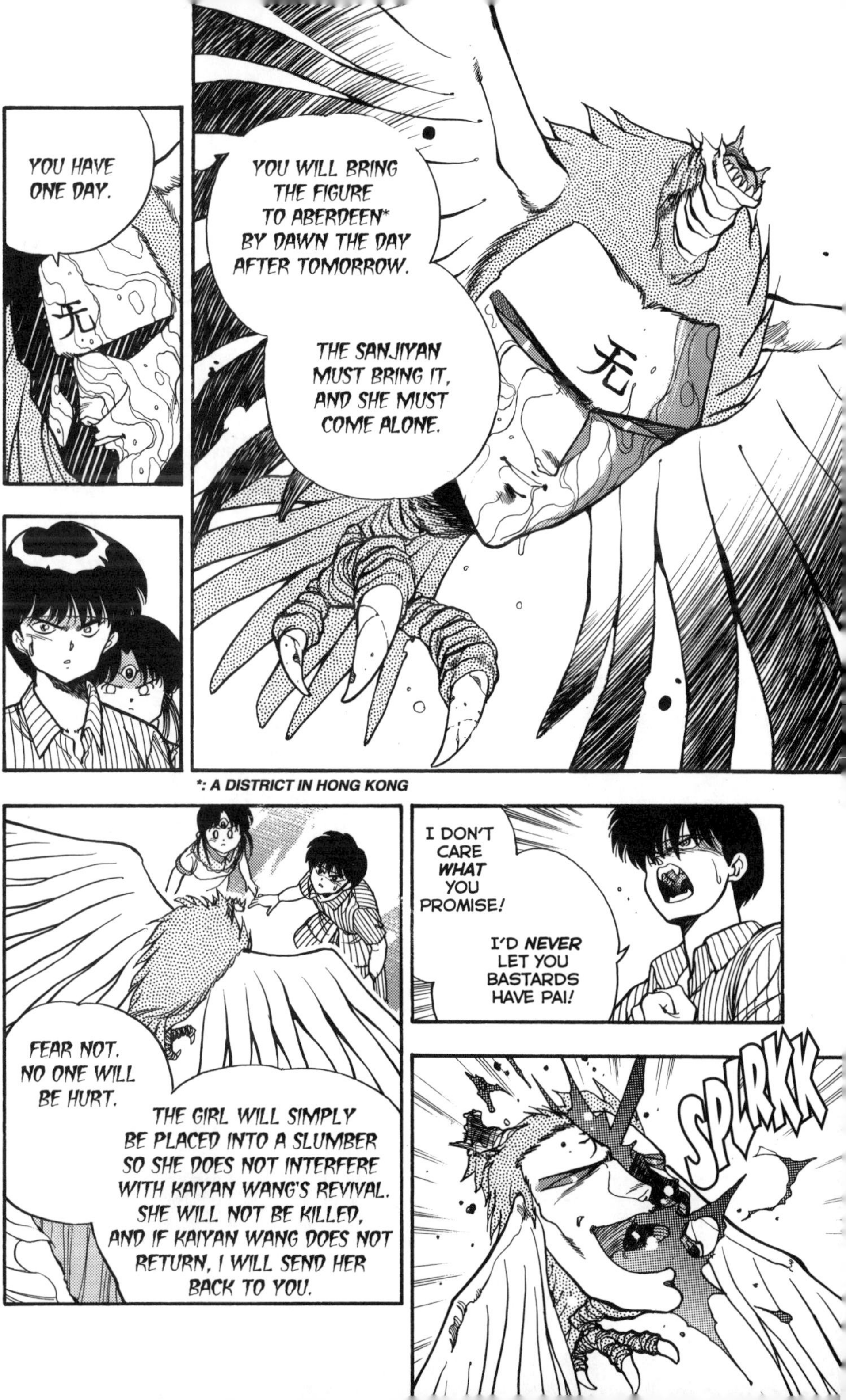
YOU HAVE ONE DAY.
YOU WILL BRING THE FIGURE TO ABERDEEN* BY DAWN THE DAY AFTER TOMORROW.
THE SANJIYAN MUST BRING IT, AND SHE MUST COME ALONE.
FEAR NOT. NO ONE WILL BE HURT.
THE GIRL WILL SIMPLY BE PLACED INTO A SLUMBER SO SHE DOES NOT INTERFERE WITH KAIYAN WANG'S REVIVAL. SHE WILL NOT BE KILLED, AND IF KAIYAN WANG DOES NOT RETURN, I WILL SEND HER BACK TO YOU.
I DON'T CARE *WHAT* YOU PROMISE!
I'D *NEVER* LET YOU BASTARDS HAVE PAI!
SPLRKK

*: A DISTRICT IN HONG KONG

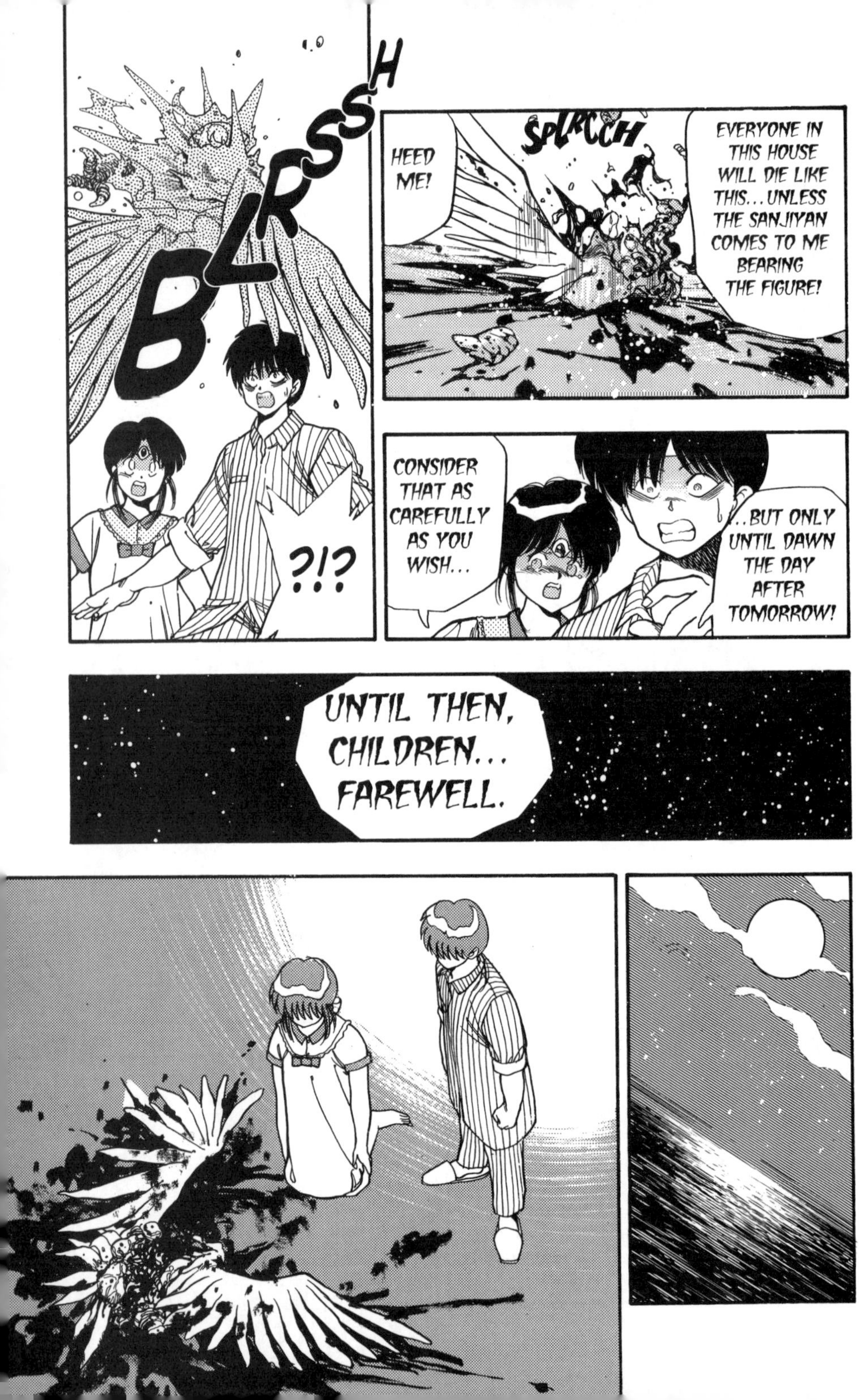
BLRSSSH
?!?
HEED ME!
SPLRCCH
EVERYONE IN THIS HOUSE WILL DIE LIKE THIS...UNLESS THE SANJIYAN COMES TO ME BEARING THE FIGURE!
CONSIDER THAT AS CAREFULLY AS YOU WISH...
...BUT ONLY UNTIL DAWN THE DAY AFTER TOMORROW!
UNTIL THEN, CHILDREN... FAREWELL.

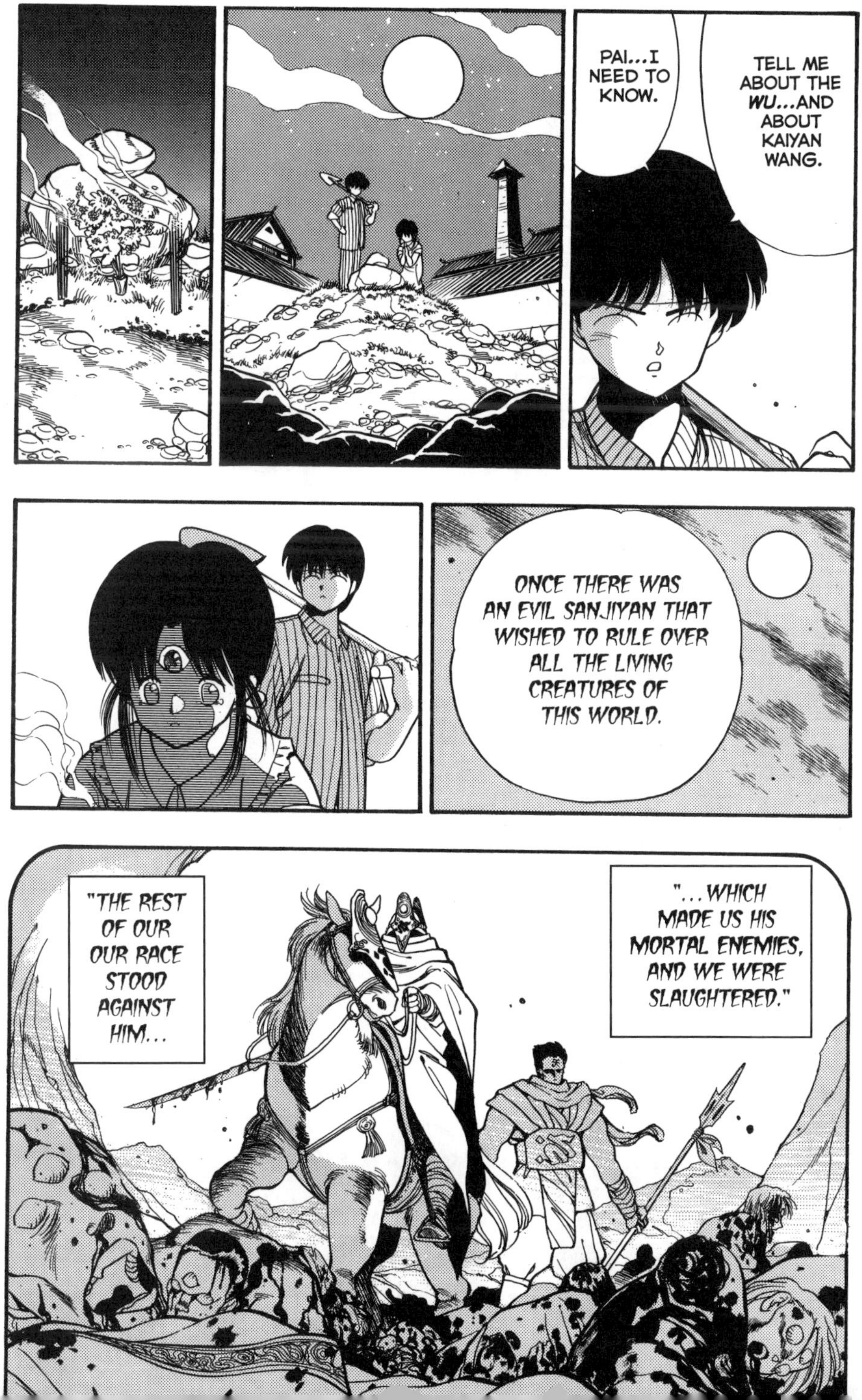
PAI...I NEED TO KNOW.
TELL ME ABOUT THE WU...AND ABOUT KAIYAN WANG.
ONCE THERE WAS AN EVIL SANJIYAN THAT WISHED TO RULE OVER ALL THE LIVING CREATURES OF THIS WORLD.
"THE REST OF OUR OUR RACE STOOD AGAINST HIM...
"...WHICH MADE US HIS MORTAL ENEMIES, AND WE WERE SLAUGHTERED."

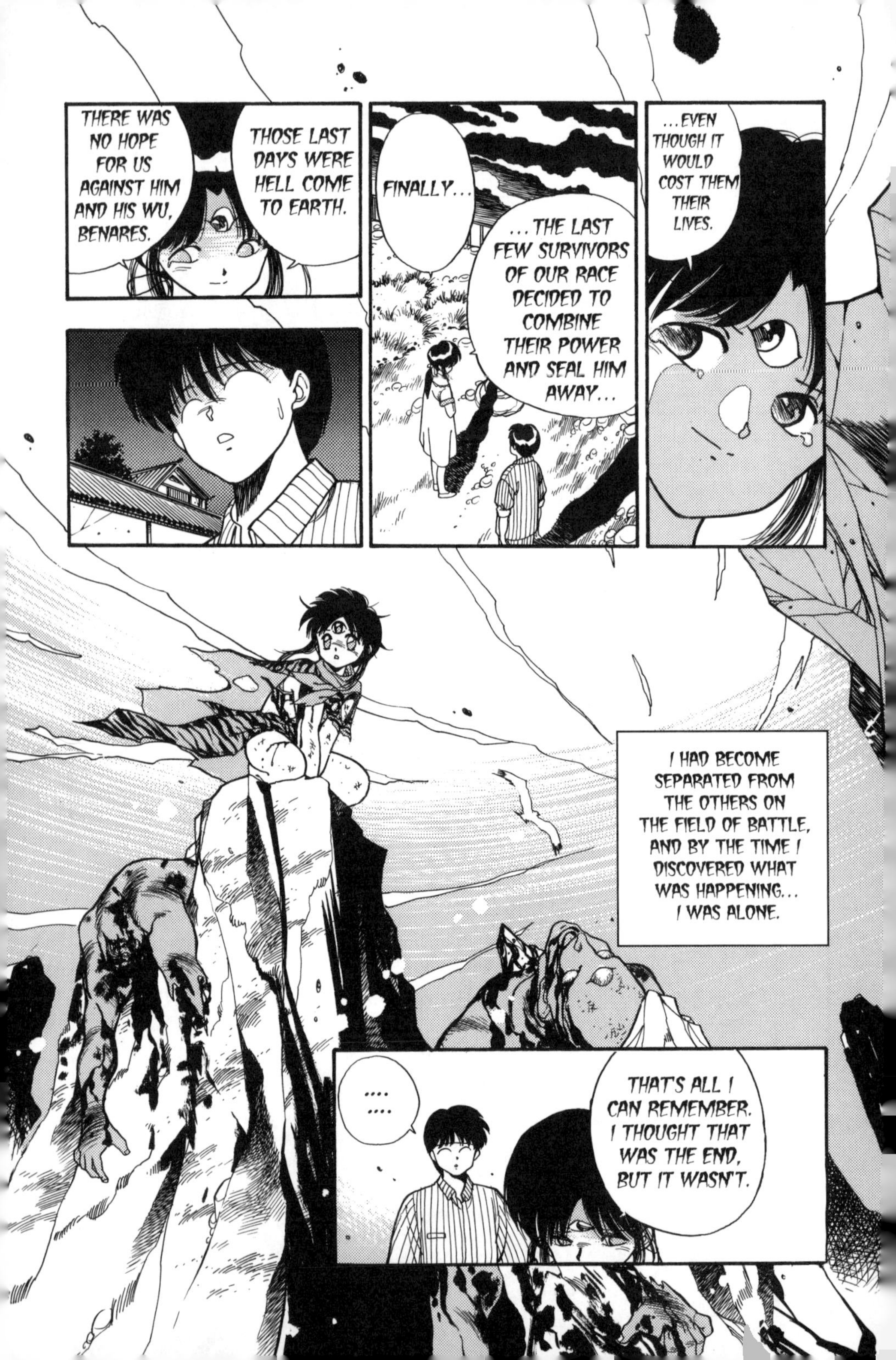
THERE WAS NO HOPE FOR US AGAINST HIM AND HIS WU, BENARES.
THOSE LAST DAYS WERE HELL COME TO EARTH.
FINALLY...
...THE LAST FEW SURVIVORS OF OUR RACE DECIDED TO COMBINE THEIR POWER AND SEAL HIM AWAY...
...EVEN THOUGH IT WOULD COST THEM THEIR LIVES.
I HAD BECOME SEPARATED FROM THE OTHERS ON THE FIELD OF BATTLE, AND BY THE TIME I DISCOVERED WHAT WAS HAPPENING... I WAS ALONE.
....
....
THAT'S ALL I CAN REMEMBER. I THOUGHT THAT WAS THE END, BUT IT WASN'T.

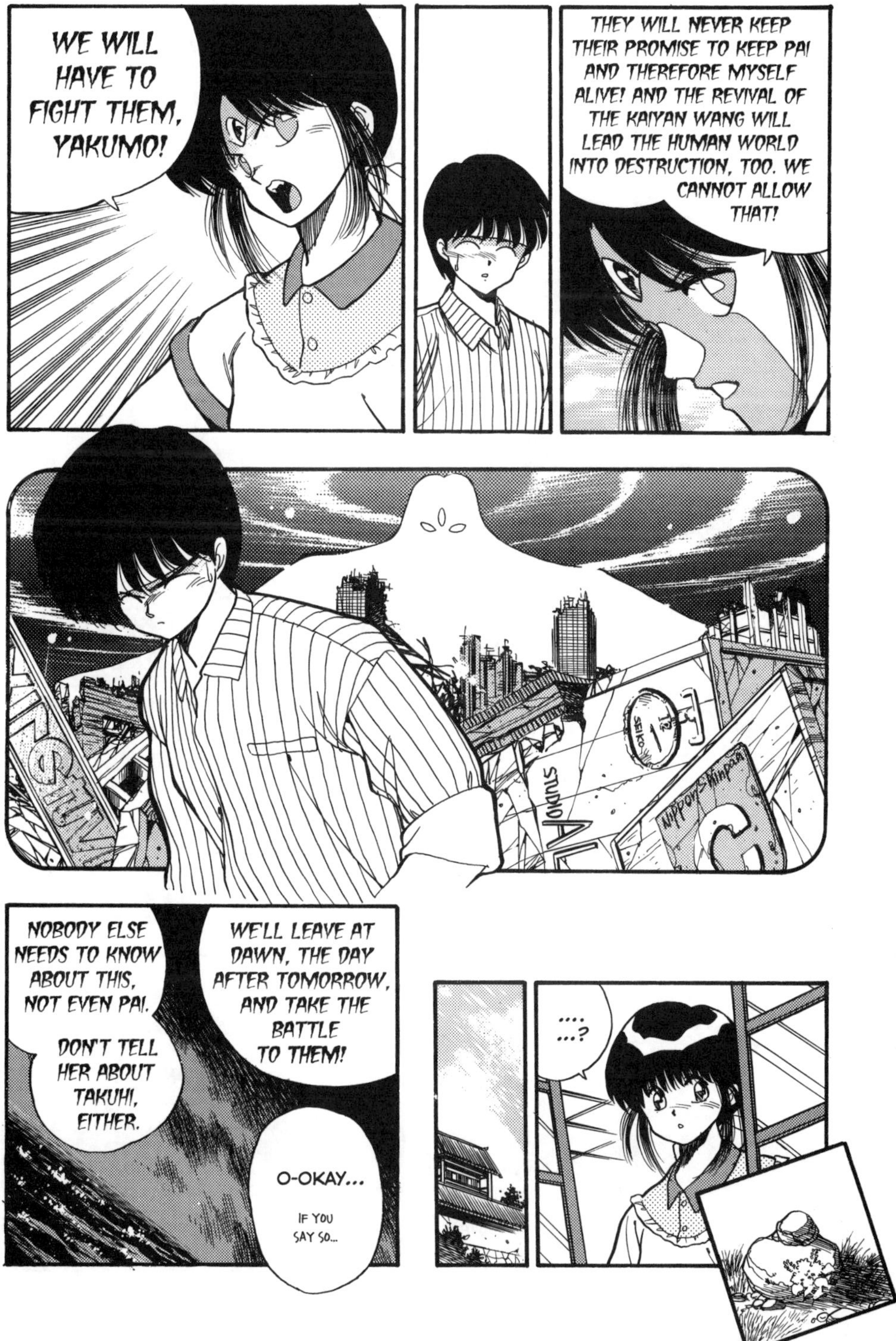
WE WILL HAVE TO FIGHT THEM, YAKUMO!
THEY WILL NEVER KEEP THEIR PROMISE TO KEEP PAI AND THEREFORE MYSELF ALIVE! AND THE REVIVAL OF THE KAIYAN WANG WILL LEAD THE HUMAN WORLD INTO DESTRUCTION, TOO. WE CANNOT ALLOW THAT!
NOBODY ELSE NEEDS TO KNOW ABOUT THIS, NOT EVEN PAI.
DON'T TELL HER ABOUT TAKUHI, EITHER.
WE'LL LEAVE AT DAWN, THE DAY AFTER TOMORROW, AND TAKE THE BATTLE TO THEM!
O-OKAY...
IF YOU SAY SO...
....
...?

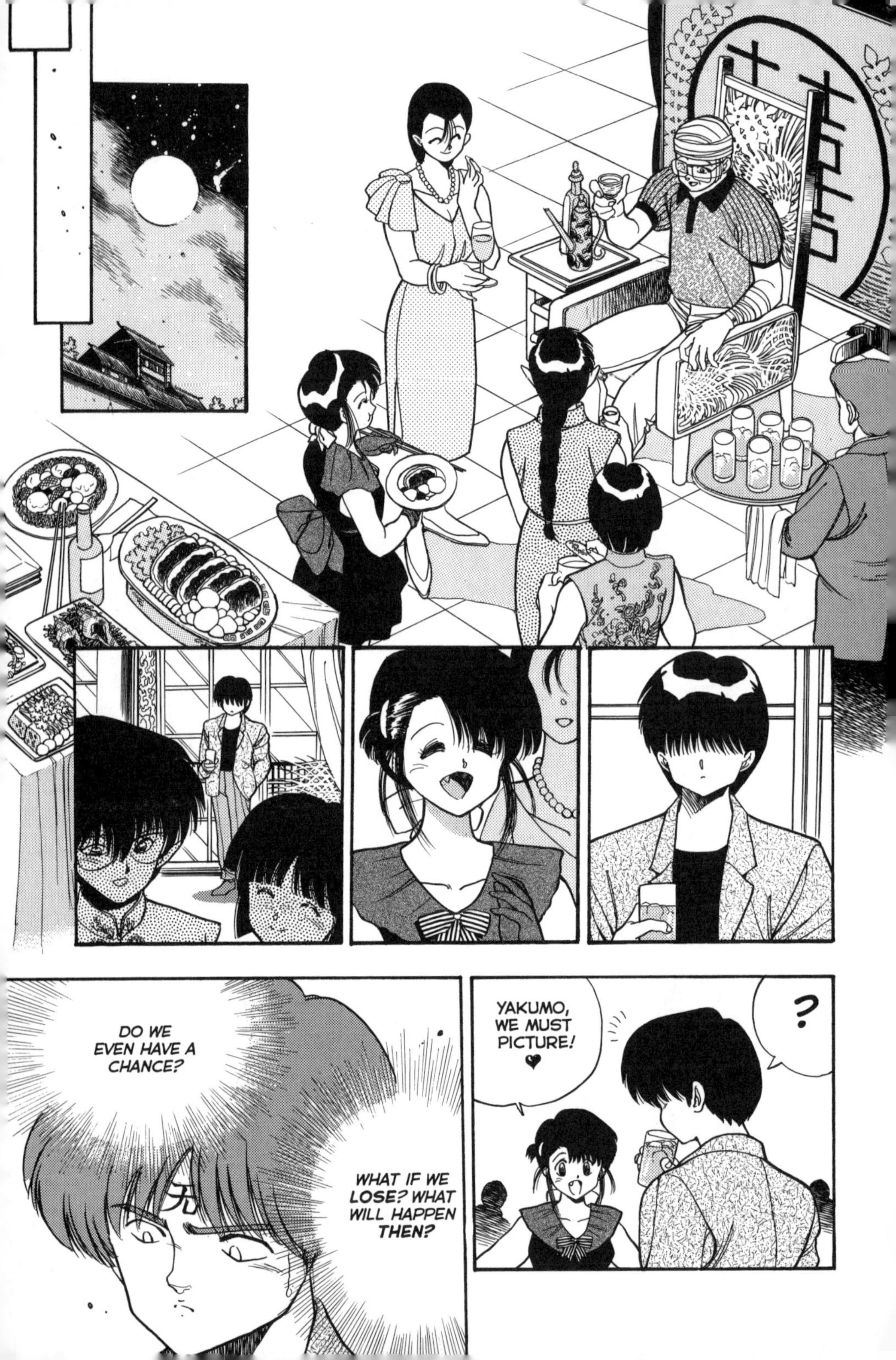
DO WE EVEN HAVE A CHANCE?
WHAT IF WE LOSE? WHAT WILL HAPPEN THEN?
YAKUMO, WE MUST PICTURE!
?

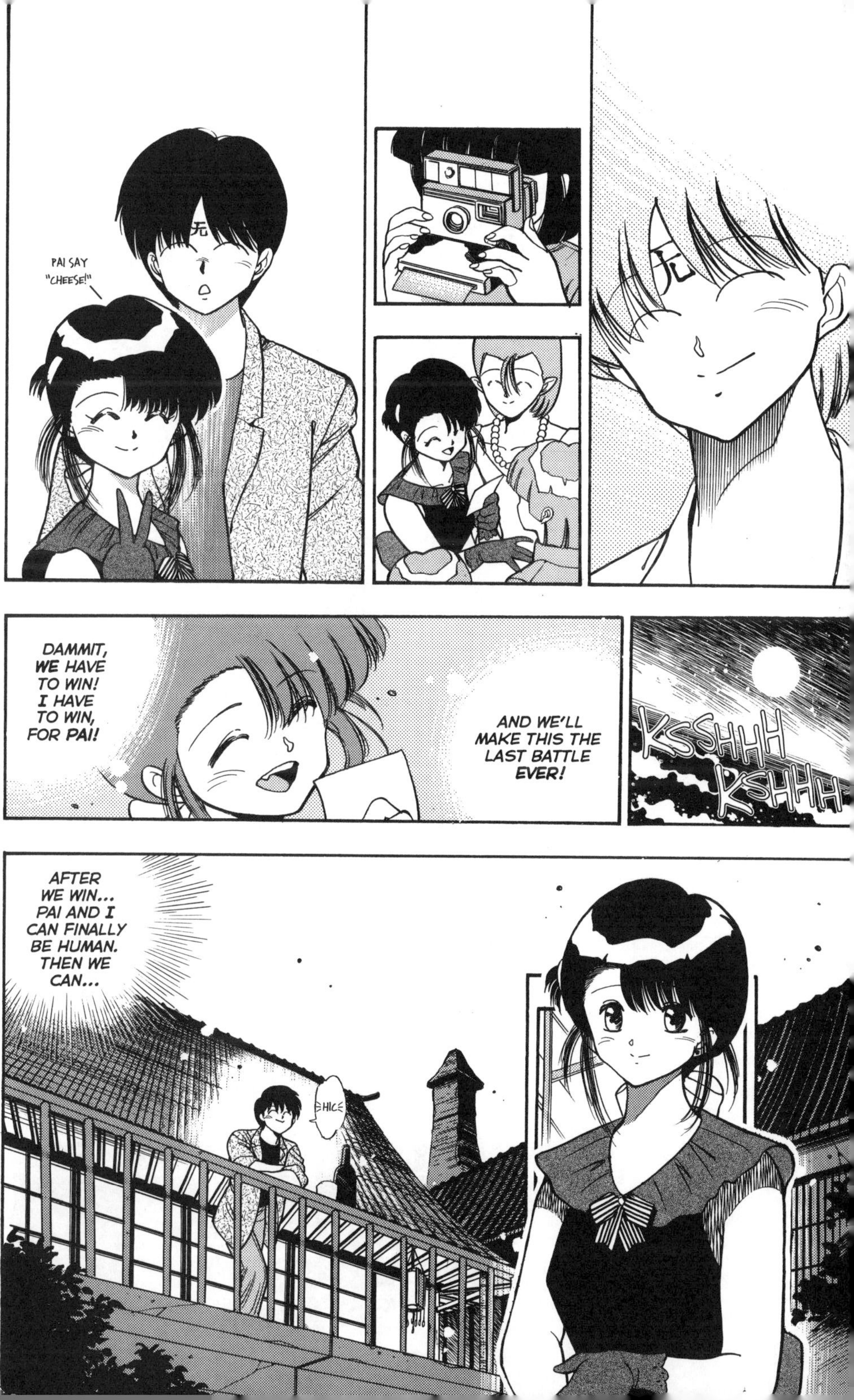

PAI SAY "CHEESE!"
DAMMIT, WE HAVE TO WIN! I HAVE TO WIN, FOR PAI!
AND WE'LL MAKE THIS THE LAST BATTLE EVER!
KSSHHH KSHHH
AFTER WE WIN... PAI AND I CAN FINALLY BE HUMAN. THEN WE CAN...
HIC

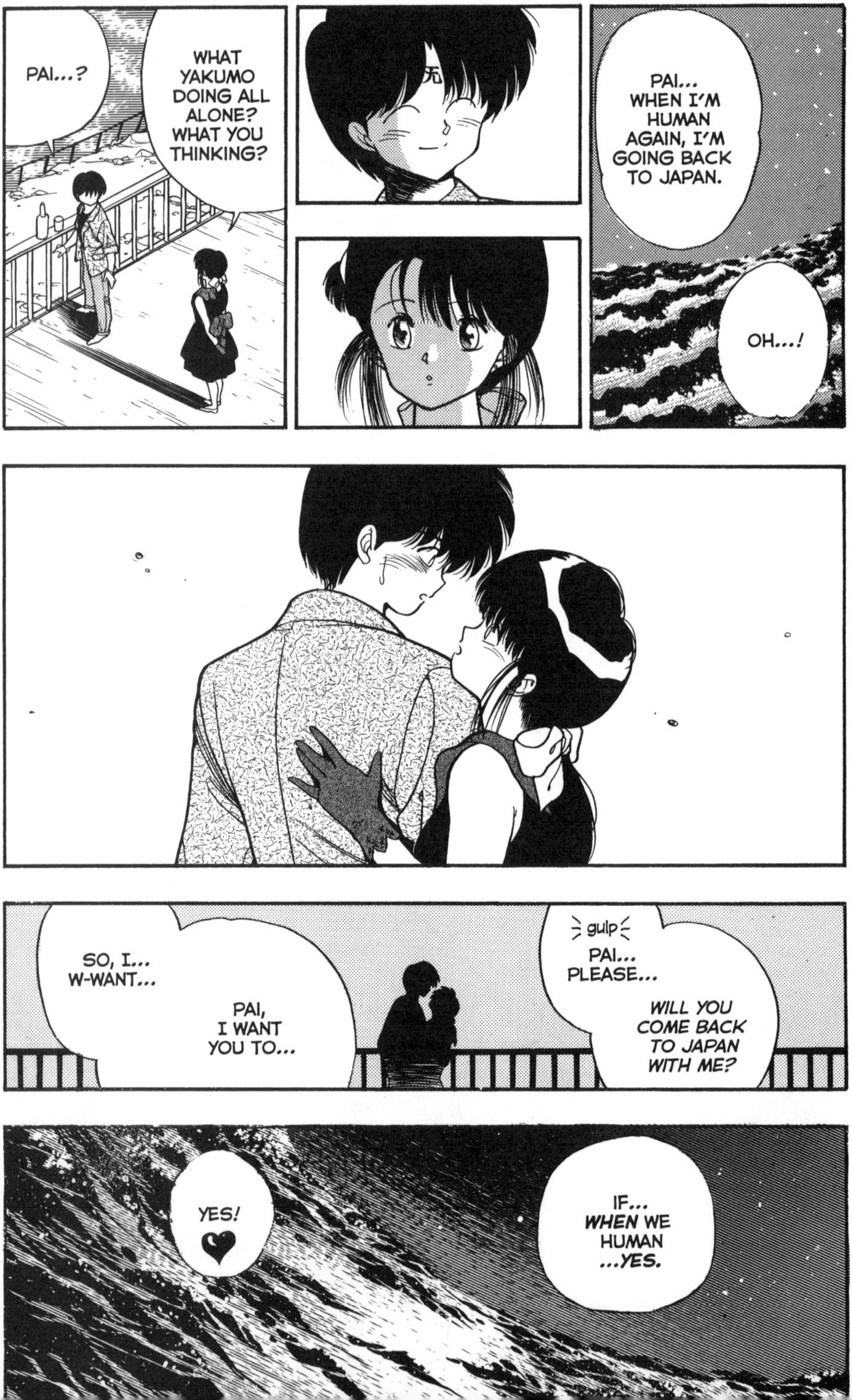
PAI...?
WHAT YAKUMO DOING ALL ALONE? WHAT YOU THINKING?
PAI... WHEN I'M HUMAN AGAIN, I'M GOING BACK TO JAPAN.
OH...!
SO, I... W-WANT...
PAI, I WANT YOU TO...
gulp
PAI... PLEASE...
WILL YOU COME BACK TO JAPAN WITH ME?
YES!
IF... WHEN WE HUMAN ...YES.

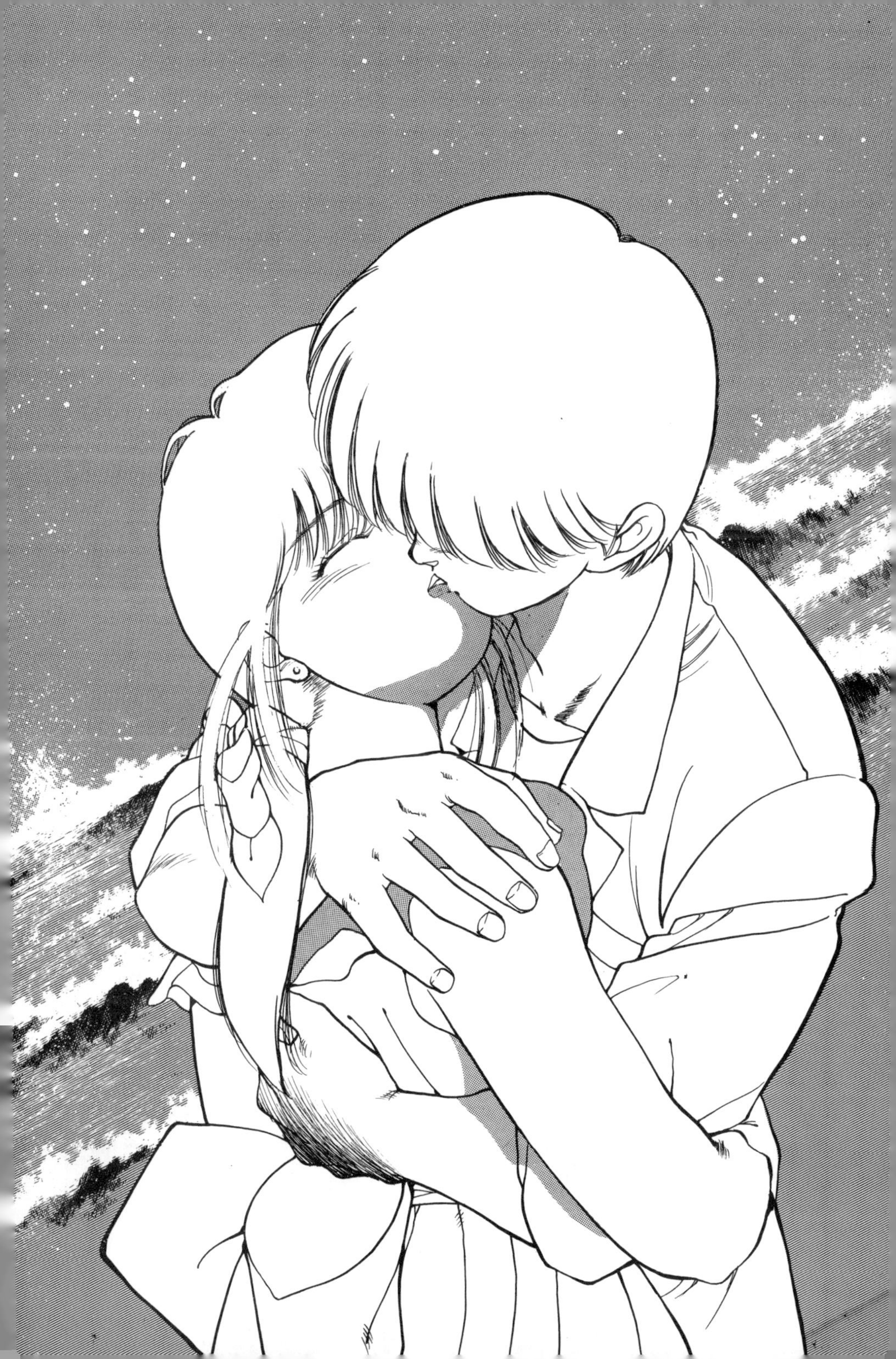

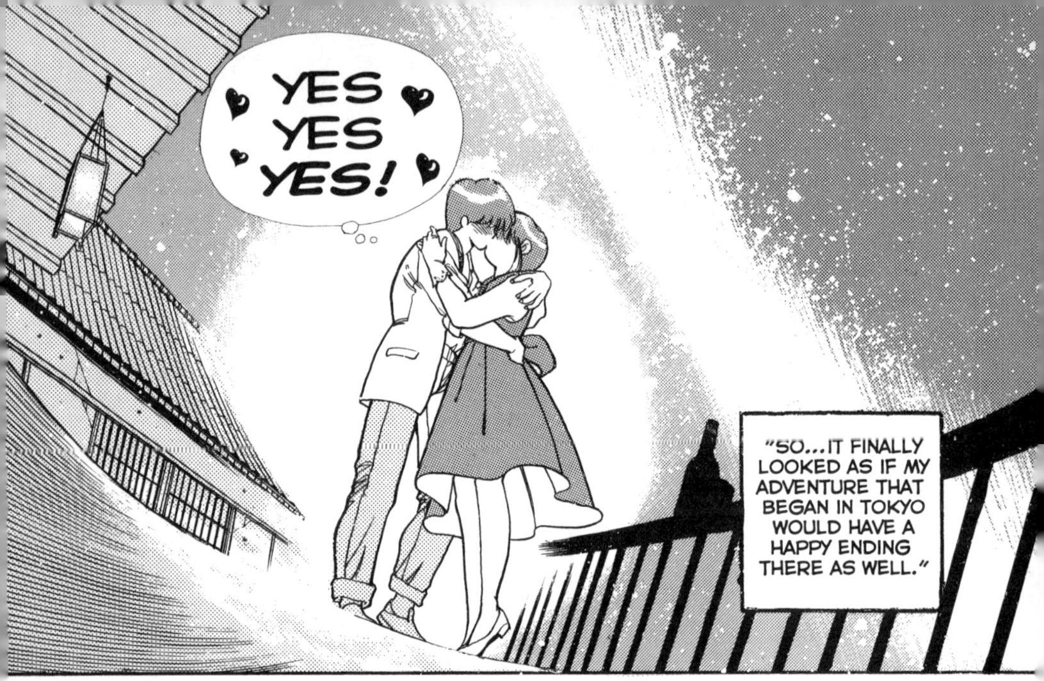
YES YES YES!
"SO...IT FINALLY LOOKED AS IF MY ADVENTURE THAT BEGAN IN TOKYO WOULD HAVE A HAPPY ENDING THERE AS WELL."

"IF...*WHEN* WE HUMAN..."

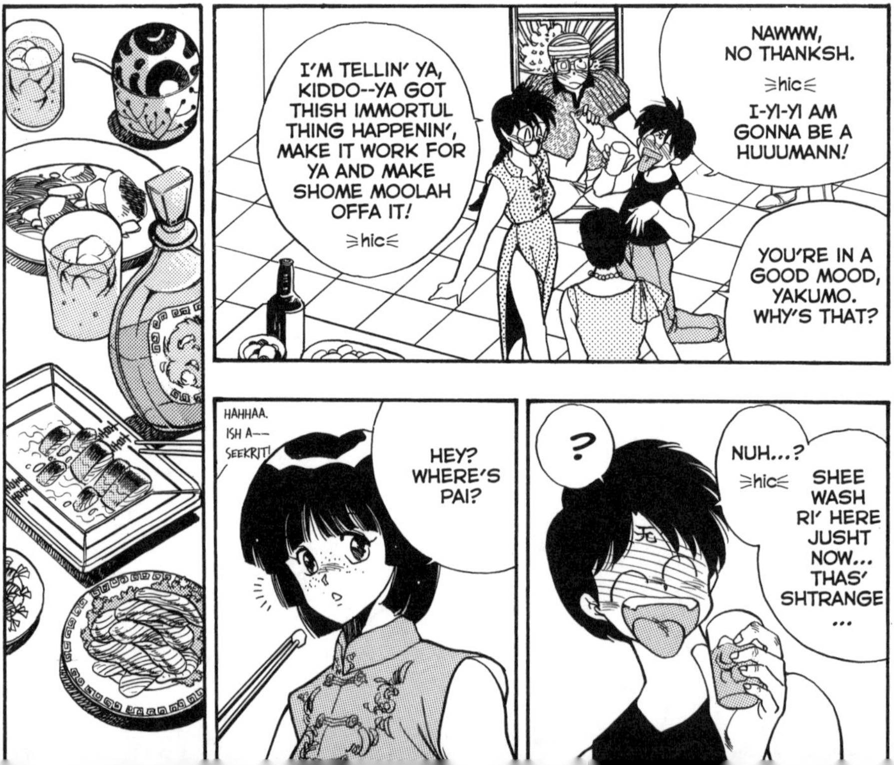
I'M TELLIN' YA, KIDDO--YA GOT THISH IMMORTUL THING HAPPENIN', MAKE IT WORK FOR YA AND MAKE SHOME MOOLAH OFFA IT! ≽hic≼
NAWWW, NO THANKSH. ≽hic≼ I-YI-YI AM GONNA BE A HUUUMANN!
YOU'RE IN A GOOD MOOD, YAKUMO. WHY'S THAT?
HAHHAA. ISH A-- SEEKRIT!
HEY? WHERE'S PAI?
?
NUH...? ≽hic≼
SHEE WASH RI' HERE JUSHT NOW... THAS' SHTRANGE ...

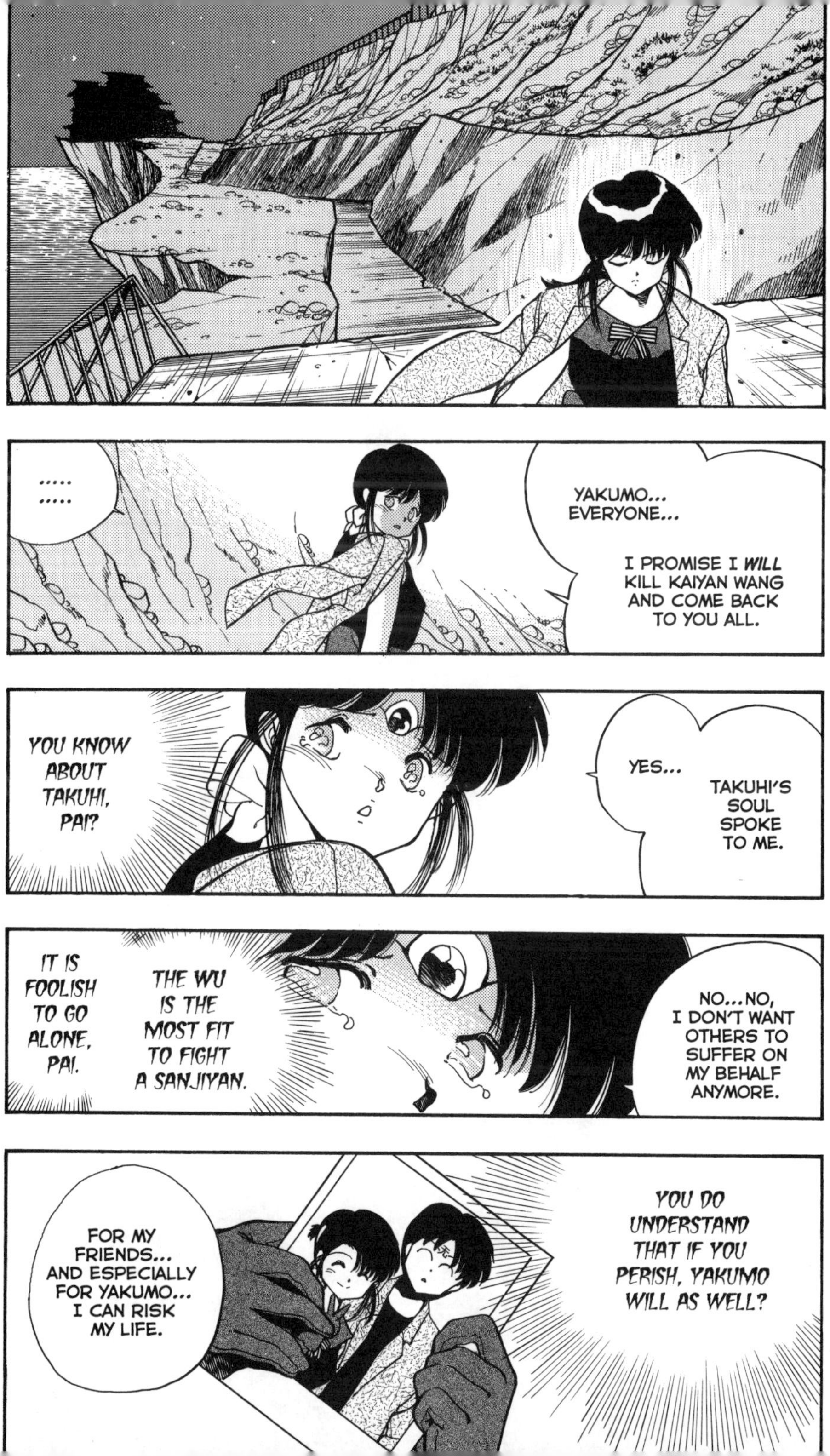
.....
.....
YAKUMO... EVERYONE...
I PROMISE I *WILL* KILL KAIYAN WANG AND COME BACK TO YOU ALL.
YOU KNOW ABOUT TAKUHI, PAI?
YES...
TAKUHI'S SOUL SPOKE TO ME.
IT IS FOOLISH TO GO ALONE, PAI.
THE WU IS THE MOST FIT TO FIGHT A SANJIYAN.
NO...NO, I DON'T WANT OTHERS TO SUFFER ON MY BEHALF ANYMORE.
FOR MY FRIENDS... AND ESPECIALLY FOR YAKUMO... I CAN RISK MY LIFE.
YOU DO UNDERSTAND THAT IF YOU PERISH, YAKUMO WILL AS WELL?

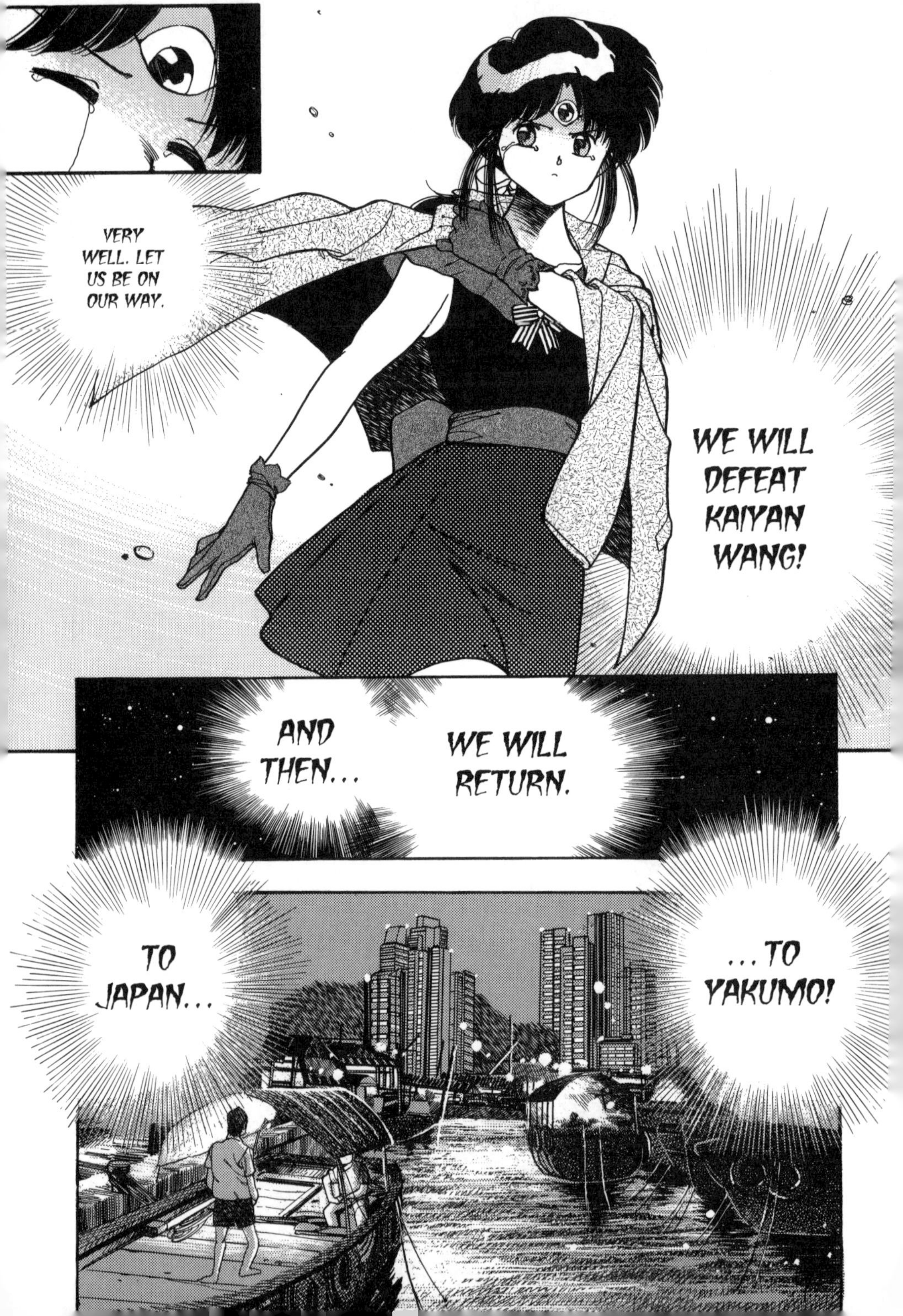
VERY WELL. LET US BE ON OUR WAY.
WE WILL DEFEAT KAIYAN WANG!
AND THEN...
WE WILL RETURN.
TO JAPAN...
...TO YAKUMO!

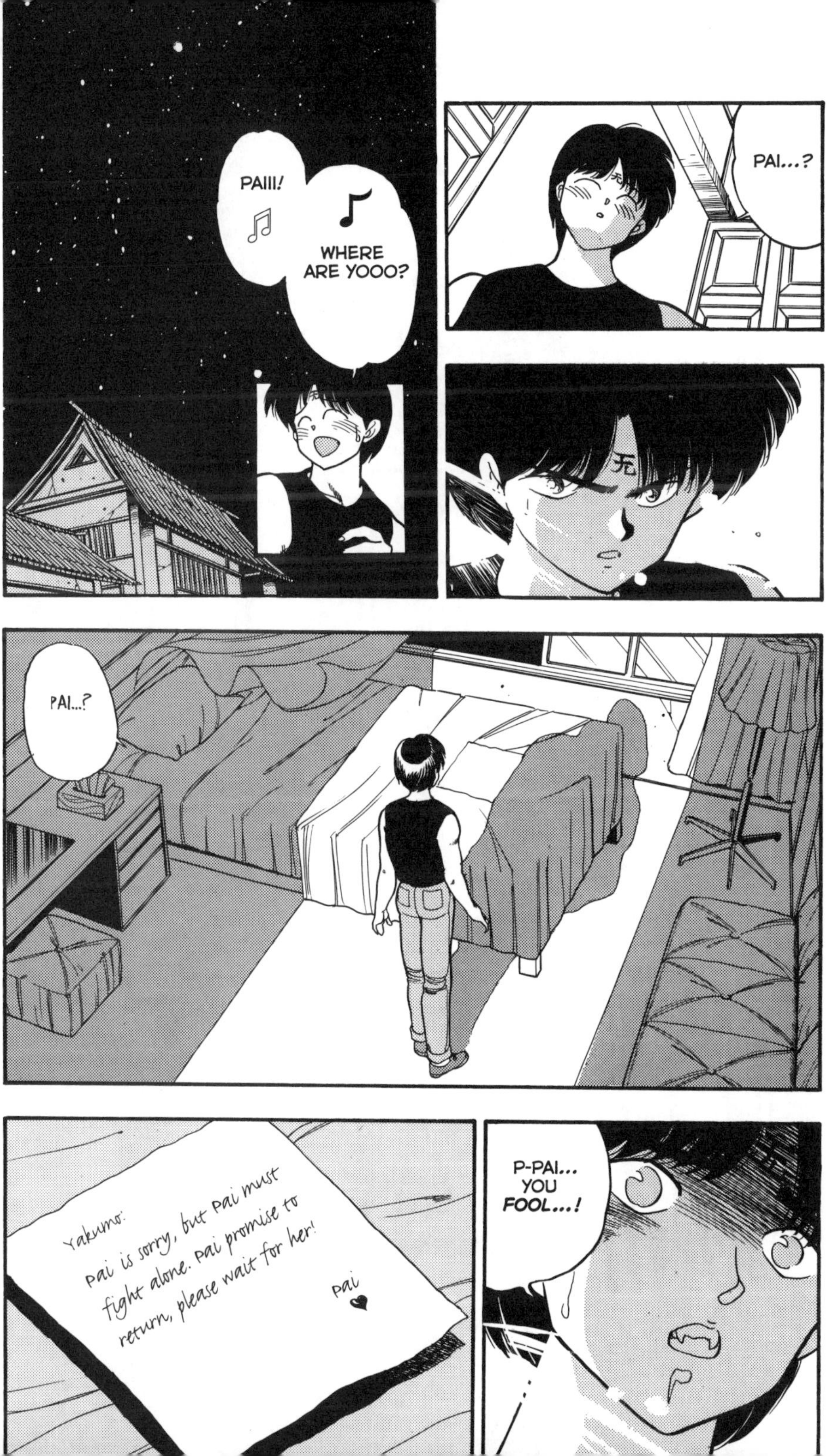
PAIII!
WHERE ARE YOOO?
PAI...?
PAI...?
Yakumo:
Pai is sorry, but Pai must fight alone. Pai promise to return, please wait for her!
Pai
P-PAI... YOU FOOL...!

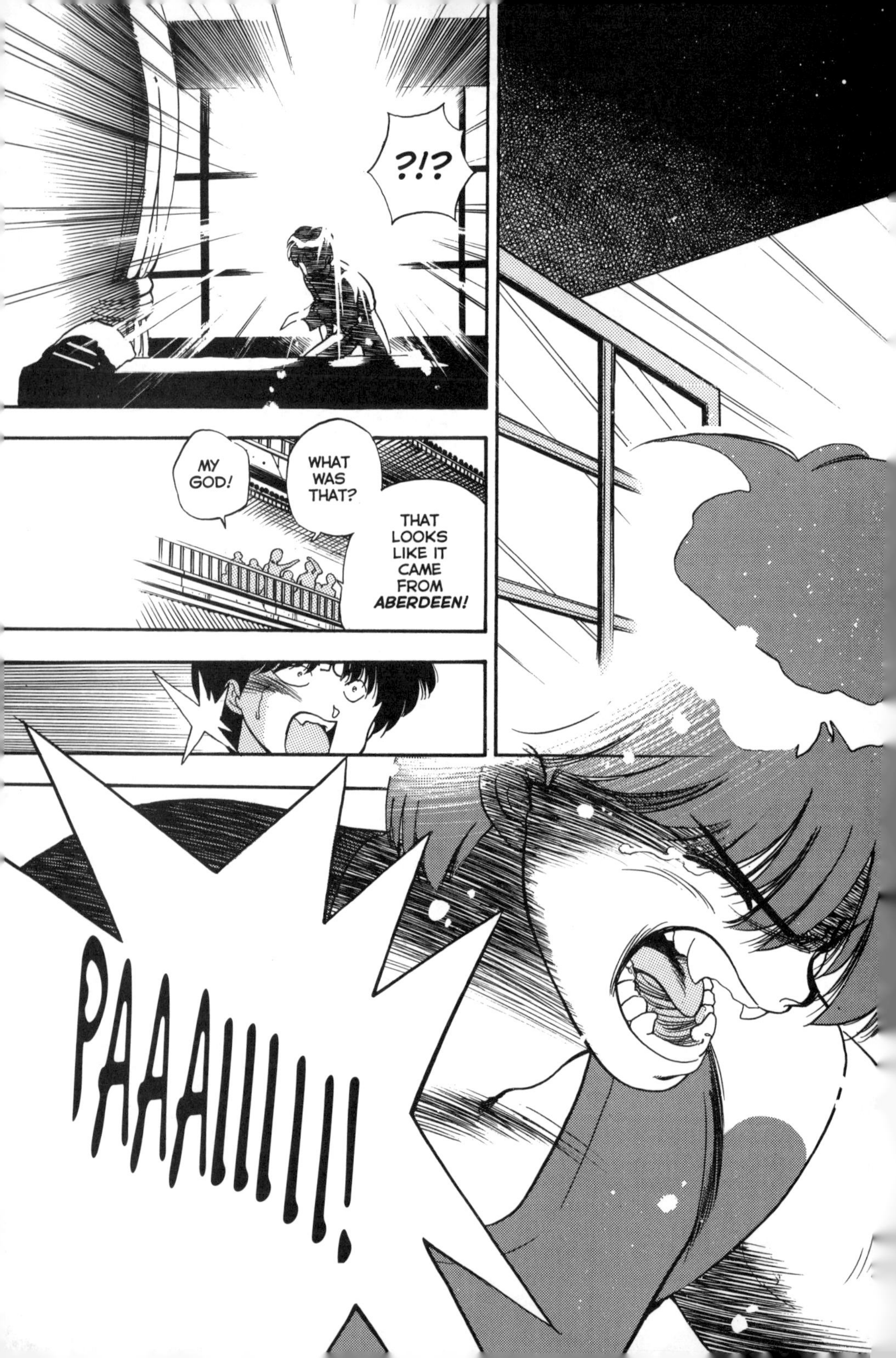
?!?
MY GOD!
WHAT WAS THAT?
THAT LOOKS LIKE IT CAME FROM ABERDEEN!
PAAIIIII!

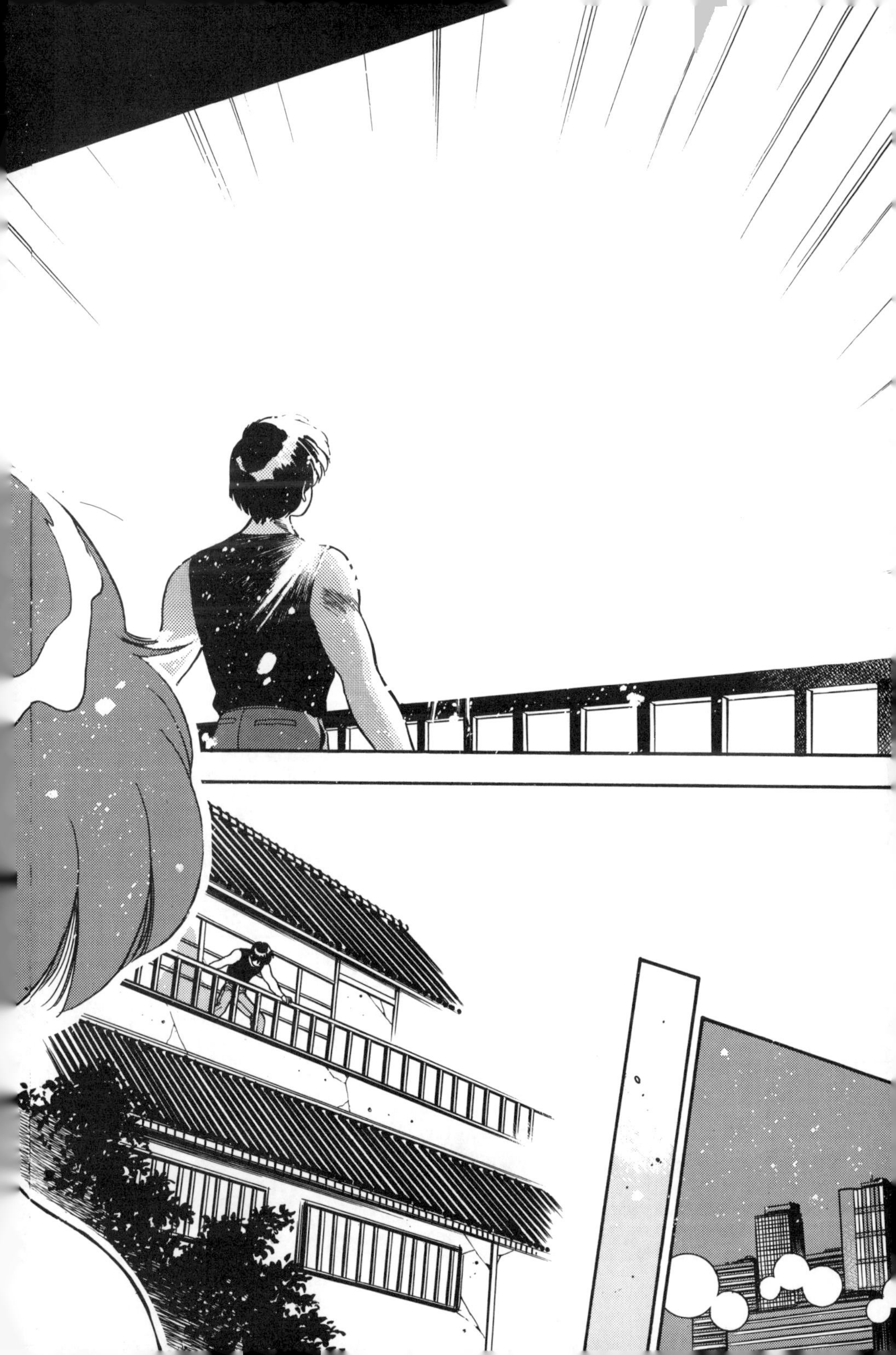

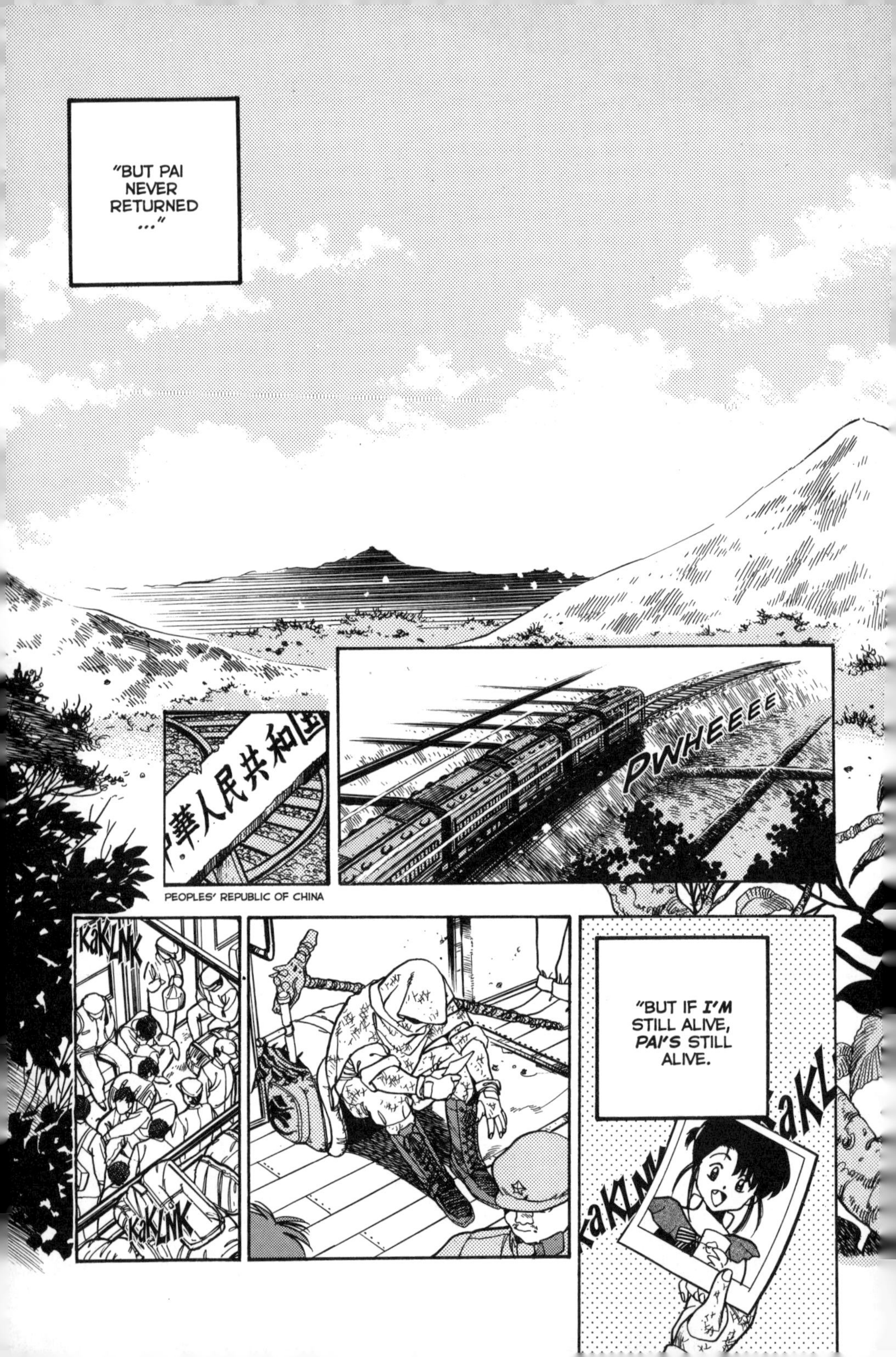
"BUT PAI NEVER RETURNED ..."
華人民共和国
PEOPLES' REPUBLIC OF CHINA
PWHEEEE
KaKLNK
KaKLNK
"BUT IF I'M STILL ALIVE, PAI'S STILL ALIVE.
KaKL
KaKLNK

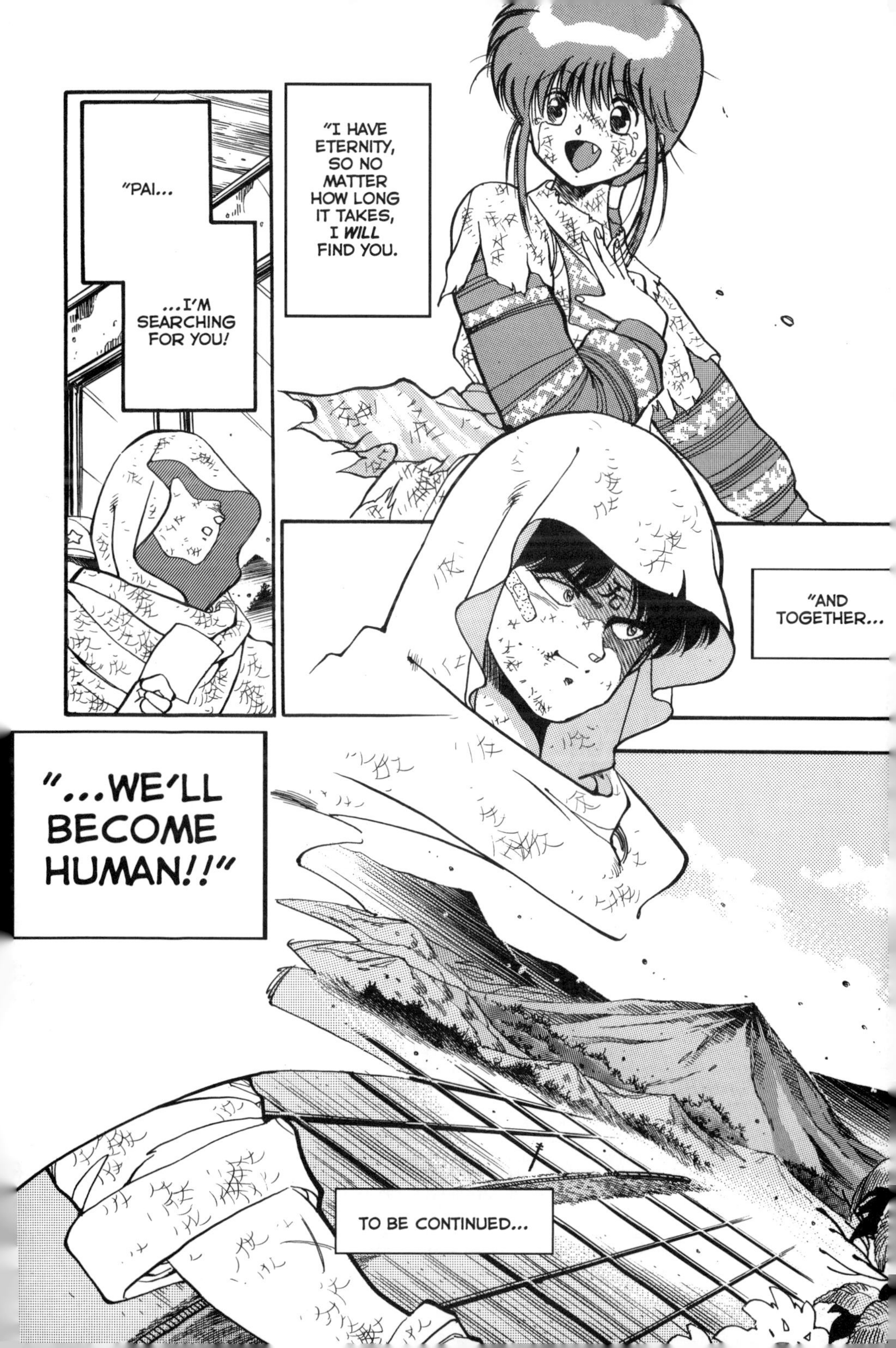
"PAI...
...I'M SEARCHING FOR YOU!
"I HAVE ETERNITY, SO NO MATTER HOW LONG IT TAKES, I *WILL* FIND YOU.
"AND TOGETHER...
"...WE'LL BECOME HUMAN!!"
TO BE CONTINUED...